MOIRA
MODEL OF INTERNATIONAL RELATIONS IN AGRICULTURE

CONTRIBUTIONS
TO
ECONOMIC ANALYSIS

124

Honorary Editor

J. TINBERGEN

Editors

D.W. JORGENSON

J. WAELBROECK

NORTH-HOLLAND PUBLISHING COMPANY
AMSTERDAM • NEW YORK • OXFORD

MOIRA

Model of International Relations in Agriculture

Report of the project group
'Food for a Doubling World Population'

Hans Linnemann *(project leader)*
Jerrie De Hoogh
Michiel A. Keyzer
Henk D. J. Van Heemst

with contributions by

Rein J. Brolsma
Jelle N. Bruinsma
P. Buringh
G. J. Staring
C. T. De Wit

1979

NORTH-HOLLAND PUBLISHING COMPANY
AMSTERDAM · NEW YORK · OXFORD

338.1
M713

ISBN: 0 444 85169 0

Publishers:

NORTH-HOLLAND PUBLISHING COMPANY
AMSTERDAM • NEW YORK • OXFORD

Sole distributors for the U.S.A. and Canada:
ELSEVIER NORTH-HOLLAND, INC.
52 VANDERBILT AVENUE, NEW YORK, N.Y. 10017

Library of Congress Cataloging in Publication Data

Main entry under title:

Model of international relations in agriculture.

(Contributions to economic analysis ; 124)
    1. Agriculture--Economic aspects--Mathematical
models. 2. Food supply--Mathematical models.
I. Linnemann, Hans. II. Series.
HD1411.M635   338.1'01'51   78-5303
ISBN 0-444-85169-0

PRINTED IN GREAT BRITAIN

Introduction to the series

This series consists of a number of hitherto unpublished studies, which are introduced by the editors in the belief that they represent fresh contributions to economic science.

The term 'economic analysis' as used in the title of the series has been adopted because it covers both the activities of the theoretical economist and the research worker.

Although the analytical methods used by the various contributors are not the same, they are nevertheless conditioned by the common origin of their studies, namely theoretical problems encountered in practical research. Since for this reason, business cycle research and national accounting, research work on behalf of economic policy, and problems of planning are the main sources of the subjects dealt with, they necessarily determine the manner of approach adopted by the authors. Their methods tend to be 'practical' in the sense of not being too far remote from application to actual economic conditions. In addition they are quantitative rather than qualitative.

It is the hope of the editors that the publication of these studies will help to stimulate the exchange of scientific information and to reinforce international cooperation in the field of economics.

The Editors

Members of the project group

R.J. Brolsma — Economist, Economic and Social Institute, Free University, Amsterdam

J.N. Bruinsma — Economist, Economic and Social Institute, Free University, Amsterdam

P. Buringh — Professor of tropical soil science, Agricultural University, Wageningen

H.D.J. van Heemst — Agronomist, Centre for Agrobiological Research (CABO), Wageningen

J. de Hoogh — Professor of agricultural economics, Free University, Amsterdam and Deputy Director of the Agricultural Economics Research Institute, The Hague

M.A. Keyzer — Economist, Economic and Social Institute, Free University, Amsterdam

H. Linnemann — Professor of development economics and planning, Free University, Amsterdam and Director of the Economic and Social Institute, Free University, Amsterdam

G.J. Staring — Soil scientist, Agricultural University, Wageningen

C.T. de Wit — Professor of theoretical production ecology, Agricultural University Wageningen, and Agronomist, Centre for Agrobiological Research (CABO) Wageningen

Research assistants

J. Kapteyn
P. Lameris
H.J. Moen
F. Soeteman
P. Veenendaal
H. Vos
G. Winters

Consultants

K.J. Beek
G. Hamming
M.J. 't Hooft-Welvaars
C.J. Jansen
J. Tinbergen
M. van der Vlis

PREFACE

This report is the result of a three-year study on the long-term development possibilities and problems of food production in the world. The starting point of the research was the question raised by the Club of Rome: is it possible to produce enough for everyone's needs, even if the world population were to double its numbers? Man's most basic needs in the material sphere may be brought together under four headings: food, shelter, health and access to education. The initial request of the Club of Rome to some Dutch scholars to analyze the long-term prospects for the world population specified these four basic needs, to be studied in their interrelations and in the setting of the world models as developed by several groups sponsored by the Club of Rome.

In the course of 1972 and 1973 a research group was formed in which a variety of disciplines were represented. It soon became evident that financial and manpower resources available did not permit a sound and thorough study of the various basic needs simultaneously. The group decided to focus its research on one of these needs in particular, i.e. on food. Consequently, the larger part of the group concentrated its research efforts on the international food situation and developed the model MOIRA. Some of the group members continued to work on the broader initial task, without engaging themselves in model building or similar quantitative work. The results of their more verbal description and analysis of the world situation are reported elsewhere.

The project focusing on the international food situation was called *Food for a Doubling World Population*; it maintained a rather loose relationship to the Club of Rome as its original inspirer. The moral support received from Dr. Aurelio Peccei and his colleagues of the Club of Rome was matched by the financial support given by various institutions. Research funds were made available by the Ministry of Agriculture and Fisheries and the Ministry of Foreign Affairs at The Hague, and by the Haak Bastiaan Kuneman Foundation. Also, several group members were made available to the project by the governing bodies of those institutions where they hold permanent posts. In addition, the Free University at Amsterdam provided office space and administrative facilities to the team. The project group wishes to express its gratitude to all persons and institutions that made it possible to undertake this somewhat venturous project.

Final responsibility for the present report rests with the
authors. It has to be stressed, however, that possible
merits of the material content of the book should go to all
members of the MOIRA group. In spite of working conditions
that often were far from ideal, everyone of them contributed
substantially to our joint venture. In the initial stage of
the research, the nucleus of the MOIRA group was formed by
the present authors except the project leader. The way in
which the model has been conceived and developed should be
attributed primarily to these three people, and as project
leader I have the privilege of thanking these colleagues in
particular for their contribution to the project. In the
discussions between De Hoogh (agricultural economics and
agricultural policies), Van Heemst (agronomy) and Keyzer
(mathematical economics), large parts of MOIRA took their
shape. Without belittling anyone's work, it is only fair to
say that in conceptualizing and modeling MOIRA the input of
Michiel Keyzer has been outstanding.

It is almost impossible to identify with precision the
contributions made by the individual group members all of
whom I cordially thank for their valuable support to the
project. Chapter 2 was written by P. Buringh, H.D.J. van
Heemst and G.J. Staring, and virtually constitutes a study
in itself; their findings play a part again in Chapter 4. In
the latter chapter, the way in which the agricultural production function is conceived bears the mark of C.T. de Wit
and H.D.J. van Heemst. Jelle Bruinsma worked closely together
with Michiel Keyzer on the mathematical formulation of the
model; he developed a model for the fertilizer industry
generating the fertilizer prices used in MOIRA, and wrote
the larger part of Chapter 8. Rein Brolsma studied institutional aspects of agricultural production and marketing, as
well as nutrition standards and food consumption norms
(Chapter 8). Income distribution was dealt with in particular
by Michael van der Vlis.

Collecting and processing of statistical data has been done
largely by the research assistants listed on the back of the
title page. Their assistance in the work is gratefully
acknowledged by the project group. The same is true for the
valuable advice given by our consultants, in various stages
of the research work. In terms of time and effort spent on
the project, two of them should be mentioned in particular:
Mr. Cornelis J. Jansen, senior economist on sabbatical leave
from the World Bank, and Dr. G. Hamming of the Agricultural
Economics Research Institute whose deep concern about the
long-term ecological implications of agricultural processes
is only very partially reflected in the present study.
To our secretary Mrs. Lioe Jacobs-Sie, and to her predecessor
Mrs. Ima Boeschoten-Schölvinck, we are all indebted for
never-failing administrative help; Mrs. Jacobs had the
courage and stamina to type and retype and retype again the
entire manuscript. Dr. Wouter Tims, who recently joined us
as Director of the newly established foundation that is to
continue the study of the world food problem (Centre for

World Food Studies, c/o Free University, P.O. Box 7161,
1007 MC Amsterdam), made many valuable improvements of an
editorial nature.

Prior to the publication of this volume, the set-up of the
analysis and a number of preliminary findings have been
published in several articles and research reports. These
forerunners of the present report, in English, were, in
chonological order:

Population doubling and food supply. Economic and Social
Institute, Free University, Amsterdam. July 1974.

'Problems of population doubling: the world food problem';
in: Gerhart Bruckmann (ed.), *Latin American World Model -
Proceedings of the second IIASA symposium on global modelling*,
October 7-10, 1974. IIASA, Laxenburg. pp. 305-310.

P. Buringh, H.D.J. van Heemst and G.J. Staring, *Computation
of the absolute maximum food production of the world*. Agricultural University, Wageningen. January 1975.

Food for a doubling world population. Report on the Club of
Rome conference organized by the Austrian College Society at
Alpbach, Tyrol, June 25-27, 1975.

'Food for a growing world population', in: Gerhart Bruckmann
(ed.), *MOIRA: Food and agricultural model - Preceedings of
the third IIASA symposium on global modelling*, September 22-
25, 1975. IIASA, Laxenburg. pp. 13-515.

'Food for a growing world population: some of the main
findings of a study on the long-term prospects of the world
food situation', in: *European Review of Agricultural Economics*, Vol. 3 (1976), pp. 459-499.

'Food for a growing world population', in: *Technological
Forecasting and Social Change*, Vol. 10 (1977), pp. 27-51.

Some of these earlier reports were published in other lan-
guages as well. They are all of a preliminary nature, as
compared to the present volume.

Finally, a word about the cooperation between agricultural
scientists and economists, as the representatives of the two
disciplines most strongly involved in MOIRA. I am sure that
I express the feelings of all members of our project group
when I state that this form of co-operation has been fruitful and stimulating for both parties - even to such an
extent that most members of the group have decided to stick
together for another period of joint research into the world
food problem. In all fairness it should be added that in the
birth process of MOIRA on occasions the economists have
forced the contributions of agronomists into a bodice that,
in the opinion of the latter, came pretty close to a strait
jacket. The reader whose background is in the agricultural
sciences should accuse the economists of our group, rather
than the agronomists, whenever he feels that the insights
obtained in his discipline are made use of in too rough a

manner.

Needless to say, that all comments and criticisms will be
welcome to our group - particularly also in view of the
intended continuation of research along these lines.

                                    Hans Linnemann, project leader

Amsterdam, January 1979

TABLE OF CONTENTS

PART I

FOOD, NATURE AND MAN

Chapter 1

OUTLINE OF THE STUDY

> *"To the poor man God*
> *dare not appear except*
> *in the form of bread*
> *and promise of work"*
> M.K. Gandhi

1.1 *AIM AND CHARACTER OF THE STUDY*

Decades have passed since Gandhi pleaded, in his words
and in his way of life, the cause of the poor and hungry.
Decades have passed, some of them heralded as *Development
Decades* for the countries where most of the world's poor and
hungry are living. Indeed, time has passed - but time does
not solve all problems. In 1967, when the greater part of
the first U.N. Development Decade had passed into history
already, a review of the development of food production and
consumption arrived at the conclusion that *the number of
people that go hungry is larger today than ever before.*[1] In
1974, the Secretariat of the World Food Conference again
observed that *the actual number of hungry persons has quite
certainly increased.*[2] The Secretariat also referred to a
preliminary forward assessment indicating that by 1985 in
countries with a combined population of 800 million people
effective demand for food would still fall short of food
energy requirements.[3]

These are alarming statements, indicating that the prospects
for the eradication of hunger and malnutrition may be very
bad indeed. Some recent studies - i.a. the Club of Rome
reports prepared by D.L. Meadows and associates[4] and by
Mesarovic and Pestel[5] - point in the same direction. In the

---

[1] Hans Linnemann, *The Plan that Failed*, Haarlem 1967; p. 3

[2] *Assessment of the World Food Situation*, U.N. World Food Conference
doc. E/CONF. 65/3; p. 55

[3] *Ibid.*, p. 7

[4] D.H. Meadows <u>et al.</u>, *The Limits to Growth*, New York, 1972

[5] M. Mesarovic and E. Pestel, *Mankind at the Turning Point*,
New York, 1974

affluent countries, however, the world food problem became a
matter of public concern primarily because of the sudden
scarcity of important basic foods and the unprecedented
price rises on the world food market during the first half
of the 1970s, revealing the uncertainty of an adequate world
food supply. In 1972 and 1973 disappointing harvests caused
major shortfalls in international trade, and the world's
stocks (particularly of grains) proved to be quite inadequate
to absorb these shortages. The tripling of international
grain prices which occured in the period 1972-1974 meant an
enormous decrease in purchasing power, particularly for the
food importing countries, and also caused food aid programmes
to be sharply reduced.

However, hunger and malnutrition are not only caused by
scarcity and high world market prices, as has happened
during the last few years. Even in times of low international
prices and increasing surpluses, as in the 1960s, large
groups of the world population are unable to obtain sufficient food. The situation on the world market is a very
crude indicator of the relation between need and availability.
Conditions on national and regional markets may be quite
different to that on the world market. Moreover, the markets
show predominantly the demand of the well-to-do. Those with
insufficient purchasing power (incomes) may still suffer
hunger and malnutrition even though the market supply is
fairly large and prices are low.

The latter fact emerges also from a close scrutiny of the
post-war development of food production and consumption.
World food production has grown faster than world population,
and in most developing countries per capita food supply has
increased somewhat over the years. Why, then, has the number
of hungry people gone up? The first and most obvious reason
is that a given percentage of hungry and malnourished people
represents an increasing absolute number when population
grows (as it does). The more fundamental reason, however, is
the persistent inequality in incomes; with few exceptions,
income distribution in developing countries is very uneven,
and has tended to worsen rather than improve over the last
decades. It is important to note in this connection that a
large part of the poorest people are working in the agricultural sector itself.

In sum, the historical record suggests that hunger and malnutrition have remained with us throughout the decades, affecting more and more people as time passes. Although the
scourge of mass starvation and famines has not recurred in
the years since the last World War, it is increasingly felt
that one cannot continue to cope with food shortages through
international trade and aid, but that countries have to rely
more heavily on their own capacity to increase food production.
But are there ways open to them which promise a better
balance between people and their nutrition? Or is the world
in its entirety coming dangerously close to the limits of
its capacity to produce food? These are questions which

require careful analysis, in order to enhance our understanding of the true causes of the world food problem.

It is to these questions that the present study addresses
itself. It attempts, firstly, to describe the world food
situation in terms of its underlying causal factors. The
second purpose is to provide considered judgements regarding
the policy measures that may redirect future developments
towards improvements of the world food situation, with
special emphasis on international policy measures. The
complexity of the world food problem, and the need to arrive
at quantitative statements, suggested the construction of a
model specifying the various interrelations relevant to the
world food sector; the model that has been developed is
called MOIRA - shorthand for Model of International Relations
in Agriculture, and the Greek name of the goddess of fate.

The study was inspired by the debate generated by the Club
of Rome publications on the Predicament of Mankind; in this
context, it may be seen as a contribution to the world-wide
efforts at global modelling. Above, reference was made
already to two such studies - both arriving at gloomy conclusions as regards the future world food situation. They
were followed by other world-model analyses offering more
hope for the fight against hunger: e.g. the study of the
Fundación Bariloche team led by A.O. Herrera[6] (originnaly
also a Club of Rome venture), and the United Nations study
by W. Leontief.[7] All of these studies are model-based and
have a long-term time dimension; also they are not confined
to the agricultural sector but deal with the entire (world)
economy. This is not the place to discuss the possible merits and
demerits of the various approaches, and to compare the agricultural sector models of these studies with MOIRA; comparative studies of this kind are being undertaken by others.[8]
Yet it may be useful to describe briefly those aspects,
elements and limitations that, in the view of the authors at
least, characterize the present analysis. Keeping in mind
these characteristics - to which we will return at length
below - may also facilitate the reading of the individual
chapters in that the overall structure and purpose is not
lost sight of.

MOIRA is a model of international relations in the field of
food and agriculture which is developed as a linkage of

---

[6]   A.O. Herrera et al., *Catastrophe or New Society? A Latin American
      World Model*, Ottawa, 1976

[7]   W. Leontief et al., *The Future of the World Economy*, New York, 1977

[8]   See, e.g., J. Clark and S. Cole, *Global Simulation Models*, London,
      1975; and S. Cole, *Global Models and the International Economic
      Order* (a UNITAR sponsored study; forthcoming).

national models. It describes the food sector of individual
countries, and links these sectors by means of an equilibrium
model of international trade in food. At the national level,
two sectors are distinguished: agriculture and non-agriculture;
the rate of development of the latter sector is (largely)
exogenous. These two sectors may have opposite or at least
diverging interests, in particular as regards the food price
level. This potential conflict of interests between the
agricultural and the non-agricultural population is incorporated in the model. The agricultural production decision
is described for the agricultural sector as a whole; the
food consumption decision is modelled for twelve income
classes per country, six classes for each sector. Average
food consumption per income class is compared with a country-
specific food consumption norm, from which the extent of
hunger or malnutrition follows. At the international level,
the role of policies of developed countries receives special
attention. Simulation shows possible developments of food
production and consumption over the next decades, both under
conditions of unchanged policies and in case of deliberate
changes in international food policy (liberalization of food
trade, world market food price stabilization at different
price levels, food aid, voluntary restriction of food consumption in the rich countries). The latter simulations may
be said - somewhat presumptuously - to indicate the direction
in which the international economic order should be changed
in order to reduce (or at least help reduce) hunger and
malnutrition in the world.

This thumbnail sketch of the main characteristics of MOIRA
requires some additional comments. MOIRA is a sector model,
with all limitations thereof. On the other hand, it also
implies that all efforts could be focussed on the sector
concerned, which is perhaps described with more care than in
some other studies. Another limitation of the present study
is that only one agricultural product is distinguished; all
production and consumption of food is expressed in terms of
consumable protein - a unit of measurement to be discussed
later on. The choice of this unit of measurement was judged
to be convenient also from an agronomic point of view, and
the integration of agronomic and economic considerations in
the description of the production decision of the agricultural
producer is possibly one of the distinguishing features of
MOIRA. In general, behaviour relations - including government
behaviour - play an important part in the present model, as
compared to other global models. Population growth is exogenous,
but migration from agriculture to non-agricultural occupations
is endogenous. Income distribution is also exogenous; the
effects of changes in non-agricultural income distribution
on food consumption can be assessed, but these changes in
income distribution cannot be generated in the model. Food
production and consumption in the centrally-planned countries
could be modelled in MOIRA in a very primitive fashion only.

Obviously, in the following chapters much more will have to
be said about these and other characteristics of MOIRA, and
about the way in which the model may be used for policy
analysis. Suffice it here to stress that MOIRA should not be
seen primarily as a forecasting or prediction model, but as
a simulation model useful for the analysis of alternative
policies. As such, it may hopefully shed some light on the
question what international food policy (or package of
policies) would seem to be more promising than others. The
criterion for comparing alternative policies is their potential, or lack of potential, to contribute to a reduction of
world hunger and to an increase in the rate of growth of
food production in the Third World.

1.2 *FOOD CONSUMPTION IN THE BASE YEAR, AND FOOD PRODUCTION POTENTIAL*

The choice of consumable protein as physical unit of
measurement (argued in Chapter 3) made it necessary to convert the base-year data on production and consumption into
this new unit. The base-year data refer to *1965*, i.e. to the
average of 1964-1966, and were taken from the FAO *Food
balance sheets: 1964-1966 average* (Rome, 1971). The method
of conversion into consumable protein is discussed in detail
in Annex 1.

Expressed in this unit, total food consumption shows the
demand made by all foodstuffs together on primary soil
production in agriculture. Processing losses (e.g. by the
production of meat on a grain basis) entail that *consumable*
does not equal *consumed*. Table 1.1 presents the regional
averages (derived from country averages) of food production
and consumption per caput expressed in terms of consumable
proteins, and compares these figures with the corresponding
values in terms of consumed proteins and consumption in
calories. Although the data of Table 1.1 are self-explanatory,
some of their implications may be spelled out explicitly:
-    in the industrialised nations (the Western market
     economies and Eastern Europe including the USSR),which
     contain 30 per cent of the world's population, more
     than half of the world's food is produced and also
     consumed. Seventy per cent of the world's population
     therefore has to make do with less than half the total
     amount of food;
-    food production per head of total population of a
     country is usually higher in countries with higher
     levels of income and wealth. In North America, for
     example, six times as much food is produced per head of
     population as in South Asia;
-    per caput food consumption in a country is closely re-
     lated to the national per caput income. In the richest
     countries the use of vegetal raw materials is four
     times as great as in the poorest countries; expressed
     in calories, however, the ratio is 1.5 : 1 because in
     the menu of the rich consumers the share of animal

products, for example, is relatively large;
- the relation between consumable protein and consumed protein varies strongly with the income level of the consumers. Between countries, the averages vary between 1.2 (below $100 p.c.) and 3 (above $1600 p.c.);
- taking into account an average food consumption norm of about 2200-2400 Kcal./day (corresponding with approximately 25 kg consumable protein/year), average food production per head of the world population was sufficient in *1965*; if it were evenly distributed no-one would need to suffer deprivation

By adding the amount of protein in non-food products (wood, cotton, wool, etc.) to total food production in consumable proteins, total agricultural product expressed in terms of vegetal proteins is obtained. The basic data are taken from the FAO *Production Yearbook*, and are converted into protein by using appropriate weights. The results are shown in column (4) of Table 1.2. (It may be noted in passing that in the model itself the share of non-food products in total agricultural output is given exogenously). Column (1) of this table shows the area of arable land in *1965*.

More interesting than these *1965* figures, however, are the findings reported in columns (2) and (4) of Table 1.2. They originate from the study described in detail in Chapter 2. On the basis of a detailed inventory of soil characteristics, rainfall, irrigation potential, temperature and sunshine, the study reported on in Chapter 2 estimated the absolute physical limit to agricultural output to be about 30 times the *1965* volume of production. A great deal of agriculturally suitable land is not yet used (see column (3)), but - above all - production per hectare could be increased considerably; see column (7).

This maximum production level is calculated - for 222 broad soil regions - for a purely hypothetical situation in which all growth circumstances that can be influenced by man are optimal. Thus, it presupposes perfect conditions as to water management, soil cultivation, fertilizer use, maintenance, pest control, environmental protection, and so on. Clearly, a hundred per cent satisfaction of these conditions - if at all possible - would require a tremendous input of capital, labour and know-how, not only in agriculture itself but also in the associated infrastructure. Also, it has to be recognized that the ecological implications of such a massive expansion of agricultural production remain rather uncertain. Therefore, the numerical findings reported in Table 1.2 represent a point of departure for further study rather than a conclusion in itself.

With due regard to its theoretical and hypothetical nature, the analysis of Chapter 2 nevertheless permits us to say with some confidence that - at least in the coming decades - world food supply need not be endangered by *upper limits* set

Table 1.1

Food production and food consumption in '1965'

	Food production[1] per caput	Food consumption[2] per caput			Ratio of consumed protein to consumable protein
	kg consumable proteins/year	in kg 'consumable' proteins/year	in kg 'consumed' proteins/year	in Kcal/day	
REGIONS					
North America	152	104	35	3180	0.34
Western Europe	49	81	33	3015	0.41
Japan	19	55	32	2501	0.58
Australia etc.	92	55	32	2942	0.59
Eastern Europe (incl. USSR)	74	74	34	3169	0.46
Subtotal: industrialised economies	*76*	*80*	*34*	*3047*	*0.42*
Latin America	47	43	24	2485	0.57
Middle East	27	32	23	2234	0.72
Tropical Africa	29	26	22	2160	0.85
Southern Asia	24	26	19	2002	0.73
China c.s.	30	30	22	2060	0.75
Subtotal: developing economies	*29*	*29*	*21*	*2100*	*0.72*
World	44	45	25	2398	0.55
INCOME CLASSES[3]					
< 100 $/cap.	24	24	19	1995	0.80
100 - 200	26	27	20	2062	0.73
200 - 400	32	32	22	2148	0.69
400 - 800	52	49	29	2718	0.59
800 - 1600	57	70	33	2988	0.47
> 1600	106	98	35	3150	0.35

[1] Of agricultural origin
[2] Fish included.
[3] Countries classified according to average per caput income in 1965, in dollars of 1965.
Note: 1965 refers to the average over the years 1964-1966.
Source: Calculations mainly based on FAO data.

Table 1.2

Actual and potentially suitable agricultural land;
actual and maximum agricultural production

	Arable land in '1965' mln. ha (1)	Potentially suitable agric. land mln. ha (2)	(1) in % of (2) (3)	Agr. prod. in 1965 10^8 kg cons. prot. (4)	Maximum agric. prod. 10^8 kg cons. prot. (5)	(4) in % of (5) (6)	(4)/(1) in % of (5)/(2) (7)
REGIONS							
North America	220	546	40	397	7159	5.6	14.0
Western Europe	129	147	88	233	2192	10.7	12.2
Japan	6	8	72	29	111	25.9	36.0
Australia etc.	59	284	21	86	2723	2.3	11.0
Eastern Europe (incl. USSR)	228	522	55	322	6042	5.3	9.6
Subtotal: industrial economies	*702*	*1507*	*47*	*1067*	*19228*	*5.5*	*11.7*
Latin America	122	695	18	173	14599	1.2	6.7
Middle East	52	111	47	35	1038	3.4	7.2
Tropical Africa	174	643	27	91	11681	0.8	3.0
Southern Asia	266	382	70	248	7520	3.3	4.7
China c.s.	111	349	32	267	3992	6.7	20.9
Subtotal: developing countries	*725*	*2180*	*33*	*815*	*38830*	*2.1*	*6.4*
World	1427	3687	39	1882	58058	3.2	8.2

Note: *1965 refers to the average over the years 1964-1966.*
Source: *Calculations mainly based on FAO data.*

by *mother nature*. The magnitude of the calculated non-
utilized capacity of the earth for food production is, in
spite of uncertainties that do exist, large enough to warrant
the conclusion that a three-to five-fold increase of the
production level is not impossible because of natural resource
constraints. It is primarily a large complex of economic,
social, and political factors that will determine the rate
of growth of agricultural production in the decades ahead.

The latter factors are studied in parts II and III of the
present volume, taking into account the technical production
relations in agriculture. The results of the analysis of
Chapter 2 also enter into the model to be described below,
in the form of a quantified estimate of natural resource
availability for agriculture at the country level. Thus,
differences between countries in natural resources for
agricultural production are incorporated in the model, and
have their implications for the relative costs of production
expansion. In this approach, natural resources for agricultural
production are seen as a given endowment, and hence as a
given factor of production at the country level.

1.3 *A MODEL OF WORLD AGRICULTURE*

A thorough analysis of the world food situation is
necessary if we are to learn on which factors the future
developments of food production and consumption in various
parts of the world will depend. Therefore, the focus of the
research effort reported in Part II lies in an attempt to
explain the circumstances and relations which characterize
world food supply and its development over time. The complexity of the linkages in national and international relations
and the necessity for quantification were the reason why
this explanation has taken the form of a mathematical model -
the model MOIRA.

Chapter 3 is devoted to a discussion of issues and aspects
of model building in general and those of MOIRA in particular.
As MOIRA is an algorithmic model, some problems associated
with this type of model are reviewed. Also, the choice of
the levels of aggregation in the model is discussed. An
appendix to the chapter is of a more technical character; it
deals with the advantages and disadvantages of cross-section
estimation, and with the choice and specification of functions.
The types of functions receiving attention correspond, of
course, with those that are used in MOIRA; however, actual
specification, estimation results, etc. are given only in
the next four chapters. These chapters deal with production,
consumption, the national market and the role of government,
and the world food market, in that order.

Chapter 4 describes the production side of MOIRA. The agricultural sector of a country is the smallest unit as far as
production is concerned; in the model, therefore, 106 production units annualy take a certain decision regarding the

level of production.

The model explains the size of agricultural output as depending
on the efforts of the farmers (the agricultural sector) to
combine so many variable production factors with the (short
term) given inputs (in particular, labour and land) that
their incomes (i.e. the value-added of the sector) are as
high as possible. The prices of end-products and of means of
production are taken as a given that cannot be influenced by
the agricultural sector; it is also assumed that the farmer
bases the expected price for his end-product on the prices
he has received in preceding years. Supply of agricultural
produce therefore depends on the endowment with natural
resources, on the amount of labour and on the prices of
inputs and output. The economic interrelations between
agriculture and other productive sectors may vary in intensity;
when these links are weaker, fluctuations in the price of
output have less influence on the volume of production. In
the extreme case of subsistence agriculture the price sensitivity of supply is nil.

Furthermore, the producer is assumed to be familiar with the
technicalities of the production process under the prevailing
natural circumstances. These technical relations are described by the model with a production function, estimated
with the aid of a cross-section over 106 countries. In this
equation, yields per hectare are assumed to be dependent on
the amount of labour and of labour-substituting capital
available per ha (the so-called operating capacity), in such
a way that enlargement of this input per ha is subject to
diminishing returns. The curve approaches asymptotically the
maximum possible level of yield per ha mentioned above,
determined *ex ante* for each of the 106 countries. This so-
called intensity-of-land-use function relates agricultural
output and operating capacity not to actual agricultural
area but to the total area of each country that can potentially be used for agricultural purposes. In effect, this
means that the two forms by which production can be augmented -
i.e., increased yields per ha and increased area of agricultural land - are not differentiated; they are described by
one and the same technical relationship. This stratagam was
adopted due to lack of data. As a result, it is impossible
to distinguish which of the two forms of production enlargement (or a combination) gives rise to the production growth
generated by the model over the course of time.

The production function is coupled to a demand function for
fertiliser; the latter is therefore considered as a production factor which is complementary to the input of labour
and labour-substituting capital.

Movement along the production function derived from cross-
section data is only possible if the level of production
technology changes. It is assumed that in the long term
technological improvement will actually occur if producers
strive to attain higher yields per ha; technological develop-

ments in the model are thus endogenously determined. In the
short term, however, the given level of technology can make
it impossible to achieve higher production. Changes in the
level of applied production techniques require time (research,
training, infrastructural investments, etc.). This time
factor is accounted for in the model by built-in limitations
to the growth rate of total production and to the rate at
which the amount of capital used per unit of labour may
change.

The size of the agricultural product in any given year is
dependent not only on decisions taken by the producers.
Change fluctuations in the harvest as a result of weather
conditions, the occurrence of disease etc., are introduced
into the model on a regional basis by assuming the repetition
of annual harvest fluctuations over a historic period.

The amount of agricultural labour used in any year is taken
as a given. In the course of time, this important production
factor is subject to change as a result of two developments:
natural population growth and the outflow of people from
agriculture to the non-agricultural sector. The model explains the latter change as being due in particular to the
income inequality between the agricultural sector and the
rest of the economy; the distribution of population over the
agricultural and non-agricultural sectors also plays a role.

Chapter 5 deals with food consumption, which is treated at a
lower level of aggregation than production. Average food
consumption per capita of a country may mask great differences within that country's borders, particularly as regards
income inequality, and throws insufficient if any light on
possible hunger. With this in mind, the consumers of each
country (with the exception of the three centrally planned
country groups) have been divided into income classes, six
for the agricultural population and six for the non-agricultural population. For each year the model thus calculates
the food consumption of roughly 1250 consumer groups.

The behaviour of the food consumer is described by a consumption function which explains per capita use of consumable
proteins as determined by per capita income and food price
levels. This function has also been estimated with the aid
of a country cross-section in which allowance is made for
the distribution of income within the respective countries.
In addition to this relation regarding the consumed volume
of primary agricultural products (measured in consumable
proteins), a second function shows the relation between the
consumer's food expenditure and the size of his income.
Combination of these two relations gives the value increase
due to processing of primary raw materials (in the form of
both processing within the agricultural sector and in the
food industry). This value increase due to processing, which
partly determines the difference between the producers'
price level of agricultural raw materials and the consumers'

food price level, is in turn strongly linked to a country's
level of prosperity.

Chapter 6 discusses the functioning of the food market at
the national level, taking into account the role of intermediaries in food trade and government policies concerning
the agricultural sector. With regard to the behaviour of
governments of the various countries, it is assumed that
they try to establish a certain distribution of income
between the agricultural sector and the rest of the economy
with the aid of the domestic food price level. This sectoral
income distribution thus reflects to some extent the political
power relations which pertain between urban and rural areas,
and which are in turn connected to the prevailing material
and institutional circumstances. Using again cross-section
analysis, an attempt has been made to link the great differences which exist between countries with regard to the
relative income position of the agricultural population with
such characteristics as agriculture's share in the national
income, population density, and actual per capita income in
agriculture. This statistical analysis can only partly explain the differences between countries; the remainder is
attributed to institutional factors which are difficult to
measure, and is therefore taken up as a structural characteristic of the government's behaviour in the country in
question. The government is thus accredited with an objective
which is endogenously generated by the model via this parity
function. From this follows the ratio which it tries to
attain between agricultural and non-agricultural per capita
incomes. From this income ratio the model derives the desirable domestic price level of food products (given the prices
of production inputs purchased by agriculture and given the
level of technology in the domestic agricultural production
process). The price level defined in this way may be considered as a market price, corrected by any other income
transfers (positive or negative) through taxation and subsidies, expressed per unit of output.

It is assumed that the government principally uses market
intervention as the method with which to achieve its agricultural income policy target. Further, that the instruments
of this price policy consist of trade policy measures which
are intended to keep clear of disruptive price influences
from the world market. Such measures (levies or subsidies on
imports and exports; quantitative restrictions on foreign
trade) have their consequences for the government budget.
Under certain circumstances the desired domestic price
policy may strand on prices that would be too high for the
national treasury (for a food-importing country at high
world market prices; for a food-exporting country at low
world market prices). The desired domestic price level will
then be impossible to maintain; if the budgetary burden is
too high, world market prices will influence the domestic
prices. The price policy in the model is therefore subjected
to budget restrictions (expressed in a percentage of the
income of the non-agricultural sector).

This also introduces the significant fact that wealthy countries (because they are rich) are better able to isolate
their domestic food markets from the world market than are
the poor countries whose much smaller budgetary capacity
will usually be far sooner exhausted.

Chapter 7 relates the functioning of the various domestic
markets to that of the world market. Developments in the
food supply sector in various parts of the world are not
independent of each other. Price formation on the world food
market brings the national markets into contact with each
other to a greater or lesser extent, dependent on the competitive conditions pertaining on the domestic market and
the restrictions on national food market policies. Moreover,
the international price level affects real national income
for as far as the latter is dependent on import expenditure
or on food export receipts. The domestic price level is the
result of the price level aimed at by government and of the
effect of the world market price. This latter variable
results from the total of demand and supply positions of the
countries in international trade. The model's iterative
procedure calculates the world market price which, partly
through its effect on national incomes and possibly also on
domestic prices, brings total consumption and supply into
equilibrium. Allowance is made for the fact that international
trade can partly bridge imbalances between demand and supply
by means of stockpiling.

The domestic price level that is related to this equilibrium
price in international trade is an important variable in
producers' decision-making regarding the size of the coming
year's supply.

Chapter 8 contains a discussion of the exogenous variables
and their rôle in MOIRA. The rate of growth of population is
completely exogenous to the model. The standard assumption
is one of a relatively fast decline in fertility, leading to
a doubling of the 1965 world population by the year 2010.
The growth rates are, of course, country-specific. The rate
of growth of non-agricultural GDP is another important
exogenous variable, and is again country-specific. The
assumed growth rates are, *grosso modo*, in line with those of
the basic scenario analyzed in the United Nations study on
The Future of the World Economy (New York, 1977).

For the poorest countries - in which the agricultural sector
is still very large - it is assumed that the rate of growth
of non-agricultural GDP cannot deviate too strongly from the
rate of growth in agriculture; the non-agricultural rate of
growth is adapted downwards if agricultural growth as generated in the model is found to be too low to be consistent
with the initially assumed non-agricultural growth rate.

A third exogenous variable discussed in this chapter is the
price level of (artificial) fertilizer. Long-term development of fertilizer prices is assumed to depend on the develop-

ment of production costs. Data on production cost structure
and transportation costs are used in a simple model (not
given explicitly in the present volume) that assumes a long-
term tendency towards an optimal situation in which fertilizer
production at the regional level takes place where it happens
to be most efficient to produce. Future fertilizer price
development is generated at this level only, and differences
between countries within a region are maintained at their
base-year magnitude. The chapter also analyzes the sensitivity
of fertilizer demand in MOIRA to fertilizer price changes.

Another exogenous factor playing a part in the simulation
runs of MOIRA is the level of food consumption that should
be realized from a nutritional point of view so as to avoid
hunger and malnutrition. Nutrition standards are discussed
in terms of the calorie norm, and in terms of the consumable
protein norm used in this study. The food consumption norm
is again country-specific.

Chapter 9 adds nothing new to the description and analysis
of the model, but tries to present a summary view of MOIRA.
The functioning of the model is illustrated with the help of
simplified arrow schemes; also, the main structure of the
computer programme is shown.

1.4 *ANALYSIS OF ALTERNATIVE SIMULATION RUNS*

The model presented in detail in Part II (Chapters 3-9)
is used in Part III to analyze the consequences of a number
of alternative international food policies. Prior to that,
the sensitivity of the model to alternative assumptions regarding the exogenous variables is studied.

Chapter 10 contains the numerical results of a selected
number of simulation runs of MOIRA. The runs that differ in
the assumed values of exogenous variables only are discussed
and compared in this chapter. This comparison provides at
the same time an opportunity to illustrate once more the
working of the model. The standard run of the model shows
what might be the future course of development of the world
food situation, given a number of specific assumptions. This
future development pattern is compared to that which results
from a simulation run based on lower rates of growth of non-
agricultural GDP. Similarly, the implications of a lower
rate of growth of population are analyzed. Another simulation
run shows the consequences of gradually decreasing income
inequalities in the non-agricultural sector, as compared to
the standard run in which income inequality remains unchanged.

The results of these and other simulation runs are shown
numerically for some of the variables only. Instead of the
original country values, the derived regional totals or
averages are given. Differences between regions in the
development patterns resulting from the simulation runs are
discussed as to their origin.

Chapter 11 is devoted to the use of MOIRA as an instrument
for the analysis of international food policies. The principal aim of such policies should be the provision of an
adequate food basket to every human being. Attention focuses
on devising acceptable strategies for fighting hunger. From
the various strategies, aspiration levels serving as intermediate objectives can be derived. Deviations of reality (as
simulated by the model) from these aspiration levels lead in
the model to corrective policy action.

Basically, the strategies analyzed fall into two classes:
measures intended to achieve a redistribution of available
food in the world, and measures intended to stimulate food
production in the developing countries. Measures of the
first type that are simulated with MOIRA comprise the (voluntary) reduction of food consumption in the rich countries,
and internationally-organized food aid on a large scale.
Measures of the second type concentrate on the functioning
of the world food market, aiming at a regulation of this
market in order to stabilize international prices. In this
context, the level at which prices will be stabilized (if
possible) is an important policy variable whose influence on
the production in developing countries is tested. Alternatively, the effect which liberalization of international trade
may have on developments in the world food situation is
examined.

In the first instance, the various policy measures are assessed as to their individual influence on the development
of world hunger (using also the standard run as a frame of
reference). Based on these findings, combinations of measures
are designed in order to determine what package of international policy measures might benefit most the development
of world food supply and the lowering of hunger in the world
during the coming three to four decades. The role of the
rich countries with regard to world food supply receives
special attention.

Chapter 12 finally, tries to give a tentative evaluation of
the study, from the point of view of the authors. What are
the possible merits and demerits of the approach that has
been chosen? What are the weak spots on which attempts at
improvement should concentrate first of all?

The outline of the study given above will hopefully allow
the reader to find his way in this volume without too much
trouble. Chapter 2 stands, largely, on its own; in as far as
its results are used in MOIRA, this is explained in Chapter
4. The hard core of the model is presented in Chapters 4-7,
and the results of the simulation runs in Chapters 10 and
11. The equations of the model are mostly given in Appendices
to the various chapters, as well as the formal analysis of
the properties of MOIRA. The computer programme in ALGOL is
available upon request.

Chapter 2

POTENTIAL WORLD FOOD PRODUCTION

2.1 *PURPOSE OF THIS CHAPTER*

The purpose of this chapter is to try and compute the absolute maximum food production of the world, the upper limit of what can be grown on all suitable agricultural land. Moreover, an assessment is made of land resources and productivity of more than 200 regions of the world, introducing at the same time the regional aspects of food production and land productivity.

The research reported in this chapter may be of broader interest than the specific use that is made of the findings in Part II of this study. The development of agricultural production depends, among other things, on the availability of natural resources. The assessment of natural resources availability presented here was made for its incorporation in the subsequent analysis, to determine the magnitude of two variables of importance in the production sphere: the total availability of agricultural land, and the hypothetical upper limit to photosynthetic food production.

The present analysis is a theoretical approach to these specific aspects of the complex food problem. It is based on measurements, appraisals and asssumptions which are presented separately, and performed at a rather high level of generalization because one is dealing with the whole world, and consequently the result is an approximation. The very high potentials of food production that are computed are realistic as such, but can hardly be obtained in practice because of a variety of other factors, including economic social and political limitations.

This chapter should not be misunderstood, conceptually nor by its purpose. The materials presented here estimate a theoretical potential of the world to produce food, under specified assumptions; the results are not intended to suggest that the absolute maximum production would be a desirable goal, or even that it could be attained in reality. Thus, it provides an input of information and estimates for others to use, to study and to improve if possible. The absolute maximum presented here is a theoretical one.

The authors of this chapters, who have published their findings earlier in a monograph of the Agricultural University

in Wageningen[1] in January 1975, are also fully aware of the
ecological aspects of increased food production. However,
relatively little is known at present about the ecological
characteristics of alternative land use patterns - too
little in any case to incorporate a full analysis on a
standardized and global basis. Further work needs to be done
here, in order to achieve proper weighing of all relevant
factors, including ecological considerations, in deciding
the future course of action and priorities for increasing
food production.

2.2 METHODS

2.2.1 Introduction

The authors studied the land resources and the
suitability and quality of the soils (Buringh and Staring),
and the climatic conditions and potential dry matter production (Van Heemst). In addition, data on the quantity of
water available for irrigation were collected from a recent
study by Moen and Beek (1974). In recent years it was generally accepted that about 1406.10^6 hectares of land are
cultivated at present and that a similar area would be
suitable for cultivation in the future, making a total area
of potential agricultural land of approximately 2800.10^6 ha
which is about 21 per cent of the land surface of the world.
Earlier studies by American specialists (The World Food
Problem, 1967; Simonson, 1967) revealed that there should be
approximately 3190.10^6 ha of potential agricultural land,
whereas some Russian soil scientists (Kovda, 1974) believe
that approximately 5000.10^6 ha of land could be cultivated.
This means about 25 per cent and 39 per cent of the land
surface, respectively.

The maximum food production on these areas has never been
estimated. Various specialists, however, have claimed that
the present food production could be multiplied by ten, and
in particular that this should not be very difficult in
(sub)tropical regions. Until recently, actual calculations
could not be made because of the absence of reliable soil
maps of the various continents. Now that the FAO/UNESCO soil
map of the world has become available, a much better basis
for assessing the land resources exists. The calculations
presented in this chapter are based on present knowledge of
soils and of modern means to bring these soils in the best
possible conditions by adding manure, fertilizers and other
production inputs, and by improving the soils by, for example,
drainage, subsoiling, or deep ploughing. This does not mean
that all land could be given a specific set of complicated
treatments for amelioration to create the ideal growing
conditions and realize a maximum yield. Many soils have
specific internal properties that will always limit growing
conditions and therefore crop production. Therefore, a

---

[1]P. Buringh, H.D.J. van Heemst and G.J. Staring, *Computation of the absolute maximum food production of the world*, Wageningen, 1975.

reduction factor is introduced if soil conditions are limiting food production.

Data on climate were collected for virtually the entire world. These data include precipitation, temperature, sunshine, relative humidity and wind. With these data the maximum photosynthesis and consequently the maximum dry matter production per hectare could be calculated. This is done on the basis of a standard crop, which has the properties of a cereal crop, for example wheat or rice, - the main food crops - and the final result is expressed in grain equivalents. Here is assumed that crop production takes place by applying modern farm management practices best suited to the prevailing local environmental conditions. Under these assumed optimal management practices there will be no degradation, accelerated soil erosion, salinization, sodication, etc.; also, there will be adequate flood protection. Plant diseases are assumed not to occur under these conditions.

Information on irrigation potential is available per country; this potential is distributed over the regions as if irrigation reaches the most suitable soils. Desalinized seawater is not considered to be a source of irrigation water, nor has anywhere been supposed that new, still unknown techniques of farm management will be introduced. The possibility of heating of soils in the cold zones is not taken into account.

The costs of food production are not studied in this chapter that does not deal with economic or social aspects, with one exception. As part of the potential agricultural land may have to be reclaimed in the future, a crude indication of the land development cost is given, in particular inasfar as these costs depend on topography, present vegetation and hydrological conditions.

2.2.2 *Land resources*

Soil conditions vary all over the world, often even over short distances. There are many thousands of soils with quite different characteristics and properties. Some soils are highly productive, others are inadequate for crop production. There are no detailed soil maps which show all soils in the world. The best map showing soil conditions of the continents is the new Soil Map of the World (1:15,000,000), compiled by a large number of competent soil scientists and published by FAO/UNESCO (1974). For the continents for which these maps are not yet available other recent maps were used. Australia (Stace, 1968), Asia (Kovda and Lobova) and Europe (Dudal, Tavernier and Osmond, 1966).

Each continent has been subdivided into 30 to 50 broad soil regions. For South America (see figure 2.1) the broad soil region map of FAO (figure 7 in Vol. IV of the Soil Map of the World) was used. For the other continents similar maps

were made, based on the soil maps of the continents. In
total 222 broad soil-units have been distinguished. A broad
soil region is a physiographic unit (see figures 2.1-2.6)
indicated with a symbol on the maps. Each region covers a
very large area with quite different soil conditions. The
area of each broad soil region was measured by the plani-
metric method on map scale 1:15,000,000. The scale of the
maps in this chapter is much smaller and these maps are
somewhat simplified. The symbols on the maps (figures 2.1-
2.6) correspond with those in the tables of the appendix to
the chapter (Tables A2.1-A2.6); the tables give the results
of our measurements and calculations. The character A refers
to lowlands, B to uplands, C to high mountain lands and D to
dry deserts and tundras. The total area of each broad soil
region (TA) is given in column 2 in the Appendix tables, and
is summarized in table 2.1 below. The total land area of the
continents is taken from data given in the Winkler-Prins
atlas (Elsevier, Amsterdam, 1954). The area of each broad
soil region as a percentage of the total area of the continent concerned is given in column 3 (TA%) of the Appendix
tables A2.1-A2.6.

Table 2.1

*Total area, by type and geographic region
(in millions of ha)*

	A Low- lands	B Up- lands	C · High mountain	D Desert, Tundra	total land area	Land per region, % of total
South America	700	810	270	–	1780	13.1
Australia, New Zealand	167	460	86	167	880	6.5
Africa	280	1682	134	934	3030	22.4
Asia	843	1521	1261	765	4390	32.4
North+Central America	662	683	160	915	2420	17.9
Europe	498	349	157	46	1050	7.7
WORLD TOTAL	3150	5505	2068	2827	13550	100.0
Land Type, % of total	23.2	40.6	15.3	20.9	100.0	

As a next step, the soils occurring in each broad soil
region were studied. Not all soils of a region can be used
for crop production; some are very poor, too stony, too
steep or too shallow, others are already used for urban or
other non-agricultural purposes (10-30 per cent). Poor land
used for extensive grazing, a part of the forested areas,
and lakes and swamps that cannot be reclaimed, are also
excluded. This means that the potential agricultural land
(PAL) that could be used for crop production is a fraction
of the area of a broad soil region. The appraisal of this
fraction (FPAL) is given in column 5 of the Appendix tables.
The area of potential agricultural land (PAL) is calculated
with the formula

$$PAL = TA \cdot FPAL$$

(2.1)

for each broad soil region. The result is given in column 6 of the Appendix tables A2.1-A2.6 and summarized below, in tabel 2.2 Although extensive grazing, cultivation of some specific crops and some commercial forestry may be feasible on land that is excluded, this production is ignored in this study.

Table 2.2

Potential agricultural land by region
(in million ha)

	Total land area (mln.ha)	Fraction(%) usable for crops	Potential agricultural land(mln.ha)	Potential agricultural land as % of World Total
South America	1780	34.4	617	16.6
Australia, New Zealand	880	25.7	226	6.1
Africa	3030	25.1	762	20.5
Asia	4390	24.6	1081	29.9
North & Central America	2420	26.0	629	16.9
Europe	1050	38.0	399	10.7
WORLD TOTAL	13550	27.4	3714	100.0
Lowland	3150	48.5	1529	41.2
Upland	5505	37.7	2075	55.9
High Mountain	2068	5.3	110	2.9
Desert, Tundra	2827	–	–	–

It should be noted that, for most continents, the fraction of total land usable for agricultural cropping differs little from the world average. Exceptions are South America and even more Europe, where higher fractions are usable. In those regions lowlands and uplands take a larger share of total land and those are, according to the figures in the lower half of the table, relatively more attractive for cropping.

Even if climate and farm management were ideal not all soils can produce the maximum production because of internal soil properties that are not optimal, and that can hardly be improved. In many regions soil conditions may prove to be a limiting factor in crop production. Therefore, a reduction factor FSC (reduction factor soil condition) is introduced. For each region this factor is appraised and given in column 8 of the Appendix tables. Now we can calculate IPAL, the imaginary area of potential agricultural land with potential production:

$$IPAL = PAL \cdot FSC \qquad (2.2)$$

This imaginary area is given in column 10 of the Appendix tables. For reasons to be explained in the next paragraph

this formula is applied only if soil conditions restrain
cultivable area more than possible water deficiencies
which are discussed below.

In other regions, where precipitation in particular during
the growing season of crops is low, water deficiency becomes
the limiting factor for crop production. The factor for water
deficiency FWD can be calculated as is explained below;
see Chapter 2.2.4. It is given in column 9 in the Appendix
tables. For regions having FWD < FSC, which means that water
deficiency is the limiting factor, the following formula is
used - instead of Chapter 2.2 - to calculate the imaginary
area of potential agricultural land IPAL in column 10 of the
Appendix tables:

$$IPAL = PAL . FWD \qquad\qquad (2.3)$$

The estimates are summarized in table 2.3, on the next page.

In water deficient regions irrigation may provide the required additional water to reach the maximum crop production.
Water resources, however, are limited and therefore only a
low percentage of the land can be irrigated. In a study by
Moen and Beek (1974), the potential irrigable area for a
great many countries was determined. The study draws heavily
on a report by the International Commission on Irrigation
and Drainage (ICID), 1969: *Irrigation and drainage in the
world, a global review,* and on some more recent publications
by FAO and individual countries. This information was adapted
and applied to the broad soil regions used in the present
study. In column 12 of the Appendix tables the potential
irrigable agricultural land PIAL is given for each region
where water is available and irrigation is needed. It is
supposed that the best soils in those regions are irrigated
first, and if enough water is available soils with some
limitations can also be irrigated. If no definite information
was available (USSR, China) the irrigation projects have
been located in the drier zones. We did not take into account
the quality of the irrigation water, the possibilities of
desalinization of sea-water, the availability of ground
water and the possibility of diverting rivers in a completely
different direction.

In regions where part of the land can be irrigated (PIAL),
the soil conditions are again the limiting factor to production for those parts that are potentially irrigable. The
soil condition factor FSC cannot be applied for the irrigated
land, because irrigation water will be applied to the best
land of the region concerned. Such land has a higher FSC
than the average FSC of all the potential agricultural land
of the region. Consequently, the FSC for the irrigated
part - called FSCI - is set at 0.8, which is considered
acceptable for such land.

The imaginary area of potential agricultural land with
potential production including irrigation (IPALI) therefore
is:

(a)   for regions where the soil condition is the limiting

factor of the non-irrigated land (FWD $\geq$ FSC):

IPALI = PIAL . FSCI + (PAL - PIAL) . FSC   (2.4)

and

(b) for regions where water deficiency is the limiting
     factor of the non-irrigated land (FSE < FSC):

IPALI = PIAL . FSCI + (PAL - PIAL) . FWD   (2.5)

The result of this calculation (IPALI) is given in column 13
in the Appendix tables and summarized in the last two columns
of table 2.3.

Table 2.3

*Imaginary potential agricultural land after correction
for soil and water deficiencies*

	Potential agr. cropland (mln ha)	Correction* factor for soil and water deficiencies	Imaginary potential agr. land (mln ha)	Possible additional land through irrigation	Total potential area incl. irrigation (mln ha)
South America	617	.54	334	8	342
Australia, New Zealand	226	.33	75	2	77
Africa	762	.40	303	11	314
Asia	1081	.42	455	127	582
North & Central America	629	.51	320	17	337
Europe	399	.53	223	28	251
WORLD TOTAL	3714	.46	1710	193	1903
Lowland	1529	.54	824	97	921
Upland	2075	.40	847	86	923
High Mountain	110	.35	39	8	47
Desert, Tundra	–	–	–	2	2

* The correction factor presented here is an average over broad regions
and soil types. The actual calculations presented in the Appendix
tables distinguish for each soil category separately a reduction factor
for soil conditions and for water deficieny, but the aggregates above
only present the results of their detailed application.

2.2.3 *Development costs*

A part of the area of potential agricultural land
PAL is already cultivated; there is, however, also much land
that can be reclaimed or improved in the future. This requires
capital inputs. In column 7 of the Appendix tables an appraisal of these capital inputs is given in five classes of
development costs. Class 1 represents very low costs of

reclamation or improvement and class 5 very high costs, because clearing of dense forest vegetation, soil conservation, terracing, levelling and/or drainage, etc. may be needed. The classes 2, 3 and 4 are intermediate. It is expected that the costs of class 1 shall be less than $200 and of class 5 approximately $3000 per hectare in US dollars of 1975. The development cost classes (DCC) are given in column 7 of the Appendix tables. The data are not used in the calculations given below. For agronomists and economists they may be of interest as tentative indication of the capital inputs required..

It should be kept in mind that the estimate of potential agricultural land is an assessment independent of the climate. An exception has been made for real desert soils without possibilities of irrigation and/or tundras (group D at the lower part of the tables).

The estimates are summarized in table 2.4 below. It should be noted that the classification is made on the basis of potential agricultural land (PAL) rather than for the part which remains after taking account of soil and water deficiencies (IPAL).

Table 2.4

*Potential agricultural land by development category
(in mln ha)*

| | Development cost category | | | | | Total |
	1	2	3	4	5	PAL
South America	45	63	184	125	200	617
Australia, New Zealand	–	–	65	137	24	226
Africa	93	287	210	163	9	762
Asia	56	245	419	246	115	1081
North & Central America	65	124	403	37	–	629
Europe	35	118	203	39	4	399
WORLD TOTAL	294	837	1484	747	352	3714
Categories as % of total	8	23	40	20	9	100
Lowland	140	426	522	263	178	1529
Upland	154	411	861	475	174	2075
High Mountain	–	–	202	9	–	110
Tundra, Desert	–	–	–	–	–	–

The table shows that land resources which appear cheap to develop are scarce, at 8 per cent of total potential agricultural land. Less than one third can be developed at less than average cost, mainly in Africa and Asia.

2.2.4 *Climate conditions and photosynthesis*

Crop production also depends on climate, which varies widely. It was attempted to estimate the theoretical potential production, that is the production of a healthy, green, closed, standard crop, well supplied with nutrients, oxygen, water and foothold, and therefore limited only by the daily photosynthetic rage which depends on the state of the sky, the latitude and the date. In order to calculate the potential production in each broad soil region many climatic data of many locations were collected. These include the monthly air temperature, precipitation, solar energy, etc. De Wit (1965) gives for a standard crop a table indicating for the middle of every month of the year the daily totals of photosynthesis on every clear (PC) and overcast (PO) day at various latitudes. PC and PO can be derived from this table for any location by linear interpolation. These totals, calculated on the basis of the light climate, can only be reached when the average temperature is reasonable. This is presumed to be the case when the average temperature is 10°C or higher. The mean monthly gross photosynthesis GP can be computed by using the formula

$$GD = ID \{F . PO + (1-F) . PC\} \tag{2.6}$$

in which

GP = gross photosynthesis expressed in kg carbohydrate per ha, per month
ID = the number of days in the month
F = the fraction of the time when the sky is overcast:

$$F = 1 - h . H^{-1} \tag{2.7}$$

h = mean monthly sum of hours of sunshine, local data
H = the monthly sum of maximum hours of sunshine, derived from meteorological tables or computed.

To convert carbohydrates of gross photosynthesis (GP) into plant dry matter (DM) with a standard chemical composition the following formula is applied (Penning de Vries, 1973):

$$DM = 0.65 . GP, \text{ or}$$
$$DM = 0.65 . ID \{F . PO + (1-F) . PC\} \tag{2.8}$$

Summing up the monthly totals for the months with an average temperature of 10°C or higher during three months or more gives the potential dry matter production PDM of the specific location in kg per hectare per year in roots, stem, leaves, flowers and fruits. The PDM as calculated for each broad soil region is shown in column 4 of the Appendix tables in 1000 kg per hectare per year. If the number of months with an average temperature of 10°C or higher is less than three the production is considered to be zero, because the growing season becomes too short for arable farming.

The standard crop that is presumed to be grown has the properties of a cereal, belonging to the group of C_3-plants.

At average temperatures between 25° and $35^{\circ}C$ a C_4-plant is
able to maintain higher growth rates than a C_3-plant can.

The potential evapotranspiration depends only on the climate
and is defined as the amount of water which will be lost
from a surface completely covered with vegetation if there
is sufficient water in the soil at all times. The potential
evapotranspiration (Eo) is calculated according to Penman.
In the calculation of Eo mean monthly weather data are used.
The actual evapotranspiration is also based on rain data and
calculated by evaluation of a monthly water balance, assuming an average of 150 mm water storage in all soils. To
obtain the initial value of the soil water storage, the
water balance programme is run for two years, and only the
values of the second year are considered. A complete description is given by Arbab (1972). Adding the monthly totals
for the months with an average temperature of $10^{\circ}C$ or
higher during three months or more gives the potential and
actual evapotranspiration of the specific location during
the growing season.The difference between potential and
actual evapotranspiration is the moisture deficit during the
growing season. This is often one of the limiting factors
for potential production. Actual transpiration is actual
evapotranspiration minus potential evaporation. Potential
transpiration is potential evapotranspiration minus potential evaporation. Actual transpiration is set at zero if the
actual evapotranspiration is less than the potential evaporation. It is assumed that the potential evaporation is 15 per
cent of the potential evapotranspiration.

Finally, the reduction factor caused by water deficiency FWD
as used in equations (2.3) and (2.5) is the ratio between
the actual transpiration and the potential transpiration. It
is determined for all broad soil regions according to local
climatic data, see column 9 of the Appendix tables, A2.1-A2.6.

2.2.5 *Maximum production of dry matter*

        In the Chapters 2.2.2 and 2.2.3 the imaginary
area of potential agricultural land with potential production
IPAL was calculated for soil conditions being the limiting
factor - using (2.2) - and for water deficiency being the
limiting factor - using (2.3). Moreover, the area of potential
irrigable agricultural land (PIAL was determined if irrigation
water is available. In Chapter 2.2.4 the potential production
of dry matter was calculated per hectare per year (PDM, see
column 4 of the Appendix tables). This provides the possibility
to calculate for each broad soil region the maximum production of dry matter MPDM.

For regions without irrigation practices the following
formula is used:

        MPDM = IPAL . PDM

$$(2.9)$$

Substitution of IPAL according to (2.2) or (2.3) gives

a)   for regions where the soil condition is the limiting
     factor (FWD $\geq$ FSC):

     MPDM = PAL . FSC . PDM   (2.10)

b)   for regions where water deficiency is the limiting
     factor (FWD < FSC):

     MPDM = PAL . FWD . PDM   (2.11)

The resulting value of MPDM is given in Column 11 of the
Appendix tables.

For regions where part of the land is irrigated, the maximum
production of dry matter MPDMI can be calculated as

     MPDMI = IPALI x PDM   (2.12)

Substitution of IPALI according to (2.4) or (2.5) gives

a)   for regions where the soil condition is the limiting
     factor of the non-irrigated land (FSD $\geq$ FSC):

     MPDMI = (PIAL . FSCI + (PAL-PIAL) . FSC) . PDM   (2.13)

b)   for regions where water deficiency is the limiting
     factor of the non-irrigated land (FWD < FSC):

     MPDMI = (PIAL . FSCI + (PAL-PIAL) . FWD) . PDM   (2.14)

The resulting value of MPDMI is given in column 14 of the
Appendix tables. When no land is irrigated (i.e. PIAL is
zero in column 12), column 14 simply repeats the number in
column 11.

Table 2.5 demonstrates the significant differences in production potential between geographic regions and also between
the four main land classes. Effects of multiple cropping
possibilities in sub-tropical and tropical areas (which
classify to a large extent with low lands and uplands) are
notable.

For almost all broad soil regions the equations (2.10), (2.11),
(2.13) and (2.14) have been used to calculate MPDM or MPDMI,
the maximum dry matter production without or with irrigation,
taking into account the limiting factors, being either soil
condition or water deficiency for non-irrigated land. For
some regions where irrigation is or can be practised over a
large part of that region a somewhat different FSCI has been
used, as showed in Table 2.5.

(a) for the broad soil regions Asia A6, South America B10,
     and Europe B5, where FSC = 0.8, FSCI is set at 0.9 because
     the best soils of these regions will be irrigated and
     those soils have a higher FSC than the average of
     column 8.
(b) for two broad soil regions (Asia B5 and B7) the FSCI =

FSC + 0.1 for the same reason.
(c)   the broad soil regions where FSC = 0.9 (Africa A2,
       Asia A3, A5, A7 and A10, North America A9, B7 and
       Europe A4, A10 and A11), FSCI is set at 0.9.

Table 2.5

Potential production of dry matter, by regions

	Potential dry matter production $(10^3$ kg/ha)[1]	Imaginary potential agricultural land (M ha)		Potential production of dry matter $(10^9$ kg)	
			incl. irrigation	excl. irrigation	incl. irrigation
South America	75.5	334	342	25216	25700
Australia, New Zealand	70.5	75	77	5297	5462
Africa	79.5	303	314	24162	24674
Asia	55.0	455	582	24946	33058
North & Central America	47.5	320	337	15213	16184
Europe	37.0	223	251	8290	9653
WORLD TOTAL	60.5	1710	1903	103124	114731
Lowland	54.0	824	921	44582	50465
Upland	67.5	847	923	57046	62087
High Mountain	38.5	39	47	1496	2005
Desert, Tundra	–	–	2	–	174

[1]Average of detailed estimates by soil regions, as shown in the Appendix tables; excluding production on land which can potentially be irrigated.

2.2.6 *Maximum production of grain equivalents*

The maximum production of dry matter per year MPDMI as calculated in column 14 of the Appendix tables can be added for each continent and for the whole world (see Appendix tables A2.7). It can be converted into a maximum cereal (grain) production, because the calculations made are based on the assumption that a standard crop (see Chapter 2.2.4) is grown. This could be rice or wheat, for example. This production is called the grain equivalent production. In order to calculate the maximum production of grain equivalents MPGE for each region, for each continent and for the whole world the following assumptions have been made.

The dry matter production consists of
(a)   roots and stubble: 25 per cent of dry matter;
(b)   straw and grain: 75 per cent of dry matter, ratio 1:1;
(c)   harvest losses: 2 per cent of grains with modern harvesting methods;

(d)   moisture content of grains: 15 per cent.

Therefore

$$MPGE = \frac{0.75 \times 0.50 \times 0.90 \times 100 \times MPDMI}{85} \qquad (2.15)$$

or

MPGE = 0.432 x MPDMI

The maximum production of grain equivalents MPGE for each
region is given in column 15 in the Appendix tables A2.1-A2.6.

2.3   *THE RESULTS AND THEIR RELIABILITY*

2.3.1 *The maps*

         The maps are simplified versions on a reduced
scale; see figures 2.1-2.6. The original soil maps of the
continents were used (see Chapter 2.2.2) which give information
on the soils occurring in each broad soil region. Sometimes
also some more detailed soil maps of specific countries were
used. In addition, maps were studied on topography, land use
and natural vegetation in some modern world atlasses. As
soon as the sheets of the Soil Map of the World (FAO/UNESCO)
on Asia, Australia and Europe are published, the corresponding maps (figures 2.4, 2.2 and 2.6) can be improved. If
more time had been available it would have been possible to
distinguish on this FAO/UNESCO Soil Map of the World some
soil regions for each country (depending on the size and the
ecological conditions of the country) in order to get specific
data for the various countries. However, it probably would
be better to study the original soil maps of the countries.

The soil Map of the World does not have an equal reliability
for all parts of the world. Therefore, the reliability of
the maps presented here is different also and not higher
than the reliability of the original soil maps. The maps have
been simplified further for this publication; parts of some
regions (groups of islands) are not shown.

2.3.2 *The calculations*

         All calculations according to the formulas men-
tioned before are made with non-rounded numbers. Therefore
some slight differences may occur if calculations are made
with the rounded numbers as given in the tables.

2.3.3 *The data on land resources*

         There are two important appraisals:

(a)   FPAL, the fraction of potential agricultural land, and
(b)   FSC, the reduction factor due to soil conditions.

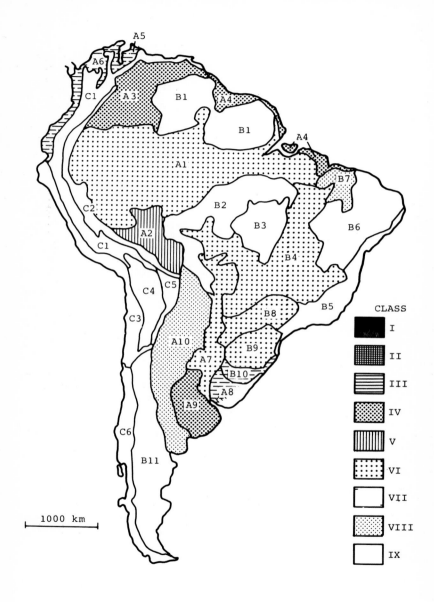

Fig. 2.1

The broad soil regions of South America

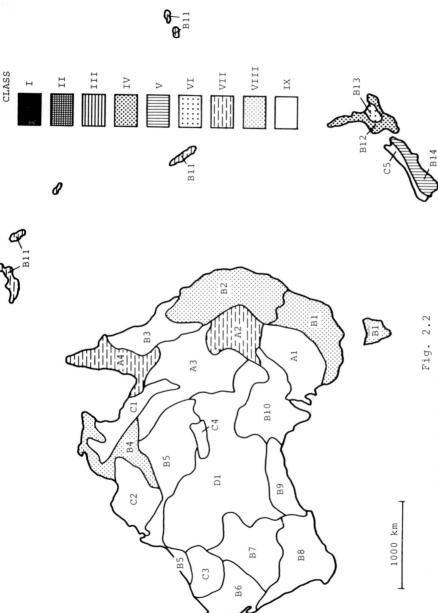

Fig. 2.2

The broad soil regions of Australia and New Zealand

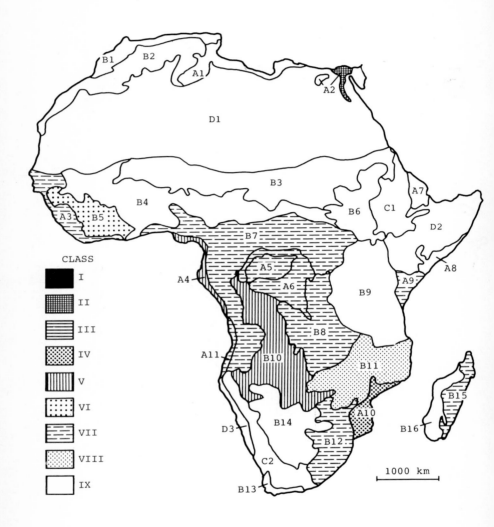

Fig. 2.3

The broad soil regions of Africa

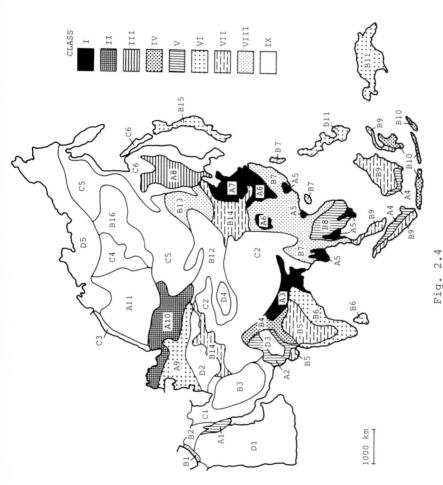

Fig. 2.4

The broad soil regions of Asia

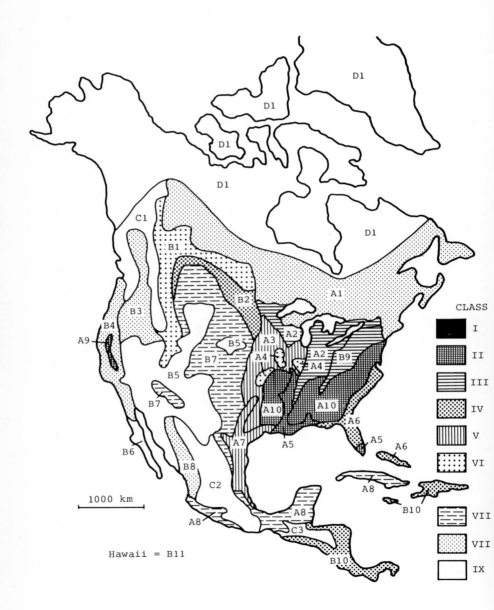

Fig. 2.5

The broad soil regions of North & Central America

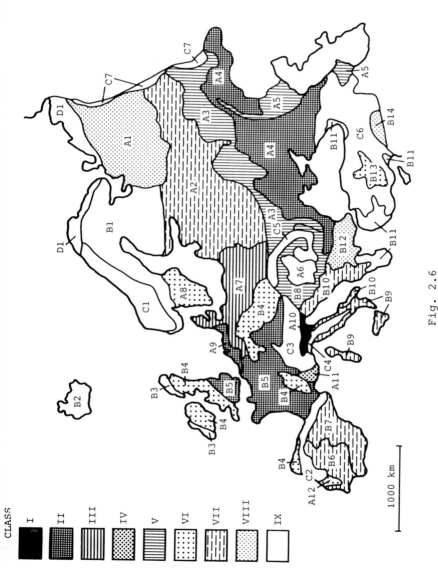

Fig. 2.6

The broad soil regions of Europe

Both are based on an evaluation of soil conditions in each
region. FPAL is also based on topography, elevation, land
use and natural vegetation. FPAL is mostly less than 0.5 and
it is never higher than 0.7, because at least 30 per cent of
the land will be needed for non-agricultural purposes. The
appraisal of FSC is based on knowledge of soil conditions
and soil productivity. When the appraisals are studied in
detail it will be evident that the climatic conditions are
not taken into account in this stage of the calculation. It
is assumed that the climate is optimal. The climatic conditions are considered separately in Chapter 2.3.5 in order
to give every specialist the opportunity to modify the
calculation by introducing his own specific appraisals or
assumptions. A disadvantage is that in some dry regions the
area of potential agricultural land (PAL) may be rather
large, but water deficiency is absolute. Examples are the
regions B5 and B7 in Australia. If there is no water for
irrigation, PAL could have been set equal to zero as has
been done for purely desert areas. The consequence is that
the total potential agricultural land PAL of some continents
and of the world as a whole is somewhat too high. Therefore,
for these totals a corrected PAL is introduced.

The potential agricultural land that can produce two or even
three crops per year is not counted two or three times to
get a potential gross agricultural land area, because the
double and triple cropping is taken into account in the
calculation of the production of dry matter (PDM).

The two hypothetical areas with potential production, IPAL
(without irrigation) and IPALI (including irrigation) have a
theoretical meaning only as they represent stages in the
calculation procedure.

In order to know the relative importance of the availability
of potential agricultural land in all broad soil regions independent of the size of the area, a calculation is made of
the hypothetical area of potential agricultural land including irrigation (IPALI) as a percentage of the total area
(TA). The data for all regions are given in table 2.6.

With these data a classification of the relative importance
of the availability of potential agricultural land was established. Nine classes are defined in Appendix table A2.9,
and for each region the class has been indicated on the maps
(figures 2.1-2.6). These maps give an impression of the
regional distribution of the potential agricultural land per
continent.

It is also possible to calculate the absolute maximum production in grain equivalents per hectare potential agricultural land by dividing MPGE by PAL for each region. This
is done for all regions (see Appendix table A2.10), except
for the mountains, dry deserts and tundras, because in those
regions the area of potential agricultural land is very
limited or zero.

Table 2.6

Imaginary potential agricultural land (incl. irrigation, IPALI)
as per cent of total area (TA), by continents and
land classes[1]

	Lowland	Upland	High Mountain	Tundra, Desert	Total
South America	28.4	16.7	3.0	–	19.2
Australia, New Zealand	13.2	11.7	1.2	–	8.8
Africa	20.4	15.2	1.5	–	10.4
Asia	33.6	17.8	2.1	0.3	13.3
North & Central America	30.4	19.3	2.5	–	13.9
Europe	31.9	24.9	3.2	–	23.9
WORLD TOTAL	29.2	17.0	2.3	0.1	14.0

[1]Source: see Appendix table A2.8

Table 2.7

Classification of soils by continents according to maximum
production in terms of grain equivalent (M ha)

	Maximum production (1000 kg/ha)					
	I >25	II >20–25	III >15–20	IV >10–25	V >5–10	VI ≤5
South America	3	185	287	108	–	12
Australia, New Zealand	–	49	19	26	68	60
Africa	5	135	335	95	92	93
Asia	69	135	214	352	51	197
North & Central America	–	48	144	87	342	–
Europe	–	4	12	224	151	1
TOTAL	77	556	1011	892	704	362

Land productivity classes for potential agricultural land, based on grain equivalents, are established (see Appendix table A2.11). In a special set of maps (figures 2.7–2.12) the regions of all continents are classified according to this system. This is a type of land capability classification, indicating the absolute maximum productivity. It is based on soil and climatic characteristics, and irrigation possibilities. Here it becomes clear that good tropical and subtropical land with irrigation possibilities is suitable for double or triple cropping. Therefore, it is classified in

a higher class than land in temperate regions on which only
one crop per year can be grown. The classification includes
only the potential agricultural land, which usually does not
exceed 50 per cent of a region.

2.3.4 *The data on irrigation*

The International Commission on Drainage and
Irrigation (and some other sources) indicate an area of 201
millions of hectares irrigated at present, which can be
expanded to 458 millions of hectares for 103 countries. Moen
and Beek (1974) have introduced some new information and
have found a potential irrigable agricultural land area
(PIAL) for the whole world of 470 millions of hectares (see
Appendix table A2.7). They also indicate that an overall
irrigation efficiency of 50 per cent could be reached, which
is approximately 10 to 30 per cent higher than the present
overall irrigation efficiency. However, an additional 10 to
30 per cent of the water supplied to the farms will be
needed for washing and leaching in order to avoid salinization and sodication. The increased irrigation efficiency
provides water for washing and leaching and consequently no
special correction factor had to be introduced. For more
details reference is made to Moen and Beek (1974).

The data on potential irrigable land for more than a hundred
countries as determined by Moen and Beek (1974) have been
converted to the data by broad soil regions. For some large
countries with a large area of potentially irrigable land
(e.g. USSR, China) it was often difficult to decide which
part of the total potential irrigable land should be allocated to the various broad soil units. There will be mistakes;
for the totals of the various continents, however, these
mistakes are not important. The numbers of column 12 (PIAL)
of the Appendix tables A2.1-A2.7 are not very accurate, in
particular for the USSR and China. Moreover, the reliability
of the data used could be improved if more information, in
particular on the potential irrigable land per catchment
area, would be available.

There are some regions where rice is grown with very large
quantities of irrigation water (e.g. Bangladesh); for such
regions no corrections were made.

2.3.5 *The data on climate and crop production*

The assumptions and calculations are based on
similar studies made for other purposes and published some
years ago or recently (see Chapters 2.2.4 - 2.2.6). The
climatic data used often cover a long, but sometimes only a
short period, whereas in some cases an interpolation of data
of some weather stations was made. In the case of a total
absence of climatic data in some regions, data were used
from locations of similar climates. The climate classification of Papadakis was used to find similar climates. In
areas with relatively good soils weather stations are often

present, which increases the reliability.

The assumption that the water storage of all soils suitable for cultivation is 150 mm had to be introduced in order to avoid very complicated calculations. It is known that some soils have a water storage of less than 50 mm, others of more than 200 mm. However, for the time being no useful differentiation could be made. If similar calculations are made in more detail, e.g. for some specific countries, this aspect surely needs more attention. The same applies to the standard crop and some other assumptions. On a world-wide scale, however, it is hardly possible to introduce a larger number of parameters as this would lead to significant complications.

There are some regions where climatic conditions are favourable for growing two or even three crops per annum, in particular when irrigation water is available. In such regions the PDM is much higher than in regions where only one crop can be grown.

It may seem somewhat extreme to assume a high level of modern farm management and a potential production of dry matter (or grain equivalents) all over the world on all land that could be cultivated. The purpose, however, was to calculate the absolute upper boundary of food production (in grain equivalents) for the whole world. It should be repeated again that many other factors will have to be taken into account in order to get results that could have some meaning in practice. For example, much food is lost by diseases and during transport and storage; for this reason a specific reduction factor could be chosen, which could vary for the various regions.

The land that is not included in these calculations because of topography, elevation, poor soil conditions or poor climatic conditions, etc. can be used and often is used by farmers, e.g. for extensive grazing. The yield is low. This was neglected, because total production of this land is small in comparison with the total potential production. In more detailed calculations for specific countries it probably cannot be neglected.

In various regions the productive season is somewhat longer than the growing season of one crop; it is, however, too short to grow two crops. As the calculations are based on all months suitable for crop production, the results are sometimes higher than could be expected in practice.

2.4 DISCUSSION OF THE RESULTS

2.4.1 Great importance of some regions

The maximum production of dry matter (MPDM) and of grain equivalents (MPGE) is strongly influenced by (a) the size of some broad soil regions with favourable soil and

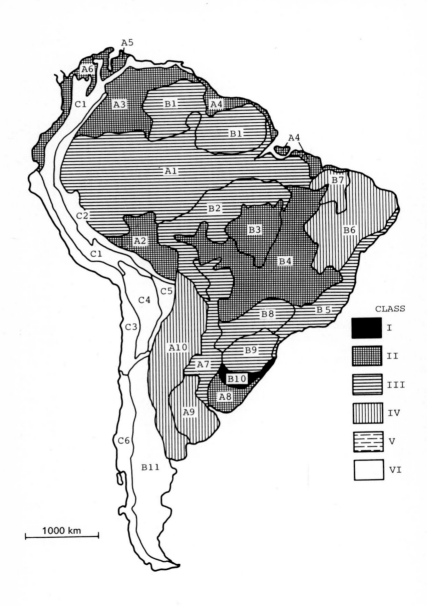

Fig. 2.7

Land productivity classes in South America

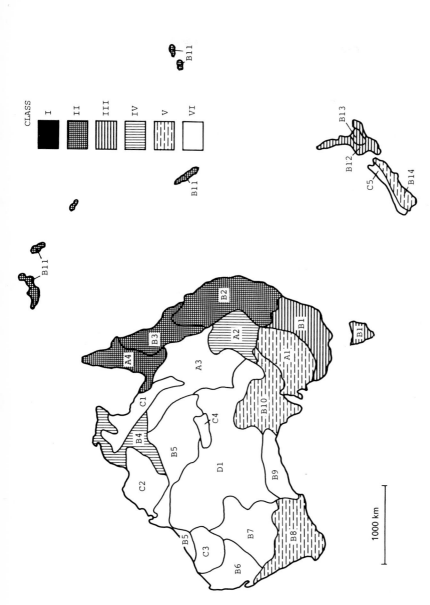

Fig. 2.8

Land productivity classes in Australia and New Zealand

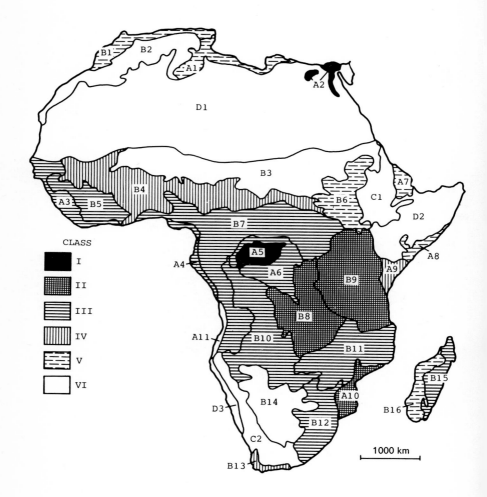

Fig. 2.9
Land productivity classes in Africa

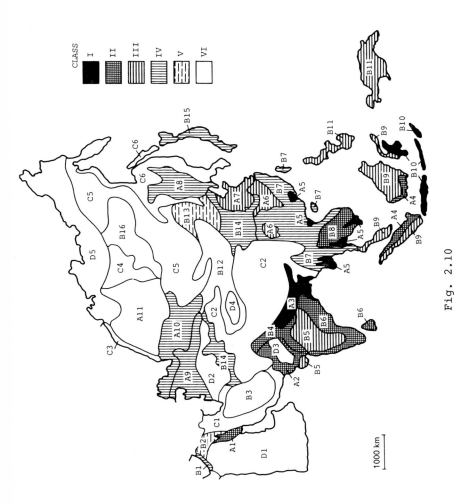

Fig. 2.10

Land productivity classes in Asia

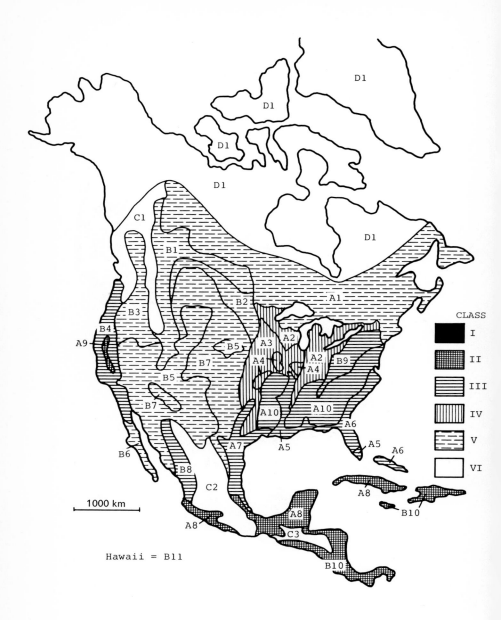

Fig. 2.11

Land productivity classes in North and Central America

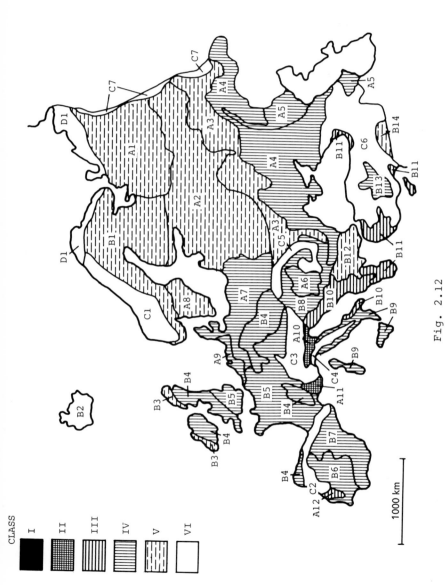

Fig. 2.12

Land productivity classes in Europe

climatic conditions, and (b) some smaller regions with excellent soils and important possibilities for irrigation. In each continent only a limited number of regions is really important for the computation. More than 50 per cent of the grain equivalent production in a continent could be obtained from 3 to 4 major regions, except for Asia where this number is 10. This means that for the world at large more than half of the maximum production could be grown in 28 out of 222 regions. Therefore, the appraisals and assumptions made for these regions have a much greater influence on the final result than those for other regions. These important regions are given special attention.

2.4.2 *The continents*

Once more attention is drawn to the fact that the environmental conditions in the various regions are not at all homogeneous. With the help of fraction of the potential agricultural land (FPAL) and the reduction factors caused by soil conditions (FSC) and by water deficiency (FWD) it was tried to eliminate this difficulty. Moreover, the calculations are based on the potential yield of a standard crop to be grown on all suitable land, whereas at the moment in practice there is sometimes a fallow-system of farming and approximately 35 per cent of the area is used to grow non-cereal crops.

South America has been divided into 27 broad soil regions. At present 4.4 per cent is cultivated and 33.5 per cent is potential agricultural land. It is the continent with the most promising possibilities for food production, although soil conditions are not as good as those in other continents, except Australia. There are very large reserve areas, e.g. the Amazone catchment area, although only half of the Amazone region has been indicated as potentially arable. Some regions (see the maps, figures 2.1 and 2.7) seem to be rather promising; however, the reliability of the data used in the calculations is often lower than the reliability of the data for other continents.

Australia has been divided into 25 broad soil regions; 3.9 per cent of the continent is cultivated and 23 per cent is potential agricultutal land. For food production this continent has the smallest possibilities, due to a shortage of water.

Africa has been divided into 32 broad soil regions. Approximately 5.2 per cent of the continent is cultivated and 23.5 per cent is potential agricultural land. After South America this continent has the best possibilities for increasing food production. The regions surrounding the Sahara desert have low potentialities because of water deficiency. The Nile valley and delta and the Congo basin are in the highest productivity class.

Asia has been divided into 54 broad soil regions (some have the same region symbol because conditions are similar). 15.6 per cent of the continent is cultivated and 20.2 per cent is considered to be potential agricultural land. There are various valeys and deltas of high quality. The coastal parts of these deltas and the costs with organic soils are often poor. The large, still uncontrolled rivers give possibilities for irrigation over very large areas, much larger than is irrigated at present. The potential irrigable agricultural land area (PIAL) is very large, at 67 per cent of the total PIAL of the world. Asia has the largest potential agricultural land area (PAL). It also seems that the USSR and China are promising; however, this might be caused partly by perhaps too optimistic a view of the soil scientists who prepared the soil maps.

North America has been divided into 34 broad soil regions. Although it would have been possible to introduce more regions, because soil and climatic conditions are known better than elsewhere, it was preferred to make the calculations in a similar way as was done for the other continents. The same applies to Europe. At present 11.3 per cent of the land is cultivated and 25.9 per cent is considered being potential agricultural land, which is almost 4 per cent higher than the estimate given in The World Food Problem (1967). There is a clear transition in the land productivity classes from east to west.

Europe has been divided into 49 broad soil regions, some being combined in the calculations. Approximately, 20.2 per cent of the land is cultivated and almost 38 per cent is considered to be potential agricultural land. This is 12 per cent more than is estimated by American specialists (The World Food Problem, 1967). This continent includes the European part of the USSR. The land productivity classes are rather high, although many soils are relatively young and have important potentialities.

Table 2.8

The absolute maximum production of grain equavalents (total and per hectare) of the continents and the world

	MPGE (10^9 kg)	% MPGE	average MPGE (kg.ha^{-1}.year^{-1})
South America	11106	22.3	18014
Australia	2358	4.7	10447
Africa	10845	21.8	14259
Asia	14281	28.6	13182
North & Central America	7072	14.2	11250
Europe	4168	8.4	10454
TOTAL	49830	100.0	13368

2.4.3 *The world*

        The total figures for the continents and the
world totals are given in Appendix table A2.7 and some
percentages in table 2.8. The total potential agricultural
land is 3419 million hectares of which at present 1406
million hectares are cultivated. South America and Africa
South of the Sahara together have more than 50 per cent of
the total reserve of agricultural land. There is no reason
to believe that there is almost no new land available for
food production, although much productive land is lost at
the present time because of misuse of land. At present
approximately 200 million hectares are irrigated. If all
available water for irrigation would be used in an efficient
way some 470 million hectares could be irrigated of which
more than 300 million hectares are in Asia alone (PIAL,
Appendix table A2.7). The diagrams in figures 2.13 (the
continents) and 2.14 (the world) give an idea about the
ratios between total area (TA), potential agricultural land
(PAL) and hypothetical potential agricultural land including
irrigation (IPALI).

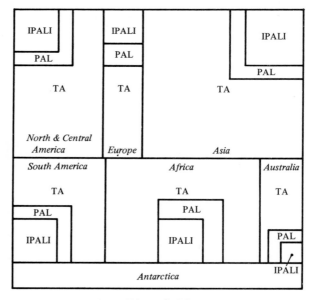

Fig. 2.13

*The land area of the continents: total area (TA),
potential agricultural land (PAL), and imaginary area of potential agricultural land
with potential production, including
irrigation (IPALI)*

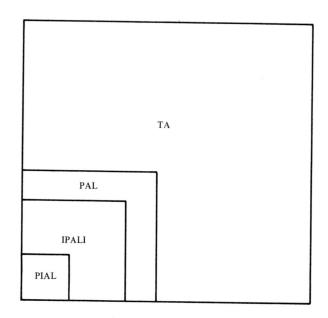

Fig. 2.14

*The land area of the world: total area (TA),
potential agricultural land (PAL), potentially irrigable agricultural land (PIAL),
and imaginary area of potential agricultural land with potential production
including irrigation (IPALI)*

Approximately 73 per cent of the total production of grain
equivalents (MPGE) could be produced in three continents
(Asia, South America and Africa). These continents have 64
per cent of the potential agricultural land (PAL) and 65 per
cent of IPALI. There are nine regions with a potential for
more than 1000 million tons of grain equivalents. The total
potential production of these nine regions (13224 M tons) is
approximately ten times the present cereal crop production,
and amounts to 37.7 per cent of the absolute maximum production of the whole world.

The absolute maximum production of grain equivalents is estimated at 49830 million tons, that is almost 40 times the
present cereal crop production (1268 million tons, average
of the period 1970-1972). The present cereal crop production, however, is grown on approximately 65 per cent of the
cultivated land area. If 65 per cent of the potential agricultural land were to be used to grow cereal crops, and the
rest for non-cereal crops, potential production would be
32390 million tons, or 30 times higher than present production.

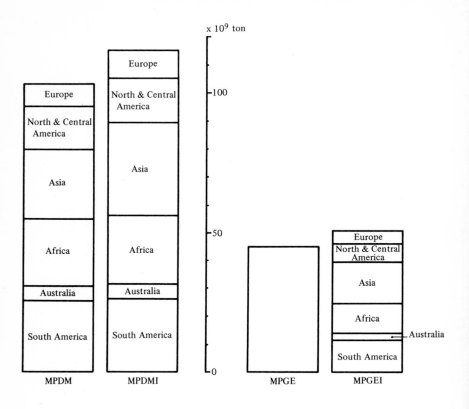

Fig. 2.15   *Absolute maximum production of dry matter without (MPDM)*
            and including irrigation (MPDMI).

Fig. 2.16   *Absolute maximum production of grain equivalents without*
            (MPGE) and including irrigation (MPGEI).

The average absolute maximum production per hectare (table 2.8), is lowest in Europe and highest in South America, mainly because of differences in climatic conditions. The average absolute maximum production per hectare and per year for the world is 13368 kg grain equivalents, whereas the present average yield is 1460 kg per ha for wheat and even less for rice.

The absolute maximum production of dry matter without (MPDM) and including irrigation (MPDMI) is given in the diagrams of figure 2.15, and for grain equivalents in figure 2.16. With full application of all irrigation possibilities the difference in maximum production in grain equivalents is only 5170 million tons or 10 per cent of the total production.

Some believe that approximately 1500 million ha of old tropical soils in the humid equatorial zone can never be used for intensive agricultural production. If so, the following calculation can be made, assuming TA=1500, FPAL=0.3, thus PAL=450. Assuming also FSC=0.4 and PDM=75, then MPDM= 450x0.4x75=13500 million tons and MPGE=5800 million tons of grain equivalents. The absolute maximum of 49830 million tons then has to be reduced to 44000 million tons of grain equivalents. This example is given to demonstrate that it is easy to make corrections if they are wanted.

All results seem to give an optimistic view of the food production capacity of the world, in particular for a layman. We repeat once again that various reduction factors have to be introduced by competent specialists in order to get realistic information on the world food problem. It should be quite clear that the computation gives no information about the present situation. No attention was given to factors in the field of economics, and to social, cultural and political obstacles. The interrelationship of some of these factors and the complexity of the world food problem should not be overlooked; they will come to the fore in Parts II and III of this report.

Finally, attention is drawn to the new type of land capability classification given in section 2.3.3. The maximum land productivity classification can be improved if more detailed information is available. It seems worthwhile, however, to make similar computations for other land capability classifications in order to know, besides the present, also the maximum capability of the land. It is beyond the scope of this study to discuss in detail the results as given in Appendix table A2.10 and in figures 2.7-2.12. In particular the maps given an instructive general view of the differences in productivity of the potential agricultural land.

2.4.4 *Some high yields obtained in practice*

It is evident that the present yields of cereal crops are below and mostly far below the absolute maximum as calculated here, because farm management is not optimal and

in large areas of the world farming is still done on a
primitive or traditional basis. However, some authors have
given data on high yields that have been obtained on experimental stations in various parts of the world.

De Vries et al. (1967) reports a rice yield (triple cropping)
in the Philippines of 26 tons and Van Ittersum (1971) of 23
tons per ha, per year. For the region including the Philippines the present study suggests a maximum yield crop of
16.8 tons of grain equivalents. This seems therefore too
low; this number is, however, an average of a much larger
area (see the map in fig. 2.5). For the best land with irrigation a maximum production of 28.6 tons/ha is calculated.
Van Ittersum (1971) also mentions yields of 11 tons of rice
per ha in West Pakistan and Kenya, whereas for these regions
the present study calculates 24.2 and 21.5 tons of grain
equivalents.

Simonson (1967) reports a maximum yield of wheat in the
North-Western United States of 14.5 tons per hectare, for
which the present study calculated 15 to 18 tons of grain
equivalents. In the south-eastern part of the State of
Washington some large farms had average yields of 10 tons
per hectare.

In the Netherlands the average yield of wheat is 5 tons per
hectare. Some farmers have harvested 8 to 9 tons of wheat,
whereas the maximum computed here would be 10.5 tons of
grain equivelents; this estimate includes the possibility of
crop growth after the grain harvest, for example turnips.

Double cropping of rice on Madagascar and in Senegal has
given yields of 16.2 and 14.0 tons/ha respectively (Agron.
Trop. 24-08-1969 and 23-10-1968). The present study calculates for these regions 17.7 and 16.9 tons/ha respectively.

A high yield of water wheat in S.W. Finland is 6.2 tons/ha
(FAO soils bul. 12, Rome, 1971) as compared to 7.2 tons/ha
calculated here.

Van Ittersum (1971) believes that the best farmers can reach
a yield of about 25 to 35 per cent below the potential one.

2.5   *A COMPARISON WITH OTHER STUDIES*

   2.5.1 *The world food problem, 1967*

        In the American report *The world food problem, a
report of the President's Science Advisory Committee,* volume
II, (1967) data are given on potential arable land. The
soils of the world are studied on a world soil map, scale
1:15,000,000, prepared by the Soil Conservation Service of
the USA. Soils are shown in 13 broad geographical groups and
boundaries from a climatic map are superimposed on the soil
map. The potentially arable land has been assessed for each
continent as shown in table 2.9 in which also the comparable

data from the present study are given. The World Food Problem table gives the continents and the USSR separately. For purposes of comparison, 25 per cent of the USSR figures are added to Europe and 75 per cent to Asia. There is not much difference between the potential agricultural land areas (PAL) in both studies. The present computations are somewhat lower for South America, somewhat higher for North America and much higher for Europe.

In the World Food Problem (1967) an additional area of 28 per cent of the total land area of the world has some grazing potential. However, this land provides only a relatively small proportion of current livestock production. As is mentioned in section 2.2, this is omitted here.

The total potential agricultural land of 3190 million hectares for the whole world is used by Meadows (1972) in his well-known first report to the Club of Rome. Some other American scientists have used also the data of the World Food Problem (1967) in their report, e.g. Simonson (1967), Revelle (1973), and Kellogg and Orvedal (1969).

2.5.2 *The study by Mesarovic and Pestel, 1974*

In the second report to the Club of Rome (Mesarovic) and Pestel, 1974), the world has been divided into ten regions. A rearrangement of the data for the 222 regions is made in order to allow a comparison with these ten regions; the results are given in table 2.10. The slight differences in total land area may be caused by some inaccuracy as a result of the very small scale of the map of the 10 regions in the second report. There are very important differences between the two studies. Mesarovic and Pestel (1974) did not indicate how their figures were obtained. Their remarks on agriculture and soils of tropical regions are pessimistic. They believe that North America and Australia are the only continents with large reserves of agricultural land, and that the tropical regions are unimportant for a solution of the world food problem. They also conclude that the possibilities of increasing the cultivated land area are limited. We do not agree with this part (Appendix III.A) of their study, nor with some remarks on irrigation possibilities and other related subjects. However, it was worthwhile to show that our data can easily be rearranged and integrated into larger regions of other studies.

Table 2.9

Comparison of the American and our calculations on potential agricultural land (PAL)

	CTA (M ha)	The World Food Problem (1967)				Our data		
		Cultivated		PAL		PAL (corrected) (M ha)	(%)	PAL (cultivated) (M ha)
		(M ha)	(%)	(M ha)	(%)			
South America	1750	77	4.4	682	38.9	596	33.5	519
Australia	820	32	3.9	153	18.7	199	23.2	167
Africa	3010	158	5.2	734	24.4	711	23.5	553
Asia	4420	689	15.6	894	20.2	887	20.2	198
North America	2110	239	11.3	465	22.9	627	25.9	388
Europe	1040	211	20.2	263	25.3	399	37.9	188
TOTAL	13150	1406	10.7	3190	24.2	3419	26.0	2013

Table 2.10

Calculations with our data for the ten regions of the second report to the Club of Rome

	TA (M ha)	PAL (M ha)	IMAPLI (M ha)	MPGE (M kg.yr^{-1})	PAL[1] (M ha)	Available[1] (M ha)
1. America	2156	533	293	5579	392	220
2. West Europe	445	143	87	1655	155	127
3. Japan	52	21	15	298	8	6
4. Australia	1120	275	97	3077	150	58
5. East Europe, USSR	2071	491	301	4472	382	280
6. Latin America	2044	692	385	12599	429	128
7. Middle East	1280	122	28	918	86	53
8. Tropical Africa	2181	658	234	9729	423	167
9. South Asia	881	360	215	7467	278	268
10. China	1278	388	193	4029	122	118
TOTAL	13508	3683	1848	49823	2425	1425
OUR TOTAL	13530	3727	1900	49830		

[1] figures from the report by Mesarovic and Pestel (1974)

Appendix 2A

NUMERICAL DATA FOR 222 BROAD SOIL REGIONS,
AND THEIR CLASSIFICATION

Explanation of the columns in the Appendix tables A2.1-A2.11.

1		Symbol of a broad soil region in a continent
2	(TA)	Area of a broad soil region (10^6 ha)
3	(TA%)	Area (TA) as percentage of the total area of the continent
4	(PDM)	Potential production of dry matter (10^3 kg.ha^{-1}.year^{-1})
5	(FPAL)	Fraction of potential agricultural land
6	(PAL)	Potential agricultural land (10^6 ha)
7	(DCC)	Development cost class
8	(FSC)	Reduction factor caused by soil conditions
9	(FWD)	Reduction factor caused by water deficiency
10	(IPAL)	Imaginary area of PAL with potential production, without irrigation (10^6 ha)
11	(MPDM)	Maximum production of dry matter without irrigation (10^6 tons.year^{-1})
12	(PIAL)	Potentially irrigable agricultural land (10^6 ha)
13	(IPALI)	Imaginary area of PAL with potential production, including irrigation (10^6 ha)
14	(MPDMI)	Maximum production of dry matter, including irrigation (10^6 tons.year^{-1})
15	(MPGE)	Maximum production of grain equivalents, including irrigation (10^6 tons.year^{-1})

Appendix table A2.1

South America

1	2 TA	3 TA%	4 PDM	5 FPAL	6 PAL	7 DCC	8 FSC	9 FWD	10 IPAL	11 MPDM	12 PIAL	13 IPALI	14 MPDMI	15 MPGE
A 1	297.8	16.7	74	.5	148.9	5	.6	.8	89.3	6611	.0	89.3	6611	2856
A 2	40.9	2.3	80	.5	20.5	4	.6	.7	12.3	982	.0	12.3	982	424
A 3	81.8	4.6	80	.5	40.9	2	.7	.7	28.6	2290	.4	28.7	2294	991
A 4	24.9	1.4	80	.5	12.5	3	.7	.8	8.7	697	1.2	8.8	707	305
A 5	10.7	.6	80	.4	4.3	4	.6	.4	1.7	137	1.1	2.6	208	90
A 6	24.9	1.4	80	.3	7.5	3	.7	.7	5.2	418		5.3	427	185
A 7	53.4	3.0	78	.6	32.0	4	.5	.7	16.0	1250	.0	16.0	1250	540
A 8	16.0	.9	72	.3	4.8	3	.8	.8	3.8	276		3.8	276	119
A 9	37.4	2.1	56	.6	22.4	2	.9	.6	13.5	754	.0	13.5	754	326
A10	112.2	6.3	64	.4	44.8	1	.8	.4	18.0	1149	1.5	18.5	1185	512
B 1	108.6	6.1	78	.2	21.7	5	.8	.8	10.9	847	.4	11.1	856	370
B 2	97.9	5.5	80	.3	29.4	5	.5	.6	14.7	1175		14.7	1175	508
B 3	46.3	2.6	78	.2	9.3	4	.5	.7	6.5	506		6.5	506	218
B 4	170.8	9.6	80	.5	85.4	3	.7	.6	51.2	4090		51.2	4099	1771
B 5	56.9	3.2	76	.3	17.1	4	.6	.8	8.5	649	.0	8.5	649	280
B 6	97.9	5.5	84	.3	29.4	3	.5	.3	10.2	740	2.7	10.2	854	369
B 7	23.2	1.3	82	.5	11.6	4	.7	.5	4.6	380		4.6	380	164
B 8	40.9	2.3	76	.5	20.5	4	.4		12.3	933	.0	12.3	933	403
B 9	35.6	2.0	74	.3	17.8	4	.6	1.0	10.7	790	.0	10.7	790	341
B10	10.7	.6	72	.1	3.2	3	.6	.9	2.6	185	.7	2.6	190	82
B11	121.1	6.8	48		12.1	3	.8	.0	.0	0		1.9	92	40
C 1	80.1	4.5	80	.05	4.0	3	.7	.4	1.6	128	2.4	2.2	173	75
C 2	39.1	2.2	78	.05	2.0	3	.7	.7	1.4	107	1.4	1.4	110	47
C 3	49.6	2.8	84	.1	5.0	3	.7	.0	.0	0	.4	.4	34	15
C 4	37.3	2.1	64	.1	3.8	3	.7		.0	0		.2	10	4
C 5	16.0	.9	44	.05	.8	3	.7	.2	.2	7	.2	.3	12	5
C 6	48.0	2.7	48	.1	4.8	3	.7	.5	2.4	115	2.6	3.2	153	66

Appendix table A2.2

Australia and New Zealand

1	2 TA	3 TA%	4 PDM	5 FPAL	6 PAL	7 DCC	8 FSC	9 FWD	10 IPAL	11 MPDM	12 PIAL	13 IPALI	14 MPDMI	15 MPGE
A 1	41.8	4.86	72	.6	25.1	4	.6	.2	5.0	361	.5	5.3	383	165
A 2	29.5	3.43	78	.5	14.7	4	.6	.4	5.9	460	.4	6.0	471	203
A 3	66.5	7.74	80	.4	26.6	4	.5	.1	2.7	213	1.0	3.4	269	116
A 4	28.8	3.35	80	.4	11.5	3	.6	.6	6.9	553	1.0	7.1	568	245
B 1	45.9	5.34	60	.3	13.8	4	.6	.7	8.3	496	.4	8.4	502	217
B 2	60.4	7.02	78	.3	18.1	4	.6	.8	10.9	848	.3	10.9	853	368
B 3	28.8	3.35	78	.2	5.8	4	.6	.8	3.5	270	.2	3.5	273	118
B 4	27.4	3.19	80	.4	11.0	3	.4	.4	4.4	351	.5	4.6	367	158
B 5	61.1	7.10	84	.2	12.2	4	.5	.0	.0	.0	.0	.0	0	0
B 6	26.7	3.11	78	.3	8.0	4	.4	.1	.8	62	.0	.8	62	27
B 7	36.4	4.23	84	.3	10.9	5	.5	.8	.0	.0	.0	.0	0	0
B 8	48.6	5.66	68	.5	24.3	3	.5	.3	7.3	496	.1	7.3	499	216
B 9	23.3	2.71	72	.1	2.3	4	.4	.0	.0	0	.0	.0	0	0
B10	43.8	5.10	64	.3	13.1	5	.5	.2	2.6	168	.1	2.7	172	74
B11	34.3	3.99	78	.4	13.7	3	.6	.7	8.2	642	.1	8.2	642	277
B12	2.8	.32	54	.5	1.4	4	.7	.9	1.0	53	.0	1.0	53	23
B13	9.6	1.12	54	.4	3.8	4	.7	.9	2.7	145	.1	2.7	146	63
B14	10.3	1.20	36	.2	5.2	4	.6	.7	3.1	111	.3	3.2	113	49
C 1	24.0	2.79	82	.05	1.2	3	.6	.2	.2	20	.1	.3	25	11
C 2	30.9	3.59	82	.05	1.5	3	.6	.3	.5	38	.1	.5	42	18
C 3	18.5	2.15	80	.05	.9	3	.6	.0	.0	0	.1	.0	6	3
C 4	6.2	.72	82	.05	.3	3	.6	.9	.2	0	.0	.2	6	3
C 5	6.2	.72	54	.05	.0	3	.6	.0	.0	10	.1	.0	10	4
D 1	166.6	19.38	—	.0		—	.0	.0	.0	0	.0	.0	0	0

Appendix table A2.3

Africa

1	2 TA	3 TA%	4 PDM	5 FPAL	6 PAL	7 DCC	8 FSC	9 FWD	10 IPAL	11 MPDM	12 PIAL	13 IPALI	14 MPDMI	15 MPGE
A 1	40.3	1.33	74	.3	12.1	2	.7	.2	2.4	179	.4	2.7	197	85
A 2	8.2	.27	84	.6	4.9	3	.9	.6	.0	0	4.2	3.8	318	137
A 3	40.3	1.33	76	.4	16.1	2	.5	.8	8.1	613	.6	8.2	626	271
A 4	14.2	.47	68	.5	7.1	2	.6	.9	4.3	290	.0	4.3	290	125
A 5	30.9	1.02	74	.3	9.3	5	.8	.8	7.4	549	.0	7.4	549	237
A 6	62.9	2.07	76	.5	31.4	4	.5	.1	15.7	1195	.1	15.7	1195	516
A 7	15.4	.51	84	.1	1.5	4	.4	.2	.2	13	.0		19	8
A 8	17.3	.57	84	.6	10.4	3	.6	.4	2.1	174	.1	2.1	174	75
A 9	15.4	.51	84	.5	7.7	2	.7	.6	3.1	259	.0	3.1	262	113
A10	26.0	.86	80	.6	15.6	2	.7	.1	9.4	749	.0	9.4	749	323
A11	8.6	.28	84	.4	3.4	2	.5	.2	.3	26	1.9		26	11
B 1	36.4	1.20	74	.3	10.9	2	.7	.1	2.2	162		3.3	249	106
B 2	99.7	3.29	74	.2	19.9	3	.5	.0	2.0	148	.6	2.1	153	66
B 3	231.9	7.65	88	.4	46.0	2	.4	.3		0	1.8		42	18
B 4	212.5	7.02	82	.5	85.0	3	.6	.6	25.5	2091	.0	26.4	2165	935
B 5	52.7	1.74	76	.6	26.4	2	.6	.1	15.8	1202	3.1	15.8	1202	519
B 6	73.1	2.41	86	.5	43.9	4	.5	.7	4.4	377		6.6	564	244
B 7	164.2	5.42	76	.4	82.1	4	.5	.7	41.1	3120	.0	41.1	3120	1348
B 8	118.8	3.92	80	.4	47.5	3	.6	.6	28.5	2281		28.5	2281	985
B 9	157.1	5.18	82	.6	62.8	1	.6	.5	37.7	3092	2.0	38.1	3125	1350
B10	155.7	5.14	80	.3	93.4	3	.6	.6	46.7	3737	.3	46.8	3744	1617
B11	119.2	3.94	80	.4	35.8	3	.5	.4	17.9	1430	1.3	18.3	1462	631
B12	75.4	2.49	76	.3	30.2	2	.6	.1	18.1	1375	1.5	18.2	1385	598
B13	8.5	.28	80	.2	2.5	2	.6	.7	1.0	78	.3	1.1	87	37
B14	114.8	3.79	80	.4	23.0	3	.5	.2	2.3	184	.4	2.6	206	89
B15	31.2	1.03	80	.4	12.5	2	.8	.5	6.2	499	.5	6.4	511	221
B16	31.8	1.05	84	.05	12.7	3	.7	.5	2.5	214	1.0	3.1	264	114
C 1	63.9	2.11	78	.05	3.2	3	.7	0	1.6	125	.4	1.6	127	55
C 2	70.0	2.31	80	0	3.5	3	.7		0	0		.3	26	11
D 1	803.7	26.52	82	0	-	-	-	-	-	-	-	-	-	-
D 2	114.8	3.79	76	0	-	-	-	-	-	-	-	-	-	-
D 3	15.1	.50	80	0	-	-	-	-	-	-	-	-	-	-

Appendix table A2.4

Asia

1	2 TA	3 TA%	4 PDM	5 FPAL	6 PAL	7 DCC	8 FSC	9 FWD	10 IPAL	11 MPDM	12 PIAL	13 IPALI	14 MPDMI	15 MPGE
A 1	12.3	.28	78	.5	6.2	4	.8	0	0	0	4.8	3.8	300	129
A 2	39.2	.89	80	.5	19.6	4	.7	.7	.5	1831	19.6	13.7	1098	474
A 3	55.9	1.27	78	.6	33.5	4	.9	.7	23.5	782	31.7	29.8	2324	1004
A 4	32.6	.74	80	.5	16.3	5	.6	.9	9.8	973	1.2	10.0	802	346
A 5	26.0	.59	78	.6	15.6	3	.9	.8	12.5	1335	7.9	13.3	1035	447
A 6	51.5	1.17	54	.6	30.9	3	.8	.9	24.7	885	15.0	26.2	1415	612
A 7	59.0	1.34	50	.6	35.4	4	.9	.5	17.7	1489	35.4	31.9	1593	688
A 8	93.3	2.12	38	.6	56.0	1	.6	.7	39.2	0	.0	39.2	1489	643
A 9	94.6	2.15	56	.5	47.3	3	.9	0	0	2215	31.0	24.8	1389	600
A10	146.5	3.33	76	.7	102.6	2	.9	.6	61.5	279	20.0	67.6	2432	1051
A11	232.3	5.28	12	.2	46.5	5	.5	.9	23.2	29		23.2	279	120
B 1	4.8	.11	76	.4	1.9	3	.8	.2	.4	93	.8	.9	66	28
B 2	24.6	.56	76	.5	12.3	2	.7	.1	1.2	0	1.9	2.6	195	84
B 3	115.3	2.62	80	.4	46.1	3	.6	0	0	605	7.2	5.8	460	199
B 4	43.1	.98	78	.6	25.9	4	.7	.3	7.8	1186	18.4	17.2	1343	580
B 5	96.4	2.19	82	.5	48.2	4	.5	.3	14.5	1702	31.0	23.8	1948	842
B 6	92.0	2.09	78	.4	36.8	4	.6	.6	22.1	1457	9.6	24.0	1872	809
B 7	248.6	5.65	64	.3	74.6	3	.7	.9	37.3	1874	26.6	40.0	2557	1105
B 8	60.7	1.38	80	.5	30.4	5	.5	.6	18.2	1111	1.2	18.5	1478	639
B 9	120.1	2.73	78	.4	48.0	3	.7	.9	24.0	1898	2.2	24.7	1923	831
B10	38.7	.88	82	.5	19.4	5	.5	.8	13.5	0		13.8	1130	488
B11	102.6	2.56	74	.5	51.3	5	.5	.8	25.7		4.6	27.0	2000	864
B12	180.4	4.10	48	.5	90.2	2	.6	0	0		10.6	8.5	407	176

Appendix table A2.4 (continued)

1	2 TA	3 TA%	4 PDM	5 FPAL	6 PAL	7 DCC	8 FSC	9 FWD	10 IPAL	11 MPDM	12 PIAL	13 IPALI	14 MPDMI	15 MPGE
B13	78.3	1.78	38	.5	39.1	2	.7	.3	11.7	446	4.1	13.8	524	226
B14	123.2	2.80	44	.4	49.3	3	.8	.5	24.6	10813.4	28.7	1261	545	
B15	51.9	1.18	46	.4	20.8	3	.7	1.0	14.5	668	4.4	15.0	689	298
B16	139.9	3.18	8	.1	14.0	3	.4	.9	5.6	45	.0	5.6	45	19
C1	104.3	2.37	72	.05	5.2	4	.6	.1	.5	38	1.8	1.8	128	55
C2	461.9	10.50	52	.05	23.1	3	.6	.1	2.3	120	4.4	5.4	280	121
C3	22.0	.50	12	.05	1.1	3	.6	.9	.7	8	.0	.7	8	3
C4	74.4	1.69	0	.05	3.7	3	.6	.0	.0	0	.0	.0	0	0
C5	433.8	9.86	16	.05	21.7	3	.6	.9	13.0	208	.0	13.0	208	90
C6	165.0	3.75	40	.05	8.3	3	.6	.9	5.0	198	1.0	5.2	206	89
D1	313.3	7.12	80	0	.0	-	-	-	-	-	.2	.2	13	6
D2	84.5	1.92	84	0	0	-	-	-	-	-	2.4	1.9	161	70
D3	27.7	.63	80	0	0	-	-	-	-	-	-	-	-	-
D4	23.8	.54	44	0	0	-	-	-	-	-	-	-	-	-
D5	315.5	7.17	0	0	0	-	-	-	-	-	-	-	-	-

Appendix table A2.5

North and Central America

1	2 TA	3 TA%	4 PDM	5 FPAL	6 PAL	7 DCC	8 FSC	9 FWD	10 IPAL	11 MPDM	12 PIAL	13 IPALI	14 MPDMI	15 MPGE
A 1	289.6	11.97	30	.4	115.8	3	.5	.9	57.9	1738	.0	57.9	1738	751
A 2	72.1	2.98	38	.6	43.3	2	.7	.9	30.3	1151	.0	30.3	1151	497
A 3	56.1	2.32	56	.7	39.3	1	.9	.5	19.6	1100	.0	19.6	1100	475
A 4	9.0	.37	44	.5	4.5	2	.6	.9	2.7	119	.0	2.7	119	51
A 5	19.1	.79	54	.6	11.5	2	.8	.9	9.2	495	.0	9.2	495	214
A 6	19.1	.79	70	.6	11.5	3	.6	1.0	6.9	481	.0	6.9	481	208
A 7	35.1	1.45	76	.6	21.1	2	.6	.7	10.5	800	1.2	10.9	828	358
A 8	58.1	2.40	80	.4	23.2	3	.6	.3	13.9	1116	1.5	14.2	1140	492
A 9	3.9	.16	64	.6	2.3	4	.9	.3	.7	45	2.0	1.0	121	52
A10	100.2	4.14	54	.6	60.1	3	.8	.9	48.1	2597	.0	48.1	2597	1122
B 1	86.9	3.59	32	.5	43.5	2	.8	.5	21.7	695	2.0	22.4	715	309
B 2	42.8	1.77	34	.6	25.7	1	.9	.6	15.4	524	.0	15.4	524	226
B 3	58.1	2.40	40	.4	23.2	3	.8	.3	7.0	279	4.0	9.0	358	155
B 4	42.8	1.77	60	.3	12.8	3	.7	.5	6.4	305	5.0	7.0	474	205
B 5	175.5	7.25	60	.2	35.1	4	.6	.1	3.5	211	5.0	7.0	421	182
B 6	11.4	.47	82	.1	1.1	3	.4	.0	.0	0	.2	.2	13	6
B 7	162.6	6.72	44	.6	97.6	3	.9	.3	29.3	1288	10.5	35.6	1565	676
B 8	26.1	1.08	80	.4	10.4	3	.7	.4	4.2	374	2.0	5.0	397	171
B 9	30.7	1.27	44	.5	15.4	3	.8	.8	12.3	540	.0	12.3	540	233
B10	44.8	1.85	80	.5	22.4	3	.8	.7	15.7	1254	2.7	16.4	1276	551
B11	1.7	.07	78	.5	.9	3	.8	.6	.5	40	.0	.5	40	17
C 1	70.7	2.92	44	.05	3.5	3	.6	.6	2.1	93	.0	2.1	93	40
C 2	72.8	3.01	78	.05	3.6	3	.6	.4	1.5	114	1.0	1.8	144	62
C 3	16.0	.66	78	.05	.8	3	.7	.7	.6	44	.0	.6	44	19
D 1	914.8	37.80	20	0	0	-	0	.9	-	-	-	-	-	-

Appendix table A2.6

Europe

1	2 TA	3 TA%	4 PDM	5 FPAL	6 PAL	7 DCC	8 FSC	9 FWD	10 IPAL	11 MPDM	12 PIAL	13 IPALI	14 MPDMI	15 MPGE
A 1	78.8	7.50	24	.3	23.6	3	.5	.9	11.8	284	.1	11.9	284	123
A 2	134.4	12.80	28	.4	53.8	2	.6	.9	32.3	903	.0	32.3	903	390
A 3	68.1	6.49	30	.5	34.1	2	.8	.6	20.4	613	6.5	21.7	652	282
A 4	114.2	10.88	44	.7	79.9	3	.9	.5	40.0	1759	32.1	52.8	2324	1004
A 5	20.6	1.96	44	.5	10.3	4	.7	.6	6.2	272	5.0	7.2	316	136
A 6	10.0	.95	48	.6	6.0	3	.7	.6	3.6	173	2.2	4.0	194	84
A 7	45.0	4.29	34	.6	27.0	2	.7	.8	18.9	643	3.1	19.2	653	282
A 8	12.5	1.19	30	.5	6.2	3	.6	.9	3.8	113	.1	3.7	114	49
A 9	4.4	1.42	36	.6	2.2	2	.9	1.0	2.0	71		2.0	71	31
A10	4.4	.42	54	.4	2.6	5	.9	.3	.8	43	2.6	2.4	127	55
A11	2.5	.24	60	.6	1.0	5	.9	.4	.4	24	1.0	.9	54	23
A12	3.2	.30	72	.3	1.9	3	.7	.4	.8	55		.9	67	29
B 1	79.3	7.56	24	.1	23.8	3	.5	1.0	11.9	285	.1	11.9	286	124
B 2	10.0	.95	0		1.0	3		.0	.0	0		.0	0	0
B 3	5.7	.54	28	.2	1.1	2	.6	1.0	.7	19	.0	.7	19	8
B 4	49.4	4.70	36	.4	19.8	1	.7	.9	13.8	498	.3	13.9	499	216
B 5	57.5	5.48	40	.6	34.5	4	.8	.9	27.6	1104	.3	27.7	1109	479
B 6	18.2	1.73	60	.5	9.1	4	.7	.4	3.6	218	4.6	3.8	228	98
B 7	25.0	2.38	68	.5	12.5	3	.6	.3	3.8	255	4.2	6.1	411	177
B 8	23.1	2.20	44	.5	11.6	3	.7	.6	6.9	305	1.9	7.8	343	148
B 9	13.8	1.31	54	.5	6.9	5	.7	.3	2.1	112	1.1	3.0	163	70
B10	18.2	1.73	50	.3	5.5	3	.7	.7	3.8	191	3.6	3.9	197	85
B11	21.8	2.08	64	.2	4.4		.7	.3	1.3	84	1.7	3.1	199	86
B12	15.0	1.43	48	.4	6.0		.7	.3	1.8	86		2.7	127	55

Appendix table A2.6 (continued)

1	2 TA	3 TA%	4 PDM	5 FPAL	6 PAL	7 DCC	8 FSC	9 FWD	10 IPAL	11 MPDM	12 PIAL	13 IPALI	14 MPDMI	15 MPGE
B13	7.5	.71	54	.5	3.8	4	.6	.1	.4	20	2.1	2.2	117	51
B14	4.4	.42	54	.5	2.2	3	.7	.3	.7	36	.0	.7	36	15
C 1	30.0	2.86	22	.05	1.5	3	.7	1.0	1.1	23		1.1	23	10
C 2	11.2	1.07	46	.05	.6	3	.7	.7	.4	18	.1	.4	19	8
C 3	19.4	1.85	32	.05	1.0	3	.7	.9	.7	22	.2	.7	22	10
C 4	5.7	.54	48	.05	.3	4	.7	.2	.1	3	.1	.1	6	2
C 5	11.2	1.07	36	.05	.6	3	.7	.9	.4	14	.1	.4	14	6
C 6	70.7	6.73	54	.05	3.5	4	.7	.2	.7	38	1.0	1.3	71	30
C 7	8.7	.83	16	.05	.4	3	.7	.9	.3	5	.0	.3	5	2
D 1	46.1	4.39	0	0	0	—	0	—	—	—	—	—	—	—

Appendix table A2.7

Continents and the World

	2 TA	6 PAL	10 IPAL	11 MPDM	12 PIAL	13 IPALI	14 MPDMI	15 MPGE
South America	1780	616.5	333.6	25224	17.9	340.7	25710	11106
Australia	680	225.7	74.2	5297	5.3	76.1	5462	2358
Africa	3030	761.2	306.5	24162	19.7	317.5	25115	10845
Asia	4390	1083.4	433.5	24966	314.1	581.6	33058	14281
North America	2420	628.6	320.0	15443	37.1	337.5	16374	7072
Europe	1050	398.7	233.1	8289	75.9	247.1	9653	4168
Antarctica	1310	0	0	0	0	0	0	0
TOTAL	14840	3714.1	1700.9	103381	470.0	1900.5	115372	49830

Appendix table A2.8

Potential Agricultural Land (including irrigation, IPALI)
as per cent of total area for all broad soil regions

	South America	Australia	Africa	Asia	North America	Europe
A 1	30.0	12.7	6.7	30.9	20.0	15.1
A 2	31.1	20.3	46.3	34.9	42.0	24.0
A 3	35.1	5.1	20.3	53.3	34.9	31.9
A 4	35.3	24.7	30.2	30.7	30.9	46.3
A 5	24.3	–	23.9	51.2	48.2	35.0
A 6	21.3	–	25.0	50.9	36.1	40.0
A 7	30.0	–	1.3	54.1	31.1	42.7
A 8	23.8	–	12.1	42.0	24.4	29.6
A 9	36.1	–	20.1	26.2	48.7	45.5
A10	16.5	–	36.2	46.1	48.0	54.5
A11	–	–	3.5	10.0	–	36.0
A12	–	–	–	–	–	28.1
B 1	10.1	18.3	9.1	18.8	25.7	15.0
B 2	15.0	18.0	2.1	10.6	36.0	0.0
B 3	14.0	12.2	0.0	5.0	15.5	12.3
B 4	30.0	16.8	12.4	39.9	18.5	28.1
B 5	14.9	0.0	30.0	24.7	4.0	48.1
B 6	10.4	3.0	9.0	26.1	1.8	20.9
B 7	19.8	0.0	25.0	16.1	21.9	24.4
B 8	30.0	15.0	24.0	30.5	19.2	33.8
B 9	30.0	0.0	24.3	20.6	40.1	21.7
B10	24.3	6.2	30.1	35.7	35.7	21.4
B11	1.6	23.9	15.4	26.3	29.4	14.2
B12	–	35.7	24.1	4.7	–	18.0
B13	–	28.1	12.9	17.6	–	29.3
B14	–	31.1	2.3	23.3	–	15.9
B15	–	–	20.5	28.9	–	–
B16	–	–	9.7	4.0	–	–
C 1	2.7	1.3	2.5	1.7	3.0	3.7
C 2	3.6	1.6	0.4	1.2	2.5	3.6
C 3	0.8	0.0	–	3.2	3.8	3.6
C 4	0.5	0.0	–	0.0	–	1.8
C 5	1.8	3.2	–	3.0	–	3.8
C 6	6.7	–	–	3.2	–	1.8
C 7	–	–	–	–	–	3.4
D 1	–	0.0	0.0	0.1	0.0	0.0
D 2	–	–	0.0	2.2	–	–
D 3	–	–	0.0	0.0	–	–
D 4	–	–	–	0.0	–	–
D 5	–	–	–	0.0	–	–

Appendix table A2.9

*Classification of the relative importance of potential
agricultural land in the broad soil regions*

Class	Importance	IPALI in % of TA
I	extremely high	> 50
II	very high	> 45 − 50
III	high	> 40 − 45
IV	moderately high	> 35 − 40
V	medium	> 30 − 35
VI	moderately low	> 25 − 30
VII	low	> 20 − 25
VIII	very low	> 15 − 20
IX	extremely low	≤ 15

Appendix table A2.10

MPGE per hectare potential agricultural land (1000 kg)

	South America	Australia	Africa	Asia	North America	Europe
A 1	19.2	6.6	7.0	20.8	6.5	5.2
A 2	20.7	13.8	28.0	24.2	11.5	7.2
A 3	24.2	4.4	16.9	29.9	12.1	8.3
A 4	24.4	21.3	17.6	21.2	11.3	12.6
A 5	20.9	−	25.5	28.7	18.6	13.2
A 6	24.7	−	16.4	19.8	18.1	14.0
A 7	16.9	−	5.3	19.4	17.0	10.4
A 8	24.8	−	7.2	11.5	21.2	7.9
A 9	14.6	−	14.7	12.7	22.6	14.1
A10	11.4	−	20.7	10.2	18.7	21.2
A11	−	−	3.2	2.6	−	23.0
A12	−	−	−	−	−	15.3
B 1	17.1	15.7	9.7	14.7	7.1	5.2
B 2	17.3	20.3	3.3	6.8	8.8	−
B 3	23.4	20.3	.4	4.3	6.7	7.3
B 4	20.7	14.4	11.0	22.4	16.0	10.9
B 5	16.4	.0	19.7	17.5	5.2	13.9
B 6	12.6	3.4	5.6	22.0	5.5	10.8
B 7	14.1	.0	16.4	14.8	6.9	14.2
B 8	19.7	8.9	20.7	21.0	16.4	12.8
B 9	19.2	.0	21.5	17.3	15.1	10.1
B10	25.6	5.6	17.3	25.2	24.6	15.5
B11	3.3	20.2	17.6	16.8	18.9	19.5
B12	−	16.4	19.8	2.0	−	9.2
B13	−	16.6	14.8	5.8	−	13.4
B14	−	9.4	3.9	11.1	−	6.8
B15	−	−	17.7	14.3	−	−
B16	−	−	9.0	1.4	−	−

Appendix table A2.11

Land productivity classes for the potential agricultural land
(productivity in 1000 kg per hectare)

Class	Land productivity	$MPGE . PAL^{-1}$
I	extremely high	> 25
II	very high	> 20 – 25
III	high	> 15 – 20
IV	medium	> 10 – 15
V	low	> 5 – 10
VI	very low	≤ 5

REFERENCES

1.   General

ARBAB, M., (1972), A CSMP-program for computing Thornthwaite's classification of climate. Rep. 8. Dep. Theor. Prod. Ecology. Agri. Univ. Wageningen.

FAO/UNESCO, (1974), Soil Map of the World, 1:5,000,000, Vol. I legend, Vol. IV South America, and the soil maps of Africa and North America. Paris.

FRAMI, K.K., and I.K. MAHAJAN, (1969), Irrigation and drainage in the world, a global review, ICID.

GANSEN, R., und F. HÄDRICH, (1965), Atlas zur Bodemkunde. Mannheim.

ITTERSUM, A. van, (1971), A calculation of potential rice yields. Neth. J. Agr. Sci. 19, 10-21.

KELLOGG, C.E., and A.C. ORVEDAL, (1969), Potentially arable soils of the world and critical measures for their use. Advances in Agronomy, Vol. 21, 109-170.

KOVDA, V.A., (1974), Biosphere, soils and their utilization. Moscow.

MEADOWS, D.L., et al., (1972), The limits to growth. London.

MESAROVIC, M., and E. PESTEL, (1974), De mensheid op een keerpunt (Mankind at the turning point). Amsterdam-Brussels.

MOEN, H.J., and K.J. BEEK, (1974), Literature study on the potential irrigated acreage in the world. I.L.R.I., Wageningen.

PAPADAKIS, J., (1969), Soils of the world. Amsterdam

PAPADAKIS, J., (1966), Climates of the world and their agricultural potentialities. Buenos Aires.

PENNING DE VRIES, F.W.T., (1972), Substrate utilization and respiration in relation to growth and maintenance in higher plants. Wageningen.

REVELLE, R., (1973), Will the earth's land and water resources be sufficient for future populations? World Population Conference, Stockholm, UNESCO, IV/13. Paris.

SIMONSON, R.W., (1967), Present and potential usefulness of soil resources. Annual Report 1967, I.L.R.I., 7-25.

U.S. DEPARTMENT OF COMMERCE, (1966), World Weather Records 1961-1960, Vol. 3. Washington.

VRIES, C.A. de, J.D. FERWERDA and M. FLACH, (1967), Choice of food crops in relation to actual and potential production in the tropics. Neth. J. Agr. Sci. 15, 241-248.

WIT, C.T. de, (1965), Photosynthesis of leaf canopies. Agr. Res. Rep. 663. Wageningen.

WMO/OMM, (1971), Climatological normals (CLINO) for climate and climate ship stations for the period 1931-1960, no. 117, TP52. Geneva.

The World Food Problem (1967), Report of the President's Science Advisory Committee, Volume II. Washington.

2.   South America

ANONYMUS, (1944), Regimen Meteorologica de la cuenca del Rio de la
    Plata, Monografia serie A sec. 2, 2e parte.
ANONYMUS, (1968, 1969), Normais Climatologicas, 1931-1960. Rio de
    Janeiro.
ANONYMUS, (1964), Valores Normales de 36 Estaciones seleccionadas,
    Climatologia de Chile, Fasciculo 1, periodo 1916-1945.
    Santiago de Chile.
BERGEIRO, J.M., (1945), Clima del Uruguay. Montevideo.
GONZALES, E., (1948), Datos detallados de Climatologia de Venezuela.
    Caracas.
Mededeling Meteorologische Dienst, (1966), serie 3 no. 3,
    Klimatologische tabellen. Zanderij 1952-1963. Paramaribo.
Min. de Agricultura Republica Argentina, (1958), Estadisticas
    Climatologicas 1941-1950, serie b, publication no. 3.
    Buenos Aires.
MORIDE E., (1927), Contribução de Estudo do Clima do Brasil.
Topographic map of South America. Groningen.

3.   Australia

Department of National Development, (1954-1962), Atlas of Australian
    Resources (with 28 maps).
STACE, H.C.T., a.o., (1968), A Handbook of Australian soil (with
    soil map). Glenside.
Staff of the Soil Bureau, (1968), Soils of New Zealand I (with 4 maps).
    Wellington.
STEPHENS, C.G., (1961), The soil landscapes of Australia (with soil
    map).

4.   Africa

British East African Meteorological Service, (1947), Mean and extreme
    values of certain meteorological elements for selected stations
    in East Africa.
BROWN, L.H., and J. COCHEME, (1969), A study of the agroclimatology of
    the highlands of Eastern Africa, FAO.
d'HOORE, J.L., (1964), Soil map of Africa (with explanatory monograph).
    Lagos.
DUBIEF, J., (1959), Le climat du Sahara. Alger.
FAO/UNESCO, Map of broad soil regions of Africa. (Not yet published).
Min. of Public Works, Egypt, (1938), Meteorological normals for Egypt
    and the Sudan, Cyprus and Palestina. Cairo.
Topographic map of Africa. Groningen.
WELTER, J., (1941), Moyennes, Mémento du Service Météorologique
    no. 7a, Hautcommissariat de l'Afrique Française.

5.   Asia

GERASOMOV, I.D., a.o., (1971), Natural Resources of the Soviet Union,
    their use and renewal.
MATAKEYAMA, H., (1964), The climat of Asia, Tokyo.
KOVDA, V.A., and E.V. LOBOVA, (?), Soil map of Asia (to the project
    of FAO/UNESCO Soil Map of the World.)

Topographic map of Asia. Groningen
U.S. Dept. of Commerce, (1962), An atlas of Chinese Climatology,
    JPRS: 16, 324. Washington D.C.

6.   North and Central America

Topographic map of North America. Groningen.

7.   Europe

Atlas Ceskoslovanski Socialistiche Republiky. Praha.
DUDAL, R., R. TAVERNIER and D. OSMOND, (1966), Soil map of Europe.
    FAO, Rome.
Institutul Meteorologic, (1961), Clima Republicii Populare Romîne,
    Vol. 2, date climatologice. Bucuresti.
K.N.M.I., (1968), Klimatologische gegevens van nederlandse stations
    no. 1: Normalen voor het standaardtijdperk 1931-1960. De Bilt.
MARIOLOPOULOS, E.G., (1937), La distribution des éléments météorologique
    en Grèce. Athènes.
STEFANOVITZ, P., and L. SZÜCS, (1960), Soil map of Hungary. Budapest.
PRASSOLOV, L.T., (1927), Soil map of the European part of the U.S.S.R.
Soil map of Romanian People's Republic, (1964).
Topographic map of Eurasia. Groningen.
ZITEK, J., (1961), Tabulky, Vydává Hydrometeorologcky. Ustav, Praha.

PART II

THE MODEL MOIRA

Chapter 3

GENERAL DISCUSSION OF THE MODEL

3.1 *INTRODUCTION*

This study relies heavily on model building and quantitative concepts. In Chapters 3.2 and 3.3 some basic issues
and problems related to model building are discussed. Chapter
3.4 describes briefly the domain of reality on which the
model is focussed. Chapter 3.5 deals with the nature of the
model in terms of the levels of aggregation that are chosen.
Appendix 3A discusses some econometric aspects of the use of
cross-section estimates. The main purpose of this chapter is
to provide some perspective to the advantages and limitations.

3.2 *DEPICTION*

In setting out to study a problem, it is necessary to
depict the domain in which the problem occurs. This may be
done in several ways: photographically, cinematographically,
or pictorially; a story may be written, or model developed.
If the picture is to be useful for future study it should,
first of all, reproduce those characteristics of the domain
that do not change over time; identification of these invariant characteristics presupposes that in the domain of
reality which is depicted certain objects can be described
as being in a static situation, i.e. in a state of equilibrium. This implies a generalization over time. The characteristics or properties of a field of reality can be formulated in terms of concepts. In using concepts, full detail
of each individual event cannot be given, and hence again
generalization is inevitable.

Any generalization has to establish which object is involved
in the event. Each object can be considered as a set of elements; in turn, the individual elements can be considered as
objects. In the process of depicting, the choice of the
objects to be depicted necessarily implies a certain level
of aggregation. A picture made at the level of individual
elements when their number is very large may soon become
unwieldy and unmanageable even though it might have a high
degree of realism. In order to be useful for further study,
any depiction requires a level of aggregation that keeps the
number of elements in the set low enough to remain manageable. In depiction, therefore, aggregation is inevitable on

both theoretical and practical grounds. A very illustration
may clarify these points. In depicting the domain of reality
studied in this volume, a striking characteristic is that
people use food. This characteristic is formulated in terms
of the concept food consumption. Although some individuals
may throw away a large part of their food and others almost
nothing, it could be assumed that all individuals physically
consume the same (high) percentage of the food available to
them; this would be a generalization - in this case over
individuals. The concept of food consumption need not be
defined as a property of the individual; it is possible to
define it as a property of the family, or of the national
population. Here the level of aggregation is at stake. If
food consumption of the national population is chosen as the
object to be depicted, there are in a world-wide picture as
many elements in this set as there are nations.

Thus, in the process of depicting reality the basic issues
that have to be faced concern (a) the static characteristics
that can be identified, (b) the extent of generalization,
and (c) the level of aggregation. These three issues are
related to each other.

Given the level of aggregation and a set of concepts (generalization), it is difficult to describe an object with the
help of mutually independent characteristics. This applies
first of all when the object is believed to be more than the
sum of the various elements referring to it, i.e. when it is
a property of the object that its component parts are some-
how related to each other. It also applies when the object
itself undergoes change. In the latter case, in particular,
it is difficult to achieve a picture that is invariant in
time. Usually it will be necessary to describe the changes
in the object and to try to relate them to other changes;
only then will it be possible to search for explanatory
factors by which the varying manifestations of reality can
be reduced to invariant characteristics through generalization, or at least depicted as such. In the simple example
given above, food consumption changes; other objects - for
instance, income and the price of food - change as well. In
depicting reality, one may assume that the changes in food
consumption are related to changes in income and in price,
and that the way in which they are related is an invariant
characteristic of reality.

In many cases it is not necessary to aim at an unconditional
depiction of reality. For instance, depicting reality may
focus on situations that can be described directly in terms
of in dependent concepts, i.e. on equilibrium situations. A
bridge can be described as it is, i.e. a static picture;
alternatively, it could be described in all possible situations: collapsing or not collapsing. In the latter case, it
is necessary to depict all possible variations in time (a
dynamic picture). More limited aims in depicting reality are
also possible. However, a purely dynamic picture is impossible since any identification of invariant characteristics
is based on a static view.

It should therefore be borne in mind that any depiction of a domain of reality is to a certain extent static and aggregated and generalizing. These aspects may be considered as inevitable but nonetheless undesirable properties of a picture; the discrepancy between reality and the inherent characterics of a picture may lead to shortcomings in the analysis that could be labelled as errors of the first order.

In this context yet another problem has to be mentioned - a problem which is the source or errors of the second order. Every picture itself will take the shape of an object: a painting, a book, a set of equations on the computer. The picture as object also has certain characteristics. Therefore, it is impossible to arrive at a picture of reality that shows exclusively the selected characteristics of reality - although these side effects or errors of the second order are not equally large for all possible *shapes* of the picture or for all problems depicted. In painting, the picture as an object necessarily has *added* characteristics such as only two physical dimensions and the quality of the paint; in econometric model building, the picture has properties that originate from the way in which functions are specified and from the quality of the data used.

Any picture of reality, no matter how detailed or complicated, remains a picture; a perfect picture of reality does not exist and cannot be made. Our depiction is not perfect.

3.3   *OUR DEPICTION: AN ALGORITHMIC MODEL*

3.3.1 *Why a model?*

A picture can be made in terms of mathematical concepts by which the usual problems of depicting or mapping have to be faced. Such a picture is then called a (mathematical) model.

A mathematical approach has a number of advantages: the limited number of basic concepts, its clarity (which makes the - formal - logical consistency of the statements easy to verify), and the restricted side effects resulting from the use of a language that is inherently restricted to necessary concepts. These advantages hold in particular as compared with verbal descriptions. Usually, however, a model builder will need such a verbal description of reality to begin with; in this case the model should not be seen as an alternative to the verbal picture but rather as the result of processing it. In addition to these advantages of a picture in terms of a mathematical model, in studying the world food problem two other reasons made it desirable to adopt this approach: the need to arrive at a dynamic picture, and the need to rely heavily on quantitative information.

The world food problem cannot properly be depicted by a set of independent and invariant characteristics that can readily be selected. Firstly, the world food situation changes, and important characteristics of it evidently change in combination with or dependent on other characteristics. Secondly, as the existing food situation is not satisfactory, some of the characteristics will have to be changed deliberately - with related consequences for other characteristics. Thus, a static description would be insufficient. It would be unwise to depict the world food situation merely by enumerating the sources of food production and the ultimate consumers, without describing the relations between production, distribution, and consumption of food, and the dynamics of their changes.

In any description in which the behaviour of man is involved, such as that of the world food situation, a dynamic picture is essential as man reacts to changing circumstances. Moreover, as human beings - and even more so human society - do not lend themselves to laboratory development and testing, a comparison of different *static* pictures is hardly worthwhile; static specifications for an ideal society are not very suitable as a guideline for policy. In short, dynamization is required. Although it is possible to give a verbal dynamic specification of the interdependent relations (even though such a description may be rather intractable), it is impossible to describe their dynamic operation and interaction in a verbal manner. A model has the advantage that it can deal with large numbers of complex relationships and can be run on a computer. A computer can store very extensive descriptions; moreover, computerization permits extensive testing and quick operation of a model.

A model also constitutes a convenient vehicle for the use of quantitative information. Such information is well-organized and has a wide geographic coverage; systematic efforts have been made by FAO and others to collect this information according to well-defined standards. Availability of information restricts the choice between possible alternative types of pictures that could be made. Within the restrictions imposed by the availability of information for the present study, the choice of a quantitative model which contains the most essential variations over time and over countries would seem to be most appropriate. Hence, also from this point of view the use of a mathematical model in depicting reality is convenient. Those forms of non-quantitative information on the world food situation that are readily available are often expressed as rather broad generalizations; it is usually possible also to incorporate this type of non-quantitative information in a mathematical model, if only by approximation.

Thus, the depiction of the world food situation attempted in this study will take the shape of a model. It should be clear, however, that the model does not pretend to reveal the solution of the world food supply problem. As will be discussed below, the model even excludes some relevant characteristics of reality. Nevertheless, it is considered

to be sufficiently realistic to improve our understanding of
the joint operation of many conditions and forces that
influence the development of world food production and
consumption.

3.3.2 *Algorithmic models*

An algorithmic model is a mathematical model formulated as an algorithm; it is a depiction expressed as a
set of (sometimes conditional) arithmetic instructions that
have to be executed consecutively. An arithmetic instruction
can be seen as an instruction to process numbers into other
numbers. In an algorithmic model, each arithmetic instruction
usually corresponds with the depiction of one specific relation between quantified phenomena. For instance, if a
theory postulates that the relations $x = 5$ and $y = 2x$ apply,
this is a depiction formulated in the third person. In an
algorithmic model, the same depiction is formulated in the
second person, i.e. as an instruction (to a computer):
assign to x the value 5, compute $2 * x$, and assign the
result to y. In other words, an algorithmic model can be
seen as (part of) a computer programme. A computer can store
these instructions; it can execute them only when all initial values (numbers) for the arithmetic operations are
provided. No picture of reality can be fully comprehensive;
within the abstraction in the form of an algorithmic model,
however, quantitative information for all instructions has
to be fully specified.

The fact that quantitative information is essential for an
algorithmic model imposes certain constraints on the model
as a picture of reality. This should be considered as a
serious side effect: not only does the model carry characteristics beyond the properties which one desires to depict,
but also it is necessarily possible to depict all relevant
properties. On the other hand, it is erroneous to think that
algorithmic models could only depict quantifiable properties: the ordering and content of arithmetical instructions
rely heavily on non-quantifiable considerations. In the
present model, for example, food consumption of the agricultural and the non-agricultural sectors is not determined
simultaneously; food consumption in the agricultural sector,
and hence its net supply of food, is determined in the model
prior to non-agricultural consumption.

Nevertheless, the dynamics of non-quantifiable factors are
difficult to render and their effects are hard to isolate.
For instance, suppose variable y to be a function of x, i.e.
$y = f(x)$. The specification of the function f and the definition of the place of this function in the whole system
make it necessary to take into account various non-quantifiable properties which determine the influence of x on y.
Suppose the function is specified in linear form: $y = ax$.
The combined effect of many non-quantifiable properties is
now subsumed in the one parameter a. Moreover, it should be
emphasized that these properties specify the form or place

of the function only once and in conjunction with each
other. This causes a side effect which should not be underestimated.

Another problem in model building is the indermediateness of
the choice between function and model approaches which could
all describe the same properties. This is aggravated by
uncertainty as to whether these alternatives have the same
impact on the dynamic behaviour of the whole systems.

An illustration (familiar to econometricians) of this problem
is the choice between a model expressed in terms of relative
changes (percentage ratio) of the variables, and a model
formulated in terms of (changes in) absolute levels. Opting
for the first approach may imply that the derivatives of
absolute levels have undesirable properties, while in the
second approach percentage rates of change and elasticities
may show unwanted patterns of development. In addition,
dynamic behaviour will certainly be influenced by the necessary *stylizing* of the lag patterns. This point will be taken
up again in the appendix to this chapter.

Furthermore, it should be noted that a continuous description
of a phenomenon is often difficult to achieve. In this case
it may be necessary to aggregate over time, i.e. to switch
to period analysis. In economics this is almost inevitable
due to the periodicity of available quantitative information. The present model depicts the phenomena on an annual
basis.

As a consequence of this aggregation it is impossible to
describe changes within the chosen period of one year.
Suppose that A influences B within one period and B reacts
to this influence within the same period. In period analysis
this can be depicted in two ways:
(a) by adding the influences to obtain the net effect and
     by inputting this to the most important influences
     (recursive system), or
(b) by considering the observed total effects as the equi-
     librium solution of two forces - that which causes the
     action of A to B and that which causes the reaction of
     B to A (simultaneous system). In the latter case cause
     and effect are indistinguishable, and in the given
     picture this distinction is irrelevant as it depicts
     the equilibrium state. In other words: lack of know-
     ledge of the phenomenon within the period causes one to
     depict the situation statically. This implies that the
     picture meets transitions between properties and con-
     tinuous change in course of time only to a limited
     extent.

The present model is mainly recursive, with certain parts
that are simultaneous; it is a bloc-recursive model. In the
next paragraph, the nature of the model is discussed mainly
in terms of the levels of aggregation that are chosen. The
influence of all constraints implicit in the choice of an
algorithmic model as the form of depiction is discussed in

more detail in the following chapters.

3.4 *THE LEVELS OF AGGREGATION IN THE MODEL*

3.4.1 *Aggregation and disaggregation*

As observed in Chapter 3.2, in depicting reality generalization and aggregation are to a certain extent inevitable. There is, however, also an upper limit to generalization and aggregation beyond which the picture becomes vague because certain essential characteristics have been neglected. In the present study, for instance, it would not be particularly useful to choose *total food consumption from now till 2010* as the object to be depicted. Obviously, many relevant characteristics of food consumption would be lost in this way. A description that would classify food consumption in time, in space, and by social stratum would generally be considered a much better picture of reality - though this depends of course on the purpose of the analysis. The larger the number of classes that is used, the greater the extent of disaggregation.

The level of aggregation to be used is not given beforehand; choosing the most proper level often is a difficult task. A phenomenon can be studied at a certain level of aggregation only when it is defined at that level. Different phenomena may be defined at different aggregation levels. When they have to be brought together in the same picture, obviously problems arise. In the context of the present study this means in fact that many phenomena are defined at too low a level of aggregation to be depicted as such (e.g. billions of food consumers; many different food products); hence, aggregation is necessary.

In order to move from a lower to a higher level of aggregation, a suitable aggregation principle is needed. Such a principle can be arrived at by establishing what the individual phenomena have in common, so that a generalization would be possible. If the aggregation is to be made over individual phenomena that can be quantified, a common dimension has to be established. For instance, apples and pears could be aggregated by using as the common dimension their weight, or their caloric value, or their money value. In studying transportation of food, weight or volume may be the common dimension which is relevant; in studying income formation or spending, the money value may be more relevant.

More intricate problems arise when the phenomena involved in the aggregation are not just a set of individual quantities, but the relationships among quantities. A theory formulated at a high level of aggregation (e.g. concerning the relationship between national food consumption and national income) is not usually fully consistent with the theory or theories formulated at lower aggregation levels (e.g. concerning the relation between food consumption and income at the individual or family level). From a purely theoretical point of

view, low levels of aggregation are usually to be preferred;
in applied research this is often impossible. The level of
aggregation used in empirical studies is frequently considered to be too high in the judgement of scholars working
on pure theory.

In practice, two types of arguments are usually put forward
to defend the choice that has been made: (a) a lower level
of aggregation than the one that was chosen would be an
unnecessary refinement; (b) theoretical or empirical information, or both, are inadequate to allow a lower level of
aggregation.

Intuitively the first argument is rather appealing, but it
is difficult to give it a solid theoretical foundation. The
cause of this difficulty is that the level of aggregation
not only determines the measure of detail of the results,
but also and primarily the functioning and operation of the
model. Except for the rare cases of perfect aggregation, the
significance of the errors due to aggregation can hardly
even be assessed beforehand. Of course, in specific cases it
remains possible to work out two different approaches to the
same problem and to judge the significance of lowering the
aggregation level by comparing the results of the two approaches.

The relevance of the second argument - inadequate information
- can hardly be denied. Still, objections to the chosen
level of aggregation could be made on the grounds that the
search for information has not been thorough enough, or that
the approach would have to be modified altogether in view of
its inherent shortcomings.

The argument of inadequate information concerning phenomena
at lower levels of aggregation has played an important part
in the approach followed in the present study. One may hope
that the first argument is - at least partly - valid as
well.

3.4.2 *The level of aggregation in time and space*

The level of aggregation in time is the time
period of one year. Most of the quantitative information is
available only at this level.

The level of aggregation in space is that of a country or a
group of countries. The number of geographical units is 106.
A lower aggregation level was impossible because of data
availability; a higher level would have been undesirable for
two reasons. Firstly, there are differences between countries
in the level of economic development and in government
policy that have to be depicted. Secondly, there is a statistical need for a large number of geographical units as
will be discussed in greater detail in Appendix 3A on cross
section estimation.

It is important to note that the 106 geographical units are classified into two groups: countries with a market economy, and centrally-planned countries. The latter are treated separately because in centrally-planned countries the distinction that has to be made in market economies between government decisions and producer decisions appears less useful. Public organizations act in a way found best from a political point of view. This makes it difficult to describe their behaviour as reacting to changed market circumstances. As the knowledge and number of instruments at the disposal of organizations increase, it becomes more difficult to depict the behaviour of those organizations.

The present study, therefore, has two types of submodels at the national level. Thus, differences between countries having the same type of national model are depicted by means of differences in the values of the variables in the model, and not by differences in the structure of the model. Model structure differs only between market-economy and centrally-planned countries. There are 103 market-economy (groups of) countries and 3 (groups of) centrally-planned countries distinguished in the present study.

3.4.3 Agricultural produce

In the present model, the agricultural production process yields two products only: food, and other products called non-food. It is assumed that there is a fixed relation between the prices of both (types of) products, and that the relation between the quantities produced of both is exogenously given.

A more detailed treatment of agricultural produce is not feasible, for several reasons:
(a) information about the application of means of production per product, and the income ensuing from it, is not available,
(b) the way in which the agricultural producer composes his production depends on highly specific factors, like the local natural conditions and the relative prices of products. Generalization here is very difficult,
(c) the determination of variations in relative prices implies the description of an equal number of markets, and therefore as many components as products. Both theoretical and empirical information on this point is grossly insufficient.

In addition, it should be realized that the total volume of food production is only to a very limited extent influenced by the food product mix of the farmer. Once it is accepted that the ratio between food and non-food products cannot be determined endogenously - for the reasons mentioned in the above paragraph -, it is in the context of the present study not particularly relevant to try to describe the factors that determine the product composition of food output and its possible changes in time. Changes in the food product

mix are substitution processes that take place within a
total food production capacity governed by other factors,
and it is the latter group of factors on which attention is
focussed in the present model.

Consequently, a unit of measurement has to be chosen in
which all agricultural production can be expressed and
aggregated in a useful way. The unit of measurement that is
chosen in this study is the weight of vegetal protein that
may be consumed directly or indirectly by man - for short,
consumable protein. This choice is based on several considerations:

(a)　all products of the agricultural sector have to be ex-
　　　pressed in terms of the vegetal production that was re-
　　　quired for them, as all agricultural production is
　　　based on the cultivation of plants and trees;
(b)　in view of the technical nature of the production
　　　process, a measure is needed indicating the biomass
　　　produced in the process of photosynthesis in terms of
　　　physical units. Thus, the concept of *grain equivalent*
　　　as often used by FAO is not suitable, as individual
　　　food products are aggregated in value terms using
　　　producer prices (relative to the wheat price) as weights;
(c)　the quantity of protein contained in the biomass pro-
　　　duced is related in a direct and well-defined way to
　　　the amount of nitrogen that had to be available in the
　　　soil. Using vegetal protein as the unit of measurement
　　　for agricultural production therefore established a
　　　direct link between production and nitrogen input, one
　　　of the most important production growth factors that
　　　can be controlled by man;
(d)　part of total vegetal production can be used for human
　　　consumption only after *processing* by animals. This part
　　　of vegetal protein production (grass, plant wastes, by-
　　　products, etc.) can be readily converted into the
　　　quantity of animal protein that is the result of it.
　　　These two forms of protein production are aggregated in
　　　the concept consumable protein.

Another unit of measurement suitable for measuring the
quantity of useful biomass in a technical sense is its
energy content or caloric value. Consumable protein is
preferred in this study, partly because of the consideration
mentioned under (c), and partly for a reason related to (d).
Conversion from vegetal material inedible for man into
edible animal products could be performed also in terms of
calories; however, conversion in terms of protein assigns a
greater weight to this indirect production from the land in
total agricultural production - a fact that seems to be more
in accordance with the relatively large share this form of
production has in the photosynthetic process as a whole.

Finally, it should be stressed that agricultural production
is measured in terms of consumable protein as it is, for the
purpose of the present study, a suitable indicator of the
volume of production - and not because proteins would constitute the most crucial element in the food package. For a

detailed discussion of the technical aspects of the use of
the concept consumable protein, the reader is referred to
Annex 1.

3.4.4 *The agricultural producer*

In the agricultural production process, the
level of aggregation is the country. For each country (or
group of countries), the agricultural sector is assumed to
be one unit as far as production is concerned. It is depicted as one large, national enterprise producing one product.
Thus, no distinction is made
(a)   between rich and poor producers,
(b)   between independent farmers of peasants and dependent
      agricultural labour force, and
(c)   between active and non-active population in agricul-
      ture.

The generalizations implied by this lack of disaggregation
are heroic indeed. Unfortunately they are felt to be inevitable in view of inadequate knowledge. The distinctions
made under (a) and (b) partly overlap each other; in both
cases, theoretical understanding of the causes of inequality
is often partial only, or very country-specific, or of
little operational value. Also, the effect of inequality on
production cannot easily be established. the scantiness of
relevant statistical data is an additional problem. Hence,
there is no choice but to depict in the model one agricultural sector in which the decision-making agent is farmer-
entrepreneur and labourer at the same time.

The distinction mentioned under (c) is again not introduced.
Firstly, it is customary in most countries that during
certain parts of the year almost all family members par-
ticipate in the agricultural production process; consequently,
the distinction between active and non-active population in
agriculture becomes vague. Secondly, even if the active part
of agricultural population could be clearly identified and
depicted as involved in the production, total agricultural
population would still be needed at the consumption side. A
transformation would be needed from active to total population; proper handling of this transformation would require
incorporating in the model a demographic sector. For the
time being, no such enlargement of the model was deemed to
be feasible.

In addition to the production factor labour, three other
factors of production in agriculture are distinguished:
labour-substituting capital goods, fertilizer, and land.
Labour-substituting capital goods - in shorthand: capital -
are defined as all those forms of equipment of labour that
increase its productive capacity but that could be substituted in the production process by an increased labour
input. Fertilizer is treated separately because it is considered to be not substitutable for or by labour; it is
assumed to be a complementary input factor directly depen-

dent on the level of production. Both variables capital and
fertilizer are discussed at some length in the next chapter.
Land is considered to be a homogeneous production factor of
constant dimension, as has been described already in Chapter
2.

3.4.5 *The consumer*

A highly important characteristic of the world
food situation is the prevalence of hunger, i.e. of inadequate food consumption. Depicting aggregate food consumption
at the national level only would obscure the fact that
within countries food consumption may be distributed very
unequally; at this high level of aggregation, hunger would
hardly come into the picture. Therefore, food consumption is
dealt with in the model at a lower level of aggregation than
food production is.

Firstly, a distinction is made between food consumption in
the agricultural sector and in the non-agricultural sector.
Secondly, within each sector consumers are classified in six
income brackets (the income distribution is given exogenously; see Chapter 5). Thus, in each geographical unit food
consumption is depicted for twelve socio-economic strata.

Consumption other than of food is not shown in the model.
Food consumption is expressed in the same unit of measurement as food production, i.e. in consumable protein. As
observed before, this does not imply that in food consumption norms only the norm for protein would be considered
essential. How food consumption norms can be formulated in
terms of consumable protein is discussed in Chapter 8.

3.4.6 *Summary*

The decisions made concerning the level of aggregation in the model may be summarized as follows. The values
of all variables are computed year by year for every geographical unit; a geographical unit is classified either as
a market economy or as a centrally-planned economy. In all
106 geographical units, one and the same product is produced
by one agricultural sector using four factors of production:
labour, capital, fertilizer, land. Of this product of agriculture, a given fraction is food.

For market economies, demand for food is formulated at the
level of the income class concerned; there are six income
classes within the agricultural sector, and six within non-
agriculture. Due to lack of data on income distribution,
demand for food in the centrally-planned economies is determined only at the sectoral level. Thus, in every year food
consumption is computed for 6x2x103+2x3 = 1242 aggregates.

Appendix 3A

CROSS-SECTION ESTIMATION

This appendix discusses some specifics of the mathematical
and statistical techniques used, in particular parameter estimation by means of cross-section analysis. The reader who
feels sufficiently familiar with the subject, can skip over
this appendix.

3A.1 *ADVANTAGES AND DISADVANTAGES OF CROSS-SECTION ANALYSIS*

     In the present study, all parameters of equations es-
timated by econometric methods have been estimated by the
method of ordinary least squares applied to a cross section
over countries. Throughout this appendix, the term cross
section refers to cross section over countries.

In the context of the present analysis, cross-section estimation has certain advantages. Firstly, it implies the
availability of a rather large number of observations -about
100. In comparison to this, the number of available time
series data is much more limited; for instance, for food
consumption measured in consumable protein there is only one
observation in time. Another advantage of cross section is
that the dispersion of the observations is rather large;
this means that the relatively large variations in variables
often occurring in long-term analysis do not lead as quickly
to great unreliability of the estimated value of the dependent variable as in the case of time-series estimation. In
other wordt, if it would be assumed that e.g. Zaire would
reach in the year 2000 the level of prosperity of to-day's
Belgium, it would seem to make sense to base a prediction of
Zaire's behaviour in 2000 not only on present-day behaviour
of Zaire but also on present-day behaviour of Belgium.

The latter example brings us to the disadvantages, or at
least the problems, associated with cross-section analysis.
Three problems need to be discussed:
(a)   the influence of country-specific factors;
(b)   the neglect of dynamic aspects, and
(c)   generalization over time is not tested statistically.

(a)   Country-specific factors
      A cross-section analysis compares the behaviour of
countries that find themselves in different situations;
these different situations are indicated by the explanatory

variables. But is the behaviour of two countries fully comparable? Most probably there are also differences between countries that are due to country-specific factors, i.e. differences that are independent of the explanatory variables. Suppose that these country-specific characteristics do not change over time. In this case, the following regression model may be formulated:

$$Y = X\beta + \alpha + \varepsilon \tag{3A.1}$$

in which

X = deterministic matrix of order N x K, where N is the number of countries, and K the number of explanatory variables (possibly including a disturbance term).

Y = vector of the dependent variable (N x 1)

β = vector of general parameters, i.e. parameters holding for all countries (K x 1)

α = vector of country-specific constants (N x 1)

ε = vector of disturbances (N x 1).

Furthermore, the classical assumptions are made:

E (ε) = 0

E $(\varepsilon\varepsilon^T)$ = $\sigma^2 1$

X has rank K < N

Even thouth it will hold only by approximation, it is assumed that X and α are independent of each other:

$X^T\alpha = 0$

Now (3A.1) is rewritten as

$$Y = [X1] \begin{bmatrix} \beta \\ \alpha \end{bmatrix} + \varepsilon \tag{3A.2}$$

Define Z = [X1]

Z is a N x (K+N) matrix of a rank <N. Thus, Z^TZ has a rank <N, and a dimension (K+N) x (K+N).

Therefore, Z is singular; consequently, the method of least squares cannot be used to estimate Y.

If we commit a specification error and estimate β according to the specification

$$Y = X\beta + \varepsilon \tag{3A.3}$$

we obtain for b as estimator of β

$$b = (X^TX)^{-1}X^TY \tag{3A.4}$$

This estimator is BLUE (Best Linear Unbiased Estimator).
Substitution of (3A.1) in (3A.4) gives

$$b = (X^TX)^{-1}X^T (X\beta + \alpha+\varepsilon)$$

$$b = \beta + (X^TX)^{-1}X^T\alpha + (X^TX)^{-1}X^T\varepsilon \tag{3A.5}$$

As we have assumed $X^T\alpha$ = 0, (3A.5) is simply

$$b = \beta + (X^TX)^{-1}X^T\varepsilon \tag{3A.6}$$

Obviously this result for b would have been obtained also
from the specification (3A.3). Thus, we may conclude that
- in spite of the specification error in (3A.3) - b is a
BLUE estimator of β.
Furthermore, for the estimated disturbance we have

$$\hat{e} = [1 - X(X^TX)^{-1}X^T]Y$$

$$E\hat{e} = E[\{1 - X(X^TX)^{-1}X^T\}(X\beta+\alpha+\epsilon)]$$

$$= E[X\beta+\alpha+\epsilon-X\beta-X(X^TX)^{-1}X^T\alpha-X(X^TX)^{-1}X^T\epsilon]$$

$$= \alpha$$

Thus, $\hat{e}$ is an unbiased estimator of α:

$$\hat{e} = \alpha + [1-X(X^TX)^{-1}X^T]\epsilon \qquad (3A.7)$$

Defining $M = 1-X(X^TX)^{-1}X^T$, we have

$$\alpha\hat{e} -\alpha = M\epsilon$$

Just as for the covariance matrix of b, we obtain for the
covariance matrix of $\hat{e}$:

$$\Sigma\hat{e}\hat{e} = E\{ \hat{e}-\alpha) (\hat{e}-\alpha)^T\} = E(M\epsilon\epsilon^TM^T)$$

$$= \sigma^2MM^T$$

As we know that M is symetric and idem potent, it follows
that

$$\Sigma\hat{e}\hat{e} = \sigma^2M^2 \qquad (3A.8)$$

It remains to be shown that the estimator $\hat{e}$ is the only one
that is BLUE.
Consider the matrix

$$M' = M-D$$

in which D is a deterministic N x N matrix. We have now the
estimator

$$\hat{e} = M'Y$$

$$= \alpha + X(X^TX)^{-1}X^T\epsilon+DX\beta+D\alpha+D\epsilon \qquad (3A.9)$$

In order to show that the first estimator $\hat{e}$ is the only one
that is BLUE, it is sufficient to demonstrate when for $\hat{\hat{e}}$ the
condition for being unbiased will be met. Taking the expected value of $\hat{\hat{e}}$, we have from (3A.9)

$$E\hat{\hat{e}} = \alpha+D(X\beta+\alpha)$$

We have an unbiased estimator if and only if $D(X\beta+\alpha) = 0$.
Assuming $X\beta+\alpha = v \neq 0$, the condition $Dv = 9$, for any arbitrary
value of v, is met only if $D = 0$. In other words, the estimator $\hat{\hat{e}}$ is unbiased if and only if $D = 0$, and in this case
$\hat{\hat{e}} = \hat{e}$.

Summing up, it may be concluded that problem (a) - concerning
the country-specific factors - may partly be solved by assum-

ing that the disturbance term of direct OLS estimation on
cross-section data is of structural nature. From a theoretical point of view, however, the generalization problem is
not fully solved.

(b)   Dynamic aspects
      MOIRA describes the development over time of a number
of variables; as indicated in section 3.3.2 it is an algorithmic model in which the numerical values of all endogenous variables follow recursively from the values of the
exogenous variables in the current period and from the
values of endogenous variables in the previous period or
periods. In this sense MOIRA is a dynamic model.

However, a fully dynamic model incorporates dynamic equations - and cross-section equations do not qualify as such.
In essence cross-section analysis is based on the method of
comparative statics. Different situations are compared, but
strictly speaking the movement from one situation to another
is not described. The dynamic aspects are, therefore, largely neglected. This is, admittedly, an important shortcoming -
also in the present approach. One cannot prove the relevance
of a static comparison between countries for the dynamic
development of one country.

In spite of all this, it is possible to bring in the dynamics
by introducing all sorts of time lags, partly on the base of
theoretical and a priori considerations, and partly on the
basis of limited empirical information concerning the delays
in adaptation that would seem to have demonstrated themselves
in the past. An attempt to dynamise the picture again is made
in MOIRA along the following lines.

Consider a cross-section relation $\bar{y} = f(x)$ in which y is
immediately determined by x in a *frictionless* situation.
The actual reaction *with friction* may be presented by

$$y = g(\bar{y}(x), y_{t-1}),$$

like e.g.

$$y_t = \alpha \bar{y}_t + (1-\alpha) y_{t-1}$$

with $o < \alpha < 1$. In a stationary state, we have $y_t = \bar{y}_t$.
Coefficients like the above α and $(1-\alpha)$ are to be considered
as the weighing coefficients of a distributed lag.[1]

As observed before, in the present analysis the parameter α
cannot be estimated directly due to an insufficient number
of observations along a time path. Suppose, however, that
also another relation $z = h(y)$ holds, and that some historical information concerning the time path of z is available.
In this case, the value of α should be chosen in such a way

---

[1] In the computer programme these coefficients bear labels starting with
WE (standing for weight), followed by the name of the variable being
weighed. Following the example given in the text, the weighing coefficient would be indicated in the computer programme by WEY.

that the resulting time path of y is (as much as possible)
in agreement with the observed time path of z.

Often there will be at least qualitative information about
the time path of variables: wild oscillations are usually
not an acceptable picture of reality, and the same is true
for sudden explosions. These and other properties of the
relationships in the model are studied in the first phase of
the simulation; we revert to the problem of dynamization in
the subsequent chapters.

(c)   Generalization over time
      The cross-section estimation generalizes over countries.
The goodness of fit or, in other words, the extent to which
the numerical data falsify the hypothesis is indicated by a
number of test statistics such as correlation coefficients
and t-scores of the parameters. These criteria only serve to
test the generalization over countries; they do not test the
generalization over time. Due to the paucity of historical
time series, generalization over time remains without empirical text.

3A.2 *SPECIFICATION OF CROSS-SECTION FUNCTIONS*

      (a) Deterministic specification

         Cross-section estimation imposes certain restric-
tion on the specification of a function. A simple example
may serve to illustrate this point.

The consumption function at the national level will often be
formulated as

      $C = \alpha Y + \beta$

in which

C = consumption at the national level
Y = national income
Generalization of β over countries, however, such as in case
of cross-section analysis, leads to problems. It would imply
that a country - be it large or small in size - has a certain
level of autonomous consumption just because it is 'a'
country.
Introducing the population size L of a country, and rewriting
the above equation on a per capita base, we get

      $\frac{C}{L} = \alpha\frac{Y}{L} + \frac{\beta}{L}$

In other words, consumption per capita would be explicitly
dependent also on the size of the country. Usually this will
be an undesirable property of relations depicting technical
processes or the behaviour of the population. In these cases
the functions will have to be neutral to scale, e.g. of
linear homogeneous farm.
A function $y = f(x_1, \ldots, x_n)$ is linear homogeneous if
$\lambda y = f(\lambda x_1, \ldots, \lambda x_n)$ for $\lambda > 0$. Choosing $\lambda = \frac{1}{x_1}$, this def-

inition yields

$$\frac{y}{x_1} = f(\frac{x_1}{x_1}, \ldots \frac{x_{i-1}}{x_i}, 1, \ldots \frac{x_n}{x_i})$$ (3A.10)

Thus, a linear homogeneous function in n variables can be rewritten as a function in (n-1) variables in which all variables are relative numbers (ratio's). The reverse also holds: a function expressed in relative numbers can be considered as a transcription of a linear homogeneous function expressed in absolute numbers. As can readily be verified from (3A.10), a linear homogeneous function can be conceived of as a function expressed in relative numbers (ratio's) multiplied by a scale factor.

All functions in the present model on which cross-section estimation is applied are linear homogeneous.

(b)   Specification of the disturbance term
        Referring to the example given in section (a) of this paragraph, consider a consumption function now specified as

$$C = \alpha Y + \beta L + \varepsilon$$ (3A.11)

in which

C = consumption at the national level
Y = national income
L = population size
ε = a homocedastic disturbance term
This function should not be estimated with a homoscedastic disturbance term as in this case the variance of the disturbance term would be independent of the size of a country. This is not acceptable, as the consumption function has to describe the behaviour of the consumer rather than the behaviour of the country.

Consequently, in the cross-section estimations the disturbance term has to be specified differently; for instance, (3A.11) could be changed into

$$C = \alpha Y + \beta L + \varepsilon L$$

or into

$$C = \alpha Y + \beta L + \varepsilon Y$$

Rewriting these functions in terms of relative values, we get

$$\frac{C}{L} = \alpha \frac{Y}{L} + \beta + \varepsilon, \text{ or}$$

$$\frac{C}{Y} = \alpha + \beta \frac{L}{Y} + \varepsilon$$

(c)   Disturbance term and correlation coefficient
        Suppose the following two functions appear in a model

$$\frac{C}{L} = \alpha \frac{Y}{L} + \beta + \varepsilon$$ (3A.12)

$$Q = g(C)$$ (3A.13)

Estimation of the first relation in its relative form is still relevant; econometric theory would recommend to compute firstly the estimated value of $\frac{C}{L}$ and to use the result, after multiplication by L, as the explanatory variable in the second relation.

Suppose, however, that (3A.13) has coefficients that are determined a priori - as in several instances happens to be the case in the present study. The accuracy of the estimate of Q then depends on the accuracy of the estimate of C. Hence, in judging the estimation results for (3A.12) it is useful to take into account not only a goodness of fit criterion for $\frac{C}{L}$ but also a similar criterion for C. For this purpose a coefficient of determination can be calculated

$$R_z = 1 - \frac{\Sigma(Z-\hat{Z})^2}{\Sigma(Z-\bar{Z})^2}$$

(3A.14)

in which Z is the variable for which the goodness of fit is to be judged, $\hat{Z}$ is its estimated value, and $\bar{Z}$ is its arithmetic average. Note that the subscipt of R^2 indicates the variable concerned; this notation will be followed in the following chapters as well.

3A.3 *THE CHOICE OF FUNCTIONS*

(a) DLUP functions

The choice of the type of functions to be used in a model depends on the characteristics that the function has to depict; in other wordt, the choice of the function depends on its (mathematical) properties. This problem cannot be discussed here at length. For the present study, the class of functions that are Directly Linearizable with respect to the Unknown Parameters (DLUP functions) is of particular importance. This section focusses on a first desctiption of some DLUP functions that are of relevance to the present model. We are interested in this class of functions as the parameters of DLUP functions can be estimated with the linear regression model (if the proper assumptions about the disturbance term are made).

(b) Deterministic specification

Consider a function

$$Y = f(X_1, \ldots, X_n)$$

(3A.15)

which is assumed to be a continuous function in the relevant value range of the variables. This function is called DLUP if there exists a monotonous transformation of Y, $Z = g(Y)$, such that $Z = \Sigma \alpha_i Q_i$, in which $Q_i = Q_i(X_1, \ldots X_n)$ and $Z = g(Y)$ are functions with a priori given parameters and α_i the unknown parameters.

Two examples by way of illustration. Firstly, specify (3A.15) as

$$Y = X_1^\beta X_2^\gamma$$

Choosing further $Z = \ln Y$ and $Q_i = \ln X_i$, we obtain

$$Z = \beta Q_1 + \gamma Q_2$$

As $Z = g(Y)$ is a monotonous transformation of Y, we also have the inverse function

$$Y = g^{-1}(Z)$$

In this example, we obtain $Y = \exp(Z)$.

A second example is somewhat more complicated; it illustrates at the same time some of the properties of the intensity of land use function that will be introduced in Chapter 4. Consider the following specifications:

$$Z = \frac{\bar{Y} \cdot Y}{\bar{Y} - Y} \qquad (Y < \bar{Y}) \tag{3A.16}$$

in which $\bar{Y}$ is a given parameter.

$$Q_1 = X_1 \tag{3A.17}$$

$$Q_2 = \sqrt{X_2 + k} - \sqrt{k} \qquad (K > 0) \tag{3A.18}$$

$$Z = \alpha Q_1 + \beta Q_2 \tag{3A.19}$$

The inverse of (3A.16) is

$$Y = \frac{\bar{Y} \cdot Z}{\bar{Y} + Z} \tag{3A.20}$$

The original function therefore reads

$$Y = \frac{\bar{Y}[\alpha X_1 + \beta(\sqrt{X_2 + k} - \sqrt{k})]}{\bar{Y} + \alpha X_1 + \beta(\sqrt{X_2 + k} - \sqrt{k})} \tag{3A.21}$$

Some comments on (3A.18) and (3A.20) are in place. Ad (3A.20): the inverse (3A.20) can be rewritten as

$$Y = \frac{Z}{1 + \frac{Z}{\bar{Y}}} \tag{3A.22}$$

As can be readily seen in this form, (3A.22) weighs the influence of $\bar{Y}$ as compared with Z. When $Z \ll \bar{Y}$, Z is almost equal to Y; when $Z = \bar{Y}$, we have $Y = \frac{1}{2}Z$; when Z increases further, Y increases less rapidly. The function (3A.22) - or (3A.20) - is a hyperbola approaching $\bar{Y}$ asymptotically; in the origin, it has a slope equal to 1.

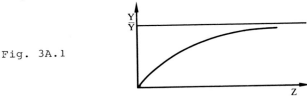

Fig. 3A.1

Thus, one of the main properties of (3A.22) is that it guaran-
tees the characteristic $Y < \bar{Y}$. It can be demonstrated that
this characteristic does not influence the substitution
elasticity of the function $Y = f(X_1, X_2)$.
Ad (3A.18): in this function the parameter k has to be considered as given a priori. If we define

$$P = \sqrt{X} \qquad\qquad\qquad (3A.23)$$

and plot this function in a system of axes with 0 as the
origin, then the transformation

$$P' = \sqrt{X+k} - \sqrt{k} \qquad\qquad (3A.24)$$

can be seen as the result of a shift of the system of axes
along the square root function from 0 to 0' as the new origin.

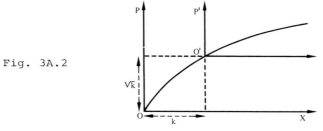

Fig. 3A.2

An advantage of (3A.24) over (3A.23) - from the point of
view of the properties desired in the present context - is
that the first derivative

$$\frac{dP'}{dX} = \frac{1}{2\sqrt{X+k}} \qquad\qquad (3A.25)$$

does not approach infinity when X becomes very small. The
first derivative (3A.25) also shows that the slope of the
function decreases when k increases. Furthermore, the absolute value of the second derivative

$$\frac{d^2 p'}{dX^2} = - \frac{1}{4}(X+k)^{-\frac{3}{2}}$$

also decreases with increasing k; thus, higher values of k
lead to a more "flat" transformation.

(c) Specification of the disturbance term

Referring to what has been said in the first paragraph of section (b) concerning DLUP functions, we have to
discuss now some of the econometric aspects. In order to
estimate the inverse of the function $Z = g(Y)$ with the help
of the linear regression model, the disturbance term has to
be specified according to

$$Y = g^{-1}(Z^S + \varepsilon) \qquad\qquad (3A.26)$$

in which $Z^S =$ the systematic component of Z, and $\varepsilon =$ the disturbance term for which the classical assumptions can be made.

In this case, the estimation would be made as if we have

$$Z = \sum_{i=1}^{H} \alpha_i Q_i + \varepsilon \tag{3A.27}$$

On theoretical grounds, however, one would usually prefer a specification

$$Y = g^{-1}(Z^S) + \eta \tag{3A.28}$$

An OLS estimation according to (3A.27) would give

$$\hat{\varepsilon} = (I - Q(Q^T Q)^{-1} Q^T)\underline{Z}$$

in which

$\hat{\varepsilon}$ = the vector fo the estimated disturbances

Q = the (NxH) matrix of the vectors Q_i,

$\underline{Z}$ = the vector of the transformed observations Z

I = the identity matrix

From (3A.28) it follows that

$$\hat{\eta} = Y - g^{-1}(\hat{Z}^S)$$

As Z^S is the systematic component of Z, we may rewrite this as

$$\hat{\eta} = Y - g^{-1}(Z - \hat{\varepsilon}) \tag{3A.29}$$

Rewriting (3A.29) again, we have

$$\hat{\varepsilon} = -g(Y - \hat{\eta}) + Z \tag{3A.30}$$

Applying (3A.30) to the earlier example of (3A.16) where

$$Z = \frac{\bar{Y} \cdot Y}{\bar{Y} - Y} \quad \text{with } Y < \bar{Y},$$

we obtain for the estimated disturbance

$$\hat{\varepsilon} = Z - \frac{\bar{Y} \cdot (Y - \hat{\eta})}{\bar{Y} - Y + \hat{\eta}}$$

Substituting Z according to (3A.16) gives

$$\hat{\varepsilon} = \bar{Y} \left(\frac{Y}{\bar{Y} - Y} - \frac{Y - \hat{\eta}}{\bar{Y} - Y + \hat{\eta}} \right)$$

$$= \frac{\hat{\eta} \bar{Y}^2}{(\bar{Y} - Y)^2 + (\bar{Y} - Y)\hat{\eta}} \tag{3A.31}$$

The OLS estimation procedure minimizes the value of $\Sigma \varepsilon^2$.
Observe, however, in (3A.31) that if for a particular observation Y approaches the given parameter $\bar{Y}$, the denominator approaches zero and a very large absolute value of $\hat{\varepsilon}$
will result - even if the disturbance term $\hat{\eta}$ is relatively
small. Minimization of $\Sigma \hat{\varepsilon}^2$ leads to parameter estimates that
pull the regression line towards the observation or obser-
vations that are close to the boundary $\bar{Y}$ in order to minimize
the $\hat{\eta}$ values corresponding with these observations because
they are heavily weighed in the summation. The $\hat{\eta}$ values
corresponding with all other observations will become large
as they have a much lower weight. Consequently, a good
statistical fit according to (3A.26), expressed in R^2_Y.

In the present example this implies that R^2_Y will be close to
R^2_Z only if $Z<<\bar{Y}$. If this would not be the case, it is doubtful whether an estimation with a disturbance term specified
as in (3A.27) with the assumption of homoscedasticity would
be appropriate. In the intensity of land use function, to be
discussed in the next chapter, the conditions $Z<<\bar{Y}$ was in
fact met, however.

In general, it may be observed that the function $Z = g(Y)$
transforms a possibly bounded value range of Y into an
unbounded value range of Z. Specification according to
(3A.26) leaves the transformation itself undisturbed, and
therefore retains this property. In estimation this implies
that an extreme observation approaching the restriction (in
the present case Y approaching $\bar{Y}$) is weighed very heavily.
Comparison of the different coefficients of determination
gives a certain check in this respect, but it is a test of a
practical nature rather than an application of a well-
defined test statistic.

Chapter 4

AGRICULTURAL PRODUCTION

4.1 *INTRODUCTION*

     Agricultural production is a process which combines
nature and human activity. But before the process of production begins, various decisions have to be made by the producer. Economic analysis describes the actions of the producer as the outcome of decisions based on the confrontation
of aims and means. This distinction between the producer's
objectives on the one hand, and his knowledge of his possibilities on the other, is adopted in the first instance.
Integration of these two facets determines the final decision
of the producer; this integration takes place in what is
described in this chapter as the *behavioural model* of the
producer.

The technical relations in agriculture are discussed first.
This is followed by a discussion of the producer's feasi-
bilities given the natural resources availability as analyzed
in Chapter 2. In the largest section of this chapter, Chapter
4.4, the agricultural production decision as it is assumed
to take place in market economies is dealt with, while
Chapter 4.5 describes the process of labour outflow from
agriculture in these countries. Finally, Chapter 4.6 indicates
in what respect agricultural production decisions in centrally-
planned economies differ from those in market economies.

The analysis is limited to the production of food from land.
Thus, the production of the fishery sector and the production of food from non-conventional sources are ignored in
the model. Obviously, fish and fish-based consumption are
too important to be neglected; altogether therefore, fish
production (in consumable protein) is estimated exogenously,
and added to total food supply. As the world fish catch
seems to have reached a plateau and may actually have declined recently due to overfishing, production of fish is
assumed to remain constant over time and equal to the base-
year catch; also, the distribution over countries is kept
unchanged. In terms of consumable protein, fish production
adds about 2 per cent to total world food production.

Non-conventional sources of food are presently of little
significance. Attempts to introduce non-conventional types
of food have not so far been very successful. The main
reason for neglecting those altogether in the present study

is that production of non-conventional forms of food is not
likely to create additional purchasing power for people
whose diets are at present meager or inadequate.[1] As the
present study intends to demonstrate, the world food problem
is not the result of constraints to produce more conventional
food, but rather the low income levels in the developing
countries keeping down effective demand for food. Industrial
production of non-conventional food - in all probability an
affair of industries of the developed countries - is not
likely to contribute to the solution of the latter problem,
but might conceivably aggravate it.

4.2   *THE TECHNICAL RELATIONS IN AGRICULTURAL PRODUCTION*

4.2.1 *The production process in agriculture*

        The process of photosynthesis constitutes the
base of all agricultural production. The food supply of
mankind ultimately depends on plant growth, since consumption of animal products incorporates the consumption of
vegetal matter processed by the animal. In the previous
chapter the magnitude of total vegetal production was described as one of the key variables in the model, expressed
in terms of consumable protein; a detailed discussion of the
measurement of *consumable protein* is presented in Annex 1.

Chapter 3 stated the reasons why the distinction between
food and non-food (including wood) products cannot be made
in the present analysis. For each country, of group of
countries, a given ratio has been assumed between the production of food measured in consumable protein, and the
production of non-food products as measured in proteins
directly required to obtain the harvested product, i.e.
required a sustain plant life. In the computer runs, this
ratio is kept constant at the observed 1964-1966 level. For
this base period, the actual percentage of food production
in total production is shown in table 4.1 for major regions.

Table 4.1

*Food production as a percentage of total agricultural
production (both measured in consumable protein),
1964-1966*

North America	82	Latin America	66
Western Europe	79	Middle East	89
Japan	62	Tropical Africa	69
Australia, New Zealand		Southern Asia	90
South Africa	40	China c.s.	90
Eastern Europe	75	WORLD	78

Source: Own calculations mainly based on FAO data.

---

[1] The introduction of significant amounts of synthetic proteins in the
world market may also have consequences for food prices. Little is known
about the relative costs of such non-conventional foods and their price
effects cannot be assessed with any degree of certainty.

Indeed, food production takes place on land[2]. The data on land availability used in the model are those of the detailed investigation reported in Chapter 2, and therefore land area is the total area suitable for agriculture, as distinct from the area actually used at present in agriculture. Consequently, also the technical production functions discussed in what follows do not explain the average yield of the actual agricultural area but production per unit of total agricultural land. This artifice is required in order to avoid the distinction between intensification of agricultural production and extension of agricultural land under cultivation. Subdivisions of this kind are rather arbitrary. Also, statistical data on land use are notoriously weak.

Thus, the model does not distinguish between two possibilities of increasing production, viz. extension of the area, and raising the yield of the area presently in use. Both processes are considered to be an intensification - via the intensity of land use function - of the total area fit for agricultural use. This approach gives expression to the assumption that the most suitable land is already in use. Hence, extension of the area as well as intensification are subject to diminishing returns. Sound objections to this generalization can undoubtedly be raised. Particularly the investment costs associated with area extension do not explicitly figure in the model, but it would in any case be extremely difficult, if not impossible, to include those in a meaningful way.

Agricultural production requires means of production, i.e. land, labour, machinery, seeds etc. As the *ruling technique* we define that specific combination of means of production which is in fact utilized to obtain a volume of product per unit of suitable land. It is considered to be chosen from among a number of known and possible techniques. Further, all producers are thought to make *realistic* choices, i.e. they will act with normal efficiency. If, for example, a certain quantity of product can be produced with ten people and one tractor, rational producers do not decide to produce it with ten people and two tractors. In technical terms the choice of techniques will always be located on the isoproduct curve (the isoquant) at the point where the available inputs give the highest output. The implications of inflexible labour supply in that context will be further discussed later in this chapter.

The technical relations of the model are obtained from cross-section estimation. These are, therefore, the result of a generalization over the techniques actually applied in

---

[2] Although the sea is large, the yield is low because of its low fertility. The long food chain between primary production and the harvestable fish and the impossibility of applying optimal harvesting strategies. The contribution of marine products to world food supplies is therefore marginal

the various countries. It implies that the range of known
techniques is described by continuous functions.

The description of the technical production process in agriculture distinguishes three components:
(a)   an absolute upper limit to food plant production per
       hectare in each geographical unit, and the total area
       suitable for agricultural production (by country);
(b)   a relation between the quantity of plant nutrients that
       must be applied in the soil and the quantity of harvested
       products - to be called the land production function;
       and
(c)   a relation between the quantity of harvested products
       and the quantity of all inputs other than plant nutrients
       into the production process - to be called the intensity
       of land use function.
The distinction between (b) and (c) derives from the observation that agricultural production factors such as labour
and many forms of capital can be substituted for each other,
while the input of plant nutrients (fertilizer) is complementary to the input unit of labour and capital.

The meaning of (a), the upper limit of production, was discussed in Chapter 2; we will briefly refer to it in Chapter
4.3. Obviously, this upper limit is of little use in depicting the possible growth of food production unless some
quantification is provided of the means of production needed
at different levels of output.

It should be noted that the technical relations do not
depend on the scale of operation; thus, production will
increase by a certain factor when the use of all means of
production (including land) increases by the same factor.
This property of linear homogeneity - see also Chapter 3.5 -
is convenient as it permits cross section estimation. In
doing so, the possibility of economies of scale at the micro
level is not denied. It does only emphasize that the size of
a country is not considered to have an impact on the technical
relations.

   4.2.2 *The land production function*

       (A) Nature of the function
              The land production function relates the
quantity of plant nutrients required for the growth of
products (that should therefore be available in the soil) to
the quantity of harvested product. The function explicitly
contains the total demand for N, P_2O_5 and K_2O at each produc-
tioon level; the actual relation is based on the observed
efficiency of these nutrients.

Nutrients can originate from organic rests like stubbles or
dung, from weathering, and from chemical fertilizer. It is
assumed that the relation between production and required
inputs of plant nutrients is universal and linear; thus,

differences between countries in the useful effect of applied
fertilizer (e.g. related to climate and soil characteristics
or on the basis of differences in the quality of management)
are omitted, and no systematic connection between production
level and marginal fertilizer productivity is assumed.

Country-specific differences in natural fertility of the
soil -as distinct from the general internal properties of
the soil -are omitted in the model as no comprehensive and
reliable estimates appeared possible. The natural supply of
nutrients is considered the same for each broad soil region.
This is justified by the observation that in most agricultural
systems where no outside resources are used, yield levels of
grain are about 1.000 kg/ha. The supply of nutrients by
recycling is proportional to the yield level. The propor-
tionality factor depends on the agricultural and socio-
economic system. It is also assumed to be constant, in spite
of the knowledge that considerable resources could be saved
by promoting recycling. Hence the need for chemical fertilizer
input(F) is simply assumed to be proportional to the yield
(Y) except for a base constant:

$$F_t = \varepsilon Y_t + \eta$$

Thus only one source of nutrients is explicitly dealt with in
the model.

The assumption of a linear relationship between production and
the required input as represented by chemical fertilizers
needs some further explanation. At first, there is the notion
of diminishing returns. But that phenomenon concerns the
situation where all inputs except the quantity of a given
fertilizer mix are kept constant. The model, however, considers
the situation where increased fertilizer use is only one
facet of a concerted amelioration effort; under these conditions the fraction of fertilizer recovered in the plant is
practically independent of the quantity that is applied.
(There is even experience where the efficiency of fertilizers
increases with increasing yield levels when the latter
result from better growth control which enables the application
of the proper amounts at the proper time).

More open to criticism is the aggregate treatment of the
three main components of the chemical fertilizer mix, viz.
N, P_2O_5 and K_2O. Especially the need for P_2O_5 is in many
situations not so much governed by the use of nutrients by
the plant, but by the rate of fixation in the soil in the
form of aluminium, iron and calcium complexes. Only in
countries like the Netherlands where over time more than
enough phosphates have been provided to saturate those
complexes, necessary amounts are now more or less related to
plant intake. On the basis of soil maps (see Chapter 2) it
would be possible to estimate how much phosphates would be
needed to *saturate* the aluminium/ iron complexes and these
amounts might be related to the available resources, but
this has not been done at the present stage of the study.

(B) Specification of the land production function

The land production function can simply be written as:

$$Y = AY.F+BY \qquad (4.1)$$

or, expressed as a demand function for fertilizer,

$$F = \frac{1}{AY} \cdot Y - \frac{BY}{AY} \qquad (4.2)$$

However, as F is not allowed to take negative values, (4.2) should properly be written as

$$F = \frac{\max \ (0,Y-BY)}{AY} \qquad (4.3)$$

In the model, the land production function is written as a demand function for fertilizer. The value of Y is determined by the intensity of land use function, to be discussed in Chapter 4.2.3; given this value of Y, the necessary amount of F follows. Therefore, the land production function (4.1) does not imply that the marginal productivity of fertilizer is constant: increasing the yield level requires the adaptation of *all* means of production - including the type of plant grown. The land production function states that, having made the necessary adaptations in all means of production, the quantity of protein produced and the quantity of nutrients taken from the soil are related linearly.

(C) Estimation of the function

The parameters of the inverse of the land production function (4.2) were estimated from cross-section data for the base period 1964-1966. The cross-section included all countries with a level of fertilizer use surpassing 0.1 kg per hectare. However, Belgium, West Germany and the Netherlands were excluded because of their very high fertilizer use per hectare due to the large use of fertilizers on intensive pastures.[3] Also, for some countries data were lacking. The total number of countries included in the cross-section estimation is 79.

With F measured in kg fertilizer (N + P_2O_5 + K_2O) per hectare of total agricultural land and Y in kg consumable protein per hectare of total agricultural land, the results of the least squares estimation were

$$\frac{1}{AY} = \ 0.56; \ t \ score \ 18.8$$

$$\frac{BY}{AY} = 14.88; \ t \ score \ \ 4.4$$

---

[3] Output from these meadows is measured in terms of the consumable protein from its animal production, and not from its vegetal base. The ratio between the two being about 1:7.

$$R_F^2 = 82.2$$

Hence, the parameters of (4.2) are AY = 1.79 and BY = 26.6.

The estimated value of the parameters of the land production function can be compared with theoretical and experimental data concerning plant growth and fertilizer use.

Without fertilizer a grain crop yields about 800 kg per hectare, corresponding with an amount of consumable protein of about 80 kg per hectare. The estimated value of BY (the intercept of the land production function) is much lower, i.e. 26.6. However, these two figures are not comparable without some modification. The variables of the land production function are expressed per hectare of total area suitable for agriculture instead of the area on which fertilizer actually has been applied. As the area of arable land in 1965 was about 40 per cent of the total agricultural land (A), the parameter BY should be in the order of magnitude of 30 kg consumable protein per hectare. The cross-section result of BY = 26.6 is not far from the expected value. Nevertheless, it is obvious that by expressing the variables per hectare of total agricultural land the contribution of the natural soil fertility to the output per hectare is underestimated substantially.

On the other hand, the slope of the function (the parameter AY) appears to be much higher than is to be expected on the basis of theoretical knowledge. As for nitrogen only, each kg of N in the form of fertilizer yields about 1.5 kg of consumable protein. Taking into account that in the base period the ratio between N and (N + P_2O_5 + K_2O) used was on average 1.9 : 2.4, one kilogram of fertilizer of this composition should yield about 0.5 kg of consumable protein. The estimated value of AY = 1.79 is at a much higher level. It is not easy to explain this difference adequately. Partly the higher outcome for the slope of the function is related to the lower outcome of BY. But there are more factors that should be considered:
(a) In countries with a relatively large livestock sector a larger part of the plant nutrients will be recycled. On the other hand, agricultural output in terms of consumable protein is relatively low in these countries because of the measurement in terms of animal consumable proteins of the production of pastures which in general are used very extensively. These two factors may have influenced the estimated parameters substantially, although the distortion cannot be assessed easily.
(b) The aggregate treatment of N, P_2O_5, and K_2O in the land production function assumes the relation between these components in the applied fertilizer package to be constant and independent of the level of fertilizer use. This assumption is a rather crude one, as has been stated earlier. If in reality the composition varies in relation to e.g. the level of N use, the estimated value of AY will not describe correctly the technical

relations.

(c) A similar observation holds for the assumption that the
     efficiency of fertilizer application and of plant
     uptake does not depend on the level of F. However, it
     cannot be checked whether the estimated value of the
     parameter AY expresses a physiological relation only or
     also systematic differences in applied technology.

In spite of these observations, the fertilizer demand function has been used in the model with the estimated parameter
values shown above.

4.2.3 *Intensity of land use function*

(A) *Nature of the function*

         The second technical relation is labelled the
intensity of land use function. It describes, for a country,
the relationship between the level of production per hectare
(and the related application of nutrients according to the
land production function) and the mix of all other inputs
per hectare. The intensity of land use function takes explicit
account of the upper limit of production per hectare; in
other words, the function is intended to describe the actual
rate of utilization of natural resources. When the actual
yield level gets nearer to the maximum production level, it
seems plausible that progressively more means of production
are required to obtain a unit increase in yield. This assumption of diminishing marginal productivity of the input mix
per unit of area of the country is of crucial importance. In
the equation the maximum possible yield acts as the asymptote,
to which the actual yield approaches with larger inputs per
hectare. The maximum yield acts therefore not only as a
limit, but also has an impact on the marginal productivity
of the input mix.

Total agricultural production (TY) of a country is therefore
considered as a function of total agricultural land (A), the
maximum yield per hectare (YASY) and a variable (Z) representing the input mix of capital (C) and labour (L):

$$TY = f(A, YASY, Z) \tag{4.4}$$

and

$$Z = g(\frac{C}{A}, \frac{L}{A}) \tag{4.5}$$

because of linear homogeneity the function for yield per
hectare (Y) - where Y = TY/A - can be written

$$Y = f(YASY, Z) \tag{4.6}$$

where actual yields depend on the maximum attainable yield
and the input mix.

The specification of the intensity of land use function and
its properties are summarized in section B, whereas the

statistical definitions and estimation results are to be found in Section C.

(B) Specification and properties of the function

The preceding discussion has suggested a form for the land intensity function in which

(a) actual yield rises asymptotically towards the maximum possible yield;

(b) the marginal productivity of the elements of the input mix (capital and labour) should be positive but declining;

(c) without any inputs in the mix (both labour and capital) output and yield should also be zero, but inputs of only labour should still result in output.

The following two specifications for yield (Y) and the input mix (Z) can be demonstrated to meet these conditions:

$$Y = \frac{YASY \cdot Z}{YASY + Z} \qquad (4.7)$$

$$Z = APY \left(\sqrt{\frac{C}{A} + BPY} - \sqrt{BPY} \right) + CPY \cdot \frac{L}{A} \qquad (4.8)$$

Specification (4.8) was obtained by simplifying an equation which was symmetrical in C and L; regression analysis suggested that the omitted variables with C/A and $\sqrt{L/A}$ were not significant. Specification (4.7) for the yield level Y is illustrated by the graph shown below.

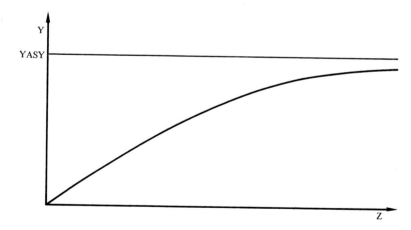

The tests which demonstrate the adequacy of these functions in terms of the three conditions imposed on them are presented in the technical appendix to this chapter.

(C) Measurement of the variables and estimation of the function

Consider first, that (4.7) which defines yield

in terms of the input mix, can be reversed:

$$Z = \frac{YASY \cdot Y}{YASY - Y} \qquad (4.9)$$

This allows estimation of Z for the base-period. From (4.8) and (4.9) we have

$$\frac{YASY \cdot Y}{YASY - Y} = APY \; (\sqrt{\frac{C}{A} + BPY} - \sqrt{BPY}) + CPY \cdot \frac{L}{A} \qquad (4.10)$$

It now remains to be seen how the variables C and L are measured. As observed in Chapter 3, it turned out to be impossible to distinguish between total agricultural population and economically active agricultural population, for statistical and demographic reasons. Agricultural labour L has been measured therefore as total agricultural population - which is, admittedly, a crude procedure.[4]

Still greater difficulties have to be faced in measuring labour substituting capital C. This variable has to be seen in fact as a measure for the *level of equipment* with which labour works. This *level of equipment* covers a wide variety of things. Partly this equipment may take a physical shape: utensils like a plough, and stocks of herbicides (both handled directly by the producer), or facilities indirectly influencing labour productivity (a drainage network, a feeder road system). Partly also this equipment may have a non-physical character: the producer's know how, and the motivation of labour. It is obvious that these various forms of equipment are hard to quantify, and equally hard to aggregate.

One of the very few indicators for which comparable data exist for many countries is the number of tractors used in agriculture. In spite of its crudeness, this indicator had to be chosen as the measure for the level of equipment of agricultural labour. As the intensity of land use function is estimated from cross-section data, the number of tractors serves only as an indicator of the variation in equipment level between countries, and not as an indicator of variation over time. The meaning of the development of the variable C over time will be discussed later on (Chapter 4.4.5 sub C).

Summarizing, the variables of the intensity of land use function are expressed in the following units of measurement. Y and YASY are measured in kg of consumable protein

---

[4]The existence or non-existence of a labour surplus is at stake here. Empirical studies have not been able to demonstrate the existence of surplus labour in agriculture; see e.g. Dale W. Jorgenson, *Testing Alternative Theories of the Development of a Dual Economy*, in: Irma Adelman and Eric Thorbecke (eds.), The Theory and Design of Economic Development, Baltimore 1966, pp. 45-60.

per hectare, A in millions of hectares, L in thousands of agricultural population, and C in number of tractors (with 1 garden tractor = 0.2 tractor). For a given value of the parameter BPY, (4.8) takes the shape of $Z = \alpha x_1 + \beta x_2$ so that α and β can be estimated with the linear regression model. The estimation proceded from different values of BPY and it was found that the correlation coefficient reached its highest value for BPY = approximately 400. The value of the parameter β turned out to be rather insensitive to variations in BPY.

For BPY = 400, the results of the cross-section estimation of (4.10) over 106 countries were:

APY = 1.12; t score 21.7

CPY = 0.051; t score 16.0

$R_z^2 = 83.2$; $R_y^2 = 86.1$; $R_{ty}^2 = 97.8$

These parameter values were used in the intensity of land use function in MOIRA. Note that in terms of output as a function of capital and labour the cross section function yields nation-specific production functions. This characterization of differences between countries is actually the main reason to introduce the variable YASY into the model. As discussed in Chapter 3A.1, it seems proper to assume that the deviation of the observed (historical) value of Z from its estimated value has structural significance. It can be asserted, for instance, that the specifics of the topography of a country (other than those taken into account in Chapter 2) will make average yields somewhat higher or lower than what would usually be the case, given a certain input mix. Also, one could think of certain specific attitudes or customs of the agricultural population of a country which bear on the agricultural output level - although the permanency of this country-specific deviation is less obvious. The deviation is defined as

$$EF_j = Z_{jo} - \hat{Z}_{jo}$$

in which

EF_j = structural deviation of country j

Z_{jo} = historical value of Z for country j in period o

$\hat{Z}_{jo}$ = estimated value of Z for country j in period o, according to the above regression equation.

In all subsequent years, this structural deviation is maintained.

(C) Short-run constraints on production change

The intensity of land use function, established by comparing various countries, is of a long-term nature. Thus, the short-term dynamics of production changes over

time are not incorporated in the function[5]. This is so
because the cross-section estimation ranges over wide variations of yield levels, whereas in reality the average
producer in a country will find the transition from one
level of yield to a higher to be arduous. Apart from the
fact that there is little, if any, scope for short-run
variations in labour inputs, there are other inflexibilities
as well. In other words, the producer encounters a more
rapidly decreasing marginal yield than this cross-country
production function reveals. In the first place, technical
characteristics of the agricultural production process may
put limits on the short-run rate of change of the production
volume. Cropping patterns cannot easily be changed from one
year to the next, and the farmer is bound by complementarities
of inputs which must be available at the appropriate time.
Change is therefore bound to be gradual, particularly at the
regional or national level.

Shifts along the intensity of land use function cannot take
place without such changes in production techniques. The
character of that function implies that in the long run the
necessary changes in the level and type of agricultural
technology will indeed take place in combination with the
higher production levels needed to raise agricultural incomes.
Long-run technical progress is therefore implicitly incorporated in the model.

In the short run, however, it may be impossible to move to a
higher level of output, given the existing level of agricultural technology of a country. Changing agricultural
techniques in practice requires time. The development,
production and distribution of new plant varieties, together
with the dissemination of the relevant information to the
producers, is a time-consuming process. The same holds for
the introduction of better methods to control diseases and
weeds, of techniques for water control, etc. And even if
significant changes in technology may occur at the farm
level, still the rate of change at the country level is
bound to be less as the entire complex of applied production
methods in agricultual changes only slowly.

In the short run, therefore a different production function
applies, as distinct from the lon-run intensity of land use
function. The short-run constraint is incorporated in the
model as follows:

(a)   Labour is considered given. For this reason, the mar-
       ginal productivity of the input mix (variable Z) de-
       creases faster in the short run than in the long run.

---

[5]In terms of Joan Robinson's critique in her *The accumulation of capital*
(London 1956) one might say that the estimated production function is a
quasi-production function, as there is no guarantee that a particular
producer (country) will in fact be able to move along the production
function. See also Joan Robinson and John Eatwell, *An introduction to
modern economics*, London 1973.

The assumption of a fixed supply of agricultural labour in the short run is discussed at greater length in Chapter 4.5.

(b)   The extent of substitution between labour and capital is subject to several constraints reflecting for example the required expansion of input producing industries and the learning process of the producer. An exogenous upper limit on the change in the capital-labour ratio, both upward and downward, is introduced:

$$\left| \frac{CE_t}{LE_t} - \frac{CE_{t-1}}{LE_{t-1}} \right| \leq UCCL$$

in which CE and LE stand for capital employed and labour employed, respectively, while UCCL = upper limit on change in capital-labour ratio.

From historical data for a substantial number of countries in the years 1965-1972, the instances of the highest observed annual changes in capital-labour ratios were selected in order to obtain a crude estimate of the value of UCCL. From a scatter diagram in which the marginal capital/labour ratio was plotted against the average ratio, it was observed that

$$\left| \Delta \frac{CE}{LE} \right|_{max} = 0.13 \frac{CE}{LE} + \left| \Delta \frac{CE}{LE} \right|_0$$

with a constant term

$$\left| \Delta \frac{CE}{LE} \right|_0 = \text{one tractor per 1000 agricultural population.}$$

Without this constant, CE_t would have to be zero if CE_{t-1} were zero.

(c)   Independent of (b), an upper limit on the annual percentage rate of growth of agricultural production has been introduced, to take into account other constraints which may not be adequately reflected in the constraint on capital/labour substitution. The limit on production growth is chosen rather arbitrarily. Historical data on long-run growth rates of national agricultural production volumes, suggest that over long periods of time agricultural primary production is very unlikely to grow by more than 4 per cent per year. The model contains this production growth constraint in the form of an upper limit on the amount of capital that can be used; the production decisions in the agricultural sector are represented in the model primarily in terms of capital use. Thus, for every year the constraint on production growth is formulated as $CE \leq CE^{max}$.

The combined effect of the constraints mentioned under (a), (b) and (c) is, that the marginal productivity of capital in

the short run is lower than the long-run marginal productivity according to the intensity of land use function.

4.3 *NATURAL RESOURCES*

Chapter 2 defined an upper limit to production in
relation to three factors: soil conditions, climatic conditions, and possibilities of irrigation. As the findings
are presented by broad soil regions, these need to be regrouped within national boundaries in order to lend themselves for inclusion in the model. Therefore national boundaries are superimposed on the soil maps for the 222 broad
soil regions and both area and maximum production estimates
have been made for the 106 geographical units of MOIRA.
Thus, for every geographical unit data for total agricultural
land area - variable A - and for the maximum production per
hectare of A - Variable YASY - were obtained. Variable A is
conceptually identical to *potential agricultural land* (PAL)
of Chapter 2. The results by geographic units for use in
MOIRA are not expressed in terms of the maximum production
of dry matter or of grain equivalents, as in Chapter 2, but
in terms of the maximum production of consumable protein per
hectare of total agricultural land. Maximum production of
consumable protein within the boundaries of a geographical
unit is the sum of the production maxima of the different
soil regions that form part of that unit. Divided by total
agricultural area, this gives the maximum production per
hectare (YASY).

The estimation procedure for the geographic units first
derives data for dry matter (MPDMI; see Chapter 2.2.5),
which are subsequently converted into figures for dry grain
yield. As in Chapter 2, it is assumed that
(a)   straw and grain constitute 75 per cent of dry matter;
(b)   the ratio between straw and grain is 1 : 1;
(c)   harvest losses amount to 2 per cent of grains.
This gives a conversion factor for dry matter to dry grain
yield of 0.75 x 0.50 x 0.98 = 0.3675.

For the conversion from dry grain yield to consumable protein
a distinction has to be made between rice and other grain
crops. Rice is assumed to have a protein content of 10 per
cent, and other grain crops a protein content of 15 per
cent. Climate and soil conditions determine whether rice or
other grain crops can be grown.

Application of these conversion factors leads to the maximum
production YASY of consumable protein per hectare of total
agricultural land, for country i:

$$YASY_i = \alpha(\beta_1 \cdot GY_i + \beta_2 \cdot RY_i) \cdot MPDMI_i$$

in which

YASY = maximum production of consumable protein per hectare
α = 0.3675 (harvestable part of the crop)

β_1 = 0.15   (protein content of grain crops other than rice)
β_2 = 0.10   (protein content of rice
GY   = share of other grains production in total production
RY   = share of rice production in total production
MPDMI = maximum production of dry matter (incl. irrigated
        area) per year

Thus, in MOIRA natural resources are seen as a fixed factor
of production. Agricultural production of a country depends
on its natural resources through the variables A_i (agricultural land available) and $YASY_i$ (maximum yield obtainable). Beyond that, weather conditions may and will vary
from year to year. In the simulation runs of the model, the
effect of weather disturbances is introduced as deviations
of the yield level from its undisturbed value. In every year
an exogenous percentage-wise disturbance is superimposed on
output levels. The disturbance factor is region-specific for
14 regions and follows a seven-year cycle. The regional
disturbances are based on historical data for output fluctuations over the period 1966-1972.

4.4 *THE PRODUCTION DECISION IN MARKET ECONOMIES*

   4.4.1 *The behaviour of the producers*
          The behaviour of the agricultural producer is
seen as the outcome of a confrontation of aims and means;
the preceding two sections described respectively the technical possibilities of the producer, and the availability of
natural resources. Against this setting the objectives of
the producer will now be discussed, together with the other
factors influencing his behaviour.

First, the general point may be made here that the model
postulates rationality of production decisions in the agricultural sector. An attempt is made to go beyond the construction of simple relations between exogenous impulses on
the one hand and final outcomes at the other. The decisions
which each farmer must and does make, form an intricate
system of relationships, that need to be reflected as well
as possible in the model; it reflects the belief that farmers
have considerable insight into the relations in their environment and do take them into consideration. This is
expressed by a number of relations in the model which reflect
the ways in which farmers arrive at their decisions. This
decision model describes what goes on in the farmer's mind
between the exogenously given conditions at one side, and
the final result (his income) at the other. The degree to
which the subject knows his environment is expressed by the
extent and the *degree of realism* of the decision model. This
determines the adequacy with which the subject reacts to his
environment.

A number of variables in this behaviour model cannot be influenced by decisions and do not result from other variables;
they are exogenous variables. The decisions of the farmer

relate to the future and thus imply a capability to foretell. In MOIRA, the existing knowledge in the sector includes knowledge of those segments of the land production function and of the intensity of land use function which are technically attainable (see Chapter 4.2). Changes in technique within those segments occur after conscious choice by the farmers. However, the farmer is not assumed to form rational expectations regarding the reaction pattern of the other actors in the system (consumers and government).

The driving force behind agricultural production decisions is the comparison made by the agricultural sector between its own standard of living and that of the non-agricultural sector. The aim is to achieve the same purchasing power as prevails in the non-agricultural sector. Even if this is not attainable, there is an effort towards the highest attainable. This behaviour assumption is a reasonable one as in virtually all countries average income per capita in agriculture is lower than that outside agriculture.

The view of the agricultural producer as combining within himself the functions of entrepreneur, labourer and financier has important implications for the way in which the behaviour model is specified. First, income that is being maximized is total value added, i.e. the sum of labour income and capital income. Rent payments are seen as transfers of income within the agricultural sector.

This view has also implications for decisions concerning the allocation of labour. A farmer may decide eventually, with his family, to leave agriculture (cf. Chapter 4.5). This can happen when the desired income has not been reached for some time. A farmer who decides not to leave agriculture will, by lack of alternatives, consider his labour and the labour of his family as fixed means of production. These will be employed as long as it yields a positive marginal income. Unemployment of farmhands, e.g. through mechanization, or more generally the implications of rural landless labour, are not considered because of the level of aggregation.

All these constraints restrict the producer in his effort towards income maximization. Still other exogenous factors, such as prices of the final product and of the means of production, will also influence his decision on planned production levels and on the corresponding quantities of fertilizers, labour-substituting capital and related means of production. The individual producer cannot influence these prices because of competition between the numerous small producers. At the sector level, this feature is introduced by taking prices as exogenous variables for the production decision.

4.4.2 *The production decision - basic structure*

The behaviour of the farmer in a market economy, which in the aggregate constitutes the picture of the be-

haviour and the decision making process of the agricultural
sector is represented in MOIRA by a set of three equations
and some related side-conditions. Two of those equations are
taken from the preceding discussion, i.e. (4.7) and (4.8);
they describe the influence of absolute maximum yields and
the input mix on realized yields, and the input mix itself
as a function of capital and labour. The third equation is
the function which defines the value added in agriculture in
relation to output, inputs and their prices. This is the
function to be maximized.

Expected income of the farmer (V*) depends on the price he
expects to obtain for his product (P*) - see Chapter 4.4.5
sub E - and the yield which can be obtained (Y) for a given
input mix, applied to total agricultural land (A) available
to the farmer, and diminished by his input costs. The latter
are only of two types: nutrients which are labelled *fertilizer*
(F) and capital (C) as labour income is considered an element
of the farmer's income.

As the decision making process for next year's agricultural
activity is supposed to take account of the current year's
prices of fertilizers (FMON) and of capital (CMON), the
function to be maximized can be written as follows:

$$V^* = (P^* \cdot Y - FMON_{t-1} \cdot F)\, A - CMON_{t-1} \cdot CE \qquad (4.11)$$

in which CE stands for capital which is to be actually employed. A side condition to this function specifies that the
use of nutrients (F) cannot take negative values.

The use of capital employed (CE) rather than capital (C) does
permit the possible existence of underutilization. Similarly,
for labour the variable LE has been introduced to allow idle
labour in the model. Therefore, the specification of the
input mix as given in (4.8) needs to be rewritten as

$$APY \left(\sqrt{\frac{CE}{A} - BPY} - \sqrt{BPY} \right) + CPY \cdot \frac{LE}{A} \qquad (4.12)$$

so that it reflects actual use of production factors in the
input mix (Z). This equation was found earlier to be subject to a side-condition concerning the maximum rate of
growth of agricultural production, and also a side condition
concerning the rate at which capital/labour substitution can
proceed. There is a third one to be added, i.e. that labour
actually employed cannot exceed the total available pool of
labour.

For convenience, the third equation of the set is repeated
here, stating the relation between acutal yield (Y), maximum obtainable yield (YASY) and the input mix (Z) as shown
by (4.7):

$$Y = \frac{YASY \cdot Z}{YASY + Z} \qquad (4.13)$$

where $Z = Z(CE, LE)$.

Agricultural labour is determined by exogenous demographic data and the labour outflow function (Chapter 4.5); thus, labour employed is given if no idle labour exists. We assume for the time being that this is indeed the case, but will discuss labour further in Chapter 4.5. Under that condition, for any given value of agricultural value added (V) the above set of equations can be graphically represented by two curves showing a relation between yield and capital employed: the iso-income curve (representing all combinations of Y and CE that lead to the same income V) and the intensity of land use curve.

Finally, the formulation of the side-condition which states that nutrient use (F) cannot be negative, is of considerable importance in the model. One can describe the behaviour of the farmer logically in two parts: one, the choices open to him without the use of nutrients, the other when nutrients (fertilizers) are applied. Graphically, these two parts can be presented as two separate lines or curves describing his choices of capital use and the levels of output or yield obtained. These two segments have an intersection at some point where a specific amount of capital is used and a specific output is obtained, but with either no fertilizer use, or some positive level of its use. It is clear that this specific output level is of interest. From the specification of the land production function (4.3) we see at once that this output level is the level BY. For the sake of convenience (4.3) is repeated below:

$$F = \frac{\max(0, \ Y-BY)}{AY} \tag{4.14}$$

The output level BY is also characterized by a specific level of capital use, which will be denoted CE_g.

Substitution of (4.14) into the agricultural income equation (4.11) gives two statements which describe income functions with or without fertilizer use (omitting time subscripts):

$$\text{If } Y<BY: \quad V^* = P^*.A.Y.-CMON.CE \tag{4.15}$$

$$\text{If } Y>BY: \quad V^* = (P^*-\frac{FMON}{AY}).A.Y - \frac{FMON.BY}{AY}.A-CMON.CE \tag{4.16}$$

Omitting for a moment the side-conditions concerning maximum growth of agricultural output and capital/labour substitution, and holding income (V) constant, the iso-income curves can be specified.

For a given value of V^* the equations of the iso-income curves can be obtained by regrouping terms in (4.15) and (4.16):

$$\text{If } Y<BY: \quad Y = \frac{V^* +CMON.CE}{P^*.A} \tag{4.17}$$

and

$$\text{if } Y>BY: \quad Y = \frac{V^* -\dfrac{FMON.BY}{AY} \ . \ A + CMON.CE}{(P^*-\dfrac{FMON}{AY}) \ A} \tag{4.18}$$

These two segments intersect at Y = BY. Differentiation of
(4.17) and (4.18) with respect to capital gives the slope of
the two segments. As a result, it is found that for positive
values of the fertilizer price (FMON) and the constant (AY),
the slope of the iso-income curve is greater for (4.18) than
for (4.17), i.e. if fertilizers are used, the slope of the
iso-income curve is steeper. One set of iso-income curves is
shown in fig. 4.1.

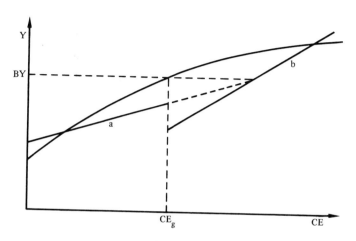

Fig. 4.1

Intensity of land use curve and iso-income curves
(segments a and b)

Next, the relationship between the intensity of land use
function (4.12) and (4.13) and the iso-income curves must be
analysed, to establish the link between income maximization
and the use of capital. Given the assumptions made, all
variables of the intensity of land use function except
capital use (CE) are known; the function therefore shows
income (Y) as determined by capital use and its curve is
shown in fig. 4.1. The maximum yield that can be obtained
without using fertilizer is BY. Putting Y = BY, we obtain
from (4.12) and (4.13) the level of capital use CE_g associated
with this yield level. As long as CE < CE_g, no fertilizer is
used (assuming, as we have done, a rational choice of production techniques). Thus, for CE < CE_g the relevant part of
the iso-income curve is the segment defined by the function
(4.17); for CE > CE_g (4.18) applies.

Note that the extent of their upward shifts for a given increase in V, measured along the vertical axis, is not the
same. Differentiation of (4.17) and (4.18) with respect to
V* shows that the upward shift of the right-hand segment (b)
of the iso-income curve is greater than that of the left-
hand side segment.

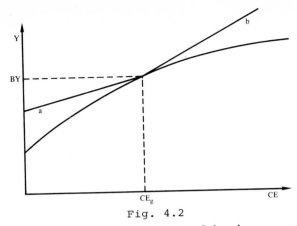

Fig. 4.2

Intensity of land use curve, and iso-incume curve
(a and b); maximum with a and b intersecting
in (CE$_g$,BY)

Maximization of agricultural GDP implies that the iso-income
curve is shifted upward until the *highest* (in terms of
income point in common with the intensity of land use curve)
is reached. Starting from the position shown in fig. 4.1 and
shifting the iso-income curve upward (without changing the
slope of the two segments), the maximum will be reached in
the position where the two segments (or their production)
intersect at Y = BY; thus, if one of the segments intersects
the intensity of land use curve in (CE$_g$, BY), then the other
half-setment passes through this point as well. Starting
from this position (fig. 4.2), the consequences of a change
in the slopes of the iso-income curve can be considered. A
change in the slopes of the curve-segments will result from
a changed price ratio between output and inputs. For instance,
a higher price of agricultural produce will lower the slopes
of the two segments. Consequently, the iso-income curve will
change clockwise (and correspond with a higher constant-
income level). Nevertheless, for a certain value range of
input and output prices, the point (CE$_g$, BY) remains the
highest point in common with the intensity of land use
function (although the value of this highest income obviously
does not remain unchanged). Still further increases of the
output price in relation to the prices of inputs would
eventually lower the slope of the segment (b) in fig. 4.2 to
such an extent that it becomes tangent to the intensity of
land use curve at a point to the right-hand side of CE$_g$, BY),
as shown in fig. 4.3. Thus (apart from the constraints
imposed) the behaviour model of the agricultural sector
leads to an investment and production decision maximizing
agricultural GDP by choosing either the point (CE$_g$, BY) -
when the two segments of the iso-income curve intersect in
this point - or the point in which the iso-income curve is
tangent to the intensity of land use curve.

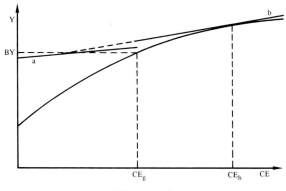

Fig. 4.3

Intensity of land use curve, and iso-income curve (a and b);
maximum with segment (b) tangent to the intensity of land
use function and optimal capital use $CE_h > CE_g$

4.4.3 *The production decision - no short-run constraints*

Two further issues need to be discussed, even
while maintaining the assumption that the restrictions on
capital/ labour substitution and on investment activity do
not apply. The first is, how the production decision of the
agricultural sector is influenced by variations in labour
supply. And secondly, how sensitive the production decision
is to change in the prices of inputs and outputs.

4.4.3.1 *Variations in labour supply*

The discontinuity in the iso-income
function necessitates distinction of three stages or steps
in the relation between labour employed (LE) and production
per hectare (Y): (a) with fertilizer use; (b) without fertilizer use, and (c) the transition from (b) to (a).

(A) Variations in labour supply (without transition)

Under the initial assumption (a), i.e. fertilizer use, (4.3)
is written as

$$F = \frac{Y - BY}{AY}$$

Substituting this in (4.11), we have

$$V^* = (P^* - \frac{FMON}{AY}) \ . \ A.Y + FMON.BY.A - CMON.CE \qquad (4.19)$$

As equations (4.12) and (4.13) together specify income as a
function of capital and labour use, the above equation can
be used to determine the partial derivative of output with
respect to labour:

$$\frac{\partial V^*}{\partial LE} = A(P^* - \frac{FMON}{AY}) \ \frac{\partial Y}{\partial LE} \qquad (4.20)$$

The term (P*-FMON/AY) is positive; otherwise zero or negative
returns to fertilizer would occur and therefore no fertilizer
would be used. Further, it follows from (4.12) that $\partial Y/\partial LE > 0$,
and therefore $\partial V/\partial LE > 0$; additional labour inputs increase
agricultural value added. The maximum value of output will
therefore be larger for higher values of labour use. As· a
consequence, labour use will increase until all labour available is employed: LE = L. Reference to this characteristic was
already made in Chapter 4.4.2.

The size of the agricultural labour force will change in the
course of time; it will most probably increase due to demographic factors, and it might decrease because of migration
from agriculture to other occupations. Such changes in the
size of the agricultural labour force can influence the
production level and the capital/labour ratio in the production process.

On the basis of the derivations contained in the appendix to
this chapter, it can be shown that additional labour employed will substitute for capital employed in agricultural
production - given a constant price ratio. Similarly, it is
found that, at given prices, an increase in labour supply
increases production, but with an elasticity less than one.
It can also be shown that the same characteristics apply
when no fertilizer is used, i.e. in case (b) referred to
above.

*(B) The transition from no fertilizer use to production with
    fertilizer use*

It can be shown (see appendix to this chapter) that when
Y = BY, changes in labour employed per hectare, within a
certain value range, will not affect the level of yield per
hectare. It is found that, for a small increase in the
amount of labour within that range, the left-hand segment of
the iso-income curve will no longer be tangent to the intensity of land use curve at Y = BY, while the right-hand
segment will not as yet be tangent to the (higher) intensity
of land use curve at Y = BY. Only further increases in
labour use will push the intensity of land use curve upward
until a situation is reached where the right-hand segment
touches the curve at the level of Y = BY. Still further
increases in labour employed will lead to production increases
(Y > BY), now requiring also the use of fertilizer. In the
transition the yield (Y) remains constant at Y = BY. In the
transition stage, the increase in the agricultural labour
available serves to replace capital employed, leaving output
and the input mix unchanged. Thus, for the limited range
over which labour employed per hectare can change, there is
no change in the yield level.

Defining labour employed per hectare as l = LE/A, we can
easily plot now the relation between the yield level Y and
the quantity of labour employed l as analyzed in the above
paragraph. This is shown in fig. 4.4.

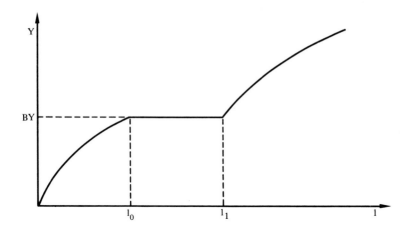

Fig. 4.4

*Labour employed per hectare and yield per
hectare (no short-run constraints).
When $l > l_1$, fertilizer will be used.*

4.4.3.2 *Sensitivity to price changes*

The sensitivity of the production decision
to changes in the prices of inputs and output can be analyzed
with the same set of equations, but still assuming that restrictions are not effective; the discussion concentrates
therefore on the case of an income maximizing decision on
investment and production in agriculture without possible
short-run constraints on the input side. It was shown before
in which way the investment decision depends, among other
things, on the price ratio between the output price (P) and
input prices (CMON and FMON). This price ratio PR is defined
in the appendix to this chapter (see Chapter 4A.3 and 4A.4)
as

$$\text{for } Y > BY: \quad PR = \frac{CMON}{P^* - \dfrac{FMON}{AY}} \qquad (4.21a)$$

$$\text{for } Y < BY: \quad PR = \frac{CMON}{P^*} \qquad (4.21b)$$

The next question is, in what way production reacts to a
change in the price ratio, given a certain level of labour
employed. Initially the case of Y = BY is excluded as at
this level the transition takes place from no fertilizer use
to fertilizer use and may change the reaction pattern.
Differentiation of yield (in the intensity of land use
function) with respect to the ratio of input and output
prices, and with respect to capital use, demonstrates (as in
the appendix to this chapter) that a change in the price
ratio leads to a change in yield level in the opposite

direction. It further shows that the absolute level of the
change in yield is larger when capital employed per hectare
is larger: the price sensitivity of production increases
when capital use increases. However, the yield level which
would be obtained without any use of capital may be achieved
with or without fertilizer. Thus two cases must be distinguished: one in which this yield is realized without fertilizer use, and one in which fertilizer would be needed to
achieve the production level even though no capital is used.

Case A: Yield level (without capital) smaller than BY

        With increasing values of the price ratio, the yield
level decreases to the level Y = BY; however, what happens
when price ratio increases further? As was observed earlier,
the slope of the iso-income curve increases; while the two
segments a and b still intersect in CE$_g$, BY), they turn
anti-clockwise, until finally the left-hand segment becomes
tangent to the intensity of land use curve in the same
point. After that, continued increases in the price ratio
would make the maximum point move away from CE$_g$, BY) along
the intensity of land use curve towards lower levels of
yields and capital use. However, over the entire value range
of the price ratio for which (CE$_g$, BY) is the maximum point,
changes in the price ratio do not affect the yield level. By
defining PR$_1$ as the price ratio at which the right-hand
segment is tangent in (CE$_g$,BY), and PR$_2$ as the price ratio
at which the left-hand segment is tangent, figure 4.5 can be
drawn. Note that the yield will not become lower than the
level Y(O), where no capital is used, as labour is given;
the level Y(O) is reached at a price ratio PR$_3$.

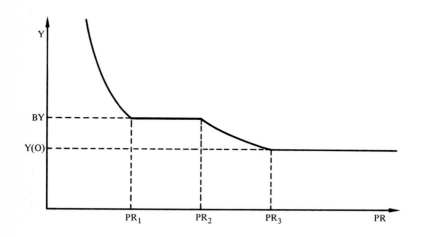

Fig. 4.5

*The relation between the price ratio PR and yield
level Y, with labour given and with Y(O) < BY*

Obviously, fig. 4.5 has important implications for the functioning of the model. The model states that the producers
react rationally to price changes. When production techniques
used are such that fertilizer is applied, higher costs of
capital use or fertilizer input will lead to lower production
levels. When (simple) production techniques without fertilizer
use are applied, a higher product price or a lower cost of
capital use will lead to increased output. However, when the
maximum yield level without fertilizer is reached, a minor
improvement of the price ratio will not immediately lead to
a decision to use fertilizer. A more substantial improvement
of the price ratio is needed to induce the producer to
switch to fertilizer-using techniques. As to very high input
price levels, as compared to the price of the output, it
should be noted that the producer may decide to use only his
own (and his family's) labour force, and thus become completely insensitive to further unfavourable price changes.

Case B: Yield level (without capital) higher than BY

       As stated before, it is uncertain whether or not the
maximum yield level without capital use and with given
labour will be lower than the level of natural fertility of
the soil, BY. Therefore, the alternative case in which this
yield level Y (O) is higher than BY needs examination. The
response curve here is much simpler and can be shown graphically at once; see fig. 4.6. As in this case there is no
transition from production without fertilizer to production
with fertilizer, or *vice* <u>versa</u>, the price ratios PR_1 and
PR_2 do not play a part in the analysis.

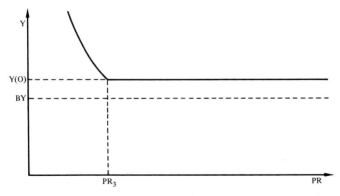

Fig. 4.6

The relation between the price ratio PR and yield
level Y, with labour given and with Y(0) > BY

In summarizing, it appears that the production decision becomes less sensitive to price fluctuations when fewer means
of production are acquired from outside the agricultural
sector (capital goods, fertilizer). In the boundary case of

an agricultural sector which is - from the point of view of
the means of production - completely isolated so that no
inputs are bought for production, the level of production is
perfectly insensitive to unfavourable price changes. In
order to avoid misunderstanding, it should be noted here
that real income of the agricultural sector will remain
sensitive to the price of agricultural produce as long as
the sector spends part of its income in the non-agricultural
sector; however, this aspect will be dealt with in the next
chapter, on consumption behaviour.

4.4.4 *The production decision - its short-run constraints*

      The intensity of land use function is essentially
of a long-term nature; in the short run, additional constraints
exist on the annual rate of substitution between capital and
labour as well as on the annual rate of increase of the production volume. As was found (in Chapter 4.4.3), additional
labour input always increases agricultural value added.
Unless the capital-labour ratio cannot change quickly enough
(see below), it will always be attractive (in terms of value
added) for the sector to employ all labour available as it is
the only input for which no price has to be paid. Thus, the
highest yield level that can be achieved in the short run is
characterized by the highest possible capital-labour ratio
and employment of all labour available.

The highest level of capital use that is feasible in view of
the constraint on substitution for labour can thus be defined
in specific terms. Similarly, one can define in precise
terms the lowest possible level of capital employed when
full utilization of all labour available is maintained. In
other words, the value range of capital use - with all
available labour employed - is restricted by specific boundary
values.

However, there is also a limit on the increase of yield to
be taken into account. This constraint is originally formulated as an upper limit to annual production growth. Every
year the behaviour model of the agricultural sector leads to
an investment decision with which a certain expected or
planned yield level (Y) corresponds. Referring to the decision
of year (t-1), this expected (*normal*) yield level must be
distinguished from the historically realized yield level
which may have been influenced by unusual weather conditions.
Because of inertia of all sorts in the sector's adapting to
technical changes, it is assumed that in year t the (expected or planned) yield level (Y) cannot surpass the value of
last year's planned level by more than 4 per cent.

It is useful to indicate the main lines of the procedure for
solving the behaviour model. Let us concisely reformulate
the problem. The agricultural sector wants to maximize its
income, given a set of prices of inputs and output. The
necessary fertilizer input is dictated by the yield level.
Together with fertilizer and capital inputs, the yield level

determines the income level. The yield level depends on
natural resources, and labour and capital input. As natural
resources are given, and total labour availability - in the
short run without alternative employment opportunities - is
also given in the short run, capital input has to be chosen
in such a way that the highest possible income level is
reached. The technical relation between yield level and
capital and labour inputs is known to the sector; there are,
however, certain short-term constraints on changes in these
inputs.

The decision on the level of capital use that maximizes
agricultural income is made by comparing the production possibilities curve (yield related to capital employed) with
the iso-income curve (combinations of yield level and level
of capital employed to which the sector is indifferent as
they lead to the same income level). The slope of the iso-
income curve is constant and depends on the price ratio
between inputs and output. The slope of the technically
determined production possibilities curve is continually
changing and decreases with increasing input levels.

With all parameters determining the slope of the iso-income
curves and the slope and level of the production possibilities
curve given, an efficient procedure for optimizing capital
employed (CE) can be designed. First the bounds on capital
use are determined; then the matter whether fertilizer
should be used may further restrict the interval. Finally a
monotonously convergent procedure is used to determine the
optimum within the given interval. The solution procedure
requires per country on the average 3 to 4 iterations.

A slightly complicating factor is, that the production possibilities curve may intersect with the Y axis below the
origin. It will be recalled that the intensity of land use
function contains a country-specific constant term EF, which
is called the structural deviation of the intensity of land
use function. This constant EF may be positive, zero, or
negative. Therefore, in case EF < 0, also Y < 0 for extremely small values of the input factors capital and labour. As
this is obviously not a desirable property, in such cases
the absolute value of EF is reduced for very low values of
the input mix (and yields) so that with positive input
levels also the yield level (Y) remains positive. In the
extreme case of a boundary maximum in the origin, the yield
level and agricultural value added may be zero; in all other
cases agricultural income corresponding with the optimum
decision on capital use is positive.

4.4.5 *The prices of agricultural produce and capital*

4.4.5.1 *Price determination*
        The prices of capital and fertilizer inputs,
the price of the agricultural product, and their ratios as
used in the model are statistically not easy to determine.

Information is available only for a few countries and special
problems arise from the measurement of agricultural produce
in terms of consumable protein. The statistical problems
could in fact not be overcome; only fertilizer price data
were found adequate and are discussed in Chapter 8.5.

The three prices - P of agricultural produce, CMON of capital
employed, and FMON of fertilizer - occur in the agricultural
value added definition and thus figure in the investment and
production decisions of the sector. Preferably, the parameters
of the model would have been estimated through a reduced-
form estimation and the results used in the structural form.
However, due to inadequate price data (and also due to the
mathematical form of the equations) the behaviour model
had to be estimated immediately in its structural form.
Still, the use of the model for projection purposes does
require estimates of the various prices for the base period.

Prices play a double role in the model; they appear as
marginal costs and marginal returns in the production decision,
and as average costs and average returns in the calculation
of value added or income. Although the marginal and the
average price need not be the same, the model assumes their
identity as if there were perfect competition. It should be
noted in particular, that in both these appearances the
prices in the model must reflect the actual prices with
which the agricultural producer is confronted. This further
aggravates the statistical problems.

As direct measurement of the capital and output prices is
impossible, their values must be computed for the base
period. With their initial values known, the model can
generate their development in subsequent years. The production decision is incorporated in the land production function, and investment decisions are represented in the model
by the agricultural income equation. These two equations are
used to determine prices of output and of capital in the
base period. In order to deal simultaneously with the two
cases of fertilizer use and no fertilizer use, the land
production function is rewritten as

$$F = k \cdot \frac{Y - BY}{AY} \tag{4.22}$$

with k = 0 or 1, with alternatively no use, or use, of fertilizer. Substituting this form into (4.11), further assuming
a given constant value of agricultural income (V) and rewriting the equation as an expression for yields (Y) along
the same lines as in (4.18), an equation is obtained similar
to (4.18), but including the new notation (with k); it is
the general form of both (4.17) and (4.18) at the same time.
Differentiation over capital use per hectare (and assuming
labour use constant), an equation is obtained which has only
the two prices as unknowns. The same applies to the agricultural income equation itself, and from the two together
prices can therefore be derived. However, this implies
the acceptance of a number of restricting assumptions, which

are that:
(a)   the equations are an accurate picture of reality;
(b)   the short-run constraints on the investment decision
       are not effective;
(c)   there is perfect foresight, so that the price of agri-
       cultural produce expected for next year is indeed
       realized;
(d) $Y \neq BY$, as in the case of their equality the price
       ratio is not uniquely determined;
(e)   yields exceed the level that would be obtained without
       capital use; in other words, the possibility of produc-
       tion levels on the Y-axis on or below the intersection
       with the intensity of land use curve is excluded.

More details are presented in the appendix to this chapter.

4.4.5.2 *The nature of technical progress*
            In the beginning of this chapter it was
stated that the technical relations in the behaviour model
purport to describe the possible production techniques in
agriculture. Chapters 4.2.2 and 4.2.3 presented two technical
relations comprising physically measurable variables only.
Next, the production decision was discussed; there, the
choice of a production technique was argued on economic
grounds, and not on the basis of autonomous shifts of the
production function confronting the producer exogenously.
Thus, technical progress in agriculture is fully embodied as
production per hectare (at the national level) increases as
a consequence of an increase in labour employed or in its
productivity in conjunction with all complementary means of
production. Changes in production techniques are thus made
endogenous and technical progress is seen as embodied in the
capital and fertilizer inputs. The decision to increase
production, for a given supply of labour, leads to a greater
need for agricultural capital goods (and possibly fertilizer),
and thus to larger outlays on capital. At a constant price
(CMON) this means a higher value of capital employed (CE).
Embodied technical progress is, therefore, in a sense put on
a par with a production increase; therefore the parameters
of the production functions do not change in the course of
time. At the end of Chapter 6 the subject of technical
progress will be taken up again.

4.4.5.3 *Base period averages and historical time
            paths*
            The base year average prices can be cal-
culated, given the values of all other variables in the
behaviour model. If this price calculation is to be made for
a series of successive years for which historical data are
avialable, a problem arises concerning capital employed
(CE). The number of tractors was used to measure CE in the
cross-section estimation over countries of the intensity of
land use function, but this crude measure was rejected as a
yardstick for annual changes in capital employed. Hence, the

time path of capital employed in the individual countries
had to be established in a different way.

It was stated above that the parameters of the technical
relations do not change over time. If for a historical
period statistical information on total yield (TY) and
agricultural labour (L) is available, and if it is assumed
that all available labour is used (LE = L), the corresponding
annual values of CE can be computed from the intensity of
land use function. This was in fact done for a base period
of seven years, 1965-1971. As production in terms of consumable proteins could not be calculated but for the base year
(1965), the FAO production index in terms of grain equivalents was used in calculating the time path of total yield.
The time series of capital use thus computed represents the
development of the effective capital stock used in agriculture. Given also the time series of agricultural income (V)
and fertilizer prices (FMON) the procedure for calculating
output and capital prices can be repeated for every year of
the base period.

The internally consistent set of time series can subsequently be used in reverse order. Given the calculated series of
output and capital prices, and given the time series of
labour (L) the model generates a realistic time series for
total and average yields (as total land is given), and for
capital employed and value added. This identification is
used to ensure that the model faithfully reproduces observed
reality. This *starting up* of the simulation model is needed
because the coefficients have been estimated by cross section
only. In order to generate a reasonable dynamic path, time
series information must be used for calibration.

Obviously, the model can no longer be used with predetermined
values of P, CMON and LE, as the values of these variables
are themselves generated in the model. In the process of
calibrating (to which we return in Chapter 6) it is tried to
make the model generate for past years values for P and CMON
close to the calculated values, and a time path of LE that
can be considered realistic. If the model generates time
series for P, CMON and LE showing close correspondence with
the above mentioned (*consistent*) time series, then it also
generates realistic time series for Y, CE and V.

4.4.5.4 *Processing of agricultural produce*

The agricultural sector is not only engaged
in the production of vegetal products but also in the processing of it. For example, the sector may convert its grain or
soya into meat by feeding cows or pigs on it. The sector
will thus earn part of its income from processing its own
(basic) products. These processed products will fetch a
higher price in the market per unit of consumable protein.
By processed products we understand in this study primarily
the products of animal husbandry.

Processing of agricultural produce can be seen as a kind of industrial transformation of raw materials. As in the case of industrial processing, the price of the final product can be considered as the sum of the price of the raw materials (in this case the vegetal proteins) and the price or value of the effort of processing. This distinction is important, as in MOIRA a distinction is made between different types of price changes of agricultural produce: (a) general price increases as caused by inflation, (b) food price increases caused by a higher level of processing, and (c) agricultural price changes other than those mentioned under (a) and (b), e.g. as a consequence of agricultural price policy.

Thus, the price (P) received by the agricultural sector for (partly processed) produce - measured of course in terms of consumable proteins - is built up from two components. For period 1 we have

$$P_1 = P_0 \cdot NPI_1 + DFPE_1$$

in which

P_0 = price of agricultural produce received by the sector in period 0
P_1 = price of agricultural produce received by the sector in period 1
NPI = general price index for non-agricultural products
DFPE = deviation of agricultural raw material prices from their base year level.

Moreover, we have to take into account the effects of possible changes in the level of processing by the agricultural sector. Such changes in the level of processing are introduced as changes in what will be called (for lack of a better word) the base price PO. For period 1 again, the development of the base price is

$$PO_0 = P_0$$

$$PO_1 = P_0 (1+GPO_1)$$

Where GPO is the rate of change in the degree of processing. In more general terms

$$PO_t = PO_{t-1} (1+GPO_1) \qquad (4.23)$$

Therefore, the price received by the agricultural sector is defined as

$$P_t = PO_t \cdot NPI_t + DFPE_t \qquad (4.24)$$

As will be obvious from its definition given above, DFPE is equal to zero in the base year. The general price index NPI is put equal to the overall price index of all non-food products. It will be discussed in more detail in Chapter 5, while DFPE is an important variable in the discussions of

Chapters 5 to 7.

The base price PO depends on the degree of processing, as far as processing takes place within the agricultural sector; in other words, PO can be seen as reflecting the quality of agricultural produce. In Chapter 5 it will be seen how the degree of processing of food is determined by the purchasing power of the consumers in and outside agriculture. The processing takes place partly in factories (i.e. outside the agricultural sector) and partly by the producing sector itself. It is assumed that the degree of processing in the agricultural sector develops at the same rate as the general degree of processing required for the total domestic market (i.e. for the two consuming sectors together).

Again, more will be said about GPO in Chapter 5. It should be noted here that the assumption of GPO being determined by the domestic market situation would seem to be a realistic one for most countries; however, its degree of realism will be lower for countries with a highly specialized and export-oriented agriculture such as the Netherlands or Taiwan.

Additional processing of food by the agricultural sector will require additional capital. This could constitute a complicating factor in the analysis presented earlier in this chapter. It is assumed, however, that processing by the agricultural sector can be described as inducing an increase in both the numerator and the denominator of the price ratio PR.

$$PR = \frac{CMON}{P - \dfrac{FMON}{AY}}$$

in such a way that the value of PR is not affected by it. In other words, the model is constructed so that an increase in PO causes an increase in CMON as well, and to an extent which leaves the value of PR unchanged. Hence, the production decision in terms of the volume of output of consumable proteins is not affected by the degree of processing. Another (minor) adjustment in CMON for inflation will be discussed in Chapter 8.

4.4.5.5 *Prices and shadow prices*

The price of agricultural produce received by the sector - variable P - is calculated over the historical period 1965 - 1971 as a shadow price, as explained above in Chapter 4.4.5.1. Nevertheless the same variable P is introduced in Chapter 4.4.5.4 as an *actual* price:

$$P_r = PO_t \cdot NPI_t + DFPE_t$$

and also used as such in computing the value added of the agricultural sector. In the first section referred to, it has been explained why this is inevitable.

The production decisions of the agricultural sector would become somewhat precarious, however, if they would be based entirely on the actual price received in the previous year. Therefore, in MOIRA a distinction is made between the price actually received by the agricultural sector (variable P), and the expected price on which the sector bases itself in making its production decision (variable P*; see Chapter 4.4.2). The latter variable is defined as

$$P^*_t = PO_t \cdot NPI_t + DFPE^{**}_t \qquad (4.25)$$

in which

DFPE** = the expected level of DFPE according to

$$DFPE^{**}_t = 0.5 DFPE^{**}_{t-1} + 0.5\, DFPE_{t-1} \qquad (4.26)$$

The choice of equal weights for the two terms at the right-hand side was made after some experiments.

4.5 *THE LABOUR OUTFLOW FUNCTION IN MARKET ECONOMIES*

4.5.1 *Measuring labour outflow*

The total agricultural labour force available is measured in terms of the total agricultural population. The occupational flexibility of the agricultural population is usually not very large; nevertheless, in all countries a continuous flow of people is observed, leaving agriculture for other occupations[6]. Labour outflows from agriculture must be taken into account in MOIRA. The present sub-section deals with the process of labour outflow in market economies; the case of the centrally-planned economies is discussed in Chapter 4.6.

Changes in agricultural labour supply are caused by agricultural population growth and by the rate of labour outflow from agriculture. In most countries the latter variable is not as such registered statistically. However, population censuses provide estimates of the agricultural (L) and non-agricultural (NPOP) population at different moments in time. Assuming that the annual natural rate of increase in agricultural population g is known, net labour outflow (NLO) over a certain period T could be computed as

$$NLO_{t,\,T} = L_{t-T} \cdot (1+g_1)^T - L_t$$

in which

NLO$_T$ = net labour outflow over a period of T years
L = agricultural population

[6] See on the topic of labour outflow J. Harris and M.P. Todaro, *Migration, unemployment and development. A two-sector analysis*, in: American Economic Review, 60 (March 1970), pp. 126-142.

g_1 = annual natural rate of increase in agricultural pop-
    ulation

T   = number of years between two censuses.

For any specific census period running from t-T to t, the
average annual rate of labour outflow LO follows - assuming
a constant g_1 - from

$$L_t = [(1+g_1) \cdot (1+LO)]^T \cdot L_{t-T}$$

or

$$LO = \frac{(\frac{L_t}{L_{t-T}})^{\frac{1}{T}}}{(1+g_1)} - 1$$

Note that LO as defined here is, strictly speaking, a rate
of change in population due to *migration*; hence, LO will be
negative when there is an outflow. Similarly, the average
annual rate of labour inflow in non-agriculture LI can be
computed as

$$LI = \frac{(\frac{NPOP_t}{NPOP_{t-T}})^{\frac{1}{T}}}{(1+g_{NPOP})} - 1$$

in which

LI   = annual rate of labour inflow in non-agriculture
NPOP = non-agricultural population
g_{NPOP} = annual natural rate of increase in non-agricultural
    population

As natural growth rates of population do not exist for the
two sectors separately, the average natural growth rate of
the entire population (g_{POP}) had to be used instead; hence
in computing LO and LI it is assumed that $g_I = g_{NPOP} = g_{POP}$.
The data on L, NPOP and g_{POP} used in the calculation are
those of the censuses of around 1960 and 1970.

4.5.2 *The labour outflow function*

        The process of labour outflow from agriculture as
represented in MOIRA, is not the result of a plan of the
agricultural sector; rather it is caused by the comparative
attractiveness of agriculture and of city life. The power of
attraction of the non-agricultural sector depends on the
ratio of average incomes in and outside agriculture, and
also on the possibility and willingness of the non-agricultural (*urban*) sector to receive and absorb the labour outflow from agriculture. When the agricultural sector is very
large in comparison to the urban sector, towns and cities
will usually be far away for most of the agricultural popu-

lation, and the urban sector may not be able to receive a
large labour inflow. It seems plausible to assume that the
relative accessibility of the urban sector, i.e. the ratio
between agricultural and non-agricultural population, does
exert an influence of its own on the rate of labour outflow.

Labour outflow from agriculture is incorporated in the model
by means of a function describing labour inflow in the non-
agricultural sector. It is nevertheless called the labour
outflow function, as in the present study the agricultural
sector is in the centre of attention. As the two factors
responsible for the pull of the non-agricultural sector -
the income ratio and accessibility - mutually reinforce each
other, a specification in multiplicative form is chosen. The
function is specified as

$$LI = ALI \cdot (TENS)^{BLI} \cdot (\frac{L}{NPOP})^{CLI} \tag{4.27}$$

in which

$$TENS = \left[\prod_{i=0}^{2} (\frac{NRVLU_{t-i}}{RVLU_{t-i}}) \right]^{\frac{1}{3}} \tag{4.28}$$

LI   = annual rate of labour inflow in non-agriculture
TENS   = ratio of non-agricultural to agricultural income
NRVLU = non-agricultural real income per capita
RVLU   = agricultural real income per capita

As before, L and NPOP are agricultural and non-agricultural
population, respectively ALI, BLI and CLI are parameters.
Real incomes per capita NRVLU and RVLU will be defined in
Chapter 5. TENS is defined in (4.28) as an average over the
past three years, as the agricultural population is assumed
not to act on the basis of the evidence of one specific
year.

The labour outflow function is estimated as a cross-country
function with average values for the period 1960-1970. Thus,
the function is estimated for 1965, if assuming that in this
year migration was equal to its average value over the
period 1960-1970. The number of geographical units in the
cross section was 96; in addition to the centrally-planned
economies, a few countries had to be excluded because of
data inadequacies. Least-squares estimation in logarithmic
form led to the following results:

ln(ALI) = -4.7313; t score 42
BLI   = 0.3543; t score 4.2
CLI   = 0.3680; t score 8.9
R^2_{lnLI} = 77.1 ; $R^2_{LI.NPOP}$ = 83.2

As was to be expected, the values of the parameters BLI and
CLI fall between 0 and 1.

4.5.3 *Some comments on the labour outflow function*

Like in the case of other functions that form
part of MOIRA, it would have been desirable to analyse the
effect of all sorts of measures and developments on the
level of labour outflow. However, an elaborate quantitative
analysis of the implications of the labour outflow function
in the context of the model is not feasible because of the
complex nature of the factors determining the variable
TENS - a complexity that will be discussed further in Chapter
6. Some brief observations, however, can be made here.

(1)   It should be noted that for TENS = 1, (i.e. equality of
       average incomes in and outside agriculture) there will
       still be a labour outflow. This is in harmony with
       actual experience, as in some countries where values of
       TENS rather close to 1 have been observed, the labour
       outflow neverteless continued due to inequalities in
       income distribution within agriculture;
(2)   At a constant ratio between total sectoral incomes, a
       labour outflow will lead to a lowering of both TENS and
       of L/NPOP. A lowering of these variables will result in
       a lowering of the labour outflow itself, but to a less
       than proportional degree;
(3)   The absolute level of the net labour outflow (NLO) is
       obtained from NLO = LI.NPOP; substituting for LI in
       (4.27), it is found that

$$NLO = ALI.(TENS)^{BLI}.L^{CLI}.(NPOP)^{1-CLI} \qquad (4.29)$$

Thus, given a constant ratio of incomes per capita and
equal natural rates of increase of population in sectors,
the net labour outflow increases with the same percentage as population as the sum of the exponents of L and
NPOP equals unity;
(4)   The development of the agricultural population is given
       by

$$L_{t+1} = L_t.(1+g)-LI.NPOP_t \qquad (4.30)$$

Dividing both sides by L_t, and substituting (4.27) for
LI, one obtains

$$\frac{L_{t+1}}{L_t} = (1+g)-ALI.(TENS)^{BLI}.(\frac{L}{NPOP})^{CLI-1} \qquad (4.31)$$

(5)   The annual rate of labour outflow from agriculture (LO)
       can be expressed as

$$LO = LI.\frac{NPOP}{L}$$

Substitution of LI according to (4.27) gives

$$LO = ALI.(TENS)^{BLI}.(\frac{NPOP}{L})^{1-CLI} \qquad (4.32)$$

An upper limit has been imposed exogenously on the annual rate
of labour outflow thus calculated. The process of labour

outflow is probably influenced by demographic factors such
as the age structure of the agricultural population. Agricultural population beyond a certain age will not usually leave
agriculture; it is mostly the younger part of the agricultural
population that is involved in labour outflow. Factors of
this nature may be responsible for the fact that the labour
outflow does not surpass a certain percentage of agricultural
population, even if conditions in agriculture are conducive
to large-scale outflows. The highest rate observed historically seems to be the 4.5 per cent annual rate of labour outflow
in the Netherlands in the recent past. For these reasons, an
upper limit of 5 per cent on the annual rate of labour
outflow from agriculture has been introduced; thus, $LO \leq 0.05$.

4.6   *AGRICULTURE IN CENTRALLY-PLANNED ECONOMIES*

It is very difficult to construct a model which is a
meaningful reproduction of reality in centrally-planned
economies. Firstly, little relevant information is readily
available or accessible. Secondly, time and resources available did not permit the research group to try and establish
the necessary cooperation with experts from the centrally-
planned countries. For these countries, the national model
of the agricultural sector in its relation to the rest of
the economy is consequently a rather crude one.

Obviously, this is a drawback - in particular as the two
geographical units with central planning, the Soviet Union
plus East European countries and China plus some adjacent
countries, comprise a considerable part of world population.
On the other hand, to the extent that these countries aim at
and realize exact self-sufficiency in food, the market
economies and the world market are not affected by agricultural production and consumption in the centrally-planned
economies. Description in MOIRA of the national agricultural
sectors of the centrally-planned countries requires the
introduction of some concepts and relations which are only
discussed in detail in the later chapters.

An important assumption about centrally-planned agriculture
is, that the agricultural sector is considered as a labour
reservoir from which the non-agricultural sector can draw
labour as needed.

It is assumed here that the National Plan first formulates
the growth rate of national income and that the planned per
capita income growth rates in agriculture and non-agriculture are equal to the national average (sectoral and personal
income distribution data are not available). Also, a constant
and given ratio between income growth and labour productivity
growth is assumed. These two growth rates determine the
desired growth of the non-agricultural labour force. The
latter increases partly because of population growth; the
remaining shortage must be filled by labour withdrawn from
the agricultural sector. There is, however, an upper limit

to agricultural labour outflow (again a maximum of 5 per
cent per annum) so that the planned income growth rate
cannot be chosen in an unrestricted manner.

The desired income level for the national economy determines
total desired consumption of food, via the consumption
function. Given the tendency towards autarky, the desired
consumption volume sets the goals for what is to be produced
domestically (i.e. within the geographical unit concerned).
The desired volume of agricultural production requires,
together with the labour force left in the agricultural
sector, an additional quantity of capital inputs. This
quantity can be computed from the intensity of land use
function, and is assumed to be made available to the sector.
However, as in the case of the market economies, the planned
increase in agricultural production cannot be more than 4
per cent annually - disregarding output variations due to
climatic factors.

If the upper limit to agricultural production growth is not
effective, the quantities of labour and capital calculated
in this way permit the realization of the desired production
level - again apart from shortfalls due to bad weather
conditions - and the demand for agricultural products can be
satisfied. Because of crop variations, a situation may arise
in which planned production will not be reached; in this
case, the centrally-planned countries have to import food.

Parameter values have been determined by calibrating the
national model on the basis of historical data, i.e. the
parameter values are chosen in such a way that for the historical period the actual development of production and
labour outflow are reproduced, given population growth. From
this, the desired rate of income growth and the rate of
increase in labour productivity can be calculated for the
historical period; the ratio between the two is assumed to
remain the same in future years. Desired rates of income
growth for future years enter exogenously.

The base year value of national income has been calculated
using the inverse of the consumption function. However, as
income distribution data for centrally-planned countries are
not available in the required format, the assumption of a
perfectly equal income distirbution had to be made. This
implies that national income as computed via the consumption
function is underestimated; as such, this fact is not important because only the income growth rates matter in determining the subsequent development of the economy. However,
it is important to note in this context that in the national
model of centrally-planned economies inadequate food consumption levels (i.e. hunger, as defined later on in this study)
will not manifest themselves as the model shows the national
average food consumption level only.

The entire structure of the model for the centrally-planned
economies in MOIRA, shows that in these countries food
supply does not present a problem from an organizational

point of view - thanks to the (perhaps not entirely realistic) assumption that the government sees to it that the required volume of food will be produced and, after that, will be distributed equally. In this case, only crop failures due to uncontrollable factors and the (largely theoretical) possibility of approaching the absolute maximum yield level might create problems. Nevertheless, it remains of interest to analyse the effect of crop failures on the world market for food.

Appendix 4A

PROPERTIES OF THE ASSUMED PRODUCTION RELATIONS

4A.1 *PROPERTIES OF THE INTENSITY OF LAND USE FUNCTION*

In Chapter 4.2.3 the specifications for yield (Y) and the input mix (Z) were written:

$$Y = \frac{YASY \cdot Z}{YASY + Z} \tag{4A.1}$$

and

$$Z = APY \left(\sqrt{\frac{C}{A} + BPY} - \sqrt{BPY} \right) + CPY \cdot \frac{L}{A} \tag{4A.2}$$

(a) For any finite value of Z, Y < YASY as

$$Y = \frac{YASY}{\frac{YASY}{Z} + 1} \tag{4A.3}$$

(b) The marginal productivity of the input mix is positive but declining:

$$Y = \frac{Z}{1 + \frac{Z}{YASY}}$$

so that Y is almost equal to Z for Z << YASY.

(c) Without any inputs in the mix, yields should also be zero; for C = L = 0, also Y = 0.

(d) Inputs of labour only still result in output; when C = 0 and L > 0, Y > 0.

(e) The marginal productivity of capital is positive and decreasing:

$$\frac{\partial Y}{\partial \left(\frac{C}{A}\right)} = \frac{dY}{dZ} \cdot \frac{\partial Z}{\partial \left(\frac{C}{A}\right)} \tag{4A.4}$$

$$\frac{\partial Y}{\partial \left(\frac{C}{A}\right)} = \frac{1}{\left(1 + \frac{Z}{YASY}\right)^2} \cdot \frac{APY}{2\sqrt{\frac{C}{A} + BPY}} \tag{4A.5}$$

$$\frac{\partial Y}{\partial (\frac{C}{A})} > 0 \quad \text{and} \quad \frac{\partial^2 Y}{\partial (\frac{C}{A})^2} < 0$$

(f)   Marginal productivity of labour decreases much less
      rapidly than of capital; in particular when Z << YASY,
      labour productivity decreases hardly with increasing
      labour input:

$$\frac{\partial Y}{\partial (\frac{L}{A})} = \frac{1}{(1+\frac{Z}{YASY})^2} \cdot CPY \qquad (4A.6)$$

As Z increases when L increases, we find

$$\frac{\partial Y}{\partial (\frac{L}{A})} > 0 \quad \text{and} \quad \frac{\partial^2 Y}{\partial (\frac{L}{A})^2} < 0 \qquad (4A.7)$$

(g)   The marginal rate of substitution between capital and
      labour is negative and independent of L; total dif-
      ferentiation of the function gives:

$$dY = \frac{dY}{dZ} \left\{ \frac{\partial Z}{\partial (\frac{C}{A})} \cdot d(\frac{C}{A}) + \frac{\partial Z}{\partial (\frac{L}{A})} \cdot d(\frac{L}{A}) \right\} \qquad (4A.8)$$

The slope of the isoproduct curve is found by putting
dY = 0, yielding

$$\frac{d(\frac{C}{A})}{d(\frac{L}{A})} = - \frac{\frac{\partial Z}{\partial (\frac{L}{A})}}{\frac{\partial Z}{\partial (\frac{C}{A})}}$$

which can be rewritten as

$$\frac{dC}{dL} = -2\frac{CPY}{APY}\sqrt{\frac{C}{A}+BPY} \qquad (4A.10)$$

For a given value of C, the slope of all isoproduct curves is
the same, shifting with rising Y parallel with the horizon
axis away from the origin.

The marginal rate of substitution does not play the crucial
role given to it in neo-classical economics as the assumption of a variable labour input is not considered realistic,
at least in the short run. In the present analysis the
optimum production conditions are not determined by the
equality of the factor price ratio and the marginal rate of
substitution.

4A.2 *VARIATIONS IN CAPITAL SUPPLY*

Chapter 4.4.3.1 discusses variations in labour supply. Equation (4.19) in the text of this chapter can also be differentiated with respect to capital:

$$\frac{\partial V}{\partial CE} = A \ (P - \frac{FMON}{AY}) \frac{\partial Y}{\partial CE} - CMON \tag{4A.11}$$

Additional capital inputs need not necessarily lead to increased value added, because of the negative right-hand side term. In fact it can be shown that, given LE, value added (V) will reach a maximum for a specific value of CE. In order to have a maximum, the two conditions

$$\frac{\partial V}{\partial CE} = 0, \text{ and } \frac{\partial^2 V}{\partial (CE)^2} < 0 \text{ have to be fulfilled.}$$

Substituting $\frac{V}{CE} = 0$, we have:

$$\frac{\partial Y}{\partial CW} = \frac{CMON}{A(P-\frac{FMON}{AY})} \tag{4A.12}$$

Thus, the slope of the iso-income curve has to equal the slope of the intensity of land use curve.

The second derivative is written:

$$\frac{\partial^2 V}{\partial (CE)^2} = A.(P-\frac{FMON}{AY}) \ \frac{\partial^2 Y}{\partial (CE)^2} \tag{4A.13}$$

Also, taking account of (4A.12) and the capital-labour substitution constraint, we can write:

$$\frac{\partial^2 V}{\partial (CE)^2} = \frac{dY}{dZ} \ . \ (\frac{\partial Z}{\partial (CE)})^2 + \frac{dY}{dZ} \ . \ \frac{\partial^2 Z}{\partial (CE)} =$$

$$= \frac{-2(YASY)^2}{(YASY+Z)^3}.(\frac{\partial Z}{\partial CE})^2 + \frac{(YASY)^2}{(YASY+Z)^2}.\frac{\partial^2 Z}{\partial (CE)^2} \tag{4A.14}$$

Furthermore, we have $\frac{\partial Z}{\partial CE} > 0$ and

$$\frac{\partial^2 Z}{\partial (CE)^2} = - \frac{\alpha}{4A^2} \ . \ (\frac{CE}{A} - BPY)^{\frac{3}{2}} \tag{4A.15}$$

so that $\frac{\partial^2 Z}{\partial (CE)^2} < 0$. Therefore, the two terms at the right-hand side of the equality sign in (4A.14) are negative.

Thus, also $\dfrac{\partial^2 Y}{\partial (CE)^2} < 0$ and also $\dfrac{\partial^2 V}{\partial (CE)^2} < 0$

The negative value of the second derivative of V with respect to CE means that, for given LE, we have a maximum for $\overline{\partial CE} = 0$.

As was stated before, $\dfrac{\partial V}{\partial LE} > 0$; the maximum value for V will thus be higher for higher values of LE. As a consequence, LE will increase until all labour is employed (see also Chapter 4.4.2).

4A.3 *THE EFFECTS OF LABOUR EMPLOYED ON CAPITAL-LABOUR SUB-STITUTION AND ON PRODUCTION*

Even if all labour is employed, changes in the agricultural labour force will occur because of demographic (incl. migration) factors. Starting from (4A.12) and multiplying both sides by A (and keeping in mind that L = LE):

$$\frac{\partial Y}{\partial \frac{CE}{A}} = \frac{CMON}{P - \frac{FMON}{AY}} \tag{4A.16}$$

Writing MP (for marginal productivity of capital) for the left-hand side, PR (price ratio) for the right-hand side, c for capital employed per hectare (CE/A) and l for labour employed per hectare (LE/A) the following functions can be derived:

$$MP = \frac{dY}{dZ} \cdot \frac{\partial Z}{\partial c} \quad \text{(from the intensity of land use function)}$$

$$dPR = \frac{dY}{dZ} \cdot d(\frac{\partial Z}{\partial c}) - d(\frac{dY}{dZ}) \cdot \frac{\partial Z}{\partial c}) \quad \text{(from (4A.16))} \tag{4A.17}$$

Further defining:

$$Y_z = \frac{dY}{dZ}$$

$$Z_c = \frac{\partial Z}{\partial c}$$

$$Z_{cc} = \frac{\partial^2 Z}{\partial c^2} \quad \text{and}$$

$$Z_{lc} = \frac{\partial^2 Z}{\partial c . \partial l}$$

We can write:

$$dZ_c = Z_{cc} dc + Z_{lc} dl$$

$$dY_z = \frac{\partial Y_z}{\partial c} dc + \frac{\partial Y_z}{\partial l} dl$$

$$Y_z dZ_c = Y_z (Z_{cc}dc + Z_{1c}dl)$$

$$Z_c dY_z = Z_c (Z_c dc + Z_1 dl)\frac{dY_z}{dZ}$$

As $\frac{dY_z}{dZ} = \frac{d^2Y}{dZ^2}$, it follows from (4A.1):

$$\frac{dY_z}{dZ} = \frac{-2(YASY)^2}{(YASY.Z)^3} = \frac{-2Y_z}{YASY+Z}$$

Substituting the above expressions in (4A.17) one obtains:

$$dPR = Y_z \left\{ (Z_{cc} - \frac{2Z_c^2}{YASY+Z})dc + (Z_{1c} - \frac{2Z_c Z_1}{YASY+Z})dl \right\} \qquad (4A.18)$$

Assuming a constant price ratio (dPR = 0), equation (4A.18) can be used to derive the effects of labour force changes (1) on the capital-labour ratio and on production.

(a) Effect of 1 on capital employed per hectare (c)
     From (4A.18) can be derived:

$$\frac{dc}{dl} = - \frac{Z_{1c} - \frac{2Z_1 Z_c}{YASY+Z}}{Z_{cc} - \frac{2Z_c^2}{YASY+Z}} \qquad (4A.19)$$

It follows from (4A.15) that $Z_{cc} < 0$; because of the additive specification of (4A.2) we have $Z_{1c} = 0$. As all other variables in (4A.19) are positive, it follows that dc/dl < 0. Obviously, then also dCE/dL < 0. Thus, additional labour substitutes for capital employed at a constant price ratio.

(b) Effect of 1 on production (Y)
     From (4A.1) and (4A.2) it follows:

$$\frac{dY}{dl} = \frac{dY}{dZ} \cdot \frac{dZ}{dl}, \text{ and}$$

$$\frac{dZ}{dl} = \frac{\partial Z}{\partial c} \cdot \frac{dc}{dl} + \frac{\partial Z}{\partial l} \qquad (4A.21)$$

As $\frac{dY}{dZ} > 0$, the sign of $\frac{dY}{dl}$ will be the same as of $\frac{dZ}{dl}$.

Using the same short-hand notation as above, (4A.21) can be rewritten:

$$\frac{dZ}{dl} = Z_c \left\{ - \frac{Z_{1c} - \frac{2Z_c Z_1}{YASY+Z}}{Z_{cc} - \frac{2Z_c^2}{YASY+Z}} \right\} + Z_1 \qquad (4A.22)$$

As $Z_{1c} = 0$, rearranging terms in (4A.22) gives:

$$\frac{dZ}{dl} = Z_1 \left\{ \frac{\frac{2Z_c^2}{YASY+Z}}{Z_{cc} - \frac{2Z_c^2}{YASY+Z}} + 1 \right\} \qquad , \text{ or}$$

$$\frac{dZ}{dl} = Z_1 \left\{ \frac{1}{Z_{cc} \cdot \frac{YASY+Z}{2Z_c^2} - 1} + 1 \right\} \qquad (4A.23)$$

Already (4A.15) demonstrated that $Z_{cc} < 0$, so that

$$Z_{cc} \cdot \left(\frac{YASY+Z}{2Z_c^2} \right) < 0, \qquad (4A.24)$$

as all other variables on the left-hand side of (4A.23) are positive. Subtracting 1 from both sides,

$$Z_{cc} \cdot \left(\frac{YASY+Z}{2Z_c^2} \right) - 1 < -1$$

Hence it follows that

$$0 > \frac{1}{Z_{cc} \cdot \left(\frac{YASY+Z}{2Z_c^2} \right) - 1} > -1$$

which implies that in the right-hand side of (4A.23) the term within the brackets is positive. As (4A.2) shows $Z_1 > 0$; thus $dZ/dl > 0$ (see (4.20)). Therefore, at given prices, an increase in labour supply increase production.

(c)   The elasticity of production with respect to labour supply.
This elasticity, ε_{yl}, is defined as:

$$\varepsilon_{yl} = \frac{dY}{dl} \cdot \frac{l}{Y}$$

and can be calculated in the present case as:

$$\varepsilon_{yl} = \frac{dY}{dZ} \cdot \frac{dZ}{dl} \cdot \frac{1}{Y}$$

The first factor on the right-hand side follows from differentiation of (4A.1); the second factor is given in (4A.21).

Substitution gives:

$$\varepsilon_{yl} = \frac{(YASY)^2}{(YASY+Z)^2} \cdot Z_1 \left\{ \frac{1}{Z_{cc} \cdot \left(\dfrac{YASY+Z}{2Z_c^2}\right)-1} +1 \right\} \cdot \frac{1}{Y} \qquad (4A.23)$$

As we have from (4A.1)

$$\frac{1}{Y} = \frac{YASY+Z}{YASY} \cdot \frac{1}{Z}$$

and from (4A.2) that $Z_1 = CPY$, we may rewrite (4A.23) as:

$$\varepsilon_{yl} = \left(\frac{YASY}{YASY+Z}\right) \cdot \left(\frac{1}{Z_{cc} \cdot \left(\dfrac{YASY+Z}{2Z_c^2}\right)-1} +1\right) \cdot \frac{CPY.1}{Z} \qquad (4A.24)$$

The three right-hand side elements are all positive with an absolute value between 0 and 1. Consequently we find $0 < \varepsilon_{yl} < 1$. Thus, at constant prices an increase in agricultural labour leads to a lesser percentage increase of production. The numerical value of the elasticity varies (see 4A.24) with the level of production.

4A.4 *PRODUCTION WITHOUT FERTILIZER USE*

The analysis presented above of the effects of variations in labour supply is limited to the case of production with fertilizer use, i.e. $Y > BY$. Now we turn to the case in which $Y < BY$ and no fertilizer is used. Obviously, text equation (4.3) reduces to $F = 0$, and instead of text equation (4.20) we have:

$$\frac{\partial V}{\partial CE} = A.P. \frac{\partial Y}{\partial LE} \qquad (4A.25)$$

whereas equation (4A.11) of this annex becomes

$$\frac{\partial V}{\partial CE} = A.P. \frac{\partial Y}{\partial CE} - CMON \qquad (4A.26)$$

Again, as $\partial V/\partial LE > 0$, all labour available will be employed so that $LE = L$. Capital employed will increase until $\partial V/\partial CE = 0$; agricultural value added will reach its maximum when, according to (4A.26),

$$\frac{\partial Y}{\partial CE} = \frac{CMON}{A.P} \tag{4A.27}$$

In other words, also in this case a maximum is reached when the slope of the iso-income curve is equal to the slope of the intensity of land use curve. Just as before, calculation of $\partial^2 V/\partial (CE)^2$ shows this quantity to be negative so that we have a maximum indeed.

When no fertilizer is used, the price ratio PR becomes PR = CMON/P. The analysis of the effects on production of variations in labour supply is made under the assumption of a constant price ratio, i.e. dPR = 0. The same assumption was made in the preceding sub-section, and all implications drawn from that analysis also hold in the present case.

4A.5 *THE TRANSITION FROM NO FERTILIZER USE TO PRODUCTION WITH FERTILIZER USE*

The preceding paragraphs discuss the cases Y > BY and Y < BY, or - in terms of the investment decision - with the cases CE > CE$_g$ and CE < CE$_g$. However, what happens at the point of transition from *no fertilizer use* to *with fertilizer use*, i.e. when Y = BY and CE = CE$_g$?. (It should be remembered that throughout this section we analyse the situation of a *free maximum* and constant prices).

It will be shown presently that when Y = BY, for a certain value range of labour employed per hectare, changes in this variable will not affect the level of yield per hectare; in symbols: dY/dl = 0, for a certain value range of l. In order to demonstrate this, let us see what happens when - starting from a position of Y < BY - the *transition point* is reached from the left-hand side. In the figure below, this point is reached for a given value of l - say, l$_o$ - when Y = BY and $\partial Y/\partial c$ = PR; the left-hand side half segment of the iso-income curve touches the intensity of land use curve in the point (CE$_{g,o}$, BY).

The transition from CE$_{g,o}$ to CE$_{g,1}$ as shown in the figure above, can be illustrated by recalling the first order maximum condition (4A.12), for Y > BY.

$$\frac{dY}{dCE} = \frac{CMON}{(P - \frac{FMON}{AY}) \cdot A} \tag{4A.12}$$

It is clear that, in the case of no fertilizer use, this simplifies (Y < BY) to

$$\frac{dY}{dCE} = \frac{CMON}{P.A} \tag{4A.28}$$

Recall also the intensity of land use function (4A.1) and

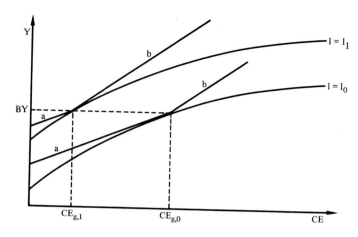

Fig. 4A.1

Intensity of land use curves, and iso-income curves
(half segments a and b); transition from no
fertilizer ($CE_{g,0}$) to fertilizer use ($CE_{g,1}$)

(4A.2); the slope of this function as shown in the figure
above is

$$\frac{\partial Y}{\partial CE} = \frac{dY}{dZ} \cdot \frac{\partial Z}{\partial CE}$$

$$= \frac{dY}{dZ} \cdot \frac{APY}{2A \cdot \sqrt{\frac{CE}{A} + BPY}} \qquad (4A.29)$$

From (4A.28) and (4A.29) we have for the maximum corresponding to $CE_{g,0}$:

$$\frac{dY}{dZ} \cdot \frac{ABY}{2A \cdot \sqrt{\frac{CE_{g,0}}{A} + BPY}} = \frac{CMON}{P.A}$$

and for the maximum corresponding to $CE_{g,1}$

$$\frac{dY}{dZ} \cdot \frac{APY}{2A \cdot \sqrt{\frac{CE_{g,1}}{A} + BPY}} = \frac{CMON}{(P - \frac{FMON}{AY})A} \qquad (4A.31)$$

In the transition from $CE_{g,0}$ to $CE_{g,1}$, the yield Y remains
constant at Y = BY. Hence, dY/dZ has the same value in
(4A.30) and (4A.31). The higher value of the right-hand side
of (4A.31) as compared with (4A.30), implies a lowering of
CE which is the only variable at the left-hand side that is

not constant. In the transition stage, the increase in the agricultural labour available serves to replace capital employed, leaving Z and Y unchanged. Thus, for the value range from l_0 to l_1, the increase in labour employed per hectare does not change the yield level; for this value range of l, we have $dY/dl = 0$.

How does production react to a change in the price ratio, given a certain level of labour employed, l? The intensity of land use function (4A.1) and (4A.2) gives Y as a function of capital and labour employed. When labour employed is kept constant, we have $dl = 0$.
Hence,

$$dY = \frac{\partial Y}{\partial c} \cdot dc$$

and

$$\frac{dY}{dPR} = \frac{\partial Y}{\partial c} \cdot \frac{dc}{dPR} \qquad (4A.32)$$

Furthermore

$$\frac{dc}{dPR} = \frac{\partial c}{\partial PR}$$

Substituting in (4A.32), we obtain

$$\frac{dY}{dPR} = \frac{\partial Y}{\partial c} \cdot \frac{\partial c}{\partial PR} \qquad (4A.33)$$

in which c is a monotonous function of PR. From the first-order condition MP = PR, we have PR = $\partial Y/\partial c$. Therefore (4A.33) can be written as

$$\frac{dY}{dPR} = \frac{\frac{\partial Y}{\partial c}}{\frac{\partial^2 Y}{\partial c^2}} \qquad (4A.34)$$

Recalling the properties of the intensity of land use function, we found from (4A.5) $\partial Y/\partial c > 0$ and $\partial^2 Y/\partial c^2 < 0$. Thus, it follows from (4A.34) that $dY/dPR < 0$; an increase in the price ratio lowers production, at a given value of labour employed. An increase in the price ratio may result from an increase of the input costs CMON or FMON, or from a lowering of the price P of agricultural produce.

We will now determine the magnitude of dY/dPR, always with given labour employed. Differentiation of the intensity of land use function with respect to c gives

$$\frac{\partial Y}{\partial c} = \frac{dY}{dZ} \cdot \frac{\partial Z}{\partial c} \qquad (4A.35)$$

and

$$\frac{\partial^2 Y}{\partial c^2} = \frac{dY}{dZ} \cdot \frac{\partial^2 Z}{\partial c^2} + \frac{d^2 Y}{dZ^2} \cdot \left(\frac{\partial Z}{\partial c}\right)^2 \qquad (4A.36)$$

Calculation of the first and the second derivative of (4A.1) shows that

$$\frac{d^2 Y}{dZ^2} = \frac{-2}{YASY+Z} \cdot \frac{dY}{dZ} \qquad (4A.37)$$

Further, substituting (4A.35) and (4A.37) in (4A.34), and dividing numerator and denominator by dY/dZ and by $\partial Z/\partial c$, we obtain

$$\frac{dY}{dPR} = \cfrac{1}{\cfrac{\frac{\partial^2 Z}{\partial c^2}}{\frac{\partial Z}{\partial c}} - \frac{2}{YASY+Z} \cdot \left(\frac{\partial Z}{\partial C}\right)} \qquad (4A.38)$$

As we had earlier from (4A.2),

$$\frac{\partial Z}{\partial c} = \frac{APY}{2\sqrt{c+BPY}}$$

and

$$\frac{\partial^2 Z}{\partial c^2} = \frac{-APY}{4\sqrt{(c+BPY)^3}}$$

Substitution of these values in (4A.38) gives

$$\frac{dY}{dPR} = \cfrac{1}{\cfrac{-APY}{4\sqrt{(c+BPY)^3}} \cdot \cfrac{2\sqrt{c+BPY}}{APY} - \cfrac{2}{YASY+Z} \cdot \cfrac{APY}{2\sqrt{c+BPY}}}$$

or

$$\frac{dY}{dPR} = \cfrac{-1}{\cfrac{1}{2(c+BPY)} + \cfrac{APY}{(YASY+Z)(\sqrt{c+BPY})}} \qquad (4A.39)$$

As can be seen from (4A.39), an increase in c reduces the value of the denominator and increases the absolute value of dY/dPR. Hence, a change in the price ratio PR leads to a change in yield level Y in the opposite direction (as we saw already), and the absolute level of the change in Y is larger when capital employed per hectare is larger. The price sensitivity of production increases when capital use increases.

Chapter 5

FOOD CONSUMPTION

5.1 *THE CONSUMPTION FUNCTION*

   5.1.1 *Consumer behaviour*
         Every human being needs food; no one can survive
without it. This book would not have been written, had food
been so plentifully available that it would be, in economic
terms, a free good. In fact, access to food is under almost
all curcumstances dependent on the capacity and the willingness of the individual or the household to make efforts for
its acquisition. In conditions of extreme poverty, virtually
all means the individual has at his disposal are needed to
meet food needs - for the sake of mere survival. With larger
available resources, not all of those need to be used for
food, but part of these means can be diverted to satisfy
other needs. In general, the demand for food depends on the
behaviour of the consumer who takes his consumption decisions
within the limits of resources available to him and taking
account of the costs and benefits derived from alternative
patterns of spending.

Consumer behaviour may thus be described as a process of
weighing all possible baskets of goods and services that
might be bought with the objective to reach an optimal
allocation of income; this process requires extensive information about a great many different goods and services. A
simpler and more direct approach to consumer behaviour is
adopted for the purpose of the formulation of the model, as
it is impossible in the present context to describe the
needs for any other goods and services than those for food.

Earlier studies have shown convincinly that the consumer's
behaviour reacts to an increase in income in two ways: the
physical quantity of food consumed will tend to increase,
and the share of processed food in the diet will increase.
The first reaction implies that more is eaten (or wasted) by
the consumer; the latter, that animal proteins and other
processed vegetal proteins replace unprocessed vegetal
proteins in the food basket. Consequently, increased purchasing power induces a rice in the consumption of consumable proteins. Although expenditure on food in money terms
increases, it does not increase proportionally with income;
thus, the share of food in total expenditure decreases with
rising income. The two food consumption curves - one in

terms of consumable proteins, the other in terms of money
spent on food - are both monotonously rising and are downwards concave. Fig. 5.1 shows the function relating consumption in terms of consumable proteins to real income; a
similar curve applies to food consumption expenditure related to income.

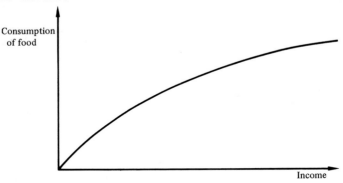

Fig. 5.1

The consumption curve relating food consumption to income

For the purpose of the analysis, income must be defined as
real income, or purchasing power. In that way price changes
of food or non-foods can be taken into account in so far as
they lead to real income changes. Price changes do not
necessarily affect real income as such changes may offset
each other. Under those circumstances total consumption expenditures (in real terms) remain the same, although their
allocation changes between goods and services through the
substitution is thought to occur mainly within the classes
of basic needs (like food, shelter, etc.) and to a much
lesser extent between these classes. It would, of course, be
better if the analysis did take account of the broad substitution effect between food consumption and all other consumption taken together. At the same time, such aggregate analysis
would not add substantively to the quality of the model as
it is in any case not designed to generate the supply of
non-food consumption goods and services, nor the prices
applicable to that part of consumption. Beyond the desire to
keep the model manageable, there would also be considerable
data and estimation problems if an extension to non-food
consumption were attempted. International cross section
analysis is of little use and the time series of consumption
measured in consumable protein are not available.

The preceding discussion of consumer behaviour is entirely
in terms of individual or household consumption and income.
However, the required statistical information exists only at
a much higher level of aggregation, and consequently a more
aggregated formulation of the consumption function is required. Total food consumption in physical terms is known

for the base year at the national level; it has been converted
into consumption of consumable proteins. Total expenditure for
food is already more difficult to obtain, and is not available for all geographical units. Income data exist at the
sector level; hence, agricultural and non-agricultural
income are known. Incomes and food consumption levels vary
greatly within each sector and it would be unrealistic to
postulate equality for the entire population of a sector.
Income distribution can affect the aggregate food consumption level and its allocation between different groups of
consumers significantly. The approach to this aspect of aggregate consumption is discussed next.

5.1.2 *Income distribution*

          As was already observed earlier, inadequate food
consumption and hunger reflect an uneven distribution of
food rather than a global shortage of food. The consumption
function of MOIRA postulates that food consumption is a
function of real income. Or, in other words, food is distributed and consumed according to purchasing power. Therefore the distribution of purchasing power, or real income,
over people is a highly important parameter and has been
strongly emphasized in the model.

Income distribution has been introduced in MOIRA already in
two of its dimensions: (a) income distribution between countries, and (b) income distribution between the agricultural
and non-agricultural sectors. A third one is now to be
added: (c) income distribution within each sector. Part of
the income distribution data needed for the present analysis
was not readily available however; the missing data had to
be derived from limited information.

The countries can be subdivided into three groups depending
on their data base:
(a)   countries for which income distribution within the two
       sectors is known and available;
(b)   countries for which only the national income distribu-
       tion is known; and
(c)   countries for which no or very little data on income
       distribution exists.
A procedure was developed to estimate for countries in group
(b) the income distribution within each of the two sectors,
using information avialable for group (a), the national
income distribution, and data on total income inside and
outside agriculture. Estimates for group (c) were made on
the basis of the distribution figures available for countries
of a similar socio-economic structure and development level.
In some cases the available information was expressed in
concepts different from those selected for the present
context, e.g. as rural income per worker rather than as
agricultural income per capita. Adaptations were made, using
information concerning countries for which both data sets
were avaiable. The income distribution estimates are obviously not particularly reliable. However, it is a far better

approach than to assume that income is distributed equally
over all people. The latter assumption is implicitly made
when the consumption function specifies only total income or
average income per capita.

For each of the two sectors (agriculture and non-agriculture), total income is given for the five income classes
defined by the quintiles, with the richest 20 per cent of
population again subdivided into the top 5 per cent and the
next 15 per cent. Thus, six income classes are distinguished
per sector, and 12 per geographical unit. The model is based
on the assumption that the distribution of nominal income
per sector (in percentage terms) remains the same over time
as in the base year. Given the income distribution per
sector, food consumption in MOIRA can now be expressed in
terms of per capita food consumption of each income class i
(i = 1, . ., 6) within each sector s (s = 1,2) country j.

As mentioned earlier (see Chapter 4.6), no income distribution data could be obtained or constructed for the centrally-
planned economies. Therefore, it was inevitable in this case
to use national averages only; consequently, the centrally-
planned economies had to be omitted from the cross-country
estimation of the consumption function. The relationship
between food consumption and purchasing power is, however,
assumed to be the same in centrally-planned countries as
applies to market economies.

5.1.3 *The consumption function in consumable proteins*

The consumption function expressed in terms of
consumable proteins can be written, at the national level,
as the sum of consumption by each income group in each
sector; consumption in each income category of each sector
is, in turn, a function of income in that income category.
For the base year, the national average per capita food
consumption is known and the income accruing to each group
is also available from data or estimates mentioned earlier.
Also, agricultural and non-agricultural population numbers
are known, and within those, the income classes can be given
their appropriate population numbers and shares.

Thus, the consumption function expressed in terms of consumable proteins is

$$\text{CONS} = \sum_{i=1}^{6} \sum_{s=2}^{2} p_s \cdot d_i \cdot \text{CONS}_{is} \qquad (5.1)$$

with

$$\text{CONS}_{is} = f(R_{is}) \qquad (5.2)$$

in which

CONS   = food consumption per capita, national average

$CONS_{is}$ = food consumption per capita, in income class i of sector s

R_{is} = real income per capita, in income class i of sector s

p_s = share of sector s in total population

d_i = share of income class i in the population of each sector.

For the base year, CONS is known and R_{is} has been determined in the way just described. Labelling the agricultural sector as sector 1, we have $p_1 = L/(L+NPOP)$, in which L and NPOP are agricultural and non-agricultural population, respectively. Obviously, $p_1 = 1-p_2$. Indicating the income class with the highest income per capita as income class 1, we have $d_1 = 0.05$; $d_2 = 0.15$; and $d_3, \ldots ,d_6 = 0.2$.

Function (5.2) is specified as

$$CONS_{is} = \left[\min \frac{R_{is}}{FP^s}, \ ACONS+BCONS \ (\sqrt{R_{is}+CCONS} - \sqrt{CCONS}) \right]$$

(5.3)

in which

FP^s = price of food per unit of consumable protein, in sector s. ACONS, BCONS and CCONS are parameters. The reasons why a specification as given above has been chosen were partly discussed already in Appendix 3A.3, and will also be clear from the discussion of the properties of the function in Chapter 5.2.2. Graphically, (5.3) is displayed in fig. 5.2.

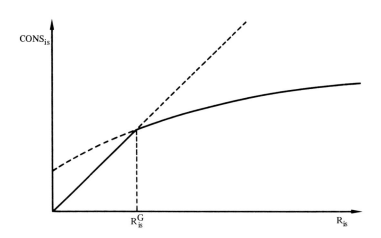

Fig. 5.2

The consumption curve in consumable protein, as specified in (5.3)

As food consumption expressed in purchasing power spent on
food ($CONS_{is}.FP^s$) cannot be larger than total real income
R_{is}, below a certain (low) income level R^G_{is} the consumption
curve is a straight line through the origin and with a slope
of $1/FP^s$. This income level R^G_{is} might be called the threshold
income. If we assume that in the base period real income per
capita of all income classes is larger than R^G_{is} (or at least
equal to R^G_{is}), we may disregard in the cross-section estimation the segment of the consumption curve to the left of
R^G_{is}. Substituting (5.3) in (5.1) we obtain

$$CONS = ACONS + BCONS \left[\sum_{i=1}^{6} \sum_{s=1}^{2} p_s \cdot d_i (\sqrt{R_{is}+CCONS} - \sqrt{CCONS}) \right]$$

(5.4)

For a given value of CCONS, (5.4) takes the shape of
CONS = ACONS+BCONS.x, and can easily be estimated with the
linear regression model. Note that prices do not explicitly
enter the consumption function at this stage.

In the cross section over countries, data on 103 geographical units were used - i.e. all units except the centrally-
planned economies. CONS is measured in kg of consumable
protein per capita, and R_{is} in 1000 dollars per capita. It
had to be assumed that the per capita GDP figures in dollars -
on which ultimately the R_{is} data are based - reflect adequately and exclusively actual differences between the levels of
purchasing power of (the various income classes in) the different countries. After trying out different values of
CCONS, it was decided to assign to it the value 0.05.

For CCONS = 0.05 the estimation results for (5.4) were
ACONS   = 16.60; t score   9.1
BCONS   = 63.84; t score 19.2
R^2_{cons} = 78.5 ; for total national food consumption

(CONS.POP), the coefficient of determination was $R^2_{cons.pop}=$
98.2. As in the case of other cross-section results, the
residuals are interpreted as country-specific disturbance
terms; thus, the base-year deviations are maintained as
structural constants, and per country the value of ACONS is
changed accordingly.

    5.1.4 *The consumption function in purchasing power*
        Turning now to the food consumption function
expressed in terms of purchasing power units spent on food
(MCONS), we can easily show how a graphical representation
of the curve should look like; see fig. 5.3.

Just like the consumption curve expressed in consumable
protein, for real income levels below the threshold income
($R_{is} < R^G_{is}$) the present consumption curve is a straight line
through the origin; now the slope of the straight-line
segment is equal to unity. For $R_{is} > R^G_{is}$, the curve is

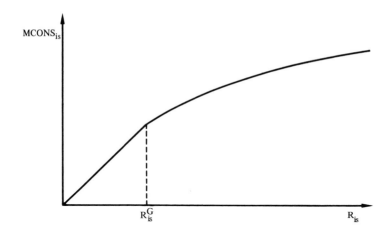

Fig. 5.3

The consumption curve in purchasing power,
as specified in (5.6) - (5.7)

again monotonously increasing and concave downwards. Also,
we know that as purchasing power increases consumption of
processed proteins will increase; hence, the value of
$MCONS_{is}/CONS_{is}$ should show a damped increase for increasing
values of R_{is}.

Therefore, the following sepcification has been chosen:

$$MCONS = \sum_{i=1}^{6} \sum_{s=1}^{2} p_s \cdot d_i \cdot MCONS_{is} \qquad (5.5)$$

with

$$MCONS_{is} = CONS_{is} \cdot FP_{is} \qquad (5.6)$$

and

$$FP_{is} = DCONS + ECONS \left(\sqrt{R_{is} + FCONS} - \sqrt{FCONS} \right) \qquad (5.7)$$

in which

$MCONS$ = purchasing power spent on food, per capita, national
average
$MCONS_{is}$ = purchasing power spent on food, per capita, in income
class i of sector s
FP_{is} = price of food per unit of consumable protein, for
income class i of sector s
$DCONS$, $ECONS$ and $FCONS$ are parameters.

Substitution of (5.6) and (5.7) in (5.5) gives

$$MCONS = \sum_{i=1}^{6} \sum_{s=1}^{2} p_s . d_i . CONS_{is} .$$

$$. \left[DCONS + ECONS \ (\sqrt{R_{is} + FCONS} - \sqrt{FCONS}) \right] \qquad (5.8)$$

A recursive estimation procedure can be followed, by sub-stituting for $CONS_{is}$ its estimated value $\hat{CONS}_{is}$ as obtained from (5.4). Thus, (5.8) has been estimated in the specification

$$MCONS = DCONS . (\sum_{1=1}^{6} \sum_{s=1}^{2} p_s . d_i . \hat{CONS}_{is}) + ECONS .$$

$$. \left[\sum_{i=1}^{6} \sum_{s=1}^{2} p_s . d_i . \hat{CONS}_{is} (\sqrt{R_{is} + FCONS} - \sqrt{FCONS}) \right] \quad (5.9)$$

For the base year, MCONS is measured as per capita expenditure on food in 1000 dollars; however, only for 40 countries were data available in the UN National Accounts Statistics. Again, for FCONS several values were tried out, and the value FCONS = 0.05 was chosen. The estimated values of DCONS did not differ significantly from zero, and the first term at the right-hand side of (5.9) was consequently dropped.

For FCONS = 0.05, the cross-section estimation results were:

ECONS $= 1.1131.10^{-2}$; t score 35

$R^2_{MCONS} = 90.0$

As $CONS_{is}$ is specified in the form $a+b\sqrt{x}$, and FP_{is} likewise in the form $c+d\sqrt{x}$, the function specifying $MCONS_{is}$ takes the shape of $(a+b\sqrt{x}).(c+d\sqrt{x}) = ac + (ad+bc)\sqrt{x} + bdx$. Thus, the desired properties of the functions for $CONS_{is}$ and FP_{is} hold also for the function $MCONS_{is} = f(R_{is})$. As the first derivative of FP_{is} with respect to R_{is} is positive, and the second derivative is negative, $MCONS_{is}/CONS_{is}$ shows indeed a damped increase for increases in R_{is}.

The food price FP_{is} reflects the degree of processing of food that corresponds with the income level of income class i of sector s. The average level of food processing of a sector's food consumption, as desired by the consumers, will be indicated by $\tilde{FP}^s$; this variable is defined as

$$\tilde{FP}^s \equiv \frac{\sum_{i=1}^{6} d_i . MCONS_{is}}{\sum_{i=1}^{6} d_i . CONS_{is}} \qquad (5.10)$$

In the model it is assumed that a sector, s food supply is characterized by a (sectoral) *average* level of processing;

in other words, although the producers and the processing industries may be aware of the variations in the *proper* level of food processing between the income classes, their food supply to a sector is characterized by an average or *standardized* level of processing only. Thus, it is assumed that there is only one type of *food shop* for the agricultural sector, and only one type (with food of a different level of processing) for the non-agricultural sector.

In addition, it is assumed that the level of food processing cannot adapt itself at once to changing market conditions. The actual level of food processing in year t is decided upon at the end of the previous year; it is assumed that it can be seen as a weighted average of last year's actual level and the *proper* average level $\hat{FP}^S$ of the previous year:

$$FP^S_t = WEFP \cdot \hat{FP}^S_{t-1} + (1-WEFP)FP^S_{t-1} \qquad (5.11)$$

in which $0 < WEFP < 1$. Thus, FP^S is a variable showing a slow adaptation only; it does not contribute to clearing the market, but it represents for the sector concerned the consumer food price in real terms reflecting the level of food processing. In the simulation runs of the model, WEFP = 0.2.

For a country or a geographical unit as a whole, the average level of food processing is given by MCONS/CONS; therefore, the annual rate of increase in the average level of food processing GPO is defined as

$$GPO_t = (\frac{MCONS}{CONS})_t \cdot (\frac{CONS}{MCONS})_{t-1} - 1 \qquad (5.12)$$

As mentioned in Chapter 4.4.5.4, it is assumed that this overall rate of increase in processing also applies to the level of food processing taking place within the agricultural sector. Thus, the base price PO received by the agricultural producer - see (4.23) - also increases by the rate GPO.

5.2   *THE DEMAND FOR FOOD IN MOIRA*

5.2.1 *Real income*

The consumption function for food, as introduced above, is a relation between food consumption and real income R. However, the model as discussed thus far does not generate the development of real income. Chapter 4 has shown how the agricultural sector creates a value added V in nominal terms, i.e. in current prices. The rate of development of non-agricultural income (more precisely: of non-agricultural output) is exogenously given; nevertheless, in order to calculate this sector's purchasing power (= real income R) the expenditure side must be taken into account, and hence the food price level. In MOIRA, income can be spent only on *food* and *other commodities*; the latter category

can be thought to include consumption expenditure as well as
savings (as far as specific investment purposes are concerned,
savings can be considered as expenditure on goods and services).

The derivation of real income can be tied together with the
formulation of the rest of the model in a rather simple
deflating procedure. It requires, in addition to the consumption function which relates consumption (in terms of
consumable protein) to real income, two definition equations:
one for total budget expenditures in terms of volumes and
current prices, the other for real income itself as the
(value) of goods and services at index-base prices. The
consumption function expressed in physical units was given
already in (5.3), and in its simple form (5.2):

$$CONS_{is} = f(R_{is})$$

The budget equation in current prices is

$$VALU_{is} = TFP^S . CONS_{is} + NPI . WR_{is} \qquad (5.13)$$

in which

VALU = current income per capita
TFP^S = current consumer price of food, in sector s[1]
NPI = general price index for non-agricultural products
WR   = consumption of non-agricultural commodities in real
       terms
Similarly, in index-base prices the budget equation is

$$R_{is} = FP^S . CONS_{is} + WR_{is} \qquad (5.14)$$

The definitions on which the variables that figure in the
budget equations are based, are discussed in the appendix to
this chapter.

Within this set of three equations, total budget expenditures and all prices are given, so that they constitute a
set of three simultaneous equations in three unknowns.
Hence, for any year t we can solve for the unknown variables:
real income, consumption in terms of consumable protein, and
all other consumption measured in volume terms (i.e. base
year prices). In the context of MOIRA in particular real
income and consumption of food in terms of consumable protein
are of importance.

The solution of the system - given explicitly in Appendix
5A -assumes that real income is above the threshold income
R^G. If the solution yields a lower value of real income, it
has to be rejected as in that case all income is spent on
food, and consequently the linear specification of the
consumption function has to be used ($R < R^G$).

---

[1] Note that the price difference between the two sectors ($TFP^1 - TFP^2$) expresses a difference in the degree of processing, and not a trade margin.

Finally, attention should be drawn to the above assumption
that all prices are given. This is obviously the case for
the price index (NPI (which is given exogenously) and for
FP^S, a lagged variable defined in (5.11). But what about
TFP^S? Note that this variable is related to FP^S in the
following manner:

$$DFPE = TFP^S - NPI.FP^S \qquad\qquad (5.15)$$

The variable DFPE was introduced already in Chapter 4.4.5.4
and is defined as the deviation of the agricultural raw
material price level from its base-year value. Here the
value of DFPE is assumed to be known; in fact, its determination will figure prominently in the Chapter 6 and 7.

5.2.2 *Properties of food consumption in MOIRA*

It is important to ascertain in some detail how
food consumption of an income class reacts to changes in
income and to changes in the food price level. The technical
analysis of these issues is presented in Appendix 5A; here
we will give a verbal summary only.

Taking the two consumption functions - one in terms of
consumable proteins and one in terms of purchasing power - as
the point of departure, it should be noted first of all that
for total food consumption both functions are linear-homo-
geneous in population and income as consumer behaviour is
expressed in per capita terms. Secondly, the slope of the
two consumption curves and the implicit income elasticity of
food consumption can be determined.

The slopes of the two curves are the first derivatives of
the consumption functions themselves for their segments
above the threshold income R^G. As the parameters of the
consumption functions were found to be positive, it follows
that the marginal propensity to consume - and consequently
also the average propensity to consume - decreases monotonously with increasing real income. The income elasticity of
food consumption is obtained by relating the slope in any
point of the consumption curve to the ratio of the corresponding absolute values of consumption and real income. The
numerical values of the parameters obtained from the cross-
section estimation can be used to show that the elasticity
of consumable protein consumption is between zero and 0.5.
It should be recalled, however, that the constant term in
the consumption function gets slightly modified for each
country as the residual obtained in the cross-section estimation is added to it (see Chapter 5.1.3). Therefore, for
certain countries the income elasticity may take a value
(slightly) higher than 0.5. In all cases the income elasticity remains within the value range between zero and
unity.

Finally, an important property of food consumption behaviour
that has to be analyzed is the reaction of the consumer to a

change in the food price. We want to establish to what
extent a change in the price of food affects food consumption, given per capita income expressed in current prices
and the non-foods general price index. As the food price
component reflecting the level of food processing - variable
FP^s; see (5.11) - changes only rather slowly, we have to
analyze primarily the effect on consumption $CONS_{is}$ of a
change in the food price component DFPE - see (5.15) - as
year-to-year changes in the food market situation express
themselves through this variable.[2]

The price elasticity can be derived by differentiating the
budget equation, assuming total income and non-food prices
as given. This leads to a formula for the price elasticity
of food consumption which is expressed entirely in known
variables and parameters; it can be demonstrated on that
basis that the price elasticity will always be between zero
and minus one. In addition, when the consumer food price increases, real income decreases and the marginal propensity
to consume increases. Hence, for increasing values of the
relevant food price DFPE the marginal rate of consumption
out of real income decreases, whereas the price of food
increases as compared to other prices. As a result, the
price elasticity increases and gradually approaches the
value minus on.

5.2.3 *The consumer and the market*

Consumer behaviour as discussed thus far has
tacitly assumed that all food is bought in the (sectoral)
food market. This may not be an appropriate assumption for
the agricultural sector which is not only a consumer but
also the main supplier of food. The implications of this
assumption and its robustness require some further argumen-
tation, in particular with reference to market economies. A
few comments will also be made with respect to consumer
behaviour in the centrally-planned economies.

5.2.3.1 *The agricultural consumer in market economies*

The agricultural sector not only produces
but also consumes food. Food consumption in the agricultural
sector can be presumed either to take place entirely through
the market, or by withholding part of own production for
home use. In the latter case, one can consider that part of
agricultural food consumption which is met from own output
(i.e. the subsistence part of consumption and production) as
being insensitive to food price changes in the short run.
If, on the other hand, all agricultural output is supposed
to move through the market, subsistence food demand would
appear to be price-sensitive. However, food prices also

---

[2] Excluding, of course, changes in food prices due to changes in the
general price level or due to the level of food processing.

determine agricultural income; an increase in the market
price of food implies a higher agricultural income in current
prices and also, to the extent that all other prices increase
to a lesser extent, in real terms. Thus, agricultural food
demand, if thought to be moving through the market, would
respond positively (or at least non-negatively) to price
changes. This would imply greater instability of the food
market than the case would be if subsistence production were
not a part of that market.

Food production for own consumptive use is usually explicitly embodied in the producer's choice of the crops to be
grown; the products grown for own use are not necessarily
the same as those produced for the market. Also, it is
doubtful whether price information reaches the agricultural
consumer rapidly enough to assume full adaptation to changing
food prices. The subsistence farmer, usually operating a
small-size farm, is certainly not integrated in the market
and should therefore not be expected to immediately adjust
his consumption level as a consequence of market price
changes. Therefore MOIRA postulates a consumption behaviour
of the agricultural sector which treats that part of output
withheld for own use as being predetermined, i.e. not directly responsive to market price changes. As was suggested
earlier (see Chapter 4.4) the agricultural sector takes its
production decisions with the intent to realize a certain
income on the basis of - among other things - a certain
price expectation. These plans and expectations imply a
planned level of food consumption. In MOIRA is is assumed
that the planned ratio between own food consumption and
total food production is maintained within the year and in
fact applied to actual food production. When no external
disturbances like weather fluctuations occur and actual
production is equal to planned production, actual food
consumption will also be equal to planned consumption. Thus,
food supply for the market equals total production less the
agricultural sector's own food consumption.

5.2.3.2 *The non-agricultural consumer in market economies*

Food consumption of the non-agricultural
sector requires the intermediary of the market. The non-
agricultural consumer determines his food consumption on the
basis of the food price and his disposable income. He is expected immediately to adjust his consumption level to the
food price level.

5.2.3.3 *The consumer in centrally-planned economies*

The functioning of the agricultural sector
in centrally planned economies as described in MOIRA was the
subject of the previous chapter (see Chapter 4.6). The model
does not generate an income distribution between agriculture
and non-agriculture for these countries: all income and

consumption magnitudes appear as national averages only. The planning method is based on a target value for real income growth; this planned income level leads to a planned food consumption level according to the consumption function. When realized income deviates from planned income, the consumption function is used again to determine actual food consumption.

5.3 *FOOD CONSUMPTION AND NUTRITION STANDARDS*

The present analysis of food consumption in an international context is distinguished from other studies by its disaggregation over 12 consuming classes per country or geographical unit (except for the centrally-planned countries). This disaggregation is essential in view of the great disparities in food consumption levels even within countries. As was observed already in Chapter 1, the world food problem is in large measure a problem of inequalities in access to food supply.

The disaggregation of food consumption in MOIRA beyond the national level allows the determination - at least in an approximate way - of the location and the extent of shortfalls in food consumption levels. A comparison of actual food consumption, in any given year, with food consumption norms or nutrition standards will show whether or not the consumption norm is met for each income class concerned. When actual food consumption levels fall short of the norm, a situation of undernourishment is identified which in MOIRA is labelled *hunger*.

The way in which the country-specific nutrition standards have been computed will be discussed in Chapter 8.6. Per income class in each country the variable *hunger* (HUNG$_{is}$) is defined as the positive difference between food norm and actual or estimated food consumption, multiplied by the population of that income class; it is measured as usual, i.e. in terms of consumable proteins. Summation of shortfalls over income classes and sectors provides an estimate of total hunger in each country; world hunger (WHUNG) follows from summation over all countries. The variable *hunger* will be discussed again in Chapter 10; it plays an important role in the world food policy scenarios presented in Part III.

Appendix 5A

DETERMINATION OF REAL INCOME AND PROPERTIES OF THE DEMAND FUNCTIONS

5A.1 *REAL INCOME*

Food consumption is determined, per income class of a sector, by real income. The function was given in (5.3) as

$$CONS_{is} = \min\left\{ \frac{R_{is}}{FP^s}, \; ACONS + BCONS \; (\sqrt{R_{is} + CCONS} - \sqrt{CCONS}) \right\}$$

where

$CONS_{is}$ = food consumption in consumable protein, per capita in income class i of sector s

R_{is} = real income per capita in income class i of sector s

FP^s = price of food for sector s

As we study throughout this section the demand behaviour of a given income class, the subscripts i and s are dropped to simplify the notation.

In MOIRA, income is spent on *food* and *other commodities*. The budget equation in current prices is

$$VALU_t = TFP_t \cdot CONS_t + \sum_j p_{jt} \cdot h_{jt} \tag{5A.1}$$

where

$VALU$ = current income per capita
TFP = current consumer price of food
p_j = price of commodity j
h_j = quantity of commodity j
The index j covers all commodities except food.

Remember that throughout this section $VALU_t$ should be read as $(VALU_{is})_t$, with

$$VALU_{is} = \frac{DISTM_{is}}{d_i} \cdot VALU_s$$

in which

$VALU_s$ = average current income per capita of sector s

$DISTM_{is}$ = share of income class i in current income of sector s

d_i = share of income class i in the population of each sector.

The definition of real income R from the budget equation *in constant prices* is

$$R_t = FP_t \cdot CONS_t + \sum_j p_{jo} h_{jt} \tag{5A.2}$$

The term *in constant prices* refers to the elimination of general price increases due to inflation.

We assume that the commodity composition of all expenditures other than on food remains constant over time so that $h_{jt}/h_{jo} = a_t$ for all j. Thus, we have

$$\sum_j p_{jo} h_{jt} = a_t \cdot \sum_j p_{jo} h_{jo} \tag{5A.3}$$

and

$$\sum_j p_{jt} h_{jt} = a_t \cdot \sum_j p_{jt} h_{jo} \tag{5A.4}$$

From (5A.3) and (5A.4) it follows that

$$\sum_j p_{jt} h_{jt} = \sum_j p_{jo} h_{jt} \cdot \frac{\sum_j p_{jt} h_{jo}}{\sum_j p_{jo} h_{jo}} \tag{5A.5}$$

The last factor at the right-hand side of (5A.5) is simply a Laspeyres price index.

In order to simplify the notation, we introduce for the latter price index NPI as the price index for non-food commodities, and WR for consumption in real terms of all non-foods; thus,

$$NPI_t = \frac{\sum_j p_{jt} h_{jo}}{\sum_j p_{jo} h_{jo}} \tag{5A.6}$$

and

$$WR_t = \sum_j p_{jo} h_{jt} \tag{5A.7}$$

Using the above two definitions, we may rewrite (5A.1) and (5A.2) as

$$VALU_t = TFP_t \cdot CONS_t + NPI_t \cdot WR_t \tag{5A.8}$$

$$R_t = FP_t \cdot CONS_t + WR_t \tag{5A.9}$$

Consider these two equations, together with the consumption function in physical units as given in (5.3),

$$CONS_t = f(R_t) \qquad (5A.10)$$

which is a monotonous function. When VALU, TFP, NPI and FP are given, (5A.8) - (5A.10) constitute a set of three simultaneous equations in three unknowns. Hence, for any year t we can solve for the unknown R, CONS and WR; in the context of MOIRA we are interested in particular real income R and consumption CONS.

The value of R is obtained as follows. Substituting in (5A.8) WR according to (5A.9), and rearranging terms, we have

$$VALU_t = (TFP_t - NPI_t.FP_t)\ CONS_t + NPI_t.R_t \qquad (5A.11)$$

Earlier we defined in (5.15)

$$DFPE_t = TFP_t - NPI_t.FP_t \qquad (5A.12)$$

in which $DFPE_t$ is the price component of the food price that is not due to (changes in) the general price level - indicated by NPI - or due to the level of food processing reflected by FP; see Chapter 4.4.5.4. Introducing (5A.12) in (5A.11) we have

$$VALU_t = DFPE_t.CONS_t + NPI_t.R_t \qquad (5A.13)$$

For $CONS_t$ we have to make use of the consumption function (5.3); to begin with, we will assume that $R > R^G$ (see fig. 5.2), i.e. we assume that not all income will be spent on food. In this case, (5A.13) becomes

$$VALU_t = DFPE_t.\left\{ACONS + BCONS\ (\sqrt{R_t + CCONS} - \sqrt{CCONS}) \right\} + NPI_t.R_t$$

$$(5A.14)$$

If we introduce the auxiliary variable

$$u = \sqrt{R_t + CCONS} \qquad (5A.15)$$

(5A.14) can be solved as an ordinary quadratic equation in u. Bringing $VALU_t$ to the other side of the equality sign, and adding the additional terms $+ NPI_t.CCONS - NPI_t.CCONS$, (5A.14) can be written as

$$\alpha + \beta.u + \gamma.u^2 = 0 \qquad (5A.16)$$

in which

$$\alpha = DFPE_t.(ACONS - BCONS.\sqrt{CCONS}) - VALU_t - NPI_t.CCONS$$
$$\beta = DFPE_t.BCONS$$
$$\gamma = NPI_t$$

From (5A.16) u can be solved as

$$u_{1,2} = \frac{-B \pm \sqrt{\beta^2 - 4\alpha\gamma}}{2\gamma} \tag{5A.17}$$

As VALU, NPI and CCONS are all positive, γ is positive, and the sign of α depends on the magnitude of $DFPE_t$. $(ACONS - BCONS \cdot \sqrt{CCONS})$. From (5A.14) we have as $BCONS > 0$ and if $R > R^G$,

$$VALU_t > DFPE_t \; . \; (ACONS + BCONS \cdot \sqrt{CCONS})$$

Hence, $\alpha < 0$, and therefore $(-\beta - \sqrt{\beta^2 - 4\alpha\gamma}) < 0$ and $(-\beta + \sqrt{\beta^2 - 4\alpha\gamma}) > 0$; consequently, one of the roots $u_{1,2}$ is positive. From this positive root we may compute R according to (5A.15) as $R_t = u^2 - CCONS$. Once R_t is known, $CONS_t$ follows from (5.3). Note also from the above equations (5A.8, 5A.9 and 5A.10) that the demand function is homogeneous of degree zero in prices and income.

The above solution is based on the assumption that $R > R^G$. If the solution would yield a value of real income $R < R^G$, it has to be rejected as we have a case in which all income is spent on food, and consequently the specification of the consumption function used in the above solution no longer applies. In this case, food consumption is determined simply as $CONS_t = VALU_t / TFP_t$, and real income follows from $R_t = CONS_t \cdot FPO$, where FPO is the food price in real terms at the minimum level of processing as corresponds with the income level R^G.

5A.2 PROPERTIES OF FOOD CONSUMPTION IN MOIRA

We turn now to a brief analysis of the properties of food consumption behaviour as depicted in MOIRA. Taking the two consumption functions - one in terms of consumable proteins and one in terms of purchasing power - as our point of departure, it should be noted first of all that for total food consumption both functions are linear homogeneous in population and income as consumer behaviour is expressed in per capita terms. Secondly, the slope of the two consumption curves and the implicit income elasticity of food consumption may be determined.

The slopes of the two curves follow immediately from the first derivative of (5.3) and (5.6); for $R_{is} > R^G$, we have

$$\frac{d(CONS_{is})}{dR_{is}} = \frac{BCONS}{2\sqrt{R_{is} + CCONS}} \tag{5A.18}$$

and

$$\frac{d(MCONS_{is})}{dR_{is}} = \frac{d(CONS_{is} \cdot FP_{is})}{dR_{is}} \tag{5A.19}$$

As explained in Chapter 5.1.4, the variable FP is assumed to adapt itself only with a certain delay, and to be the same for all income classes of a sector. Thus, in the consumption function as used in /MOIRA, FP_{is} is replaced by FP^S, and (5A.19) can be written as

$$\frac{d(MCONS_{is})}{dR_{is}} = \frac{BCONS.FP^S}{2\sqrt{R_{is}+CCONS}} \qquad (5A.20)$$

Given the positive values of BCONS and CCONS, we see from (5A.18) and (5A.20) that the marginal propensity to consume - and consequently also the average propensity to consume - decreases monotonously with increasing real income R_{is}, for $R_{is} > R^G$. For the straight-line segment of the consumption curves, i.e. for $R_{is} < R^G$, we know that all income is spent on food; the marginal (and the average) propensities to consume are constant and equal to

$$\frac{d(CONS_{is})}{dR_{is}} = \frac{1}{FP^S} \qquad (5A.21)$$

and

$$\frac{d(MCONS_{is})}{dR_{is}} = 1 \qquad (5A.22)$$

The income elasticity of food consumption is obtained by relating the slope in any point $(R_{is}, CONS_{is})$ of the consumption curve to the ratio of the corresponding absolute values of $CONS_{is}$ and R_{is}. For $R_{is} < R^G$, both elasticities are equal to unity. For $R_{is} > R^G$, we have from (5A.18) for the income elasticity ε.

$$\varepsilon_{CONS,R} = \frac{BCONS}{2\sqrt{R_{is}+CCONS}} \cdot \frac{R_{is}}{CONS_{is}} \qquad (5A.23)$$

and from (5A.20) for the short-run income elasticity of real expenditure on food

$$\varepsilon_{MCONS,R} = \frac{BCONS.FP^S}{2\sqrt{R_{is}+CCONS}} \cdot \frac{R_{is}}{CONS_{is}.FP^S} \qquad (5A.24)$$

Dividing numerator and denominator at the right-hand side of (5A.24) by FP^S, we find that the two elasticities are equal.

Substitution of $CONS_{is}$ in (5A.23) according to (5.3) gives

$$\varepsilon_{CONS,R} = \frac{BCONS.R_{is}}{2\sqrt{R_{is}+CCONS} \cdot \{ACONS+BCONS(\sqrt{R_{is}+CCONS}-\sqrt{CCONS})\}}$$

or, after rearranging terms,

$$\varepsilon_{CONS,R} = \frac{BCONS.R_{is}}{2\{(ACONS-BCONS\sqrt{CCONS})\sqrt{R_{is}+CCONS}+BCONS.CCONS\}} + \frac{1}{2}$$

Dividing both numerator and denominator by BCONS.R_{is}, we obtain

$$\varepsilon_{CONS,R} = \frac{1}{\dfrac{2\{(\dfrac{ACONS}{BCONS} - \sqrt{CCONS})\sqrt{R_{is}+CCONS}+CCONS\}}{R_{is}} + 2}$$

$$(5A.25)$$

The numerical values of the parameters as obtained from the cross-section estimation show that

$$\frac{ACONS}{BCONS} - \sqrt{CCONS} > 0$$

Consequently, the left-hand side term in the denominator of (5A.25) is positive for $R_{is}>0$; thus, we have for the income elasticity of food consumption, for $R_{is}>R^G$, $0 < \varepsilon_{CONS,R} < 0.5$ given the parameter values mentioned before. It should be recalled, however, that the parameter ACONS is slightly modified for each country as the residual obtained in the cross-section estimation is added to it (cf. Chapter 5.1.3). Therefore, for certain countries the denominator of (5A.25) may contain a negative term, and the income elasticity may take a value (slightly) higher than 0.5. In all cases the income elasticity remains within the value range $0 < \varepsilon_{CONS,R} < 1$.

An important property of food consumption behaviour that has to be analyzed next is the reaction of the consumer to a change in the food price. Recalling the equations (5A.12) and (5A.13), we have, for any year t,

$$VALU_{is} = DFPE.CONS_{is}+NPI.R_{is} \qquad\qquad (5A.26)$$

$$TFP = NPI.FP^S+DFPE \qquad\qquad (5A.27)$$

We want to establish to what extent a change in the price of food affects food consumption, given per capita income VALU (expressed in current prices) and the non-foods general price index NPI. As the food price component reflecting the level of food processing FP^S changes only rather slowly, we have to analyze the effect on $CONS_{is}$ of a change in DFPE as year-to-year changes in the food market situation express themselves through this variable.

Taking the total differential of (5A.26), with VALU and NPI given, we have

$$0 = CONS_{is} \cdot d(DFPE) + DFPE \cdot d(CONS_{is}) + NPI \cdot dR_{is}$$

or

$$-CONS_{is} \cdot d(DFPE) = \{DFPE + NPI \frac{dR_{is}}{d(CONS_{is})}\} \, d(CONS_{is})$$

and also

$$\frac{d(CONS_{is})}{d(DFPE)} = \frac{-CONS_{is}}{DFPE + NPI \frac{dR_{is}}{d(CONS_{is})}} \qquad (5A.28)$$

From (5A.28) the price elasticity of food consumption $\varepsilon_{CONS,TFP}$ is obtained by multiplying both sides by $TFP/CONS_{is}$:

$$\varepsilon_{CONS,TFP} = \frac{-TFP}{DFP + NPI \cdot \frac{dR_{is}}{d(CONS_{is})}}$$

Adding in the denominator $NPI \cdot FP^S$ to the first term and deducting it from the second term, we have, using (5A.27)

$$\varepsilon_{CONS,TFP} = \frac{-TFP}{TFP + NPI \, (\frac{dR_{is}}{d(CONS_{is})} - FP^S)}$$

and, dividing by TFP,

$$\varepsilon_{CONS,TFP} = \frac{-1}{1 + \frac{NPI}{TFP} \cdot (\frac{dR_{is}}{d(CONS_{is})} - FP^S)} \qquad (5A.29)$$

As we saw above in (5A.21), the marginal propensity to consume $d(CONS_{is})/dR_{is}$ has a maximum value of $1/FP^S$, for $R_{is} < R^G$, for $R_{is} > R^G$ its value decreases with increasing R_{is}. Hence, for its reciprocal we have

$$\frac{dR_{is}}{d(CONS_{is})} \geqq FP^S \qquad (5A.30)$$

and consequently for the price elasticity of food consumption

$$-1 < \varepsilon_{CONS,TFP} < 0$$

In addition, when the consumer food price TFP increases, real income R decreases and the marginal propensity tc consume $d(CONS_{is}) / dR_{is}$ increases. Hence, for increasing values of DFPE both $dR_{is} / d(CONS_{is})$ and - obviously - NPI/TFP decrease. From (5A.29) we see that for increasing values of DFPE the price elasticity $\varepsilon_{CONS,TFP}$ approaches the value - 1.

For the reason set forth in Chapter 5.1.1, the substitution elasticity is assumed to be zero.

Chapter 6

THE AGRICULTURAL SECTOR IN ITS NATIONAL CONTEXT

6.1 *THE FOOD MARKET*

After the discussion of the production side of MOIRA in Chapter 4 and the consumption side in Chapter 5, Chapters 6 and 7 deal with the structure and functioning of the food market - national and international. These chapters describe the approach followed in MOIRA in terms of general equilibrium theory with perfect competition but with amendments to account for distortions prevailing in the food market.

The model structure contains two important deviations from the usual (free trade) general equilibrium approach. First, changes in stocks take place which reduce year-to-year price fluctuations; stock changes are essential for an adequate description of the (world) food market. Second, the model allows for government intervention in international food trade. National governments may by way of tariffs or subsidies create differences between domestic food prices (per unit of consumable protein) in different countries. MOIRA generates food price differences between the national (domestic) markets endogenously, although those must remain within certain limits.

Still, the basic structure remains characterized as a general equilibrium approach. The equilibrium solution itself will be analyzed in Chapter 7.

6.2 *INTERMEDIARIES, THE PRODUCER FOOD PRICE, AND PRODUCER INCOME*

The discussion of the place of the agricultural sector in the national economy pays particular attention to the income distribution between agriculture and non-agriculture, and hence on the conflicting interests of the *rural* and the *urban* sectors; in addition, it focusses on the role of the government in this context.

The price received by the agricultural sector for its output is a crucial factor determining the income position of this sector as compared to the non-agricultural sector. Disregarding for the moment government intervention - to which we turn in the next section - the producer price depends on the agricultural supply and demand position in any particular

year. It is important to note that net agricultural supply
is inelastic in the short run, and that the demand for food
by (non-agricultural) consumers is not very price-sensitive.
This structure of the market suggests that autonomous fluctuations in supply (e.g. because of weather variations) may
entail rather large price fluctuations. It might almost be
said that the market structure implies price determination
to the producer by the consumer.

Relations between producers and consumers are largely of an
indirect nature. The flow of goods from the agricultural
producer to the consumer takes place through the intermediary of other persons and organizations, to be referred to
as *intermediaries*. The activities of these intermediaries
are: collecting trade (sometimes combined with money lending),
storage, transport, processing, wholesale and retail trade.
All these links in the chain between producers and consumers
do appropriate for themselves a part of the food price paid
by consumers. Thus, the food producer receives only part of
the price paid by the consumer and the difference accrues to
the intermediaries.

The economic character of the price margin accruing to the
intermediaries is not necessarily the same everywhere, nor
need it be the same for the various links in the chain. It
is useful to distinguish two elements: one part of the
margin reflects the costs incurred by the intermediaries in
bridging the difference in location, in time, and in level
of processing between production and consumption of food,
whereas the remainder depends on the relative (monopsonistic
or monopolistic) power they hold in the markets in which
they are buying or selling. Particularly the first stage
intermediaries which deal with the individual producers are
sometimes seen to be able to realize high profit margins
because of lack of competition in small, local markets and
because they can buy at the time of the harvest when prices
are lowest and credits fall due. Relatively strong monopsonistic positions of middlemen can be expected in areas
with inadequate transport and marketing infrastructure.

The intermediaries of the food market are considered part of
the non-agricultural or urban sector. The income distribution between agriculture and non-agriculture (including
the intermediaries) depends therefore on the physical conditions of topography, on the state of existing infrastructure, and on the institutional situation and the socio-
economic order. Competition within the collecting trade and
transport sectors can be expected to be less in a developing
country as compared to an industrialized economy. Therefore,
apart from the price difference due to the actual cost of
intermediation (which defies assessment) there is little
point in trying to explain the total margin received by
intermediaries on the basis of those real costs alone.

The intermediaries are made a part of the non-agricultural
sector as defined in MOIRA. The entire margin accruing to

them (whether real cost or profit) is part of non-agricultural income, although it is not known to which income classes this income accrues. The model therefore makes the simplifying assumption that the profit margin is distributed entirely in proportion to food consumption (within the non-agricultural sector) - in other words, as if the entire non-agricultural sector functions as intermediary. This renders the level of the profit margin irrelevant as each non-agricultural consumer receives a *subsidy* on food consumption equal to the margin. The only relevant remaining issue is, how much the non-agricultural sector actually pays to the food producer. That is discussed in Chapter 6.4.

6.3 *GOVERNMENT POLICIES CONCERNING THE AGRICULTURAL SECTOR*

6.3.1 *Government policy regarding food prices*

Almost nowhere in the world is the determination of food prices left entirely to the free play of supply and demand. In nearly all countries the government intervenes, in some form or other, with the pricing of major food items. These government policies differ from country to country, depending on the objectives of public policy and on the trade position of the country concerned. Some of the more important reasons for government intervention in food markets are:

(a) to protect producers, or consumers, or both, against large price fluctuations in food markets;
(b) to maintain low food prices to the consumer in order to keep the cost of living of the non-agricultural population low for reason of international competitiveness or to forestall political instability in the cities;
(c) to achieve a reasonable income level for the agricultural population, in order to improve rural living conditions and to ensure continuity in domestic agricultural production;
(d) to promote the production of agricultural commodities for export, and improve the balance of payments;
(e) to reduce agricultural output when surplusses threaten to disturb the market.

These objectives are not by necessity mutually consistent; they are unlikely to be achieved - nor need to be relevant - all at the same time. The focus of national food price policies may differ from country to country and from time to time depending on the economic position such as the general level of economic development, the net trade position for food in the world market, the relative size of the agricultural sector, etc.

In the rich, industrialized countries agricultural price policy usually aims at the protection of incomes of a relatively small agricultural population. This policy expresses the political will (and the economic possibility) in the rich countries to provide a reasonable share in the national income to agriculture and the countryside.

In the developing countries the share of agriculture in the total labour force and in national income tends to be large; also, the food price level is of far greater importance for real income and the standard of living of the non-agricultural population as a greater part of income is normally spent on food. In many developing countries, government food price policies tend to give priority to the interests of the urban population. Rural populations are socially and politically less powerful and vocal than their urban counterparts.

The formulation of the model requires that government policies be seen to focus on one issue of central importance. Therefore MOIRA postulates that governments, in some way or other, make efforts to maintain an income distribution between agriculture and non-agriculture corresponding to the political desirability, is described here as the outcome of a conflict of interests within a nation over the distribution of income (rural/agricultural versus urban/non-agricultural; intermediaries versus producers; intermediaries versus consumers, although the latter is in our case not relevant). Which interests dominate and to what extent they dominate, will depend on the political power of each group, and this in turn depends heavily on the institutional character of the country.

Although the role and functions of governments differ between countries, - ranging from active policies regarding food prices to the mere sanctioning of the outcome of the free play of market forces - the model labels all institutional influences affecting the food price level as *government policy*, thus ascribing all price deviations to *government*. (As discussed above in Chapter 6.2, in the present two-sector model price differences between the rural and the urban sector may be disregarded).

Price is an important variable both in describing consumption and production of food. The institutional factors or *government* in our terminology, that also play a role in the price formation for food in the national market require to be reflected in the model of the food supply system. That is the subject of the following subsections.

6.3.2 *Income distribution between agriculture and non-agriculture*

A.   *The disparity in rural and urban income*

The actual distribution of income between the agricultural and the non-agricultural sector as observed in the various countries, is considered to be the final outcome of the play of a combination of market and political forces. In this study, the political elements in the process are considered predominant, so that the sectoral income distribution becomes the result of a political decision-making process with respect to income distribution.[1] This must then

---

[1] See also for a discussion of this issue Joan Robinson and John Eatwell, *An introduction to modern economics*, London 1973, Ch. 5.

also be postulated for the base period of the analysis
(1964-1966); differences in the sectoral income distribution
between countries in the base period are due, in large
measure, to differences in the relative power positions of
the two sectors agriculture and non-agriculture (in this
study also referred to occasionally as the rural and the
urban sector, respectively) and their representatives. These
power positions are themselves partly a consequence of the
material circumstances under which the sectors operate.

The description of government policies concerning the income
distribution between agriculture and non-agriculture, requires therefore that the model contains some variables
which indicate the material circumstances that shape the
power position. These indicators can be used as explanatory
variables, in a cross-section analysis of the base-year
data,' in an effort to explain the ratio between per capita
incomes in the two sectors. By selecting indicators whose
development can be traded endogenously in the model, variations over time and between countries in government policies
directed towards income distribution objectives (and hence
towards domestic food price objectives) can also be generated endogenously.

Some comments on this approach are in place:
(a)   The cross-section analysis will reveal a central ten-
      dency only as there are other factors at play as well,
      e.g. institutional differences between countries;
(b)   The results may be unsatisfactory - yielding a partial
      explanation only or at their worst even misleading ex-
      planations - because of the possible deviation between
      actual and desired income ratios due to the particular
      world market situation in the base year. In other
      words, the position of the world food market in the
      base year may influence the sectoral income distribu-
      tion in a way not desired by the government but beyond
      its capacity to correct because of constraints to the
      government's income distribution policy;
(c)   The statistical explanation of the sectoral income dis-
      tribution target of the government by a number of model
      variables raises an important issue in terms of its
      interpretation. A perfect statistical explanation would
      make the government's income and food price policies
      totally endogenous and would imply that the government
      has no freedom of manoeuvre whatsoever. This is not an
      acceptable procedure. Nevertheless, it remains imper-
      ative to take full account of the actual power position
      of agriculture versus non-agriculture in the analysis
      of the government policy target for sectoral income
      distribution. It would be quite inappropriate to dis-
      regard the existing insights in the income distribution
      process and to omit relevant variables from the expla-
      nation of existing income differences between the two
      sectors.

Therefore, appropriate treatment of the disparity between
rural and urban income in MOIRA requires dealing with two

problems that can only be partially solved:
(a)   Cross-section analysis over countries, using economic
      magnitudes as explanatory variables, cannot fully ex-
      plain the variations in income disparity between the
      sectors. To the extent that this is considered due to
      institutional factors of a national character, it would
      be permissible to interpret the disturbance term as a
      country-specific indicator of a structural nature;
(b)   A fully endogenous explanation of the disparity deprives
      the national government of any margin of freedom in its
      sectoral income policy. This drawback is dealt with in
      some simulation runs of the model by introducing a more
      active government policy exogenously by way of delib-
      erate changes in the country-specific disturbance term.

B.   *The income disparity equation*
      Three explanatory variables are introduced in MOIRA
which are considered to represent the material conditions
underlying agriculture's political weight, and a fourth
variable (the unexplained residual) serves as a catch-all
for country-specific institutional circumstances. The level
of disparity aimed at by the government is assumed to be
related to the following variables in the model.

(a)   *The per capita income of the agricultural sector.*
      The higher the per capita income, in absolute terms,
the smaller the disparity with urban per capita income. The
reasons for selecting this explanatory variable are the following:
(1)   a higher per capita income in agriculture implies that
      this sector constitutes a larger market for the products
      of the non-agricultural sector, and a reduction of
      agricultural income would be detrimental to non-agri-
      cultural development;
(2)   at higher income levels in agriculture more goods and
      services will be exchanged between the two sectors;
      consequently, there will be a stronger incentive to
      improve (rural) infrastructure;
(3)   an improved rural infrastructure will increase com-
      petition between the intermediaries (in MOIRA part of
      the non-agricultural sector) with which the agricul-
      tural sector has to deal;
(4)   infrastructural improvements will lead to more communi-
      cation which will increase the farmer's awareness of
      income disparities; it will enable farmers to organize
      themselves better and to increase their political
      powers.

(b)   *The share of agriculture in gross domestic product*
      The larger the share of agriculture in total GDP, the
smaller will be the disparity. Here, argument (a.1) will
carry additional weight. Also, in the case of a larger share
of agriculture in total domestic product the non-agricultural sector itself will more strongly depend on agriculture as
processor of agricultural produce.

(c) *The population density*
     The higher the density of population, the smaller will
be the income disparity between agriculture and non-agriculture. A higher population density reinforces the arguments
(2), (3) and (4) under (a).

(d) *Other (institutional) factors*
     It is likely that, in addition to the above three vari-
ables, many other factors play a part in determining the income disparity. The social and political organization of a
country will probably exert an important influence of its
own. Also, a certain margin of freedom for an active government policy concerning the level of disparity is desirable.
Any government policy is, moreover, a subject to policy
constraints which impinge upon its success in achieving its
objectives, particularly when the country is exposed to
strong forces from outside. These factors cannot be identified and isolated in the cross-section analysis; their
combined effect is, in the main, assumed to remain constant
for each country and equal to the base year value.

As the above variables (b) and (c) are considered to reinforce
variable (a) - rather than to constitute separate factors -
a multiplicative specification of the income disparity
equation seems appropriate. Similarly, the choice of a
multiplicative disturbance term appears reasonable.

For almost all countries, the dependent variable is larger
than one; in four cases only a value lower than unity was
observed for the base year. Therefore, a lower limit to the
value of the dependent variable is assumed; for this reason
the constant EPAR is introduced. This constant term functions as an asymptotic lower limit to the dependent variable
and its value was set at 0.8. The income disparity equation
has therefore been specified as

$$PAR_j =$$
$$APAR(RVLU_j)^{BPAR} \cdot (\frac{NV_j}{V_j})^{CPAR} \cdot \left(\frac{L_j+NPOP_j}{A_j}\right)^{DPAR} \cdot PARDIST_j + EPAR$$

$$(6.1)$$

in which

PAR   = the ratio between per capita income in non-agri-
          culture and per capita income in agriculture
RVLU   = real income per capita in agriculture
NV   = non-agriculture GDP
V   = agricultural GDP
L   = agricultural population
NPOP   = non-agricultural population
A   = total agricultural land
PARDIST = ratio between the observed value of (PAR_j-EPAR) and
          its explained value, i.e. the estimated disturbance

term assumed to represent all other country-specific
factors influencing the level of income disparity.

For the base period 1964-66, the cross-section estimation over
100 countries resulted in the following parameter estimates:

ln (APAR)	=	-0.34;	t-score	0.8
BPAR	=	-0.88;	t-score	10
CPAR	=	-0.17;	t-score	5.8
DPAR	=	-0.17;	t-score	3.5

$$R^2_{\ln(PAR-EPAR)} = 61.0$$

$$R^2_{(PAR-EPAR)} = 65.0$$

All parameter estimates have the expected sign. It should be
noted that population density is measured per unit of total
agricultural land (A). This area is smaller than the total
area suitable for human settlement, but is certainly much
closer to the latter area than the total land area of a
country would be.

6.3.3 *Instruments of government policy and their impact*

A variety of instruments is usually available to
influence the terms of trade of the agricultural sector, in
order to achieve and maintain a politically desirable income
distribution.

In actual practice, manipulation of the price level of agricultural output is the level most commonly used in agricultural income policy; still, changes in the income distribution
can also be effected through the prices of the means of production used in agriculture (e.g. subsidies on fertilizer or
energy use, cheap loans, etc.). The latter kind of price
measures are usually thought of more in terms of their presumed stimulating effect on technological improvement and
long-term development in the agricultural sector. The nature
of such measures is, therefore, similar to infrastructural
improvements (such as opening up of isolated area, irrigation, land reform, research and extension work, institutions for agricultural credit) which aim at the gradual
restructuring of production conditions and methods in agriculture. For the present analysis it should be noted that
government policies of this kind are also very important for
the absolute and relative income position of agriculture in
the long run.

Both the direction and magnitude of direct government intervention in the pricing of agricultural produce and the long-
run government policies regarding the agricultural sector
will reflect the political priorities of the society concerned. Both express the relative social and political
weight attached to the interests of the agricultural population. It may even be justified, to assume both types of

policy to run somewhat parallel.

The assumption of parallelism between the different elements
of the government's policy towards agriculture - all origi-
nating from the same underlying *attitude* or socio-political
climate -is made explicitly in MOIRA by singling out the
government's agricultural price policy as *the* instrument for
influencing the distribution of income between agriculture
and non-agriculture. In this setting the price received by
the agricultural producer is defined as the actual market
price of the produce when leaving the agricultural sector,
corrected for possible positive or negative income transfers
(expressed per unit of output) that may reach or leave the
sector through other channels than the domestic market price
(e.g. through public investments in the agricultural sector,
through subsidies and direct or indirect taxes). This definition of the producer price also applies to the base
period; it should be noted that the initial level of producer prices could not be obtained directly from statistical
data but had to be derived as shadow prices from other data
series and from their interrelations in the model.

The *all-inclusive* producer price defined above can be influenced by the government in two ways: through intervention
in the market, and by measures outside the market mechanism.
In the latter case, price formation takes place in the free
market, and the agricultural producers receive a variable
subsidy (or pay a tax) on top of the market price. This
system of so-called deficiency payments could in principle
absorb a substantial part of the government's financial
means when world market food prices are low, and requires
extensive administrative controls which are difficult to
implement in developing countries. For that reason, manipulation of market prices appears to be the appropriate
policy instrument and this approach is also followed in
MOIRA.

Virtually all countries engage in international trade in
agricultural products. Agricultural trade can be controlled
at the national border. Agricultural trade policy is therefore included in the model as the major policy instrument to
manipulate the domestic price level. The common variants of
trade policy are:
(a)   tariffs - or subsidies - on imports or exports
(b)   an import or export quota system
(c)   manipulation of the exchange rate
The use of these instruments enables the government to
create and maintain differences between the domestic agricultural price level and international prices, albeit within
certain limits. Administrative controls over domestic prices
beyond the indirect means listed above are not envisaged in
MOIRA; the policy in the model is a policy *at the border*.

The government's border price policy incorporated in MOIRA
consists of taxes or subsidies on imports and exports. It is
assumed that the two other instruments have their equiva-

lences in terms of tariff policy.

The use of tariff and subsidy policies to influence the
income distribution between agriculture and non-agriculture
has consequences for the government budget: import tariffs
and export duties are receipts of the government, and subsidies are expenditures. In MOIRA, the current government
budget is considered part of the non-agricultural sector;
thus, the budgetary consequences of agricultural tariff
policy have a direct impact on non-agricultural income.
Further, they are reflected indirectly in food consumption
of the urban sector, and obviously also in the sectoral
income distribution. The distribution of tariff revenue (or
of the subsidy burden) over the income classes of the non-
agricultural sector raises a number of problems which are
discussed in Appendix 6A.2.

The budgetary effects of a tariff policy are permissible
only within specific bounds. Although positive budgetary
effects may be welcome to the government, their burden is
passed on to the urban population in the form of taxes and
there are obvious limits to tax increases. Furthermore, a
government is limited in its subsidy policies by their costs
to the budget. Therefore, the total amount of subsidy on
agricultural imports or exports that can be paid in any
specific year is defined in MOIRA as a certain maximum
fraction of the government budget. This budget constraint
implies that a tariff policy requiring subsidies cannot
always be fully pursued.

In MOIRA, the budget constraint on agricultural trade policy
is formulated in terms of the maximum percentage of non-
agricultural GDP that can be allocated to foreign trade
subsidies. This fraction, set at 3 per cent of non-agricultural income, can be translated into the maximum amount
available for subsidies by multiplying with per capita
income outside agriculture and total non-agricultural population. In case of an export subsidy, the amount of subsidies involved is equal to the (positive) difference between
the domestic price level and the world market price level,
multiplied by the quantity exported. The latter amount is
bounded at the upside by the former.

As a result, given an agricultural price policy *at the
border* together with an upper limit to the sum total of
subsidies, the domestic food price (which the government
wants to control) cannot deviate by more than a specific
maximum from the world market price level. Therefore, the
budget constraint constitutes a limiting factor to the
government's sectoral income distribution policy.

There may be other factors as well which restrict the government's agricultural price policy. One of those may be the
availability of foreign exchange for agricultural imports.
The quantity of imports which a government considers desirable in view of its domestic price policy may exceed the

foreign exchange which it is able to allocate for this
purpose. Although an import quota policy can always be
translated into a tariff policy, the numerical translation
of a constraint on the quantity imported into a constraint
in terms of a difference between domestic and world market
prices is computationally complex.[2]For this practical reason
the foreign exchange constraint on agricultural trade policy
has been disregarded.

The degree of realism of the model in its description of the
functioning of the government's price policy can be improved
by way of some additional restrictions. This price policy at
the border cannot be assumed to be all-embracing, highly
sensitive and accurate, and operating without delay. Amendments are necessary on these points.

First, it is unlikely that the government will fully control
all (prices of) agricultural imports or exports. For some
less important agricultural products no tariff policy may be
applied, possibly because the product concerned does not
compete directly with domestic products. Also, some smuggling may occur if the world market price differs significantly from the domestic price. It is therefore to be expected that there will be some *seepage* of the world market
price level through the national tariff (or subsidy) walls -
whether the government likes it or not. It is assumed,
therefore, that the actual domestic price level may deviate
from the price level desired by the government in the context
of its agricultural income policy. For this purpose a seepage
factor is applied to the difference between external prices
and desired domestic prices which is included in the equation
for actual domestic prices.

Second, it is unlikely that the government will adjust the
level of tariffs (or subsidies) to each and every change in
world market prices. It will certainly wish to achieve and
maintain the desired income ratio between agriculture and
non-agriculture, but minor deviations from this ratio will
be tolerated. In other words, the use of the tariff instrument will be adjusted only when otherwise the deviation from
the desired disparity would exceed a specified tolerance
margin. This margin of tolerance is expressed as a fraction
of the desired disparity ratio.

The policy modifications outlined in the two preceding paragraphs can be integrated as follows:
(a) Within the margins of tolerance, a world market price
     change leads to an equal change in the domestic price.
     As will be obvious, the larger the tolerance margin of
     the income disparity ratio, the more a situation of
     free trade is approached; if the tolerance margin is
     made wide enough, a free-trade situation arises.

---

[2] See M.A. Keyzer, *Analysis of a national model with domestic price
policies and quota on international trade*, IIASA Research Memorandum
no. 77-19, Laxenburg 1977.

(b)   Outside the margins of tolerance a world market price
       change will lead to a change in tariff policy, which
       intends to limit the domestic price change; however,
       some seepage may occur which moves domestic prices
       somewhat closer to external prices.
(c)   Intensification or expansion of tariff policy, to
       offset larger world market price changes, is limited by
       the budget constraint and beyond these limits the
       domestic price level can no longer be protected and
       world market price changes have to be followd.

Finally, it is not realistic to postulate price policies
without delays. Most policy changes are effected with a
certain delay over time. The government's agricultural price
and income policy as outlined above will no doubt be characterized by a certain degree of inertia. This is reflected in
MOIRA by way of a pattern of distributed lags in the policy
responses.

6.4 *THE POSITION OF THE AGRICULTURAL SECTOR RECONSIDERED*

   6.4.1 *Summary of the pertinent assumptions*
           The functioning of the food market at the national
level can now be described in a systematic way, drawing on
the previous discussion of supply, demand and policy intervention. The most pertinent characteristics of MOIRA are
repeated here for convenience.

(a)   The agricultural sector produces a total yield (TY) of
       which a constant fraction is total food yield (TFY).
The consumption function indicates the sector's plans for
the consumption of a certain part of its total food yield.
Food supply to the non-agricultural sector equals total food
yield minus the sector's own food consumption; total supply
to the (non-agricultural) food market (CTY) is completely
inelastic in any given year.

(b)   The agricultural income level is influenced by the
       governments food price policy, which takes the form of
levying taxes or paying subsidies on imports or exports of
food, within certain constraints.

(c)   The food price policy is formulated in terms of the
       price of unprocessed food which is identical to the
price of unprocessed food which is identical to the price
of agricultural raw materials.

(d)   International trade takes place in unprocessed food;
       only trade in food is considered. There is one world
market food price which is exogenous for all countries.

(e)   The domestic market demand for food by the non-agricul-
       tural sector depends on that sector's income and the
food price level. Sector income is influenced by total

receipts or payments associated with the government's food tariff policy; the consumer food price is influenced by the price policy for unprocessed food.

(f)   The profit margin of the intermediaries in food trade is allocated to the non-agricultural sector and income classes in proportion to their consumption of food, i.e. as if it were a subsidy on food.

The set of model assumptions specified above all serve to simplify the structure of the model. In addition, the lack of statistical data with a world-wide coverage concerning prices, trade margins, tariff revenue, etc. in the field of food and agriculture dictated further constraints on the effective inclusion of those essential variables in the model. Similarly, strong assumptions had to be made with respect to the accuracy and meaning of the statistical information available for the base year. The three major suppositions of this nature are:

(g)   Differences in value added (expressed in dollars) in the base year reflect fully and exclusively existing differences in purchasing power and material well-being between countries (used, for example, in estimating the parameters of the consumption function and of the disparity equation).

(h)   Differences between countries in the consumer price per unit of consumable protein in the base year reflect fully and exclusively existing differences in the average degree of food processing between those countries (used for example in estimating the consumption function in terms of purchasing power).

(i)   Government policy in the base year with respect to the per capita income ratio between agriculture and non-agriculture has been fully effective so that the desired ratio in fact has been realized (used in estimating the income disparity equation).

The assumptions (g) - (i) are needed not only for the estimation procedures referred to, but also to arrive at a full set of initial values per country for the simulation runs.

To conclude this section, a short comment on the assumptions is in place. Assumption (d) suggests homogeneity of the world food market (only unprocessed food is traded), and only one market (one world market food price) in which all participating countries are price takers. (That implication will later on be relaxed). Assumption (d) has been made partly for practical reasons, and partly on the basis of theoretical considerations. The practical reasons are that it is hardly possible to differentiate between partially separated markets in which the various participants try to pursue specific interests, as the theoretical, statistical and computational problems involved would be highly complex and difficult to solve.

Further, theoretical considerations may actually lend some
support to what has been assumed. World food market developments are largely the result of the domestic agricultural
policies of the various governments regarding the internal
income distribution in their country; these internal policies
determine to a large extent how much food moves through the
world market. Of course, countries may have certain wishes
as regards the price of food imports or exports, and they
may use to a certain extent a food stock policy to offset
major short-term variations (see Chapter 7). Nevertheless,
in view of the limited arsenal of domestic policy instruments
it is very unlikely that a market-economy country could
freely manipulate its foreign trade in food for the sake of
a completely different policy aim, such as e.g. regulating
the quantity exported in order to maximize foreign exchange
receipts. It seems to be more realistic to assume the pre-
dominance of internal policies in the field of income distribution, as is done in MOIRA.

An important corollary to the assumptions (d), (g) and (i)
is that for the base year tariff revenues or subsidy costs
are nil by definition. The development over time of the
domestic food price in subsequent years is discussed in
Chapter 7.

In order to obtain the necessary base-year values for non-
agricultural income, the consumer price of food, etc., the
(possibly rather strong) assumptions (g) to (i) had to be
made. Non-agricultural value added in dollars as reported in
international statistics is supposed to be an accurate
measure for non-agricultural income (assumption (g)); given
its equality to real income for the base year, the two
consumption functions could be estimated. Assumption (h)
states that base-year differences between countries in the
consumer price of a unit of consumable protein are entirely
due to differences in the level of food processing; hence
the deviation from the basic price is zero. The prices in
the base year now follow from the two consumption functions.
Finally, assumption (i) stating that the sectoral income
distribution in the base year was exactly in conformity with
the country's political wishes implies that the zero-level
deviation was also desired and that - also in view of assumption (g) - the desired income ratio can be measured as from
the base-year data.

6.4.2 *The rural/urban conflict*

In the preceding discussion the development of
the agricultural sector is described almost exclusively in
terms of its depencence on the price the agricultural producer receives for his produce. Any increase in the price
received by the food producer has to be borne by the non-
agricultural sector - and mainly by the urban population -
which means a sacrifice for them. In this setting, the
problems of hunger and material underdevelopment look truely
insurmountable. A high food price provided to the agri-

cultural producer could mean starvation for the urban prole-
tariat, and a low food price could increase hunger to the
rural population and increases migration to the urban slums.

No doubt this bleak picture appropriately reflects the reality of many poor countries; nevertheless it may be too one-
sided, omitting some more positive possibilities which also
form part of reality. Some amendments may therefore be
needed even if those will not dramatically change the picture.
A first amendment concerns the distribution of the food
trade margins. For model purposes it was assumed that the
trade margins of the intermediaries are distributed (in
proportion to food consumption) over the entire population
of the non-agricultural sector. But this need not necessarily be the case; in fact, it is very well possible that the
intermediaries in a developing economy earn significantly
higher than average incomes. An increase of the food price
received by the agricultural producer may well be under
appropriate institutional measures, at the expense of the
intermediaries forming part of a high-income class. To the
extent that such action is possible, the price stimulus for
the agricultural sector would not endanger the low food
consumption levels of the poor urban population. A policy
along these lines could be simulated in MOIRA as a (modest)
reduction in income inequality in the urban sector.

6.4.3 *Stimuli from agriculture for non-agricultural development*

A second comment on the rural/urban conflict in
MOIRA is related to a weakness in the model structure that
cannot easily be cured. It concerns the consequences of food
processing by both agriculture and the urban sector, and of
the expenditure of the agricultural sector on inputs (capital
and fertilizer).

An increase in the price of food to the consumer is associated with an increase in the degree of processing of the
food consumed; only part of this increase in processing will
take place within the agricultural sector itself (as will be
reflected in an increase of the price received by the farmer).
Processing is a productive activity, and increased processing
by the non-agricultural sector should therefore lead to
increased non-agricultural incomes. However, as non-agricultural income is exogenous - apart from tariff receipts -, no
such income increases are included in MOIRA, even though the
consumer has to pay the increased food price (according to
the sector's level of income).

A similar type of *leak* exists with regard to the agricultural
sector's expenditure on inputs in the production process. In
MOIRA, the urban sector does not benefit from input purchases
by the agricultural producers. It must be admitted that this
way of modelling is too partial in nature. From a macro-
economic point of view *money costs* cannot be separated from
returns to other economic subjects.

To improve MOIRA on this point would require a rather elaborate description of production (inter-)relations in the
urban sector, and for the time being an extension of the
model along these lines could not be realized.

6.4.4 *Calibration of the model*

          Finally, a third amendment to the exclusive anta-
gonism between the rural and urban sectors in MOIRA is in
place - an amendment that is in a very limited sense incorporated in the model. The driving force for agricultural
development in MOIRA is a higher price for agricultural
output which will stimulate additional investment and production increases in this sector. It should also be noted
that in the model's approach all factors leading to production increases under the condition of a constant input of
labour are considered to be capital inputs (investments). In
other words, in the model as described thus far all *investment* in agriculture (either by the government or by the
agricultural producers themselves) takes place exclusively
on the basis of profitability considerations.

Several objections could be raised if this approach would
remain unqualified. First, governments may well act according
to other criteria than profitability alone. Second, government investment may affect production costs of the agricultural
producer. Third, government investment may influence the
price received by the agricultural sector without affecting
the consumer food price in the urban sector. Fourth, the
price received by the producer in the base period is calculated as a shadow price: under the assumed behaviour of the
producer and given his production function, the price of
output has to be consistent with a given (observed) combination
of production volume, labour supply and income.

Agricultural development and production growth may in fact
be hampered by factors which could be eliminated with little
effort in terms of investment outlays, or with a once-for-
all type of investment. A land redistribution programme
might be a case in point. If in the analysis of the agricultural production function the stock of physical capital in
agriculture could have been measured directly over time, a
non-investment improvement of this kind would have implied a
shift of the production function. If, on the other hand, we
have to compute a time series of the development of capital
stock from a given production function and given time series
of output volume and labour input - as had to be done in
structuring MOIRA - the above *non-investment* improvement
would be measured nevertheless as an upward shift of the
capital stock estimate; as in fact the capital costs for the
sector remain almost unchanged, this in turn implies a
lowering of the cost of capital use per unit of capital.

Similarly, other efforts undertaken by the government or
private organizations may directly influence the price
received by the agricultural producer. A more efficient

organization of the agricultural transport network or of the
agricultural credit system may favourably affect the producer price while consumer prices remain unchanged.

Thus, the shadow prices for agricultural output and for
capital use to be specified for MOIRA must be indicative of
the economic climate in which agriculture operates. Improvement of the socio-economic climate for agriculture will
necessarily be possible only at a certain cost, but these
costs may be low in comparison to the returns. Both the
shadow prices for output and for capital use may therefore
be affected by the kind of efforts just discussed - measures
like organizational changes and other improvements that
together may be described as disembodied technical progress.

The computation of these shadow prices for the period 1965-
1971 was described in Chapter 4.4.5. In order to have the
model generate the historical time path for variables such
as agricultural income and output in this period, a calibration procedure was introduced which can be interpreted as
the introduction of disembodied technical progress (see
Appendix 6A.1).

For every year from 1965 till 1971 the *historical* producer
price and capital cost are fed into the producer's decision
model, and compared with the value generated by the model.
The geometric mean of the ratios between historical and
generated value is then taken as a calibration parameter -
which could possibly be interpreted as a disembodied technical progress parameter although it is in fact a general
residual development factor of the model. Because of its
arbitrariness the values of these parameters (which range
from 0.5 to 2) are levelled off towards 1 (unity) at a rate
of 10 per cent per year; therefore, after 1980 they do not
play a significant role any more. In short, the calibration
parameters hardly describe technical progress, but they are
needed to give to the (cross-sectionally estimated) model an
acceptable start.

The parameters are country-specific correction factors and
may in fact be considered as *exogenous* growth incentives (or
possibly disincentives, depending on their values); these do
not affect the consumer food price in the urban sector. Disembodied technical progress in agriculture could modify the
earlier picture in which agricultural growth incentives
would always have to be paid for by the urban population.

Appendix 6A

MODELLING OF INCOME DISTRIBUTION AND PRICE POLICY

In this appendix, the relationships described verbally in
Chapter 6 are presented in their mathematical form.

6A.1 *INCOME AND PRICE POLICY*

The budget constraint and subsidy policy:

Assuming that in the base year subsidies are zero, and that
only raw materials are traded internationally, the amount of
subsidies in the case of net exports (EX) can be described
in terms of the difference between DFPE (domestic food price
difference) and DFP (world market price difference); the total subsidy cost equals EX (DFPE - DFP). The budget constraint
is expressed in terms of the maximum percentage of non-agricultural GDP that can be allocated to this purpose. This
fraction (UBUDG) multiplied by non-agricultural per capita
income (NVLU) and the population of that sector (NPOP)
provides the estimate of maximum available resources. Thus,
the inequality

$$(DFPE - DFP) \; EX \leqq UBUDG \cdot NVLU \cdot NPOP \qquad (6A.1)$$

applies. It should be noted once more, that the prices are
defined as deviations from base-year price levels of unprocessed foods: DFPE = TFP - FP.NPI as introduced in Chapter 5 -
see (5.15) -, and DFP = difference between current and base-
year price of agricultural raw materials on the world market.

The maximum per unit subsidy for a given export level can be
derived from (6A.1):

$$Q = \frac{UBUDG \cdot NVLU \cdot NPOP}{EX} \qquad (6A.2)$$

and it follows also that, if EX > 0,

$$DFPE \leqq DFP + Q \qquad (6A.3)$$

For an importer the inequality sign is reversed.

Tolerances and seepages:

Seepages which reduce the effectiveness of government price

policies are defined as:

$$DFPE = DFPE* + \delta(DFP-DFPE*) \tag{6A.4}$$

in which DFPE* is the desired domestic price and $0 < \delta < 1$.

Functioning of the model:

Foreign trade (EX) is defined as the difference between domestic market supplies (CTY) and consumer demand (per capita, NCONS, multiplied by non-agricultural population NPOP):

$$EX = CTY - NCONS \ . \ NPOP \tag{6A.5}$$

Tariff receipts (TR) amount to:

$$TR = (DFP - DFPE) \ EX \tag{6A.6}$$

Tariff receipts increase non-agricultural income per capita:

$$NVLUE = NVLU + \frac{TR}{NPOP} \tag{6A.7}$$

in which NVLUE is nominal disposable per capita income in the non-agricultural sector. This variable is used in the consumption function and also in the disparity function.

Nominal income of the agricultural sector (V) is defined as the difference between outputs and inputs each multiplied by their prices:

$$V = P \ . \ TY - PCOST \tag{6A.8}$$

The *normalization* of output (TY) to abstract from year-to-year production swings leads to the substitution of TY* for actual TY. Agricultural per capita income (VLU), also normalized, is then defined as:

$$VLU* = \frac{P \ . \ TY* - PCOST}{L} \tag{6A.9}$$

in which L represents the agricultural population.

The desired per capita income level in agriculture (VLUPOL) can be expressed in terms of non-agricultural income and the desired parity ratio (PAR*):

$$VLUPOL = \frac{NVLUE}{PAR*} \tag{6A.10}$$

The desirable food price level (PPOL) can be written in equation form parallel to equation (6A.9):

$$VLUPOL = \frac{PPOL \ . \ TY* - PCOST}{L} \tag{6A.11}$$

and, rearranging terms and using (6A.10):

$$PPOL = (\frac{NVLUE}{PAR^*} + \frac{PCOST}{L}) \ / \ \frac{TY^*}{L} \qquad\qquad (6A.12)$$

The model contains the assumption that the value of the target variable $PPOL^*_{t+1}$ is determined by its current year level:

$$PPOL^*_{t+1} = PPOL_t \qquad\qquad (6A.13)$$

Earlier (in chapter 4) the price of the agricultural product at the stage where it leaves the sector (P) is defined as its basic price (allowing for the degree of processing, PO) corrected for general inflation (NPI) plus the deviation (DFPE) from the basic price:

$$P = PO.NPI + DFPE \qquad\qquad (6A.14)$$

The government's price policy affects P through DFPE, and the desirable level of the latter follows from equations (6A.13) and (6A.14):

$$PPOL^*_{t+1} = PO_{t+1} \ . \ NPI_{t+1} + DFPE^*_{t+1} \qquad\qquad (6A.15)$$

The general rate of (non-agricultural) inflation is assumed to be known and therefore exogenous to the model. The basic price PO changes over time as a result of income changes which alter the degree of processing. Its value for the next year is therefore not predetermined and the assumption must be made that the degree of food processing remains the same between the current and next year. Thus, the equation for the desired price for government parity policy purposes is written as:

$$DFPE^*_{t+1} = PPOL^*_{t+1} - PO_t \ . \ NPI_{t+1} \qquad\qquad (6A.16)$$

The current consumer price of food (TFP) was defined in Chapter 5 as the price effect of processing (FP) corrected for inflation, plus the deviation (DFPE) from the basic price:

$$TFP = FP \ . \ NPI + DFPE \qquad\qquad (6A.17)$$

and the desired consumer food price can therefore be defined as:

$$TFP^*_{t+1} = FP_{t+1} \ . \ NPI_{t+1} + DFPE^*_{t+1} \qquad\qquad (6A.18)$$

Margins:

Finally, the question must be answered concerning the effect of the margins accruing to intermediaries on prices and incomes. Assuming that these margins (M) do increase the consumer food price:

$$TFP' = TFP + M \qquad\qquad (6A.19)$$

non-agricultural income increases as well, by (TFP' - TFP)CTY, in which CTY represents the supply of food to the non-agricultural sector from domestic sources. The level of processing is not affected by the margins, but the income of the non-agricultural sector rises by (DFPE' - DFPE)CTY. Recalling the budget equations for each income class:

$$NVLU_i = DPFE . CONS_i + NPI . R_i \tag{6A.20}$$

in which food consumption per capita (CONS) and real income (R) figure, it follows from the assumption of margins being distributed according to food consumption that for each income class the modified per capita income is defined as:

$$NVLU' = DFPE' . CONS_i + NPI . R_i \tag{6A.21}$$

As also applies that

$$NVLU'_i = NVLU_i + (DFPE' - DFPE)CONS_i \tag{6A.22}$$

substituting for NVLU' in both equations (6A.21) and (6A.22), gives again the equation (6A.20), which is the original budget equation. Thus, the modified budget equation is not in any way different from the original one and the assumption about the distribution of the margins permits bypassing the problem of the unknown profit margins.

Technical progress:

The effects of disembodied technical progress are introduced by defining the shadow (or planning) price of output (P_t^*) and the shadow price of capital use (CMON$_t^*$) as a function of the actual price in each country:

$$P_t^* = P_t(1+\alpha) \qquad (-1 < \alpha < 1) \tag{6A.23}$$

and

$$CMON_t^* = CMON_t(1+\beta) \qquad (-1 < \beta < 1) \tag{6A.24}$$

The parameters of these equations are estimated for the base period of the model (1965-1971), in the course of the calibration procedure.

6A.2 *DISTRIBUTION OF TARIFF REVENUE OVER INCOME CLASSES*

As stated in Chapter 6.3.3, the positive or negative budgetary effects of a country's agricultural tariff policy are assumed to be passed on to the entire non-agricultural population. In this appendix, the distribution of tariff revenue (or of the subsidy burden) over the six income classes of the non-agricultural sector is discussed.

Income distribution within a sector is exogenously given (see Chapter 5); the obvious assumption would be to assume

that tariff revenue will be distributed likewise. However,
this assumption raises problems that cannot easily be solved,
as will be shown presently.

Total tariff receipts in a country follow from (6A.6) and
(6A.5), and amount to

$$TR = (DFP - DFPE) (CTY - NCONS . NPOP) \qquad (6A.25)$$

in which

TR   = tariff revenue
DFP   = deviation of the world market food price from its base
          year level
DFPE   = deviation of the domestic food price from its base
          year level
CTY   = total market supply of food by the agricultural sector
NCONS   = per capita food consumption in the non-agricultural
          sector
NPOP   = population of the non-agricultural sector

Note that the tariff receipts as defined here are zero in
the base year. All variables should be read as carrying a
time subscript and, except for DFP, a subscript j indicating
the country concerned. Nominal income per capita of the non-
agricultural sector NVLU has to be *corrected* for the additional
income derived from tariff receipts (which may be positive
or negative). The *corrected* income level NVLUE is called the
disposable nominal income per capita of the non-agricultural
sector, and is defined as in (6A.7):

$$NVLUE = NVLU - \frac{TR}{NPOP} \qquad (6A.26)$$

Substitution of TR in (6A.26) according to (6A.25) gives us

$$NVLUE = NVLU + (DFP-DFPE) . (\frac{CTY}{NPOP} - NCONS) \qquad (6A.27)$$

The above equations hold at the sector level, i.e. for the
non-agricultural sector as a whole. As consumption, in its
relation to income, is determined at the level of the various
income classes, the variable NVLUE has to be determined for
the income classes as well. Now we introduce the assumption
(referred to above) that the tariff receipts will be distributed according to the - exogenously given - income distribution. First of all, we define the ratio r_i between the
income per capita of an income class i of the non-agricultural sector and the average income per capita of this
sector: $r_i = NVLU_i/NVLU$. Obviously, this ratio is known. The
assumption now introduced is:

$$NVLUE_i / NVLUE = r_i \qquad (6A.28)$$

Multiplying both sides of (6A.27) by r_i, we have

$$NVLUE_i = r_i \left\{ NVLU + (DFP-DFPE) . (\frac{CTY}{NPOP} - NCONS) \right\} \qquad (6A.29)$$

From the discussion of the consumption function in Appendix 5A, we have to recall the budget equation (5A.13); as in the present analysis we confine ourselves to the non-agricultural sector (sector 2 in MOIRA), we use the label $NVLU_i$ for $VALU_{i2}$ and $NCONS_i$ for $CONS_{i2}$. Moreover, in writing down the budget equation we want to bring out clearly that consumption is a function of real income R, as in (5.3). We have, therefore, from (5A.13):

$$NVLU_i = DFPE \cdot NCONS_i(R_{i2}) + NPI \cdot R_{i2} \qquad (6A.30)$$

However, disposable income in an income class of the non-agricultural sector is $NVLUE_i$, rather than $NVLU_i$; when the allocation of tariff receipts to the income classes is taken into account, (5A.30) should be read as

$$NVLUE_i = DFPE \cdot NCONS_i(R_{i2}) + NPI \cdot R_{i2} \qquad (6A.31)$$

From (6A.29) and (6A.31) it follows that

$$r_i \left\{ NVLU + (DFP-DFPE) \cdot (\frac{CTY}{NPOP} - NCONS) \right\} =$$

$$= DFPE \cdot NCONS_i(R_{i2}) + NPI \cdot R_{i2} \qquad (6A.32)$$

Average food consumption per capita in the non-agricultural sector NCONS is a weighted average of per capita food consumption in the six income classes of this sector:

$$NCONS = \sum_{i=1}^{6} d_i \cdot NCONS_i \qquad (6A.33)$$

in which d_i = the share of income class i in total population of the sector. Substituting for NCONS in (6A.32) the right-hand side of (6A.33), we find that (6A.32) is a set of six simultaneous non-linear equations with six unknowns.

This simultaneity is cumbersome from a theoretical point of view. In order to deal with the allocation of tariff receipts in a more simple way, the following assumption is made: (a) total market supply of food by the agricultural sector CTY is distributed over the six income classes of the non-agricultural sector according to a certain key (which will be discussed below), and (b) tariff receipts are distributed according to the food surplus or deficit of an income class that results from the domestic supply to that income class and its own consumption. The implication is that in MOIRA every income class of the non-agricultural sector is an importer or exporter of food (rather than the non-agricultural sector as such), subject however to the national food price policy.

Per capita food supply by the domestic agricultural sector to an income class of the non-agricultural sector will be indicated by $CTYC_i$; this new variable is defined as

$$CTYC_i = q_i \frac{CTY}{NPOP} \qquad (6A.34)$$

in which q_i (i=1, ..., 6) is the distribution key which we will discuss below. The second part of the above assumption allows us to specify now the tariff receipts per income class TR_i as

$$TR_i = (DFP-DFPE)(CTYC_i-NCONS_i)\ NPOP_i \qquad (6A.35)$$

Disposable nominal income per capita of income class i of the non-agricultural sector $NVLUE_i$ is defined as

$$NVLUE_i = NVLU_i + \frac{TR_i}{NPOP_i} \qquad (6A.36)$$

Substitution of TR_i in (6A.36) according to (6A.35) gives us

$$NVLUE_i = NVLU_i + (DFP-DFPE)(CTYC_i-NCONS_i) \qquad (6A.37)$$

and from (6A.31) and (6A.37) it follows that

$$NVLU_i+(DFP-DFPE)(CTYC_i-NCONS_i) = DFPE.NCONS_i+NPI.R_{i2}$$

or

$$NVLU_i+(DFP-DFPE)CTYC_i = DFP.NCONS_i+NPI.R_{i2} \qquad (6A.38)$$

This is an important equation that will come up time and again in Chapter 7. Its mathematical form is convenient: after substitution of $NCONS_i$ by R_{i2} according to the consumption function (5.3), we can directly solve (6A.38) for R_{i2} using the procedure outlined in Chapter 5.2.1 - as $CTYC_i$ and the other variables at the left-hand side are known. The economic content of (6A.38) is also easily understood: at the (right-hand) expenditure side of the balance equation we see that the food consumed is valued at the world market price, while at the (left-hand) income side per capita class income is corrected for the class' share in the costs or benefits of the country's income (parity) policy.

Solving (6A.38) for R_{i2} requires that $CTYC_i$ be known; therefore, we have to return to what we have called the distribution key q_i, and we have to see how its value is to be determined. Let us recall that we tried to distribute tariff revenue in proportion to income. In this approach the ratio r_i between the class average and the sector average played a rôle; see (6A.28). In the present formulation of the problem, maintaining the ratio r_i would imply - see (6A.26) and (6A.35) while bringing them on a per capita basis - the following relationship:

$$(DFP-DFPE)(CTYC_i-NCONS_i) = r_i (\frac{CTY}{NPOP}-NCONS)(DFP-DFPE)$$

or

$$CTYC_i = NCONS_i + r_i (\frac{CTY}{NPOP} - NCONS) \qquad (6A.39)$$

and, in view of (6A.34)

$$q_i = \frac{NCONS_i - r_i (\frac{CTY}{NPOP} - NCONS)}{\frac{CTY}{NPOP}} \qquad (6A.40)$$

Also, from (6A.34) it can be inferred - after taking Σi - that there is a restriction on q_i, i.e. $\sum d_i.q_i = 1$ in which d_i is the (given) population share of class i.

For a given set of values of $CTYC_i$ it is not certain that the equality (6A.39) will hold. This could possibly be realized through an iterative procedure for determining q_i; however, the computation of the world market price bringing equilibrium between demand and supply is already in itself an iterative procedure repeated for each individual year, as will be seen in Chapter 7. This accumulation of iterations would considerably increase the computer time needed. Therefore, instead of adhering to (6A.40), we define q_i in a slightly different way by introducing a time lag:

$$q_{it} = \max \{0, \frac{NCONS_{i,t-1} + r_i (\frac{CTY_{t-1}}{NPOP_{t-1}} - NCONS_{t-1})}{\frac{CTY_{t-1}}{NPOP_{t-1}}}\}$$

$$(6A.41)$$

Market supply of food is in MOIRA allocated to the non-agricultural income classes according to (6A.41). In plain words this means that food supply is allocated to the income classes in such a way that if the distribution key q_{it} has been applied in the previous year (t-1) then in that year we would have had: class food export / sector food export = class income / sector income.

In the base year, tariff revenue is nil by definition; therefore, tariff revenue is always accurately distributed in the base year. In all following years, q_i is calculated annually for every income class of the non-agricultural sector. If a country in any year exports food, it is very likely that $q_i > 0$. If a country strongly relies on food imports, we may find for a very poor income class that

$$NCONS_{i,t-1} < \left| r_i (\frac{CTY_{t-1}}{NPOP_{t-1}} - NCONS_{t-1}) \right|$$

with, consequently, $q_{it} = 0$. However, this case remains an improbable one.

Summarizing, the approach outlined above has certain drawbacks. Firstly, the distribution of tariff receipts is not necessarily equal to that of income - although the deviations will not be great as long as the variables show a gradual development over time. Secondly, it is possible that within one country some income classes are food exporters while other classes are food importers; this is in itself not a very realistic picture. The computational advantages of the present approach, however, outweigh these drawbacks because the net demand for food by a country can directly be computed at a given level of the world market price, without any iterative procedure.

Chapter 7

THE WORLD FOOD MARKET

7.1 *WORLD MARKET SUPPLY AND DEMAND*

The previous chapters of Part II dealt with production, consumption and price formation of food in the setting of the national economy. The present chapter will show how the *national models* are interrelated; the interaction of the national models constitutes the depiction of the world food market as given by MOIRA.

Chapter 6 stated that the demand side of the world market is formed by the non-agricultural consumers, grouped together in six income classes per country. At the supply side, we have total net supply of food by the agricultural sector of the various countries (variable CTY_j). All this applies to market economies only; the centrally-planned economies are assumed to pursue, and substantially realize, self-sufficiency in food (see Chapter 4.6). Therefore, when in this chapter we refer to countries, it is always market-economy countries that are meant.

In any year, food supply to the world market is given and therefore totally price-inelastic (disregarding changes in stocks, for the time being), while on the other hand food demand is price-elastic. In MOIRA, there are 103 market-economy countries or geographical units; therefore, world market food demand originates from 103 x 6 = 618 income classes as consuming units. The sum total of the food quantities demanded by these income classes has to be made equal to the sum total of the quantities supplied by the agricultural sectors of the individual countries, by means of an adaptation of the world market price level.

Two assumptions made in the model deserve explicit mentioning. The first of these is the assumption of a homogeneous market in which no market party has monopolistic or monopsonistic power. This is a strong assumption, particularly with respect to important suppliers such as the U.S.A. Secondly, it is assumed that no transactions take place on the world market until equality between demand and supply is *guaranteed*; in other words, all transactions take place at the equilibrium price. However usual it is to make this assumption, it is obviously not always close to reality.

As the possibility of an equilibrium on the world food

market depends in very large measure on the elasticity of
food demand, we will first of all in the next section deal
at some length with the demand side of the world market.
Chapter 7.3 will then discuss the equilibrium mechanism,
including the role of food stocks. Before going into more
technical details, however, it may be useful to indicate now
already the main lines of the adaptation process working
towards equilibrium, and the role of the demand function in
this process.

To begin with, we have to recall some of the findings and
equations of Chapter 5 in which food consumption was discussed. In this chapter it was shown that for any income class
in in country j the magnitudes of food consumption $CONS_{ij}$,
all other expenditure WR_{ij} and real income R_{ij} can be determined from a set of three simultaneous equations; see (5A.8) -
(5A.10). The solution gives us $CONS_{ij}$ as a function of the
variables nominal income per capita $VALU_{ij}$, the general
price index NPI_j, and the domestic food price level $DFPE_j$.

To simplify the notation and to avoid the use of a double
subscript, the variables referring to the non-agricultural
sector were relabeled in Chapter 6, adding the letter N at
the beginning of the label. Substantially, Chapter 6 introduced a modification of nominal income per capita as one of
the determining factors of the consumption level; by corr-
ecting it for possible tariff receipts or subsidy payments,
disposable nominal income per capita $NVLUE_j$ came to be one
of the explanatory variables instead of $NVLU_j$; see (6A.26).
For the non-agricultural sector, the budget equation of the
consumer (5A.13) thus takes the form, for an income class i,

$$NVLUE_i = DFPE \cdot NCONS_i(R_{i2}) + NPI \cdot R_{i2} \qquad (6A.31)$$

as was shown in Appendix 6A.2. The relation between nominal per
capita income before and after correction for tariff revenue
was specified as

$$NVLUE_i = NVLU_i + (DFP-DFPE)(CTYC_i - NCONS_i) \qquad (6A.37)$$

in which

DFP   = world market food price (as deviation from its base-
        year value)
$CTYC_i$ = per capita food supply by the domestic agricultural
        sector to income class i.
Except for DFP, all variables in (6A.31) and (6A.37) should
be read as carrying the country subscript j. The same applies
to the function specifying per capita food consumption as
determined by income, the general price level and the food
price; in terms of the variables referring in particular to
the non-agricultural sector, the solution of the simultaneous equations (5A.8) -(5A.10) gives us (taking into account
the modifications introduced in the previous chapter; see in
particular Appendix 6A):

$$NCONS_i = f(NVLUE_i, NPI, DFPE) \qquad (7.1)$$

As observed before, for any year t world market food supply
is given, and world market demand has to adapt itself. The
magnitudes of $NVLU_t$ and NPI_t are given exogenously, and
consequently adaptation of demand has to be achieved through
changes in DFPE or NVLUE or both. How does the adaptation
mechanism operate in the model? Chapter 6 has elaborated the
point that governments will try to maintain a desired domestic food price level DFPE, but their policies will not
necessarily be (fully) successful because of certain constraints. To the extent to which these policies are not
effective, the domestic food price will have to follow the
change in the world market price DFP, and non-agricultural
food demand adapts itself in the direction required for
achieving equilibrium between world market supply and demand.

However, also in case the domestic price policy can be
pursued effectively an adaptation of demand will take place,
through the effect of a domestic food price policy on disposable nominal income NVLUE. In this case, the non-agricultural consumer will find his income affected by a (positive or negative) change in tariff revenue - see the second
term at the right-hand side of (6A.37) above - that will
bring his demand for food more in line with the world market
situation. Thus, the world market price level functions as
an adaptation mechanism whether or not domestic food price
policy succeeds in maintaining DFPE.

Nevertheless, it is worth noting that under certain conditions
the adaptation mechanism may work very weakly only. A country
that is, at its prevailing domestic price level, about 100
per cent self-sufficient in food will hardly be affected by
a change in the world market price (although part of the
world market price change will always seep in; see Chapter
6). In this case $NVLUE \approx NVLU$, because in (6A.37) the value
of $(CTYC_i - NCONS_i)$ is very small. The same applies to all
countries with very high income levels, as the value of the
second term at the right-hand side of (6A.37):
$(DFP-DFPE)(CTYC_i-NCONS_i)$ will be small in comparison to that
of the first term $NVLU_i$, because of the relatively low ratio
between trade in food and total income.

In Appendix 5A.1 it has been pointed out that the demand
function (7.1) has a linear isoquant, as can also be seen
from (6A.31). This implies that the non-agricultural consumer is indifferent to any form of taxation proportional to
food consumption when the tax revenue is distributed again
as a subsidy on food consumption. (Recall that this point
also came up in Chapter 6.2 in connection with the trade
margins of the intermediaries operating in the food market).
Although this statement may seem to be a tautology, it
should be realized that it does not necessarily follow from
(7.1) as such. It implies that, introducing a tax rate τ on
consumption, the left-hand side of (7.1) may also be written
as

$$f(NVLUE_i - \tau.NCONS_i, NPI, DFPE - \tau);$$

the resulting consumption level $NCONS_i$ will remain the same:

$$f(NVLUE_i - \tau \cdot NCONS_i, NPI, DFPE - \tau) = f(NVLUE_i, NPI, DFPE)$$

The way in which the demand side is specified in MOIRA makes it clear that the non-agricultural consumer will always be affected by (a change in) the world market price level; imports or exports of food will take place at the world market price, and the urban consumer has to pay this price - either in the form of the domestic food price or by means of an income transfer. In the extreme case of a country in which the agricultural sector produces at subsistence level only (CTY=0; domestic food supply to the non-agricultural sector is nil), urban food consumption is totally insensitive to the domestic food price level: what is not paid for through the food price, will have to be paid for through taxes. In other words, in cases where $CTY_i \approx 0$ tariff policy primarily influences the income distribution between agriculture and non-agriculture, and affects only marginally the level of food consumption of the non-agricultural sector because of the absence of a substitution effect.

These are the main lines along which the equilibrium mechanism operates in MOIRA; this issue will be taken up again in Chapter 7.3. Before that, we have to analyze the demand function more closely. This will be done in the next section.

7.2   *THE DEMAND SIDE OF THE WORLD MARKET*

7.2.1 *Analysis of the demand function*

In the above section, we already recalled the two important equations (6A.31) and (6A.37) in which the disposable nominal income per capita of an income class i of the non-agricultural sector of a country j $NVLUE_{ij}$ figures. Introduction of one of these expressions for $NVLUE_{ij}$ into the other expression results in the elimination of this variable, and - as was shown in Appendix 6A.2 - we obtain after rearranging terms

$$NVLU_i + (DFP - DFPE)CTYC_i = DFP \cdot NCONS_i + NPI \cdot R_{i2} \qquad (6A.38)$$

To simplify the notation, the country subscript j is again suppressed. At the left-hand side of (6A.38) we have the (exogenously given) nominal income per capita, corrected for the costs or benefits of the income policy pursued; at the right-hand side food consumption is valued at world market price, and real income is multiplied by the (exogenously given) general price index.

The explicit solution of (6A.38) is largely a matter of calculus, and is discussed in Appendix 7A.1. We will need this result only later on in the chapter. Presently, for a further analysis of demand behaviour, we first take the total differential of (6A.38), keeping in mind that $NCONS_i$

is a monotonous function of R_{i2} as was shown in Chapter 5.
For R_{i2} we will write in this chapter NR_i; NR_i thus stands
for non-agricultural real income per capita in income class
i. For given values of $NVLU_i$, $CTYC_i$ and NPI, the differential
of (6A.38) is

$$(dDFP - dDFPE).CTYC_i = DFP.dNCONS_i + NCONS_i.dDFP +$$

$$+ NPI.\frac{dNR_i}{dNCONS_i} . dNCONS_i$$

or, after collecting terms,

$$(CTYC_i - NCONS_i) . dDFP = CTYC_i . dDFPE +$$

$$+ (DFP + NPI\frac{dNR_i}{dNCONS_i}).dNCONS_i \qquad (7.2)$$

From (7.2) we see how $NCONS_i$ changes as a consequence of a
change in the world market price DFP:

$$\frac{dNCONS_i}{dDFP} = \frac{(CTYC_i - NCONS_i) - CTYC_i \frac{dDFPE}{dDFP}}{DFP + NPI\frac{dNR_i}{dNCONS_i}} \qquad (7.3)$$

This can be considered as a differential equation in the
variable $NCONS_i$. We shall do so in order to allow the construction of a phase diagram.

Let us first look at the denominator of the term at the
right-hand side of (7.3). The value of the denominator is by
definition positive, as can be shown as follows. In Chapter
5.2.2, we found that

$$\frac{dNR_i}{dNCONS_i} \geq FP^S$$

in which FP^S is the basic component of the food price within
a sector, reflecting the degree of processing of food. In
view of the above inequality, we also have

$$DFP + NPI \frac{dNR_i}{dNCONS_i} \geq DFP + NPI . FP^S \qquad (7.4)$$

The expression at the right-hand side of the inequality sign
in (7.4) is the absolute level of the world market price of
the (processed) food consumed in the country concerned. By
definition, this price level cannot be negative; by implication, the effect of a change in the world market price on
the domestic food price in a country j is subject to the
condition

$$DFPP_y = \max (-NPI.FP_j^s, DFP)$$

in which

$DFPP_j$ = the maximum (downward) change in the domestic food
price level in country j.
The denominator at the right-hand side of (7.3) is, therefore,
necessarily positive. But what about the value of the numerator? Here we will have to distinguish three cases, depending
on the value of dDFP/dDFP.

Case A: the domestic food price level is not at all affected
by (changes in) the world market price level. In this
case, dDFPE / dDFP = 0; consequently, (7.3) becomes

$$\frac{dNCONS_i}{dDFP} = \frac{CTYC_i - NCONS_i}{DFP + NPI \dfrac{dNR_i}{dNCONS_i}} \tag{7.5}$$

We have seen already that $CTYC_i$ is given, as supply by the
agricultural sector is completely inelastic in the short
run. Depending on the algebraic sign of the numerator at the
right-hand side of (7.5), we have again three possibilities.
(a)   Suppose $(CTYC_i-NCONS_i) > 0$, hence, income class i is an
exporter of food. The expression at the right-hand side
of (7.5) is positive, and an increase in the world food
price leads to increased food consumption as a result
of increased income of class i. The lower the (absolute)
value of $(CTYC_i-NCONS_i)$, the smaller will be the positive response of $NCONS_i$.
(b)   Suppose $(CTYC_i-NCONS_i) < 0$; in words, income class i is
an *importer* of food. An increase in the world market
price now reduces disposable income, and food consumption per capita decreases. Again, the effect on $NCONS_i$
will be smaller for lower absolute values of
$(CTYC_i-NCONS_i)$.
(c)   Suppose $(CTYC_i-NCONS_i) = 0$; this is the case of exact
self-sufficiency. The right-hand side of (7.5) is zero,
and a change in DFP has no effect on consumption per
capita.

The three possibilities (a) - (c) are illustrated by fig.
7.1. In the initial situation P, we have $(CTYC_i-NCONS_i) > 0$
and the demand curve has a positive slope. Subsequent increases in DFP will bring point P closer to the vertical
line $CTYC_i$, along the demand curve, but the movements towards
the vertical line will become smaller and smaller. It is
impossible for the demand curve to intersect with the vertical line of exact self-sufficiency; as soon as point P
would be on $NCONS_i = CTYC_i$, consumption is totally insensitive to DFP. A demand curve with two segments, one with a
positive slope and one with a negative slope, is impossible
according to (7.5). Therefore, an income class cannot - in
the short run - cross the vertical line in fig. 7.1 and
change from an exporter into an importer, or vice versa.

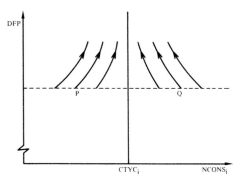

Fig. 7.1

Phase diagram of the relation between world market price and food consumption (arrows indicating direction of change); case A

In case A we find that the food demand curve of an importing class (initial situation Q) has the usual negative slope, while the demand curve of an exporting class has a positive slope. For both classes we find that an increase in the world market price leads to a consumption change in the direction of 100 per cent self-sufficiency in food.

Case B: the domestic food price level totally follows the (changes in) the world market price level. Here we have dDFPE/dDFP = 1; thus, (7.3) may be written now as

$$\frac{dNCONS_i}{dDFP} = \frac{-NCONS_i}{DFP + NPI \dfrac{dNR_i}{dNCONS_i}} \qquad (7.6)$$

The marginal response of food consumption to a change in the world market price is the same as that to a change in the domestic food price. Whether an income class i is food-exporting or food-importing, its demand curve for food has a negative slope because the right-hand side of (7.6) is negative. This case is illustrated by fig. 7.2.

Case C: the domestic food price level partly follows the (changes in) the world market price level. This case implies that dDFPE/dDFP = δ, with 0<δ<1. Introducing δ in (7.3) gives us

$$\frac{dNCONS_i}{dDFP} = \frac{(1-\delta)\ CTYC_i - NCONS_i}{DFP + NPI \dfrac{dNR_i}{dNCONS_i}} \qquad (7.7)$$

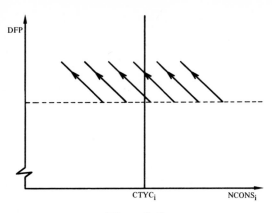

Fig. 7.2

*Phase diagram of the relation between
world market price and food consumption
(arrows indicating direction of change);
case B*

or

$$\frac{dNCONS_i}{dDFP} = (1-\delta) \ \frac{CTYC_i - NCONS_i}{DFP + NPI \ \dfrac{dNR_i}{dNCONS_i}} + \delta \ \frac{-NCONS_i}{DFP + NPI \ \dfrac{dNR_i}{dNCONS_i}}$$

$$(7.8)$$

As can be seen immediately, (7.8) is a weighted average of
the solutions (7.5) and (7.6). It will be recalled that the
parameter δ was introduced already in Chapter 6.3.3, (and
Appendix 6A.1), as a seepage factor or indicator of the
degree of free trade pursued by a country. If we widen the
value range of δ to include the two extremes discussed as
Case A and Case B, we may consider (7.7) as the general
formulation of the demand response with $0 \leq \delta \leq 1$. We will
have to say more about (7.7) in the following sections of
this chapter.

7.2.2 *Further properties of the demand function*

The previous discussion has shown that as long as
domestic prices and production are unchanged, an exporter
remains exporter and an importer remains importer. This
analysis was implicit, however, because it did not determine
the conditions for an income class to be exporter or importer.

Let us now take a closer look at the demand function, and
study the sign of the first derivative as given in (7.7):

$$\frac{dNCONS_i}{dDFP} = \frac{(1-\delta)CTYC_i - NCONS_i}{DFP + NPI\dfrac{dNR_i}{dNCONS_i}}$$

with $0 \leq \delta \leq 1$. As we saw already in the previous section, the sign of $dNCONS_i/dDFP$ is determined by the value of the numerator of the right-hand side quotient:

$$\frac{dNCONS_i}{dDFP} > 0 \quad if \quad (1-\delta)CTYC_i - NCONS_i > 0$$

or

$$\frac{dNCONS_i}{dDFP} > 0 \quad if \quad \frac{CTYC_i}{NCONS_i} > \frac{1}{1-\delta}$$

Calling $1/(1-\delta)$ the degree of sensitivity of the domestic food price level, we may state that food consumption will react positively on a price increase in the world market as long as the degree of self-sufficiency in food is greater than the degree of sensitivity of the domestic food price.

However, this finding does not allow us to make more general statements about the slope of the demand curve for any particular income class as $NCONS_i$ is obviously not a parameter. Therefore, we shall try to reformulate the above taking into account (a) that the domestic food price DFPE is unknown, and (b) that in (7.7) the expression $(1-\delta)CTYC_i$ figures – rather than $CTYC_i$.

As regards the domestic food price DFPE, we recall the definition (6A.4) stating that in any year

$$DFPE = DFPE* + \delta (DFP-DFPE*) \tag{7.9}$$

in which

DFPE* = the intended or desired value of DFPE for the year under consideration, i.e. the upper or lower bound of the margin of tolerance (see Chapter 6.3.3).

From (7.9) we have

$$DFPE - \delta.DFP = (1-\delta)DFPE* \tag{7.10}$$

so that for a given value of δ the right-hand side of (7.10) can be computed.

We introduce now the auxiliary variable NVLUB, which is defined as

$$NVLUB_i \equiv (DFPE-\delta.DFP)CTYC_i+NPI.NR_i\Big((1-\delta)CTYC_i\Big) \tag{7.11}$$

Rearranging terms gives us

$$NVLUB_i + (DFP-DFPE)CTYC_i =$$
$$DFP.(1-\delta).CTYC_i + NPI.NR_i\left((1-\delta)CTYC_i\right) \qquad (7.12)$$

This equation may usefully be compared with (6A.38):

$$NVLU_i + (DFP-DFPE)CTYC_i = DFP.NCONS_i + NPI.NR_i(NCONS_i)$$

The comparison shows that $NVLUB_i$ is to be interpreted as the value of nominal income per capita at which the food consumption level will be equal to $(1-\delta)CTYC_i$. As NPI and $CTYC_i$ are known, as well as DFPE*, substitution of (7.10) in (7.11) allows us to calculate $NVLUB_i$ for a given value of δ; hence, $NVLUB_i$ can be considered as a known parameter.

From (7.12) and (6A.38) it follows that

$$NVLUB_i - NVLU_i = DFP[(1-\delta)CTYC_i - NCONS_i] +$$
$$+ NPI \{NR_i\left((1-\delta)CTYC_i\right) - NR_i(NCONS_i)\} \qquad (7.13)$$

As regards the sign of the first derivative of the demand function, determined by $(1-\delta)CTYC_i - NCONS_i$, it can be shown that

(a) $(1-\delta)CTYC_i - NCONS_i > 0 \iff NVLUB_i - NVLU_i > 0$

(b) $(1-\delta)CTYC_i - NCONS_i = 0 \iff NVLUB_i - NVLU_i = 0$ (7.14)

(c) $(1-\delta)CTYC_i - NCONS_i < 0 \iff NVLUB_i - NVLU_i < 0$

A formal proof of this statement is given, for $\delta = 0$, in Appendix 7A.2; it corresponds with case A of Chapter 7.2.1, and the slope of the demand function may be either positive or negative (and occasionally exactly zero). For positive values of δ, the importance of the term $(1-\delta)CTYC_i$ diminishes, and as δ comes closer to unity $NVLUB_i$ becomes smaller and smaller, and the slope of the demand curve will tend to be negative. For $\delta = 1$ we have again case B of Chapter 7.2.1 and the slope of the demand curve is necessarily negative.

Thus far, we have analyzed the properties of the demand function on the basis of the structure of the model and the properties of the consumption function, but without referring to the specification of the consumption function. For a further analysis of the demand function, we have to take into account the specification of the consumption function as it has been discussed in Chapter 5. From this chapter we recall that the consumption function has two segments: (a) below the (low) real income level R_{is}^G the function is linear, as all income is spent on food, and the marginal propensity to consume food is equal to 1; (b) for real income levels above R_{is}^G the consumption function implies a marginal propensity to consume smaller than 1, and falling with higher income levels. The specification is given in (5.3); we repeat here this equation, writing $NCONS_i$ and NR_i for the variables referring to the non-agricultural sector (and dropping, for the convenience of writing, the superscript of FP):

$$NCONS_i = \min \left[\frac{NR_i}{FP}, \ ACONS+BCONS(\sqrt{NR_i+CCONS} - \sqrt{CCONS}) \right]$$

(7.15)

The real income level below which all consumption is food consumption is indicated again as NR^G, and the corresponding level of food consumption as $NCONS^G$. On the basis of the specification of the consumption function, Appendix 7A.1 shows that the explicit[1] form of the demand equation is:

if $\quad NCONS_i > NCONS^G$,

then

$$NCONS_i = ACONS+\frac{BCONS}{2.NPI} \left[-DFP.BCONS+\sqrt{(DFP.BCONS)^2+4.NPI.X} \right] -$$

$$- BCONS \sqrt{CCONS} \qquad (7.16)$$

in which the auxiliary variable X is defined as

$$X = NVLU_i+(DFP-DFPE)CTYC_i+NPI.CCONS-DFP(ACONS-BCONS\sqrt{CCONS})$$

(7.17)

else $(NCONS_i \leq NCONS^G)$:

$$NCONS_i = \frac{NVLU_i - (DFP-DFPE)CTYC_i}{DFP+NPI.FP} \qquad (7.18)$$

It should be noted here, that the above demand equation has been derived under the assumption that the world market price cannot become negative for any country, which implies a lower boundary on DFP:

$$DFP \geq \frac{-NVLU_i}{CTYC_i} + DFPE \qquad (7.19)$$

In addition to the derivation of the above specification of the demand function, Appendix 7A.1 gives a formal proof of the following properties of it (always assuming $dDFPE/dDFP = \delta$, with $0 \leq \delta \leq 1$):

(a)   for both value ranges (both segments) of the demand function

---

[1] Except that the dependent variable is the classification criterion.

$$\lim_{DFP \to \infty} \frac{dNCONS_i}{dDFP} = 0$$

The change in per capita food consumption, as a consequence of a change in the world market price level, approaches zero if DFP increases infinitely.

(b)   for both value ranges (both segments) of the demand function

$$\lim_{DFP \to \infty} NCONS_i = (1-\delta)CTYC_i$$

The absolute level of per capita food consumption, in income class i, approaches the level of $(1-\delta)CTYC_i$ if DFP increases infinitely.

(c)   if per capita food consumption responds positively to a change in the world market price, i.e. if $dNCONS_i/dDFP>0$, then $d^2NCONS_i/dDFP^2 < 0$; when the first derivative of the demand function is positive, the second derivative is shown to be necessarily negative. As has been shown above, the first derivative is positive when $NVLUB_i-NVLU_i > 0$; therefore, in this case the demand curve is rising and is concave downwards. In view of (b) we thus find that the demand curve approaches asymptotically the level $(1-\delta)CTYC_i$ *from below* when DFP increases infinitely; see fig. 7.3.

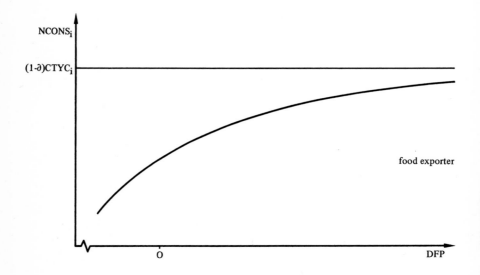

Fig. 7.3

The demand curve for food, of an income class i, when $NVLUB_i > NVLU_i$ (with $0 < \delta < 1$)

(d)   if per capita food consumption responds negatively to a
      change in the world market price, i.e. if $dNCONS_i/dDFP<0$,
then the sign of the second derivative cannot be determined
at once. For larger absolute values of the first derivative,
i.e. for $dNCONS_i/dDFP < -BCONS^2/NPI$, the second derivative
of the demand function is negative: $d^2NCONS_i/dDFP^2<0$. However, in the opposite case of $dNCONS_i/dDFP > -BCONS^2/NPI$ we
find that the second derivative is positive. Thus, when the
first derivative is negative, i.e. $NVLUB_i-NVLU_i < 0$, the
demand curve has the following properties: it is always
falling, it is concave downwards for the lower value range
of DFP, it is concave upwards for the higher value range of
DFP, and it approaches asymptotically the level $(1-\delta)CTYC_i$
from above when DFP increases infinitely. This is illustrated
in fig. 7.4.

(e)   if per capita food consumption responds positively to a
      change in the world market price ($dNCONS_i/dDFP>0$; fig.
7.3), it can be shown that at higher levels of per capita
income $NVLU_i$ food demand is less sensitive to price changes.
In the opposite case of a negative response of demand to
world market price changes (fig. 7.4), a higher per capita
income $NVLU_i$ does not necessarily imply a lower sensitivity
to price changes.

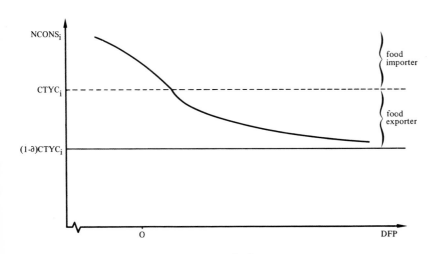

Fig. 7.4

The demand for food, of an income class i,
when $NVLUB_i < NVLU_i$ (with $0 < \delta < 1$)

7.2.3 *The demand function in the model*

        As has been discussed at some length in Chapter
6, the parameter δ indicates the *degree of free trade* pursued
by a country (and therefore by all income classes of a

country). The value of δ depends on the actual internal
situation in the country concerned. In certain situations,
the domestic food price will follow the changes in the world
market price (δ=1), while in other situations tariffs or
subsidies will be changed so that the domestic food price
does not, or not entirely, follow the changes in the world
market price (δ<1).

The above figures 7.3 and 7.4 illustrated the shape of the
demand curve for a given value of δ (o < δ < 1). However, as
δ will have different values for different value ranges of
DFP, the graphic picture of the demand function of an income
class in the context of the entire model is more complex. It
has to take into account that
(a)   within the margins of tolerance around the desired
       domestic price level no (change in) tariff policy will
       be put into practice (δ=1);
(b)   outside the margins of tolerance a world market price
       change will lead to a smaller change in the domestic
       food price level, because of an adaptation of tariff
       policy (0 < δ < 1; the case of δ=0 is judged to be im-
       possible because changes in DFP will always *seep in* to
       a certain extent);
(c)   there is an upper limit to the total amount of subsidy -
       negative tariffs - that can be spent on food price
       policy; beyond this budget constraint, the domestic
       price has to follow again the world market price (δ=1).

The discontinuity in δ introduced here causes a discontinuity
in DFPE as a function of DFP. This is not desirable as it
might theoretically endanger the existence of equilibrium on
the world market. However, in the simulation runs the margin
of tolerance is set at a very narrow level so that the
discontinuity hardly occurs when the world market price
changes.

Keeping in mind these variations in δ we are now in a position
to give a schematic picture of the demand function in MOIRA,
for an income class i of the non-agricultural sector. Fig.
7.5 shows the case of a *food importer* that only at very high
world market prices turns into an exporter of food (case 1).
The opposite case of an *exporting* income class is shown in
fig. 7.6; only at low world market prices this income class
will become food-importing (case 2). A few comments on the
two figures are in place.

In the initial situation of any specific year the desired
domestic price level DFPE* corresponds with a certain world
market price level DFP given the existing level of tariffs
or subsidies in the country concerned (which may or may not
be zero). Within the upper and lower bound of the tolerance
margin, a change in DFP will not lead to a change in tariff
or subsidy policy; over the entire range of the tolerance
margin a change in the world market price will be fully
passed on to the domestic price level. If in fig. 7.5 DFP
will fall below the lower bound of the tolerance margin
(i.e. below A), tariffs on food imports will be increased;

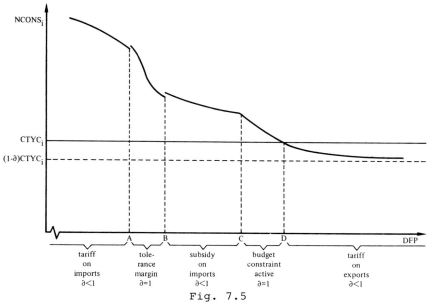

Fig. 7.5

The demand for food of an income class i
with $NCONS_i > (1-\delta)CTYC_i$ (case 1)

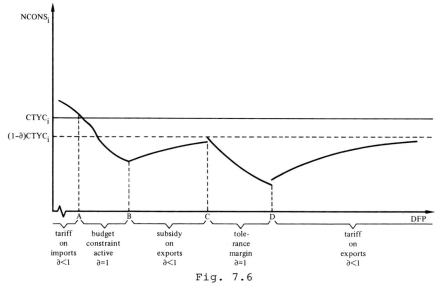

Fig. 7.6

The demand for food of an income class i,
(case 2)

the slope of the demand curve will be reduced, in comparison
to a situation in which δ = 1. Similarly, for a level of DFP
higher than B, subsidies on food imports will be increased
as long as the budget permits, and the slope of the demand
curve will be reduced as a consequence. Budgetary resources
are exhausted when the world market price is as high as C;
at higher price levels, changes in DFP will again have their
full impact on the domestic price, and food demand decreases
more rapidly until imports become nil at D. At even higher
levels of DFP the income class will be exporting food. When
the country concerned becomes an exporter of food it will,
however, introduce an export tariff to protect its domestic
price level against further upward pressure. The demand
curve at these very high price levels will approach the
level of $(1-\delta)CTYC_i$, as has been shown earlier. Note that
the transition from the range of the active budget constraint
($\delta=1$) to tariff on exports (δ < 1) in fig. 7.5 depends on
the country becoming an exporter (and not an individual
income class of the country), and is therefore determined at
the country level.

With the appropriate modifications, the same comment applies
to fig. 7.6. Note that the demand curve can cross the level
of $(1-\delta)CTYC_i$ only when δ = 1, i.e. within the value range
of the tolerance margin or of the active budget constraint.
The segments of the demand curve falling between B and C,
and to the right of D, form part of asymptotes approaching
the level $(1-\delta)CTYC_i$. The change in the direction of the
concavity of the left-hand side of the two demand curves is
introduced at an arbitrary point.

Having analyzed the demand side of the world market for
food, we now turn to the equilibrium mechanism.

7.3 *THE EQUILIBRIUM ON THE WORLD FOOD MARKET*

7.3.1 *MOIRA as a general equilibrium model*

7.3.1.1 *Assumptions*

        The demand side in MOIRA can be looked at
as a general equilibrium model under pure exchange. To
clarify this we recall briefly the main assumptions.
(a) Only one agricultural and one non-agricultural com-
     modity are distinguished.
(b) The agricultural consumer owns all factors of pro-
     duction in agriculture, so that he gets the total value
     added of the sector as primary income. The same assump-
     tion is made for the non-agricultural sector.
(c) The agricultural sector is assumed to produce its own
     food separately so that its food consumption plan is
     made up together with its food production plan, with a
     time lag of one period. Thus, the net food supply to
     the non-agricultural sector CTY is predetermined. This
     is the food endowment of the non-agricultural sector.
(d) A domestic food price policy is pursued for the non-

agricultural sector. The (possibly negative) tariff receipts resulting from this policy are redistributed
over the income classes of the non-agricultural sector.
(e) It is assumed that no price difference exists between
the world market price and the domestic price of the
non-agricultural commodity.
(f) The output of the non-agricultural sector is predetermined and the non-agricultural commodity is taken as
numéraire (the price index for the non-agricultural
commodity NPI is kept constant over the simulation
period).

7.3.1.2 *Budget equations for the two sectors.*

From the assumptions listed above the
budget equations may be derived which have been introduced
and discussed before. These equations merely represent the
accounting relationship that expentiture = income. For the
non-agricultural sector (sector 2), we have

income_2 = endowment with non-agricultural product +
        + net tariff receipts
income_2 = NV + TR

or, substituting TR according to (6A.25)

$$\text{income}_2 = NV + (DFP-DFPE)(CTY-NCONS.NPOP) \qquad (7.20)$$

and

expenditure_2 = expenditure on food + expenditure on
           non-food
expenditure_2 = TFP.NCONS.NPOP+NPI.WR_2.NPOP $\qquad (7.21)$

where WR_2 stands for per capita consumption (in sector 2)
in real terms of all non-foods; see (5A.8). As the domestic
food price TFP is defined - see e.g. (5.15) - as

TFP = NPI.FP + DFPE

the expenditure side can be rewritten as

$$\text{expenditure}_2 = DFPE.NCONS.NPOP+NPI(WR_2+FP.NCONS).NPOP \qquad (7.22)$$

As expenditure is equal to income, we have for sector 2,
from (7.20) and (7.22)

$$NV+(DFP-DFPE)CTY-DFP.NCONS.NPOP = NPI(WR_2+FP.NCONS)NPOP \qquad (7.23)$$

The price to be determined on the world market is the price
for agricultural raw materials, which is only measured as a
deviation from its base-year value, i.e. DFP. The budget
equation (7.23) holds for all prices DFP such that
$DFP + NPI.FP_o \geq 0$.

Turning now to the budget equation for the agricultural sector (sector 1), we have to remark first of all that in this case we are interested only in the expenditure on non-agricultural commodities as the demand for agricultural commodities is predetermined. For this purpose we use the term net income, defined as

$$\text{net income}_1 = \text{total receipts from the non-agricultural sector} - \text{committed expenditure for purchase of inputs}$$
$$\text{net income}_1 = P.CTY - PCOST$$

with PCOST, the sum of the sector's production outlays, defined as before (see Chapter 4.4.2):

$$PCOST = FMON_{t-1}.F.A + CMON_{t-1}.CE$$

As the producer price P is built up by different components, $P = NPI.PO + DFPE$ - see (4.24) -, we have

$$\text{net income}_1 = (NPI.PO+DFP)CTY - PCOST \tag{7.24}$$

Also,

$$\text{expenditure}_1 = \text{expenditure on non-foods}$$
$$\text{expenditure}_1 = NPI.WR_1.L \tag{7.25}$$

where L is the agricultural population, and from (7.24) and (7.25) the balance equation for the agricultural sector follows:

$$(NPI.PO+DFPE)CTY - PCOST = NPI.WR_1.L \tag{7.26}$$

7.3.1.3 *The budget equation for a country*

Summation of the two sector balance equations (7.23) and (7.26) gives us the balance equation at the country level:

$$NV + DFP.CTY - DFPE.CTY - DFP.NCONS.NPOP + NPI.PO.CTY + DFPE.CTY - PCOST =$$

$$= NPI.WR_2.NPOP + NPI.FP.NCONS.NPOP + NPI.WR_1.L$$

or

$$(DFP+NPI.PO)CTY + NV - PCOST = (DFP+NPI.FP)NCONS.NPOP + NPI(WR_1.L+WR_2.NPOP) \tag{7.27}$$

Note that NV-PCOST is the net endowment with the non-agricultural commodity for final demand purposes; because NV is given, a higher PCOST only implies a lower net endowment. This is not a very realistic feature, admittedly; it is a result of the fact that non-agricultural output is taken as given.

The budget equation shows, however, that every country will
spend exactly the amount it earnes when measured at the
world market prices of the two commodities (DFP,1). Therefore, Walras' Law holds; note that domestic food prices DFPE
do not occur in the budget equation (7.27). Moreover, demand
is a continuous function of price (disregarding the discon-
tinuities due to *jumps* of the parameter δ at the extremes of
the tolerance margin; see Chapter 7.2.3), so that a competitive equilibrium on the world market can be shown to exist.
A formal proof could be given, but we have shown already
that an autarkic equilibrium would exist for DFP $\rightarrow + \infty$
(see Chapter 7.2.1).

We shall not formally investigate the matter whether other
stable equilibria exist, but pursue the more pragmatic
approach of devising an algorithm to compute something we
still call an equilibrium - although intermediate adjustments of domestic policies may be needed.

7.3.2 *The equilibrium mechanism in MOIRA*

The world market for food can be visualized in
two equivalent ways. One possibility is to consider all non-
agricultural consumers as the actors at the demand side of
the market, while the supply side consists of all owners of
food. However, as in different countries prices are expressed
in different units it is somewhat difficult to speak of one
(world) market in this case. Another view is to restrict the
definition of the world market to the net inflows and outflows of food crossing national borders: exporting countries
are suppliers to the world market, and importing countries
act at the demand side. In this case it is easier to en-
visage the functioning of the world market in which trading
companies, governments or both, are the market parties.

From a computational point of view, both approaches or views
are equivalent. At a given level of the world market price,
demand can be calculated for each country. From this, net
demand (= demand - supply) follows directly. A positive net
demand can be labelled as import, and a negative net demand
as export. There is equilibrium on the world market when aggregate net demand is zero. When in the following pages the
term supply is used, it refers to supply from production and
not to export supply (which is the sum of negative net
demands). Analogously, the term demand is used for consumer
demand and not for import demand.

At a certain world market price level, market parties will
want to export or import a certain quantity of food. As long
as the sum total of intended demand exceeds the sum total of
supplies, the world market price will decrease; in the
opposite case, the price will increase. The traditional
assumption is that no transactions will take place unless
and until total supply and total demand have been equated by

the required price change. Although this assumption (tâtonnement) is debatable, we will adhere to it in MOIRA. All
international transactions in food will take place at the
equilibrium price level.

The theoretical considerations underlying the approach
chosen in MOIRA may be summarized as follows:
(a)   In a two-sector model in which one of the two goods is
      the *numéraire*, realization of a market equilibrium for
      one of the goods implies at the same time an equilibrium
      situation for the other good. In MOIRA, we concentrate
      for this reason on the equilibrium of the food market.
(b)   An equilibrium situation on the (food) market is not
      necessarily a unique equilibrium.
(c)   When, in a model with two goods, there is more than one
      point of equilibrium, there will be at least one equi-
      librium point which is stable - in the sense that in
      the neighbourhood of this point the excess of demand
      for this good will be reduced when the price of it
      increases.
(d)   When a general one-period, static equilibrium model is
      used in a period-by-period descriptive context, an
      algorithm has to be devised selecting one equilibrium
      point out of the stable equilibrium points that are
      possible. This selection mechanism will always have an
      element of arbitrariness in it. However, it is prefer-
      able to show this arbitrary decision quite explicitly,
      rather than to make the computer select one such point
      and pretend this point to be unique.
(e)   In MOIRA, the area in which an equilibrium can establish
      itself is a closed value range around the price of last
      year. If no stable point of equilibrium can be established
      within this range, it is assumed that we have a situation
      of a structural gap on the world market and that, as a
      consequence, the market parties (countries) will have
      to adapt their policy (see Chapter 7.3.3).[2]

The assumptions on which the equilibrium mechanism in MOIRA
is based may be listed as follows:

(a)   If, within a certain value range of the world market
      price, the aggregated demand curve and the aggregated
supply curve intersect, and if a lowering of the price leads
to a lowering of the surplus of supply over demand (and a
price rise to a lowering of the excess of demand over supply),
then a market equilibrium will establish itself when the
world food price enters this value range. This may be illustrated graphically; see fig. 7.7.

For the value range from A to C, equilibrium will be achieved
at the level B; for the range to the right of C equilibrium

---

[2]This approach is admittedly not in accordance with pure competitive
theory, as in this theory the tâtonnement does not have any descriptive
content.

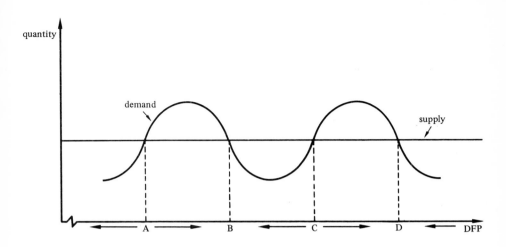

Fig. 7.7

*Supply and demand curves for the world
market, and the possibilities
for equilibrum*

will result at the level D. For the range to the left of A,
no equilibrium can be realized. In A and C there is indeed
equilibrium, but as it is not reached gradually it is not
stable so that these points are not relevant. As fig. 7.7
shows, when supply is completely inelastic the slope of the
demand curve has to be negative near to a relevant point of
equilibrium.

(b)   As stated before, all international trade takes place
      at one and the same world market price level; as long
as there is no equilibrium the ownership of the commodities
involved (food) does not change. This so-called *tâtonnement*
assumption is in fact slightly modified, however; it is
assumed that intended market supply may be changed during
the process of *tâtonnement* or negotiation, by means of
building up or running down food stocks (see Chapter 7.3.2
below).

(c)   At the beginning of a negotiation process the world
      food price is at its (equilibrium) level of last year.
Therefore, the fact that in principle at more than one point
equilibrium could be reached does not present a computational
problem; starting from an initial world market price level
only one new equilibrium price will be arrived at. Note that
the initial price may be lower than A in fig. 7.7; if in the
value range to the left of A the demand curve does not
intersect the supply curve any more, the price mechanism
will not be able to establish equilibrium between demand and
supply. From a practical point of view this case is identical

with the one in which the demand and the supply curve do not
intersect at all.

In terms of the MOIRA variables, total food consumption of
all non-agricultural sectors together is called WCONS and is
defined as

$$WCONS = \sum_j (\sum_i d_{ij} \cdot NCONS_{ij}) NPOP_j \qquad (7.28)$$

with

$$NCONS_{ij} = f(DFPE_j, NPI_j, NVLUE_{ij})$$

where DFPE and NVLUE are, as described before, functions of
DFP. The slope of the aggregated or macro demand equation is
therefore given by

$$\frac{dWCONS}{dDFP} = \sum_j \left[\sum_i d_{ij} \cdot \frac{dNCONS_{ij}}{dDFP} \right] \cdot NPOP_j \qquad (7.29)$$

Obviously, it is the weighted average of the term $dNCONS_{ij}/dDFP$ for all (non-agricultural) income classes in all countries that determines whether the slope of the macro demand
function is positive or negative.

(a) If $\delta_j = 1$ for all values of j (i.e. in all countries),
     we know that $dNCONS_{ij}/dDFP < 0$; the demand curve of
every income class i,j will intersect the line $NCONS_{ij} = CTYC_{ij}$. The macro demand curve has necessarily at all points
a negative slope, and will intersect (as an equilibrium
exists) the macro supply curve only once. Because of the
negative slope of the macro demand curve, this point of
intersection will be the equilibrium point.

(b) If $\delta_j < 1$ for certain or all values of j, $dNCONS_{ij}/dDFP$
     is not necessarily negative. In the present-day world,
the macro demand curve is very likely to have a negative
slope as the most important exporting countries - and only
for exporters we may have $dNCONS_{ij}/dDFP > 0$ - are high-
income countries: United States, Canada, Australia. As was
pointed out in Chapter 7.2.2, at high-income levels the
positive response of food consumption to a price change
(i.e. with $\delta_j < 1$) is of small magnitude only, and may
easily be more than offset by the negative response of
demand in (most) other countries. However, theoretically it
is possible - especially in case of abrupt policy changes -
that the world market price remains within a value range for
which no point of intersection between the demand curve and
the supply curve exists (in fig. 7.7 for the values of DFP
lower than A). In such a case, there is a structural gap
(surplus or deficit) in the year concerned.

We have to conclude, therefore, that it is possible for the
world market not to lead to an equilibrium situation (for a
given value range of the world market price) if the domestic

food price level of the countries dealing on the world
market does not follow in sufficient measure the variations
in the world market price. The next section discusses how
this problem is dealt with in the model.

7.3.3 *The effects of a structural gap on the world market for the national economies*

If the *normal* reaction pattern embodied in
the demand functions at the income class level does not lead
to an equilibrium in the world market, obviously other
forces must become operative in order to enforce equilibrium.
Two such factors are distinguished in MOIRA: (a) an adaptation of the parameter δ_j, and (b) the manipulation of food
stocks.

(a) *No stock changes, but adaptation of* δ_j

Let us assume that a structural shortage exists in the
world market. This implies that importing countries will not
be able to buy as much as they would like to import at the
prevailing world market price. This, in turn, means that the
domestic price cannot be maintained at the desired level but
will have to increase - particularly when the funds available for import have been exhausted. Market conditions will
make a price rise inevitable.

For an exporting country, it is less obvious that a structural shortage will enforce a domestic price increase. Here
it is not the market conditions as such, but rather the
income-parity policy that forces the country to allow its
domestic food price to rise. Taxes on exports at a very high
price would strongly favour the non-agricultural income
groups while in fact it is agriculture that made these high
foreign exchange earnings possible. This would lead to a
strong deviation from the normal income-disparity ratio, and
it may be assumed that for this reason the agricultural
sector will be able to successfully aim at an increase in
the domestic food price level. Both in importing and in
exporting countries, a structural shortage in the world
market will lead to a higher value of δ, meaning that the
change (increase) in the world market price level will be
followed more closely.

In the opposite case of a structural surplus in the world
market, for similar reasons δ will increase - notably for
exporting countries. Exporters will not be able to sell all
they want at the prevailing price, and market forces will
exert a downward pressure on the domestic price level. The
income-disparity argument works in the same direction. In
importing countries, on the other hand, these arguments do
not hold. A lowering of world market prices already favours
the non-agricultural population because of higher tariff
receipts, and it is unlikely that the sectoral income distribution will be disturbed even further by allowing the
domestic food price level to decrease.

Summarizing, we may say that in case of a structural shortage in the world market domestic prices will increase everywhere. In case of a structural surplus, domestic prices in
exporting countries will decrease. A disequilibrium in the
world market therefore implies that domestic prices will
have to follow the world market price more closely (δ will
be larger), except in the case of importing countries under
conditions of a structural surplus. An increase in δ implies
that the macro demand function is more likely to have a
negative slope; if the value of δ increases more and more, a
point of equilibrium will always be found.

This is in fact the procedure followed in MOIRA for arriving
at an equilibrium situation. Between two successive years
prices should in principle be within bounds of ±100 with
respect to last year's price. Within these boundaries δ is
increased until either equilibrum is reached or $\delta = 0.95$. If
the latter occurs, equilibrium is searched for outside the
boundaries.

(b) *Stock changes*

     Countries may also react to world market changes by
adaptation of food stocks; in point of fact, they will do so
not only in the case of a threatening disequilibrium in the
world market, but rather use this device more generally as a
policy measure offsetting part of the fluctuation in market
conditions. In case of rising prices, an importing country
will be inclined to use up part of its food stock. An exporting country, too, may run down its stocks in as far as
this does not spoil the market. In case of expected surpluses, an exporter may decide to build up stocks rather
than to sell at very low prices; an importer may also enlarge
its food stock if the world market price is considered to be
unusually low or if higher prices are expected in the future.

All this implies that at the level of the world market both
sellers and buyers will even out part of a surplus or a
shortage by building up or running down food stocks. In
terms of the market situation it means that supply is being
adapted to a certain extent. Obviously, the possibility of
using up food stocks is limited by the fact that stocks
cannot become negative.

In MOIRA, the buffer function of food stocks is assumed to
take place at world market level; there are no regional or
national food stocks in the model, and hence the possibility
of exhaustion of local stocks is not considered. The costs
of building up and maintaining stocks is not taken into
account explicitly; these costs do not affect the income
levels in individual countries, but are assumed to be borne
by existing stabilization funds of which in the long run
income and expenditure are by and large in balance. In other
words, it is assumed that stabilization funds already exist.
Empirical data about food stock fluctuations and production
fluctuations clearly point in this direction; stock changes
and production changes show a strong correlation, and food

stocks are very large as compared to the volume of world food trade (their ratio usually being larger than 1).

We may summarize this by saying that in MOIRA a central authority is assumed to exist that buys and sells food in exchange for non-agricultural product (*money*). As the authority is supposed to be an outside actor, it performs a partial slack function. This approach was chosen in order to avoid such questions as where actually the stocks are being held and who finances them. As a consequence, the income flows in the model are not fully closed. This conflicts with the general equilibrium approach, so that in further work this shortcoming must be cured.

The introduction of food stocks modifies, of course, the availability of food. In any year, the initially planned net exports to the world market (assuming no change in the world market price level) will as a rule not be equal to the initially planned imports of food. It is assumed now that part of the gap between intended net exports and intended net imports is covered by a positive or negative change in stocks; the parameters in MOIRA indicating the fraction of the gap that is covered by a stock change are called the stabilization fractions and are labeled STABWEA and STABFR, respectively.

STABWEA takes care of a part (usually 90 per cent) of the output fluctuations caused by weather disturbances, while STABFR covers a part (usually 80 per cent) of the remaining supply/demand gap. The consequences of weather fluctuations are dealt with separately because it has been assumed that traders are aware of past weather conditions and tend to buffer out these fluctuations. The numerical values of the two stabilization parameters are chosen somewhat arbitrarily. The above values have been chosen in order to reach reasonable price and stock fluctuations over the historical period.

As can easily be understood, the results from MOIRA would become quite unstable if the two parameters would be set at very low values. Therefore, it is important for an improvement of the model to get a better understanding of the role of stocks in food trade. To come back to MOIRA as it actually is: after the stock adjustment has taken place, the price adjustment procedure as described before is called and a world market equilibrium is computed.

Appendix 7A

THE DEMAND FUNCTION; FOOD TRADE

7A.1 *THE DEMAND FUNCTION AND ITS PROPERTIES: EXPLICIT SOLUTION*

7A.1.1 The demand function

Recall the budget equation in its modified form as derived in Appendix 6A.2; instead of R_{i2} we write NR_i in (6A.38):

$$NVLU_i + (DFP-DFPE)CTYC_i = DFP.NCONS_i + NPI.NR_i \qquad (7A.1)$$

The specification of the consumption function was given in Chapter 5; we repeat (5.3), writing $NCONS_i$ instead of $CONS_{i2}$:

$$NCONS_i = \min\left(\frac{NR_i}{FP^s},\ ACONS+BCONS(\sqrt{NR_i+CCONS}-\sqrt{CCONS})\right) \qquad (7A.2)$$

In view of this specification, we have to distinguish between the two value ranges of the consumption function, as it was done also in Chapter 5 and Appendix 5A. (The superscript of FP will not be repeated in this Appendix).

(a) $NR_i \geq NR^G$

From (7A.1) and (7A.2) we have

$$NVLU_i + (DFP-DFPE)CTYC_i =$$
$$DFP\left[ACONS+BCONS(\sqrt{NR_i+CCONS}-\sqrt{CCONS})\right]+NPI.NR_i \qquad (7A.3)$$

Adding on both sides of (7A.3) the tern $NR_i.CCONS$, we obtain after rearranging terms

$$NPI.(NR_i+CCONS)+DFP.BCONS.\sqrt{NR_i+CCONS}\ +$$
$$+\ DFP(ACONS-BCONS\sqrt{CCONS})\ -\ NPI.CCONS-$$
$$-\ \left[NVLU_i+(DFP-DFPE)CTYC_i\right] = 0 \qquad (7A.4)$$

This is a quadratic equation in $\sqrt{NR_i+CCONS}$. We define the

root multiplied by 2NPI as U*; hence, $U^* = 2NPI.\sqrt{NR_i + CCONS}$.
If the discriminant of the quadratic equation is not negative,
we have from (7A.4):

$$U^*_{1,2} = \frac{-DFP.BCONS \pm \sqrt{(DFP.BCONS)^2 + 4NPI[NVLU_i + (DFP-DFPE)CTYC_i +}}{+NPI.CCONS-DFP(ACONS-BCONS\sqrt{CCONS})]} \qquad (7A.5)$$

We have to verify now whether or not the discriminant could
be negative. We define an auxiliary variable X equal to the
expression between [ ] in (7A.5):

$$X \equiv NVLU_i + (DFP-DFPE)CTYC_i + NPI.CCONS-DFP(ACONS-BCONS\sqrt{CCONS}) \qquad (7A.6)$$

From (7A.1) we see that the sign of the expression
$[NVLU_i + (DFP-DFPE)CTYC_i]$ is the same as that of $(DFP.NCONS_i + +NPI.NR_i)$. Is the latter expression necessarily positive?
For DFP > 0 it is positive indeed, but what happens if DFP < 0?
As we are discussing the case of $NR_i \geq NR^G$, we know that
$NCONS_i \leq \frac{NR_i}{FP}$, and therefore $DFP.\frac{NR_i}{FP} \leq DFP.NCONS_i$ when
DFP < 0. Consequently, also

$$DFP \frac{NR_i}{FP} + NPI.NR_i \leq DFP.NCONS_i + NPI.NR_i$$

Earlier already (Chapter 7.3.1.2) it has been stated that
DFP + NPI.FP > 0, and therefore we have (also for DFP < 0):

$$DFP.NCONS_i + NPI.NR_i > 0$$

As a corollary, we find a lower limit to the effective value
of DFP at the national level; as it is required that
$NVLU_i \geq -(DFP-DFPE)CTYC_i$, the lower limit to DFP(DFP < 0) is:

$$DFP \geq \frac{-NVLU_i}{CTYC_i} + DFPE \qquad (7A.7)$$

Substituting now the right-hand side of (7A.1) in (7A.6), we
have

$$X = DFP.NCONS_i + NPI.NR_i + NPI.CCONS-DFP.ACONS+DFP.BCONS\sqrt{CCONS}$$

As we are dealing with the case $NR_i \geq NR^G$, we know that
$NCONS_i > ACONS$; as moreover BCONS and CCONS are positive, we
find that $X \geq 0$.

This result has two implications:
(1)   for $NR_i \geq NR^G$ the discriminant of (7A.5) is not negative,
       and we have two real roots U*;
(2)   the product of the two roots is not positive, as
       $U^*_1.U^*_2 = -X/NPI$. Thus, one of the roots is positive (U^*_1)

and the other negative (U_2^*). In (7A.5) the largest
value is obtained by taking the positive sign before
the square root of the discriminant. This gives us the
positive root U_1^*.

Summarizing, we find that for $NR_i \geq NR^G$ the system yields
one and only one positive solution:

$$U_1^* = -DFP.BCONS + \sqrt{(DFP.BCONS)^2 + 4NPI.X} \qquad (7A.8)$$

Substitution of this result in $U^* = 2NPI.\sqrt{NR_i+CCONS}$ gives us
the value of $\sqrt{NR_i+CCONS}$, and further substitution of this
finding in the consumption function (7A.2) leads to $NCONS_i$.

(b) $NR_i < NR^G$

From (7A.1) and (7A.2) now follows

$$NVLU_i+(DFP-DFPE)CTYC_i = DFP.NCONS_i+NPI.FP.NCONS_i$$

and we find at once the value of $NCONS_i$ as

$$NCONS_i = \frac{NVLU_i+(DFP-DFPE)CTYC_i}{DFP+NPI.FP} \qquad (7A.9)$$

Also in this case, the restriction (7A.7) on the value range
of DFP holds.

The explicit solution obtained under (a) and (b) is mentioned
in the main text of Chapter 7 under equations (7.16) - (7.18).

7A.1.2 *Properties of the demand function*

In this section, we want to analyze the behaviour
of the first and the second derivative of the demand function.
We start from the explicit solution given by (7.16) - (7.18).
For DFPE we substitute the expression in terms of DFP and
DFPE* as given by (7.10).

Firstly, we take the case $NCONS_i \geq NCONS^G$; using (7.10) we
repeat (7.16) and (7.17):

$$NCONS_i = ACONS + \frac{BCONS}{2.NPI} \left[-DFP.BCONS + \right.$$

$$\left. + \sqrt{(DFP.BCONS)^2+4.NPI.X} \right]-BCONS\sqrt{CCONS}$$

$$\qquad (7A.10)$$

with

$$X = NVLU_i + \left[(1-\delta)DFP-(1-\delta)DFPE* \right]CTYC_i+NPI.CCONS-$$

$$-DFP(ACONS-BCONS\sqrt{CCONS}) \qquad (7A.11)$$

Differentiation with respect to DFP gives

$$\frac{dNCONS_i}{dDFP} = \frac{BCONS}{2.NPI} \left[-BCONS + \right.$$

$$\left. + \frac{BCONS^2.DFP+2NPI[(1-\delta)CTYC_i-ACONS+BCONS\sqrt{CCONS}]}{\sqrt{(DFP.BCONS)^2 + 4NPI.X}} \right]$$

(7A.12)

We determine now what value the first derivative will take when the world market price DFP increases towards infinity.

$$\lim_{DFP \to \infty} \frac{dNCONS_i}{dDFP} = \frac{BCONS}{2.NPI} (-BCONS + \frac{BCONS^2+0}{BCONS})$$

$$\lim_{DFP \to \infty} \frac{dNCONS_i}{dDFP} = 0$$

(7A.13)

What level of $NCONS_i$ corresponds with this limit? We introduce the auxiliary variable Q:

$$Q \equiv -DFP.BCONS+\sqrt{(DFP.BCONS)^2 + 4.NPI.X}$$

Hence, from (7A.10),

$$\lim_{DFP \to \infty} NCONS_i = ACONS-BCONS\sqrt{CCONS} + \frac{BCONS}{2.NPI} \lim_{DFP \to \infty} Q$$

(7A.14)

$$Q = \frac{[-DFP.BCONS + \sqrt{(DFP.BCONS)^2 +4.NPI.X}]}{-DFP.BCONS - \sqrt{(DFP.BCONS)^2 + 4.NPI.X}} *$$

$$* [-DFP.BCONS - \sqrt{(DFP.BCONS)^2+4.NPI.X}]$$

$$Q = \frac{(DFP.BCONS)^2- (DFP.BCONS)^2- 4.NPI.X}{-DFP.BCONS - \sqrt{(DFP.BCONS)^2+ 4.NPI.X}}$$

or, dividing numerator and denominator at the right-hand side by DFP,

$$Q = \frac{-4.NPI \frac{X}{DFP}}{-BCONS - \sqrt{BCONS^2 + 4.NPI \frac{X}{DFP^2}}}$$

Consequently, in view of (7A.11):

$$\lim_{DFP \to \infty} Q = \frac{4.NPI[(1-\delta)CTYC_i-ACONS+BCONS\sqrt{CCONS}]}{2BCONS}$$

(7A.15)

Substitution of (7A.15) in (7A.14) gives

$$\lim_{DFP \to \infty} NCONS_i = (1-\delta)CTYC_i \qquad (7A.16)$$

In words: when DFP approaches infinity, $NCONS_i$ approaches asymtotically towards $(1-\delta)CTYC_i$.

This result was obtained for $NCONS_i \geq NCONS^G$. Turning now to the case $NCONS_i < NCONS^G$, we rewrite (7.18) using (7.10):

$$NCONS_i = \frac{NVLU_i + [(1-\delta)DFP - (1-\delta)DFPE^*]CTYC_i}{DFP+NPI.FP} \qquad (7A.17)$$

Differentiation of (7A.17) with respect to DFP gives

$$\frac{dNCONS_i}{dDFP} = \frac{(DFP-NPI.FP)(1-\delta)CTYC_i - NVLU_i}{(DFP+NPI.FP)^2} -$$

$$- \frac{[(1-\delta)DFP - (1-\delta)DFPE^*]CTYC_i}{(DFP.NPI.FP)^2}$$

or

$$\frac{dNCONS_i}{dDFP} = \frac{(NPI.FP+DFPE^*)(1-\delta)CTYC_i - NVLU_i}{(DFP+NPI.FP)^2} \qquad (7A.18)$$

It follows immediately that we have, also for $NCONS_i < NCONS^G$,

$$\lim_{DFP \to \infty} \frac{dNCONS_i}{dDFP} = 0$$

The corresponding value of $NCONS_i$ follows at once when we devide the numerator and denominator of (7A.17) by DFP:

$$\lim_{DFP \to \infty} NCONS_i = (1-\delta)CTYC_i$$

which is again the same result as in the first case.

Furthermore, we want to establish the sign of the second derivative of the demand function. This is done most conveniently starting from the first derivative as given by (7.7), i.e. without bringing in for the moment the specification of the consumption function. We repeat (7.7) for convenience:

$$\frac{dNCONS_i}{dDFP} = \frac{(1-\delta)CTYC_i - NCONS_i}{DFP+NPI\dfrac{dNR_i}{dNCONS_i}} \qquad (7.7)$$

Writing D for the denominator of the expression at the right-hand side, the second derivative is

$$
\frac{d^2NCONS_i}{dDFP^2} = \frac{-D\cdot\dfrac{dNCONS_i}{dDFP}}{D^2} -
$$

$$
- \frac{\left[(1-\delta)CTYC_i-NCONS\right]\left[1+NPI\cdot\dfrac{d^2NR_i}{dNCONS^2}\cdot\dfrac{dNCONS_i}{dDFP}\right]}{D^2}
$$

or, dividing numerator and denominator at the right-hand side by D, and using (7.7),

$$
\frac{d^2NCONS_i}{dDFP^2} = \frac{-\dfrac{dNCONS_i}{dDFP}-\dfrac{dNCONS_i}{dDFP}\left[1+NPI\cdot\dfrac{d^2NR}{dNCONS^2}\cdot\dfrac{dNCONS_i}{dDFP}\right]}{D}
$$

and therefore

$$
\frac{d^2NCONS_i}{dDFP^2} = \frac{-\left[2\dfrac{dNCONS_i}{dDFP}+NPI\cdot\dfrac{d^2NR_i}{dNCONS_i^2}\cdot\left(\dfrac{dNCONS_i}{dFP}\right)^2\right]}{DFP+NPI\cdot\dfrac{dNR_i}{dNCONS_i}}
$$

$$(7A.19)$$

In Appendix 5A it was shown that $dNCONS_i/dNR_i > 0$, for both segments of the consumption function; the denominator of (7A.19) is always positive. The sign of the second derivative depends, therefore, on the sign of the numerator. At this stage, we have to introduce again the specification of the consumption function, and to distinguish between its two value ranges.

(a) $NCONS_i \geq NCONS^G$

As was shown in (5A.18), $dNR_i/dNCONS_i = 2\sqrt{NR_i+CCONS}/BCONS$. The second term in the consumption function is $\sqrt{NR_i+CCONS}$; we may rewrite this term as $\tfrac{1}{2}BCONS^2(2\sqrt{NR_i+CCONS}/BCONS)$ which allows us to obtain the result

$$
\frac{d^2NR_i}{dNCONS_i^2} = \frac{2}{BCONS^2}
$$

The value of the numerator of (7A.19) is, therefore,

$$
-\left[2\frac{dNCONS_i}{dDFP}+\frac{2\cdot NPI}{BCONS^2}\cdot\left(\frac{dNCONS_i}{dDFP}\right)^2\right]
$$

As the second term is always positive, we have:

if $\dfrac{dNCONS_i}{dDFP} \geqq 0$

then $\dfrac{d^2NCONS_i}{dDFP^2} < 0$

For the value range of the first derivative $dNCONS_i/dDFP < 0$, we have two possibilities for the sign of the second derivative. The second derivative is positive if

$$2\,\frac{dNCONS_i}{dDFP} < -\frac{2.NPI}{BCONS^2} \cdot \left(\frac{dNCONS_i}{dDFP}\right)^2$$

or

$$1 > -\frac{NPI}{BCONS^2} \cdot \frac{dNCONS_i}{dDFP}$$

Thus,

$$\frac{d^2NCONS_i}{dDFP^2} > 0, \qquad \text{if} \qquad 0 > \frac{dNCONS_i}{dDFP} > -\frac{BCONS^2}{NPI}$$

Similarly

$$\frac{d^2NCONS_i}{dDFP^2} < 0, \qquad \text{if} \qquad \frac{dNCONS_i}{dDFP} < -\frac{BCONS^2}{NPI}$$

(b) $NCONS_i < NCONS^G$

From (5A.21) we recall that $dNR_i/dNCONS_i = FP$. Hence, $d^2NR/dNCONS_i^2 = 0$. The numerator of (7A.19) in this case is reduced to

$$-2\,\frac{dNCONS_i}{dDFP}$$

and the sign of the second derivative is opposite to that of the first derivative.

7A.2 *FOOD TRADE IN RELATION TO INCOME LEVEL*

Consider again (7A.1), for a consumption level $NCONS_i$:

$$NVLU_i + (DFP-DFPE)\,CTYC_i = DFP.NCONS_i + NPI.NR_i\,(NCONS_i)$$

together with the definition of an auxiliary variable $NVLUA_i$:

$$NVLUA_i \equiv DFPE \cdot CTYC_i + NPI.NR_i(CTYC_i) \qquad (7A.20)$$

in which

$NVLUA_i$ = nominal per capita income at which total food supply
by the domestic agricultural sector to income class i
will be consumed by income class i.

From these two equations it follows that

$$NVLU_i - NVLUA_i = DFP(NCONS_i - CTYC_i) +$$
$$+ NPI\left[NR_i(NCONS_i) - NR_i(CTYC_i)\right] \qquad (7A.21)$$

We want to determine what can be said about the sign of
$(NVLU_i - NVLUA_i)$, given the sign of $(NCONS_i - CTYC_i)$; and
vice versa. This will lead to a formal proof of the lemma
stating that

(a) $CTYC_i > NCONS_i \iff NVLUA_i > NVLU_i$

(b) $CTYC_i < NCONS_i \iff NVLUA_i < NVLU_i$

(c) $CTYC_i = NCONS_i \iff NVLUA_i = NVLU_i$

This lemma is identical with the lemma used in Chapter 7.2.2
for $\delta = 0$. The more general case of Chapter 7.2.2 with
$0 \leq \delta < 1$ can be demonstrated along the same lines by introducing the auxiliary variable NVLUB as defined in (7.11)
instead of NVLUA. Here we limit ourselves to $\delta = 0$.

We start from the situation in which the sign of
$(NCONS_i - CTYC_i)$ is known.

(a)   Assume $NCONS_i > CTYC_i$

    In Appendix 5A.2 it was shown that $NR_i \geq FP.NCONS_i$; see
(5A.30). The equality sign applies in case all income is spent
on food. This inequality may also be specified for the consumption level $(NCONS_i - CTYC_i)$. The corresponding income level
is $NR_i(NCONS_i - CTYC_i)$; note that the latter expression indicates
an income level, and that it should not be read as a multiplication. Thus,

$$NR_i(NCONS_i - CTYC_i) \geq FP.(NCONS_i - CTYC_i)$$

Multiplying both sides with -NPI, gives

$$-NPI.NR_i(NCONS_i - CTYC_i) \leq -NPI.FP.(NCONS_i - CTYC_i)$$

In view of the lower boundary on the world market price DFP,
we know that $DFP+NPI.FP \geq 0$, so that

$$DFP(NCONS_i - CTYC_i) \geq -NPI.FP.(NCONS_i - CTYC_i)$$

Thus, from the last two statements

$$DFP(NCONS_i - CTYC_i) \geq -NPI.NR_i(NCONS_i - CTYC_i) \qquad (7A.22)$$

Compare (7A.22) and (7A.21), and note that indeed $(NVLU_i-NVLUA_i)$ will have the same sign as $(NCONS_i-CTYC_i)$ if

$$-NPI.NR_i(NCONS_i-CTYC_i) \geq -NPI[NR_i(NCONS_i)-NR_i(CTYC_i)]$$

or, after deviding both side by $-NPI$, if

$$NR_i(NCONS_i-CTYC_i) \leq NR_i(NCONS_i)-NR_i(CTYC_i) \qquad (7A.23)$$

Using the properties of the consumption function, it is easy to show that (7A.23) holds indeed. If $NR_i(NCONS_i) < NR^G$, the consumption function is linear, and so is $NR_i = NR(NCONS_i)$; hence, in this case in (7A.23) the equality sign applies. If $NR_i > NR^G$, the consumption curve is monotonously rising and concave downwards; consequently, $NR_i = NR(NCONS_i)$ is monotonously rising and (weakly) concave upwards. We apply now the theorem of mean value. There are two cases

(1) $(NCONS_i - CTYC_i) \leq CTYC_i$, and
(2) $(NCONS_i - CTYC_i) > CTYC_i$

ad (1) $(NCONS_i-CTYC_i) \leq CTYC_i$; see fig. 7A.1

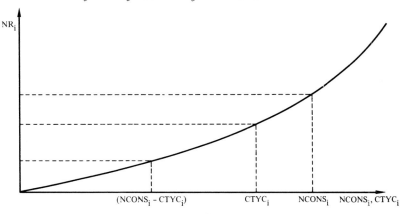

Fig. 7A.1

Income-consumption curve with $(NCONS_i - CTYC_i) \leq CTYC_i$

The theorem of mean value states:

$$\frac{NR_i(NCONS_i-CTYC_i)}{NCONS_i-CTYC_i} = NR'(\phi), \text{ with } \phi \in (0,NCONS_i-CTYC_i)$$

and

$$\frac{NR_i(NCONS_i) - NR_i(CTYC_i)}{NCONS_i - CTYC_i} = NR'(\psi), \text{ with } \psi \in (CTYC_i, NCONS_i)$$

Thus, for $(NCONS_i - CTYC_i) \leq CTYC_i$ we find that $\psi \geq \phi$ and there-fore $NR'(\psi) \geq NR'(\phi)$. Hence,

$$NR_i(NCONS_i) - NR_i(CTYC_i) \geq NR_i(NCONS_i - CTYC_i).$$

ad (2) $(NCONS_i - CTYC_i) > CTYC_i;$ *see fig. 7A.2*

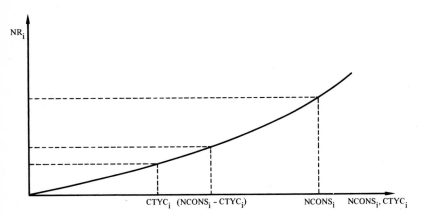

Fig. 7A.2

Income-cnsumption curve with $(NCONS_i - CTYC_i) > CTYC_i$

According to the theorem of mean value, we have in fig. 7A.2

$$\frac{NR_i(CTYC_i)}{CTYC_i} = NR'(\phi), \text{ with } \phi \in (0, CTYC_i)$$

and

$$\frac{NR_i(NCONS_i) - NR_i(NCONS_i - CTYC_i)}{NCONS_i - (NCONS_i - CTYC_i)} = NR'(\psi), \text{ with}$$

$$\psi \in = \left((NCONS_i - CTYC_i), NCONS_i \right)$$

From the latter result, we have

$$NR_i(NCONS_i) = NR_i(NCONS_i - CTYC_i) + CTYC_i \cdot NR'(\psi)$$

Deducting now from both sides of the equality sign $NR_i(CTYC_i)$, while

$$NR_i(CTYC_i) = CTYC_i \cdot NR'(\phi),$$

we obtain

$$NR_i(NCONS_i) - NR_i(CTYC_i) = NR_i(NCONS_i - CTYC_i) +$$
$$+ CTYC_i [NR'(\psi) - NR'(\phi)]$$

In this equation, the last term at the right-hand side is positive, as $CTYC_i > 0$ and $NR'(\psi) > NR'(\phi)$. Thus, also in the case of $(NCONS_i - CTYC_i) > CTYC_i$, we find

$$NR_i(NCONS_i) - NR_i(CTYC_i) > NR_i(NCONS_i - CTYC_i)$$

It has been demonstrated now that (7A.23) holds; it has been shown, therefore, that if $NCONS_i > CTYC_i$, then $NVLU_i > NVLUA_i$.

(b) Assume $NCONS_i < CTYC_i$

Multiplication of both sides of (7A.21) by -1 shows that in the present case the proof of the lemma is exactly similar to that of case (a). If $NCONS_i < CTYC_i$, then $NVLU_i < NVLUA_i$.

(c) Assume $NCONS_i = CTYC_i$

From (7A.21) it is obvious that in this case $NVLU_i = NVLUA_i$.

This concludes the necessity proof of our statement about the sign of $(NVLU_i - NVLUA_i)$ when the sign of $(NCONS_i - CTYC_i)$ is known. An additional sufficiency proof is not required, as the analysis of Appendix 7A.1 has shown that the demand function has a unique solution for all acceptable parameter values (including those of $NVLU_i$ and $NVLUA_i$).

Thus far, we have demonstrated that

if	$CTYC_i > NCONS_i$,	then	$NVLUA_i > NVLU_i$
if	$CTYC_i < NCONS_i$,	then	$NVLUA_i < NVLU_i$
if	$CTYC_i = NCONS_i$,	then	$NVLUA_i = NVLU_i$

Expressed in a system of axes, this implies that the second and fourth quadrant are excluded (empty sets). This property of the system is not affected by the choice of any of the two variables (income level or consumption level) as the independent variable. Hence, the conditions just specified may also be reversed: if $NVLUA_i > NVLU_i$, then $CTYC_i > NCONS_i$; and so on. This completes the proof of the theorem stated in the beginning of Appendix 7A.2.

Chapter 8

THE EXOGENCUS VARIABLES

8.1 *INTRODUCTION*

A model seeks to explain variations of variables by
searching for invariable relationships between them (the
structure), and showing the possible dependency of those
variations. In this manner the variation of one part of the
model's variables will be explained (endogenous variables)
but not the variations of another part (the exogenous variables). This does not negate the possible existence of
causal relationships by which endogenous variables exert an
influence on exogenous ones. For several reasons, however,
these relationships will not be described.

One of these reasons (and perhaps the most important) is
lack of knowledge: the explanation of a variable nearly
always requires its own model and its onw research effort.
Therefore, a researcher is usually confined to one sector,
and has to describe this sector given the development of its
environment; the model builder will usually translate the
latter condition in the variation of certain exogenous
variables. This implies that certain influences, i.e. the
impact of the function and results of the study object on
its environment (say the exogenous variables) will not be
described or, in other words, will be neglected. In other
instance, more knowledge is available and the model builder
might not be justified in neglecting these relationships.

For example: if we wish to report on food consumption in a
certain country but the factors underlying population growth
in that country are not known to us, we shall have to treat
population as an exogenous variable. This will imply that of
the two relationships (the influence of population on food
consumption and vice versa), the latter will have to be
neglected and only the first will be taken into account:
food consumption is described, taking population growth as a
given. An illustration is given in fig. 8.1.

In this scheme f is a relationship (e.g. $y = ax + z$) which
explains variations in y from variations in the endogenous
variable x and the endogenous variable z. Arrow b represents
all influences exerted by endogenous on exogenous variables
which are either neglected or non-existent.

It should be emphasized that what is exogenous is dependent

Fig. 8.1

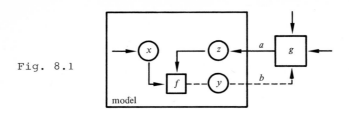

on the scope of the study object. For example, the price
which the farmer receives for his product is an exogenous
variable in his own thinking, but it is an endogenous variable in the model as a whole. To sum up, exogenous variables
have three characteristics: they are indispensable for the
explanation given in the model; the explanation of the
variable itself is beyond the knowledge of the model builder;
and relationships of type b are neglected.

Below we shall discuss some of the more important exogenous
variables in the model. The sensitivity of MOIRA simulation
results for alternative assumptions regarding some of the
exogenous variables will be discussed in Chapter 10.

8.2   *POPULATION GROWTH*

The growth rate of population per country is an exogenous variable in MOIRA. Although many divergent views
exist on population growth, there seems to be a consensus
that a doubling of world population will occur within about
35 years, that is - starting from 1975 - before the year
2010. Even if fertility rates declined rapidly, this would
only produce a strongly lagged effect on aggregate population.
Mortality rates might be influenced by starvation; this
effect is neglected in the model.

Population growth has in MOIRA a direct impact in two ways.
First, on the demand side, as the size of the population and
its distribution over income groups influences food consumption and thereby food deficits (cf. Chapter 5). Second, on
the supply side: the natural growth rate of population
influences the size of agricultural population and thereby
agricultural output (cf. Chapter 4).

The growth rate of population is therefore an important
variable for the model. Many demographic theories exist to
explain this growth rate, in particular its decline from a
rather high to a rather low level. One of the demographic
transition theories is the threshold hypothesis[1] according
to which fertility rates will decrease and stabilize at a
certain level when a particular threshold in economic growth

---

[1] See UN, *The Determinants and Consequences of Population Trends*
   (New York, 1973) Vol. 1

has been attained. Below this threshold, population will
increase, principally due to a decreasing mortality rate,
caused by the fact that economic growth is usually accompanied by better nutrition, health care etc. Attempts to
define threshold characteristics and to identify cause and
effects have not yet been successful. On the contrary,
recent experiences support the view that fertility rates
might decrease while average incomes are far below the so-
called threshold level, provided that modern commodities and
services are distributed among a large majority of the
population[2].

On the whole, people seem to behave fairly rationally and
seem to hold certain expectations (length of life of children, security for old age etc.). Fertility rates therefore
vary very slowly. This could be considered as a partial
justification of our exogenous treatment of population
growth.

In this study use is made of the most recent United Nations
population projections, which have been adjusted by the
World Bank[3]. These give growth rates for five-year periods,
based on different assumptions, for the period 1970 until
2000, for each IBRD-member country and on a regional basis
for non-Bank member countries. To these figures we have
added another series for the year 2005, calculated on the
basis of trends per country. The countries were subsequently
regrouped according to our country basis (of 106 countries)
and the five-year base was changed to one-year figures in
order to smooth the abrupt change in growth rates every five
years.

Of the three IBRD variants the *fast fertility decline* variant (projection A) has been used in the standard simulation
run of MOIRA. The decrease in fertility assumed in the fast
variant is shown in table 8.1.

Table 8.1

Pattern of the assumed fast fertility decline

Gross Reproduction Rate (GRR)	Rate of Annual Decline (in %)
< 1.5	1
1.5 - 2.0	2
2.0 - 2.6	3
2.5 - 3.0	2
> 3.0	1

[2] See W. Rich, *Smaller Families Through Social and Economic Progress* (Washington, 1973).

[3] K.C. Zachariah and R. Cica, *Population Projections for Bank Member Countries 1970 - 2000* (World Bank, Development Economic Department, Pop. and Human Res. Div.).

The *moderate decline* variant follows an intermediate course, between the fast variant and a constant GRR[4]. Both projections follow the same decrease in the mortality rate. The population levels corresponding with the *fast* and the *moderate* fertility decline variants are shown in Table 8.2. According to the more 'optimistic' projection A adhered to in MOIRA, world population will double in the year 2010. The ratio of population in developed and less developed countries changes from 1:2:25 in 1970 to 1:3:8 in 2010. Only 10% of the increase occurs in the developed countries, and the remaining 90% in the less developed countries (incl. China).

Table 8.3

Projected population of specified countries under projection A in millions

	1970	1980	1990	2000	2010	% growth 1970-2010
Asian centrally planned economies	803	951	1,105	1,265	1,467	75
India	538	674	818	975	1,156	115
Pakistan (incl. Bangla Desh)	132	117	239	307	409	210
Indonesia	121	161	208	260	324	166
Brazil	93	121	150	181	217	134
Nigeria	55	72	94	120	151	175
Mexico	51	71	97	125	161	215
Philippines	37	51	71	93	121	226
Thailand	36	50	68	87	111	210
Turkey	35	46	57	70	85	143

8.3 *NON-AGRICULTURAL GDP*

As previously discussed in Chapter 7, MOIRA is essentially a two sector type of model in which an agricultural output is exogenous and taken as numéraire. Non-agricultural GDP is therefore an exogenous variable and probably the most important one as it equals primary non-agricultural income, which directly influences food consumption, migration and government policy. The lack of a solidly based feedback from agricultural development to non-agricultural production is probably one of the main limitations of this study. This is, however, a drawback of any model with specific sectoral emphasis.

The growth rates of non-agricultural GDP are exogenously specified for five year periods until 2010. In order to

---

[4] GRR is the sum of age-specific birth rates of women of 15 to 49 years, restricted to female births only. It is a measure of the average number of daughters a woman would have if she experienced a given set of age-specific birth rates throughout her reproductive years.

Table 8.2

Projected population by region (in millions)

	(A) fast fertility decline					(B) moderate fertility decline				
	1970	1980	1990	2000	2010	1970	1980	1990	2000	2010
North America	226	247	271	290	310	226	248	275	298	323
Western Europe	395	426	457	489	524	395	428	464	503	548
Japan	104	117	126	132	140	104	117	126	132	140
Rest of the Developed Market Economies	42	51	60	70	83	42	51	62	76	92
Eastern Europe	348	378	407	432	464	348	380	412	438	472
Sub total developed countries	1,115	1,219	1,321	1,413	1,521	1,115	1,224	1,339	1,447	1,575
Latin America	292	385	492	604	742	292	388	508	648	829
North Africa and the Middle East	134	181	244	317	409	134	183	252	344	468
Main Africa	264	344	442	555	698	264	344	452	594	780
South and S.E. Asia	1,016	1,303	1,633	1,992	2,440	1,016	1,313	1,709	2,209	2,861
Centrally Planned Asia	803	951	1,105	1,265	1,467	803	973	1,172	1,398	1,682
Sub total less developed countries	2,509	3,164	3,916	4,733	5,756	2,509	3,201	4,093	5,193	6,620
TOTAL	3,624	4,383	5,237	6,146	7,277	3,624	4,425	5,432	6,640	8,195

avoid artificial jumps from one five-year period to the
next, on the base of this information a smoothed series of
yearly growth rates is generated (procedure SMOOTH1 and
SMOOTH2 in the simulation program)[5]. For countries with non-
agricultural GDP per capita below $400 (in $ of 1965) the
resulting non-agricultural GDP is checked against a norm (to
be discussed below), and the smallest of the two is the
effective non-agricultural GDP. Table 8.4 shows the share of
agriculture in total GDP of a country.

Table 8.4

Agricultural (V) and total GDP in 1976: selected countries

Country	V 10^6 $	GDP 10^6 $	V/GDP in %
USA	20,838	694,637	3
Japan	11,908	90,932	12
India	18,354	39,951	46
Brazil	6,810	22,720	30
Ghana	916	2,298	40

Source: U.N. *Yearbook of National Accounts Statistics 1968.*

8.3.1 *Growth rates of non-agricultural GDP*

The assumed growth rates of non-agricultural GDP
are based on projections of total GDP. Any set of long-term
GDP projections is based to a large extent on a subjective
assessment of growth potentials and prospects, and is for
that reason open to criticism; obviously, the same is true
for the growth rates of non-agricultural GDP assumed in the
simulation runs of MOIRA.

The GDP projections underlying the non-agricultural growth
rates used in the simulation runs are taken from one of the
preparatory studies for the United Nations Global Model. The
final report on this model, *The Future of the World Economy*,
by Wassily Leontief *et al*, shows GDP growth rates only for
the entire period of 1970-2000. The preparatory study referred to above[6] gives ten-yearly GDP growth rates for
fifteen regions of the world. The regions were selected by
means of such criteria as GNP per capita, the percentages of
urban population and the share of manufacturing in GNP. The
Leontief-team relied for its projections on estimates of the
World Bank[7] which take into account changes in the economic

---

[5] This smoothing also applies to the exogenous growth rates of population
and of fertilizer prices.

[6] W. Leontief, *Impact of Prospective Environmental Issues and Policies
on the International Development Strategy.*

[7] IBRD, *Additional External Capital Requirements for Developing Countries*
(Washington DC), March 1974.

relations subsequent to the recent increase in oil prices. The different variants (high, medium and low) take as their starting point assumptions concerning the capacity and speed of adjustment of the developing countries to the new relations. The GDP growth rates assumed in the medium-variant are (in percent per annum) on the average, for the two blocks of the developing and the developed countries, respectively:

	1970-80	1980-90	1990-2000	2000-2010
Developing countries	5.8	6.6	6.5	6.0
Developed market economies	5.0	4.9	4.5	3.6

For our purpose, these overall growth rates had to be translated into growth rates of non-agricultural GDP only. As the rate of growth of agricultural income is, historically speaking, always in the long run lower than that of all other sectors combined, the overall growth rates were revised upward in order to arrive at non-agricultural growth projections. For the richest developed countries, with a small agricultural sector, these upward corrections were virtually zero; for poor countries with a large agrarian sector the upward corrections amounted to a few percentage points. The crudeness of the resulting estimates will be obvious from the procedure just described. Table 8.5 shows the resulting growth rates of non-agricultural GDP; the country estimates on which Table 8.5 is based are used in the so-called standard run of MOIRA discussed in Chapter 10.

Table 8.5

Average growth rate non-agricultural GDP, central run

Region	1975-'85	1985-'95	1995-'05
North America	4.1	3.9	3.5
European Community	4.1	3.9	3.4
Other Western Europe	5.6	5.7	5.5
Japan	6.1	4.8	4.1
Australia etc.	5.3	5.6	5.2
Latin America	7.1	7.2	7.2
Middle East	11.6	9.0	7.1
Tropical Africa*	6.1	6.0	7.2
Southern Asia*	4.9	3.9	4.5
Sahel*	2.5	6.7	6.7
WORLD	5.0	4.8	4.5
Developing countries	7.6	7.1	6.8
Developed market economies	4.5	4.2	3.8
Centrally planned economies	6.5	6.4	5.8

*The influence of the corrections due to the upper limit on non-agricultural GDP growth (see 8.3.2) can be detected.

8.3.2 *Upper limit on non-agricultural GDP growth in the poorest countries*

The growth of non-agricultural GDP is in point of fact not independent from the expansion of the agricultural sector. This is true in particular for the poorest countries. In these countries, the non-agricultural sector is dependent on agriculture to such an extent that its growth is closely related to that of the agricultural sector. In MOIRA the poorest countries are defined as those with a per capita income in the non-agricultural sector of less than $400 per annum (in $ of 1965). For the poorest countries it is assumed that the growth of non-agricultural GDP - which is in principle exogenously given - cannot surpass a certain norm.

This norm for non-agricultural GDP growth is derived from a Kuznets-type of relationship between the share of agriculture in total GDP, on the one hand, and the level of per capita income and the sectoral distribution of the labour force on the other. The relation is specified as

$$\frac{V}{GDP} = anv \left(\frac{L}{NPOP}\right)^{bnv} \left(\frac{GDP}{L+NPOP}\right)^{cnv} \tag{8.1}$$

in which

V   = agricultural gross domestic product
GDP = (total) gross domestic product
L   = agricultural population
NPOP = non-agricultural population, while
anv, bnv and cnv are parameters to be estimated.

The results of an OLS cross-section estimate over the 88 countries for which data were available are as follows:
ln (anv) = -2.009;   t-score 23.33
bnv   = 0.215;   t-score 3.90
cnv   = -0.356;   t-score 5.03
$R^2_{ln\left(\frac{V}{GDP}\right)}$ = 77.42 and $R^2\left(\frac{V}{GDP}\right)$ = 70.83

Given these parameter values, equation (8.1) is used for determining the upper limit of non-agricultural income growth for countries below the $400 level. The residual obtained in the estimation procedure is again interpreted as a country-specific deviation remaining constant over time. If we denote the share of agricultural income V in total income GDP as S (hence S = V/GDP), and if $\hat{S}$ stands for its estimated value, the structural deviation for country j is

$$(S_j/\hat{S}_j)_{1965}$$

We multiply the term at the right-hand side of (8.1) by

$$eps_j = (S_j/\hat{S}_j)_{1965} \cdot (1-marge).$$

Now it is assumed that the resulting relationship remains valid over time for the poorest countries, i.e. for any year t we have for country j

$$(S_j/\hat{S}_j)_t \geq S_j/\hat{S}_j)_{1965} \cdot (1-marge) \tag{8.2}$$

The value of the parameter marge is put at 0.2 in order to allow for a maximum deviation of twenty percent from the structural level of the share of agriculture in GDP. As non-agricultural gross value added NV is defined as NV = GDP-V, we can derive the upper limit of non-agricultural income as

$$NV_{max} = \left\{ \frac{V}{anv.eps} \cdot (\frac{NPOP}{L})^{bnv} \cdot (L+NPOP)^{cnv} \right\} \frac{1}{1+cnv} - V \qquad (8.3)$$

When in any particular year the exogenous growth rate of non-agricultural income according to 8.3.1 would lead for one of the poorest countries to a level of NV surpassing that of NV_{max} according to (8.3), the latter value is chosen instead.

8.3.3 *Growth rates in centrally planned economies*

In Ch. 4.7 it was explained how Centrally Planned Economies have been dealt with. The desired growth of non-agricultural GDP and growth of labour productivity have been treated as exogenous variables. The magnitude of growth rates in the base period is calculated in a calibration procedure.

In the simulation runs we shall take the growth rates des-cribed under Chapter 8.3.1 as the exogenous growth rate of GDP. If we assume that growth rates of GDP and of labour productivity have a fixed ratio, the latter can be taken as given. For this purpose the ratio calculated in the base period is used. If it is assumed that increase in labour productivity occurs exclusively in the form of embodied progress, the fixed ratio between the two growth rates implies that the capital-labour ratio is varying.

8.3.4 *Alternative growth rates*

To study the influence of uncertain income develop-ments in sectors other than agriculture, simulation runs under various assumption concerning non-agricultural growth rates have been carried out. One of these assumptions is the *low income growth* variant, in which the assumed growth rates are reduced to half their original value.

8.4 *CHANGES IN PRICE OF THE NON-AGRICULTURAL COMMODITY*

The model uses the non-agricultural GDP as numéraire so that all prices are expressed in units of non-agricultural GDP. This variable is expressed in US$ of 1965. In order to avoid the problem of expressing non-agricultural GDP - i.e. the variable NV - in constant prices for non-agricultural goods and variable prices for agricultural goods, the vari-able has been expressed in current prices during the cali-bration period. Therefore, the price increases for non-

agricultural commodities has to be introduced into the
model. For each country a so-called US$ inflation rate
(GNPI) had to be determined as the yearly percent change in
the produce of the price index for non-agricultural commodities multiplied by the exchange rate index. This GNPI cor-
rects price increases of non-foods via the non-foods price
index NPI; see the determination of real income in Chapter
5.2, eqs. (5.19)-(5.21).

The necessity to use *$-inflation* is illustrated by the fol-
lowing example.

Year	$-exchange rate	Cost of living index (non-foods) in pesos country	NPI non-food price index
t	1$ = 25 pesos	100	100
t+1	1$ = 30 pesos	150	125

Despite an appreciation of the dollar, its purchasing power
decreases because of rapid inflation. Cost-of-living indices
have been derived from the FAO Production Yearbooks and
multiplied by the *current* exchange rates given in the
Financial Accounts of the IMF. The NPI's found at the end of
the caliberation period are kept constant (until 2010),
since after this period the model either generates the
variables itself or has real exogenous values at its disposal.

8.5   *FERTILIZER PRICES*

Fertilizer is dealt with in the model as one aggregate
over different types of fertilizer. It enters the model as
the exogenous variable *average fertilizer costs*. In this
section we shall discuss the availability of artificial
fertilizer, and the prices paid by the farmers in each
country in the period 1965-2010.

8.5.1 *Fertilizer market and industry*

More than 90 percent of the supply of artificial
fertilizer is produced in the developed countries (incl.
Eastern Europe and USSR). This picture is being changed,
however, by faster growth in the less developed countries
(showing a growth rate of about 14 percent, compared with an
average of 5 per cent in developed countries). The distribution of consumption is shown in Table 8.6

In 1972/73 the ratio between the quantities of N, P_2O_5 and
K_2O was about 1:.6:.5. The LDC's have to rely on imports for
55 per cent of their consumption. The import bill for fertilizers amounted in 1970 to $550 millions, in 1973 to $1 bil-

Table 8.6

Total consumption of fertilizers (in million metric tons)

	1972/1973				Growth*'72-'80(%)			1980/1981 (est)			
	N	P	K	total	N	P	K	N	P	K	total
DC	16.8	13.4	10.4	40.6	4.2	3.2	3.3	23.3	17.1	13.4	53.8
LDC	6.6	3.1	1.8	11.5	8.4	15.0	16.4	12.7	9.7	6.0	28.2
CPE	12.6	6.1	6.6	25.3	6.8	9.5	8.8	21.4	12.7	13.0	47.1
World	36.1	22.6	18.7	77.4	6.0	7.2	7.0	57.4	39.4	32.4	129.2

*Postulated Annual compound growth rates.

lion (5.8 million tons) and in 1974 to $1.8 billion (4.9
million tons).

The artificial fertilizer industry - especially nitrogen -is
characterized by strong, fairly regular cycles in the level
of investments and product prices. The industry is capital-
intensive and economies of scale are only feasible in the
case of very large units. For technical reasons, however,
such units can operate effectively only at a high load
factor which reduces their flexibility (i.e. their ability
to adjust to demand by varying the load factors). The result
is a fairly inelastic supply in the short term. In the past,
price fluctuations have been heavy: a shortage or surplus of
1 to 1.5% caused a price change of more than 50%. Competition among suppliers is keen. The industry reacts immediately to demand, adjusting its capacity through investments.
This is feasible in the medium term because building times
are relatively short (2-3 years; somewhat longer in the
developing countries).

8.5.2 *Influence of price on demand*

The influence of the exogenous fertilizer price
on the endogenous fertilizer demand in MOIRA will be discussed below (as relations of type (a) shown in fig. 8.1).
The influence of demand on physical availability will be
examined in 8.5.3; these relations belong to type (b) as
shown in fig. 8.1.

The farmer's think model

We refer again to the farmer's *think model* as described in
Chapter 4.4.2, and repeat equation (4.17) defining his
income. As to fertilizer use, the farmer reacts to the price
of artificial fertilizer only; it enters his income equation
as an average cost FMON per unit of F.

$$V^* = (P^* \cdot Y - FMON_{t-1} \cdot F) \cdot A - CMON_{t-1} \cdot CE \qquad (8.4)$$

Fertilizer demand as such is not included in the farmer's

investment decision in the sense that F is not an independent
instrument variable in his model (in constrast to the quantity of capital goods that will be employed). In MOIRA, the
demand for fertilizer F depends directly on the level of
production Y via the linear land production function (4.7)
and therefore on capital employed CE.

The order of magnitude of fertilizer costs

The place which fertilizer costs occupy in costs as a whole
can be illustrated by figures derived from agricultural sector accounts (see Table 8.7).

The first row of percentages given in Table 8.7 shows fertilizer costs as fraction of the total purchases made by the
agricultural sector as a whole in other sectors (including
imported agricultural products such as seed, feed etc.). In
developing countries this represents a larger part of total
costs than in developed countries.

This percentage is far lower for the individual farmer when
fertilizer costs are measured against total intermediate
deliveries of agricultural products inside the agricultural
sector; see row 4 (we assume for the moment these deliveries
to be equally distributed over the sector). In the Netherlands,
in 1973/74, fertilizers accounted for only 470 million
guilders (= 5%) out of a total of 9,490 million guilders for
non-factor costs. The total value available to the agricultural sector (whether for productive or consumptive expenditure) can also be taken as the frame of reference (row 6).
Fertilizer costs form only a small percentage of this amount
(< 5%). In developed countries the percentage is slightly
higher than in less-developed countries, due to greater
fertilizer consumption per farmer; in other words: agricultural GDP affects relatively far fewer people.

Artificial fertilizer and balance of payments

A large portion of the fertilizer consumed in developing
countries has to be imported. Any price increase therefore
has an immediate impact on the foreign reserve position of
these countries and might limit the availability of fertilizers. In general, we can distinguish three elements which
require foreign exchange: the build-up of domestic production capacity in the less-developed countries, which are
mostly dependent on the developed countries for capital
goods; the import of raw materials or crude fertilizer; and
finally the largest component to date, viz. the import of
manufactured fertilizer. The figures given in Table 8.8 give
some impression of the order of magnitude of current imports.

For most countries the percentage of fertilizer imports in
total exports is roughly 2%. The exceptionally high 8.9% for
Pakistan in 1970 had decreased to 2.8% in 1971. The OECD has
estimated the funds necessary for investment in local production (which should eventually replace or supplement imports)
at $750 million in 1970 (= 1.3% of total exports of develop-
ing countries). After the recent price increases, fertilizer

Table 8.7

The place of fertilizer costs

	INDIA 1967		INDONESIA 1968		MEXICO 1967		USA 1968		NETHERLANDS 1968	
	10^6 rupees	1 or (1+2) in % of	10^6 rupees	1 in % of	10^6 pesos	1 in % of	10^6 dollar	1 in % of	10^6 guilders	1 in % of
1. Fertilizers	1847		13561		1188		2125		416	
2. Manure	1962		..		..		..		..	
3. Total net intermediate consumption*	5124	37	51323	26	3460	34	19462	11	4637	9
4. Intermediate consumption of agricultural production of domestic origin	25937		36512		2479					
5. 3 + 4	30161	12	87835	15.4	5939	20	..	..	..	..
6. Agricultural GDP at market price	117843		930560		32480		25604		5622	
7. Gross output of national farmer	122967	1.5	981885	1.4	35940	3.3	45066	4.7	10259	4.1

*'net': total intermediate consumption minus 4.

Table 8.8

Imports of artificial fertilizer by less-developed countries* in 1970, in mln. $ and as percentage of total foreign trade

Country	Fertilizer crude	Fertilizer manufactured	Total fertilizer imports	Imports total	Exports total	Fertilizer imports as % of exports
LDC all	62.6	579.3	642	56300	55100	1.2
LDC Africa	8.6	62.7	71.3	11020	12600	0.6
LDC America	17.7	222.8	240.5	18940	17280	1.4
LDC Asia	36.3	292.0	328.3	25470	24760	1.3
India	13.9	63.6	77.5	2124	2026	3.8
Brazil	8.1	70.6	78.7	2849	2739	2.9
Mexico	7.0	5.7	12.7	2461	1402	0.9
Philippines	2.9	10.5	13.4	1286	1119	1.2
Indonesia	0	16.7	16.7	1000	1009	1.6
Sudan	0	4.7	4.7	311	293	1.6
Pakistan	4.0	60.4	64.4	1171	723	8.9

*Compiled from U.N. *Yearbook of International Trade Statistics 1972-1973* (New York, 1974)

purchases require about 2 per cent of the total export receipts of all developing countries. Such a percentage does
not seem to be excessively high for the developing countries
as a whole; nevertheless, for individual countries fertilizer import needs may create a serious problem in future
years. As our model describes only part of the economy and
international trade, and does not generate balances of
payments, this subject will not be elaborated upon here.

A qualitative analysis

The sensitivity of fertilizer demand to price changes will
be analyzed now on the basis of its partial elasticity (i.e.
with constant P and CMON) and for non-zero consumption
levels of fertilizer (i.e. $Y > BY$, $P > FMON/AY$ and $BY \geq Y(O)$;
see Chapter 4.4.3. The elasticity of fertilizer demand F.A.
with respect to fertilizer price FMON is by definition

$$\varepsilon_{F.A, FMON} = \frac{FMON}{F.A} \cdot \frac{d(F.A)}{dFMON} \tag{8.5}$$

As shown in Chapter 4, a change in FMON leads to a change in
the price ratio PR (at constant P and CMON), and a change in
PR leads to a change in the production decision in terms of
the planned yield level Y. This change in Y again implies a
change in the required level of fertilizer input F.
Hence,

$$\frac{dF}{dFMON} = \frac{dF}{dY} \cdot \frac{dY}{dPR} \cdot \frac{dPR}{dFMON} \tag{8.6}$$

Let us see what the three expressions at the right-hand side
of (8.6) stand for.

From (4.7) the land production function $F = \max (O, Y-BY)/AY$,
we have

$$\frac{dF}{dY} = \frac{1}{AY} \tag{8.7}$$

$\frac{dY}{dPR}$ has been calculated in Chapter 4.4.3.2, with labour employed LE given and under optimal behaviour implying

$PR = \frac{\partial Y}{\partial c}$ with $c = CE/A$, it was found - see (4.54) - that

$$\frac{dY}{dPR} = \frac{\dfrac{\partial Y}{\partial c}}{\dfrac{\partial^2 Y}{\partial c^2}} \tag{8.8}$$

We repeat (4.34a):

$$PR = \frac{CMON}{(P\dfrac{FMON}{AY})}$$

and find by differentiation (with constant P and CMON):

$$\frac{dPR}{dFMON} = \frac{PR^2}{AY.CMON} \tag{8.9}$$

Substituting (8.7) - (8.9) in (8.6) and the latter into (8.5) gives:

$$\varepsilon_{F.A, \ FMON} = (\frac{\partial Y}{\partial c} / \frac{\partial^2 Y}{\partial c^2}) . \frac{FMON}{CMON} . \frac{PR^2}{AY^2} . \frac{1}{F} \tag{8.10}$$

All terms at the right-hand side except for the first one, are positive (for CMON > 0, see Chapter 4.4.5).

With $\dfrac{\frac{\partial Y}{\partial c}}{\frac{\partial^2 Y}{\partial c^2}}$ < 0, the price elasticity of fertilizer demand ε

is also negative in line with our expectations. By increasing use of F and unchanged use of capital goods, sensitivity to price changes (FMON) diminishes. The same applies to a higher product price P. We want to determine also, how ε is influenced by the level of CMON and by the level of capital use C.

$\dfrac{FMON}{CMON} . \dfrac{PR^2}{AY^2}$ can be written as:

$$\frac{CMON}{\dfrac{P^2.AY^2}{FMON} + FMON - 2P.AY}$$

Higher costs of capital use (CMON) therefore cause fertilizer demand to be more sensitive to price changes.

$$PR = \frac{\partial Y}{\partial c} = \frac{dY}{dZ} . \frac{\partial Z}{\partial c} \tag{8.11}$$

$$\frac{\partial Z}{\partial c} = \frac{APY}{2\sqrt{c+BPY}} \tag{8.12}$$

$$\frac{dY}{dZ} = \frac{YASY^2}{(YASY+Z)^2} \tag{8.13}$$

Rewriting (4.39) gives:

$$\frac{dY}{dPR} = \frac{-2(c+BPY) . (YASY+Z)}{(YASY+Z) + 2APY . \sqrt{c+BPY}} \tag{8.14}$$

Substituting (8.12) and (8.13) in (8.11) and combining (8.11) and (8.13), we obtain:

$$\frac{\frac{\partial Y}{\partial c}}{\frac{\partial^2 Y}{\partial c^2}} \cdot PR^2 =$$

$$\frac{-APY^2 \cdot YASY^4}{+2(YASY+Z) \cdot \left\{ (YASY+Z) + 2APY \cdot \sqrt{c+BPY} \right\}} \qquad (8.15)$$

Substitution of (8.15) in (8.10) reveals that ε decreases with increasing capital use (C).

Fertilizer consumption is now tested as to its sensitivity to changes in agricultural product prices P. Again, we use a partial elasticity, with constant prices (CMON and FMON) of the inputs.

$$\varepsilon_{F.A,P} \equiv \frac{P}{F} \cdot \frac{dF}{dP} \qquad (8.16)$$

As before, we have to analyze a chain of reactions:

$$\frac{dF}{dP} = \frac{dF}{dY} \cdot \frac{dY}{dPR} \cdot \frac{dPR}{dP} \qquad (8.17)$$

From the definition of PR it follows:

$$\frac{dPR}{dP} = -\frac{PR^2}{CMON} \qquad (8.18)$$

(8.7), (8.8) and (8.18) substituted in (8.17), and (8.17) in (8.16) give:

$$\varepsilon_{F.A,P} = \left(\frac{\frac{\partial Y}{\partial c}}{\frac{\partial^2 Y}{\partial c^2}}\right) \cdot \frac{P}{AY} \cdot \frac{PR^2}{CMON} \cdot \frac{1}{F} \qquad (8.19)$$

This elasticity is positive. Analogous to the case of $\varepsilon_{F.A,FMON}$, it can be deduced that higher FMON and CMON cause sensitivity to increase, while greater use of capital goods C leads to a decrease of sensitivity. For the sake of completeness we give - without derivation - the following elasticities: the sensitivity of fertilizer demand to the ratio of fertilizer price and product price (under constant capital costs CMON).

$$\varepsilon_{F.A,\frac{FMON}{P}} = \frac{1}{F} \cdot \frac{\frac{\partial Y}{\partial c}}{\frac{\partial^2 Y}{\partial c^2}} \cdot \frac{AY.CMON}{P} \cdot \frac{(FMON/P)}{(FMON/P-AY)^2 \ (FMON/P+AY)}$$

$$(8.20)$$

This elasticity is negative, implying a decreasing demand for fertilizer when fertilizer price rises in relation to product price. Finally, we give the partial income elasticity (with all prices fixed):

$$\varepsilon_{F.A,V} = \frac{V}{F.A.} \cdot \frac{1}{(P.AY-FMON)} \tag{8.21}$$

The marginal cases

(A)   FMON $\geq$ P.AY   or   P $\leq$ FMON/AY

The elasticities are 0 (viz. $\frac{dF}{dY} = 0$ since Y $\leq$ BY). Marginal revenues of fertilizer use no longer counterbalance marginal costs. Fertilizer will therefore no longer be used and unemployment is likely to occur (see Chapter 4.4.3). This is illustrated below; compare figs. 8.2 and 8.3 with figs. 4.2-4.4 and 4.7 in Chapter 4. The yield level Y(O) is the yield level with capital employed CE=0. Increasing PR (e.g. by increasing FMON) causes segment a to rotate counter-clockwise. The optimum will be found either at S or on the segment Y(O), S depending on the slope of b.

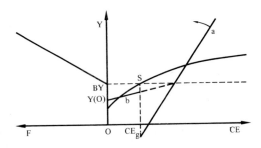

Fig. 8.2

Intensity of land use curve, iso-income curve
(segments a and b), and land production curve; case BY $\geq$ Y(0)

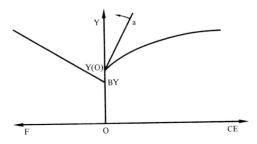

Fig. 8.3

Intensity of land use curve, iso-income curve
(segment a), and land production curve; case BY $\leq$ Y(0)

As long as $P > FMON/AY$ and $PR \geq \frac{\partial Y}{\partial c}$ in $Y(O)$, the optimum lies
in $(O, Y(O))$ with income $V = Y(O) \cdot (P-FMON/AY) \cdot A + (FMON/AY) \cdot A \cdot BY$.
However, if P becomes $\leq FMON/AY$, fertilizer consumption
looses its meaning; the optimum will then be in (O, BY) with
income $V = P \cdot A \cdot BY$, and unemployment will results.

(B) $P > FMON/AY$, but $BY \geq Y > Y(O)$.

In this case $\frac{dF}{dY} = 0$ and therefore the demand elasticities are zero.

(C) $Y(O) > BY$.

Now $\frac{dY}{dPR} = 0$ at $Y = Y(O)$, while for $Y > Y(O)$ we have
$\frac{dY}{dPR} < 0$. See Chapter 4.4.3.2 and fig. 4.9.
Similarly, we find that if
$Y > Y(O)$ and $Y(O) > BY$, then $\frac{dF}{dPR} = \frac{1}{AY} \cdot \frac{dY}{dPR} < 0$.

Note that a rising PR $(= \frac{CMON}{P-FMON/AY})$ can be due to: increasing
CMON, increasing FMON or decreasing P. If in the last two cases
the limit $P = FMON/AY$ is passed (still with $Y(O) > BY$), Y in
fig. 8.3 will drop from $Y(O)$ to BY, and fertilizer use decreases to zero.

8.5.3 *The impact of demand on price and availability of fertilizer*

What influence on the price and availability of
fertilizer is exercised by the demand generated in the
model? (In terms of the scheme of fig. 8.1, we are dealing
now with relations of type b). A proper answer to this
question requires an analysis of demand and supply, which
should be confronted on the fertilizer market. The effects
of such a confrontation on fertilizer prices and on investment decisions by entrepreneurs (and consequently on future
availability of fertilizer) ought to be investigated. As was
mentioned under Chapter 8.1 above, however, a detailed
investigation would require its own model and research
effort. We have therefore been compelled to treat fertilizer
as an exogenous variable in the form of the fertilizer price
(in which the influence of possible physical limitations
should also be reflected). Here too, we have had to neglect
the influence of endogenous on exogenous variables. An
attempt to justify this approach is made below.

Long-term price developments

MOIRA is a long-term model; as far as fertilizer costs are
concerned, our attention will also be focussed primarily on
long-term developments. We have already seen that fertilizer
costs constitute a small part only of the total production
value of the sector. It is therefore of particular interest

to find out whether in the long term structural changes are
likely to change this fact. A good description of the market,
the investments etc. could explain short-term fluctuations
in market prices (which could be wide), but is not strictly
necessary for the above-mentioned purpose.

Long-term adjustments

We have already stated that we do not attempt to explain the
size of investments. The response time of the fertilizer industry, i.e. the time needed to adapt production capacity to
changes in demand, is assumed to be so short that any description of long term developments should concentrate on
structural changes. In this view, possible shortages of
capacity become short-term bottlenecks. Capacity size is
determined by demand factors. The assumption of a short
response time seems justified in view of the fact that by
far the greater part of production (90%) occurs in developed
countries where short construction times (2 to 3 years)
entail relatively short adjustment times.

It seems feasible to anticipate that the present long construction times in less developed countries will shorten as
time goes by, due partly to the increasing knowledge and
infrastructure which they will attain as they enlarge gradually their share in world production.

Physical limitations

It is assumed that during the period under consideration (up
to 2010), capacity increase will not be limited in any way
by bottlenecks in the supply of inputs (phosphate rock,
hydrogen sources such as oil, gas, etc.). This can be illustrated with the aid of some figures. With an annual overall
growth rate of 5% during the period 1972-2010, a world
consumption (excl. CPE) of 52 million tons in 1972 and a
distribution over N, P_2O_5 and K_2O of 2:1:1 (roughly the
ratios of world consumption during the last few years), a
cumulative consumption is arrived at of 3,000, 1,500 and
1,500 million tons, respectively. Roughly speaking, the
three types of fertilizer require per ton respectively
45,000 ft^3gas, 3.5 MT P-rock and 1 MT K_2O as input. During
the period 1975-2010, therefore, 135 x $10^{12}ft^3$gas, 5.25 x
10^9MT P-rock and 1.5 x 10^9MT P-rock and 1.5 x 10^9MT K_2O are
required. Compiling figures from numerous sources, we obtained
the following estimates of reserves in the world (excl. CPE):
6,500 * $10^{12}ft^3$gas; 1,700 * 10^9bbls oil = 10,200 * $10^{12}ft^3$gas;
1,400 * 10^9bbls shale oil and tar sands = 8,400 * $10^{12}ft^3$gas
and 3,700 * 10^9MT coal = 100.000 * $10^{12}ft^3$gas; altogether an
equivalent of 125,000 * $10^{12}ft^3$gas as source of hydrogen.
Further: 47.8 * 10^9MT P-rock and 36 * 10^9MT K20. The cumulative demand calculated above, expressed as fraction of
these reserves, amounts to 0.1%, 11% and 4.2%, respectively.
An increase of 5% per annum means a fourfold increase of
consumption in 2000 and 6.5 times the consumption of 1972 in
2010 - figures that would seem to be plausable. With regard
to reserves, their magnitude is dependent on many factors.
Exploration is normally carried out only to the point where

the needs for the next two or three decades are thought to
be covered. In determining the quantity of reserves the
price plays an important role, particularly in the case of
P-rock and Potassium. A doubling of the price may mean a
five- or sixfold increase of commercially recoverable reserves. On a world-wide scale, the petro-chemical industry
uses about 5% of fossil fuel production as raw material,
almost 25% of which is destined to become fertilizer via the
ammonia production. Therefore, the computed 0.1% does not
seem to constitute too heavy a burden. As to phosphate rock,
80 to 85 percent of world production is destined for phosphate fertilizers, and 90-95% of Potassium production is
used for potassic fertilizers. Again, covering the calculated
needs of 11% and 4.2%, respectively, of world reserves
should be feasible.

8.5.4 *Long-term price developments*

        Price projections are established partly analytical-
ly, partly on fictitious prices (see Chapter 8.5.5). In
Chapter 8.5.3 we have explained why our interest is focused
mainly on long-term developments at the supply side. These
are analyzed by describing long-term average costs which
could be considered as lower limits to prices. On the regional level we attempt to indicate potential production possibilities. However, instead of explaining actual investments
we assume the existence of a long-term tendency to an optimal situation, in which production occurs where it happens
to be most efficient. This should be kept in mind in inter-
preting the results.

A schematic survey

The object is to indicate growth rates of the fertilizer
price per ton paid by the farmer (in constant 1965 dollar
prices). Our method is to follow step by step each stage
from raw material to end product delivered at farm gate, and
to calculate the average costs for each step.

Firstly, the world (excl. CPE) has been divided into 18
regions; for each region, on the basis of long term developments of the various cost components, potential production
costs for a number of standard products have been calculated
on a five-yearly basis (up to 2010). After describing interregional transportation possibilities and related costs,
combined production and transportation costs have been
minimised in order to arrive at the *supply region* for each
region of resp. phosphate-rock, N-, P_2O_5 - and K_2O fertilizer. Interregional transport and a distribution margin have
been taken into account in calculating farm gate prices.
Finally, prices of different categories of fertilizer products
have been combined into one price which serves as the basis
for the growth rate calculation. Historical prices per
country, together with this regional index, give the price
projections per country.

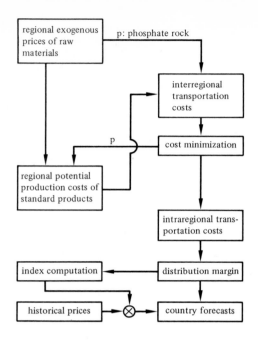

Fig. 8.4

Block diagram of computations

The regions

We are forced by lack of data to change from country level
to regional level. In this way, differences between countries belonging to the same region are neglected as far as
price developments are concerned. As to the price level,
historical differences (1965) have been maintained. Regions
have been chosen for a certain degree of homogeneity as to
infrastructure, possession of raw materials, GNP per capita,
etc. Countries have been grouped around suitable seaports.

Potential production costs

The potential production costs have been calculated for each
region for N-, P_2O_5 and K_2O- fertilizer separately. For each
category a standard product and a standard production unit
has been selected which is representative for its category,
i.e. it contains the constant components in an ever-varying
product-mix and its use presumably remains necessary during
the period considered. These products are: Urea, Triple
Superphosphate (TSP) and Muriate of Potash. Only integrated
industries have been considered, i.e. intermediary and final
product are manufactured in the same place (except for P-
rock).

An analysis of all production processes provides a series of
technical coefficients. Distinction is made between several
cost groups, i.e. investment related costs (including all
investments costs of grassroots plants, written off over a
ten-year period), interest, maintenance, taxes, insurance
etc. Each year, 22% of investment costs should be repaid.
Regional cost differences are reflected by regional indices
(e.g. US Gulf Coast=100, Indian Ocean=140 etc.). In the
course of time these indices approach the level of the
developed countries. In addition to investment costs, feed-
stocks are the most important costs. In the N-industry four
possible H-sources have been distinguished: natural gas,
naphtha, fuel oil and coal, for all of which investment
costs differ considerably. The most advantagous process is
determined on the basis of input prices and of investment
costs for each region per five year period. The costs of
utilities (electricity, steam, chemicals etc.) have been
taken as proportionate to size of production. In the production process, labour related costs represent only a minor
item; for several reasons, they are considered as fixed
costs. A pre-tax return on investment of 20% has been regarded as normal. An important factor in inputing costs is
the utilization factor, which might vary considerably among
different regions. Again, we use a regional index (e.g.
North America 90, India 55 etc.), which increases in time to
the level prevailing in developed countries.

Feedstock prices

In this context, raw materials include gas, naphtha, fuel
oil, coal, P-rock, sulphur and sylvite ore. We have projected the prices of these inputs per region, using existing
projections and taking into account such factors as the
ultimate reserves in every region, lead times of mines, etc.

Inter- and intra regional transport

Possible trade flows are computed on the basis of ocean
transport costs. These have been calculated with the aid of
an equation[8] giving costs per ton as a function of the number
of *at-sea* days. Corrections are applied depending on the
type of commodity (P-rock transport is cheaper than transport of final product) and the number of canal-passages. Also,
we take costs of energy into account. The number of *at-sea*
days could be derived from the distances between regional
seaports and the speed of transportation.

Production takes place either in the region concerned or in
another region, while transport is possible either over sea
or over land. *Supply regions* are subsequently determined by
minimizing combined production and transport costs.

For intraregional transport costs we take average rail
freight for an average commodity transported over an average
distance in each country. By weighting with the consumed

---

[8] Blakeslee L.L., Heady E.O., Framingham C.F., *World Food Production,
Demand and Trade*, Iowa State University Press, Iowa 1973

quantity of fertilizer in each country, the regional costs can be calculated.

Distribution margin

The distribution margin consists of wholesale and retail profits, duties and taxes, storage, packing, overhead etc. These elements differ widely among countries, and depend on the infrastructure, degree of rural development, government interference (state corporations, subvention policy), etc. It is not possible to introduce these structural differences by using real factors only, and historical percentages have therefore been used.

Growth rates

The three categories of fertilizer have been combined according to the ratio 2:1:1, representing the composition of world consumption during the last few years. All prices are subsequently transformed into indices in order to obtain growth rates. Regional indices are utilized for the computation of country projections. To obtain historical prices, 1965 country prices have been calculated on the basis of data given in the FAO Annual Fertilizer Reviews and some USDA-country studies. Historical differences between countries are therefore maintained to a certain extent.

Some results

Our main finding is that fertilizer prices are not likely to rise considerably during the coming years. The world fertilizer price index (1965=100) shows a breach in the period 1970-1975 with a jump to about 150, then it steadily rises to about 150 in 1990 and subsequently decreases to 140 in 2000. It appears that the rising costs of raw material will be largely compensated by increasing efficiency (mainly by a growing utilization factor and decreasing differences in investment costs).

In the production process for ammonia (the basis product for nitrogen fertilizer, the present predominant use of gas might in several regions be replaced by coal as feedstock (after 1985-90 in India, and Japan, for example). Regional differences in production costs are reflected in changes in the supply regions. In addition to traditional suppliers new ones will enter the fertilizer market and, after one or two decades, could outrun the others. North Africa, the Middle East and Venezuela could become important suppliers of nitrogen fertilizer: North Africa for Europe, Western Africa and even Argentina; the Middle East for India, Pakistan, Indonesia, South-East Asia and Eastern Africa; Venezuela for almost all Latin America. Phosphate production in Israël, Jordan, Senegal, Uganda, Peru and Brazil could become important.

8.5.5 *Price alternatives*

Wide fluctuations in fertilizer prices could act as a disincentive to the farmer. To study the consequences of price fluctuations, a cyclical variation that approximates the fluctuations in real market prices is applied to calculated trend prices. The historical fluctuation in nitrogen prices during the past twenty years is taken as the cyclical variation. The pattern of fluctuation could be described as a sinus with a period of eight years, deviations from the trend amounting to 75% in the upward and 45% in the downward direction. Introduction of these variations in fertilizer prices allows us to study the implications of policy measures such as fertilizer price stabilization.

8.5.6 *Costs of use of capital goods*

After the discussion at some length of the role and determination of fertilizer prices FMON, the question may come up why capital costs CMON are treated differently. Therefore, a short summary of what has been said before about CMON may be in place. CMON represents both average capital costs in income determination and marginal capital costs in the investment decisions of the agricultural sector. CMON cannot be identified with costs of use of capital goods in the usual sense. This is due to its measurement as a shadow price (see chapter 4.2.4); it implies that CMON stands for the cost of usage of all physical and non-physical means which determine the degree of equipment of a unit of labour. CMON is an artificial intermediary variable in the computations. As the non-agricultural commodity is used as numéraire, changes in CMON reflect quantity changes. The determination of exogenous variations in this variable is meaningless: the variations in CMON are endogenously derived, in contrast to variations in FMON. This endogenous change is determined by alterations in the general rate of inflation (GNPI), and variations due to a changing degree of food processing. CMON varies in such way that a changed GPO (and PO and P) causes no changes in the price ratio PR; production decisions therefore remain unchanged (see 4.6). Finally, a yearly component is added, that can be considered (see chapter 6.5.3) as a bridging variable between the calibration period and the simulation period. In a general sense CMON hardly changes during the simulation run.

8.6 *NUTRITION STANDARDS*

8.6.1 *The variable 'hunger'*

In any study devoted to the food problem, hunger should be a most important criterion. Hunger can be defined as the positive difference between an exogenously determined nutritional norm and the endogenously calculated food consumption per income class, when consumption is less than the norm. (In Chapter 10 the concept of hunger will be broken down into gross and net hunger).

Average food consumption per capita of world population is
apparently sufficient to meet an individual's normal needs
(see table 8.2). In order to plot the course of hunger, one
must first determine the distribution of purchasing power
among countries and, within each country, among income
classes per sector. On this basis, the consumption in each
of 1272 classes has to be ascertained (see Chapter 5). This
consumption per income class then has to be checked against
a norm. The determination of this norm is the subject of
this section. Only one norm per country will be set.

The norm will in the first instance be derived from the
concept of health (the *medical norm*). Subsequently, this
medical nutrition norm is translated into an *economic nutrition norm* with the aid of the average food package used in
the reference period 1964-1966. In calculating this economic
nutrition norm, allowance is made for variations per country
in consumption behaviour and facilities. The nutrients which
a body absorbs provide the nourishing substances of which
the body has an inadequate supply. The human being's demand
for energy is met by the burning of nutrients such as carbohydrates, fat, alcohol and protein. There are various methods
by which the minimum needs for these nutrients can be determined (i.e. determination of the necessary amount of energy
or of the necessary amount of a particular nutrient). For
example, diet-surveys or laboratory research can be used to
determine the use of a certain nutrient or the amount of
energy. Also, the minimum amount that a human being needs in
order to keep healthy could be taken as the point of departure, as experiments have been performed to determine this
minimum (for example, by means of the balance method). These
methods give rise to several technical and conceptual problems (such as what is healthy, etc.). One of the most important problems relates to the ability of the human body to
adapt within certain limits to a surplus or deficit of
certain nutrients. The body is able to experience a deficit
without much harm for a fairly short period. In the long
term, the weight and composition of the body will adjust to
the food package, thus making it difficult to determine a
norm.

To some extent, therefore, neglect of the influence of the
endogenous variable (i.e. actual consumption) on the exogenous norm is justified. As we do not trace weight and age
composition of the population nor changes in the food package,
we are forced to keep the medical and economic norms constant
during the entire period 1965-2010 (i.e. the norm computed
from 1965 data).

8.6.2 *The energy norm*

        Nutritionists have so far concentrated their at-
tention mainly on energy and proteins, for which they have
attempted to establish norms. We shall make use of an energy
norm as a medical nutrition norm, for the following reasons:

First, a sufficient supply of energy is an absolute necessity for the efficient functioning of the body. Everything
else is subordinate to this requirement insofar as, in a
calorie-deficient diet, vegetal and animal proteins will not
be converted into human protein but will be burned to meet
the demand for energy. A diet that contains sufficient
protein according to a protein norm could still cause protein deficit diseases if it cannot satisfy the demand for
energy. The reverse case does not apply.

Secondly, the protein norm has been a matter of continuous
discussion since the early 1930s. This was due to the assumption that many children in the world suffer from protein
deficiency. Only recently has the view been accepted that
this might have been at least partly a misconception. It
appears in practice that deficiency diseases are caused by
the intake of too little food. The idea of a *protein gap* has
thus been abandoned. Experiments have been adjusted to this
changed insight, with the consequence that assessments of
protein needs have decreased considerably as the years went
by. The protein norm can be expressed in a percentage of the
energy requirement; this is done by calculating the protein
norm in calories, the norm itself being denoted in grams. An
average gram protein provides 4 kcal. The FAO takes a percentage of five for protein of optimal quality, allowing for a
maximum of 8 percent for protein of bad quality. In practice
the percentage appears to be fairly constant but at a higher
level (see table 8.12). The FAO has carried out a cross-
section research in 80 countries[9], according to which animal
and vegetal proteins together provide a caloric contribution
to the diet that invariably amounts to 10 percent. Nevertheless, the FAO maintains a percentage of five, due to a low
protein norm and a high energy norm (see below). The FAO has
used different methods with which to calculate these norms.
The protein norm has been determined with the aid of laboratory experiments, the energy norm on the basis of nutrition
surveys.

Finally, it should be noted that a surplus of protein is not
harmful for man since any excess will be secreted; on the
other hand, however, a surplus of calories could cause
serious diseases.

8.6.3 *Determination of the calorie norm*

Energy is needed for the basic metabolism and for
physical activity. Calories are converted into energy during
the burning process which occurs in the fat-free part of the
body. The energy requirement is expressed in the amount of
kcal needed per kilogram body weight. This differs according
to age (a child needs more than an adult because of growth;
on the other hand, an older person needs less than an adult)
and according to sex (a female body contains more fat).
These differences are determined by means of an index with

---

[9] FAO *Nutrition Letter*, Vol. 7, No. 3 (July-September 1969).

Table 8.10

Energy requirements
(rounded-off in units of 50)

Country: MALAWI
Body weight: M: 58 kg
F: 52 kg

Age groups	Requirements in kcal/day	Adjustment according weight, age	Population distribution percent	Total energy kcal/day
Children				
0 - 1	970	970	4.7	4559
1 - 4	1350	1350	11.0	14850
4 - 7	1830	1830	9.1	16653
7 - 10	2190	2190	8.3	18177
Male adults				
10 - 13	2600	2600	3.8	9880
13 - 16	M * 0.97	2250	3.4	7651
16 - 20	M * 1.02	2366	4.1	9702
20 - 40	BW Male * 40	2320	13.7	31784
40 - 50	M * .95	2204	3.8	8375
50 - 60	M * .90	2088	2.4	5011
60 - 70	M * .80	1856	1.3	2412
70 and +	M * .70	1624	.5	812
Female adults				
10 - 13	2350	2350	3.8	8390
13 - 16	F * 1.13	2203	3.4	7492
16 - 20	F * 1.05	2047	4.1	8395
20 - 40	BW female * 37.5	1950	13.9	27105
40 - 50	F * 0.95	1853	3.9	7225
50 - 60	F * 0.90	1755	2.6	4563
60 - 70	F * 0.80	1560	1.9	2964
70 and +	F * 0.70	1365	.7	955

Total 197495

Per capita requirement at consumption level 1975

10% waste 198

Per capita requirement at retail level 2150

Source: Own computations with reference to an example of the Nutrition Department of the FAO.

as basis the standard man (age 20-39, weight 65 kg) or
standard woman (age 20-39, weight 55 kg). FAO estimates
energy requirements for the standard man and woman at resp.
3000 and 2440 kcal/day (or 46 and 44.3 kcal per kg. body
weight).[10] On the medical side, the criticism has been voiced
that 3000 kcal/day implies that the standard man either
works in a factory or is a homo sportivus.[11]If he is neither,
he seems destined to fall victim to one of the degenerative
diseases of Western civilisation. In accordance with Banerjee
and De Wijn[12]we have taken 40 and 37.5 kcal/kg body weight,
arriving at resp. 2600 and 2060 kcal/day with moderately
tiring activities.

With the aid of the population composition of each country,
a calorie norm has been derived for each one. In this calculation allowance has been made for waste of food as a
consequence of loss during cooking, etc., assumed to be 10
percent. An example of such a computation is given in Table
8.10, and part of the results are shown in Table 8.11.

Table 8.11

Average weights and required calories

Country	Average weight MALE	Average weight FEMALE	Required calories in kcal/day/caput cons. level	Required calories in kcal/day/caput retail level
USA	70	58	2190	2400
Japan	57	49	1942	2150
Nigeria	60	52	2010	2200
Zaire	55	48	1887	2050
Brazil	60	55	2074	2300
India	55	45	1878	2050
China	58	51	2000	2200

Source: Own calculations based on WHO data.

In the less developed countries the norm is lower since the
average weight in these countries is less than that in developed countries and the composition of the population is also
quite different (more children, etc.).

---

[10] *Energy and Protein Requirements* (Report of a joint FAO/WHO Ad Hoc
Expert Committee, FAO, Rome 1973).

[11] Stock, M.J. and J.P.W. Rivers, *Human Protein and Energy Requirements,*
The Lancet, September 19, 1973, p. 732 and
Wijn, Dr. J.F. de, *Assignment Report on the Applied Nutrition Programme,*
Indonesia, WHO, November 1972, 0. 19.

[12] Banerjee , S. *Study in Energy Metabolism,* Indian Council Medical
Research Special Rep. Series no. 43, New Delhi 1962, and
Wijn, Dr. J.F. de, and Staveren, W.A. van, *De Voeding van Elke Dag,*
De Erven Bohn, Haarlem 1973.

8.6.4 *The consumable protein norm*

All computations in the model refer to consumable protein making it necessary to convert the calorie norm into a protein norm. In addition, it is our intention to turn from a purely medical norm to a more economic norm which makes some allowance for the sorts of food that are supplied and consumed in each country. The transition from a protein norm to a consumable protein norm is intended to indicate the amount of consumable protein to which every person should have access if his or her basic needs are to be met. This is due to the fact that the consumer is not able to purchase this minimum food package in any desired form (e.g. in vegetal form, which means high efficiency). Instead, the consumer is confined to the measure of processing which is customary in a specific region (e.g. animal protein, packed food, etc.). The calorie norm is translated into a consumable protein norm in the following manner:

consumable protein norm = calorie norm . average protein content of calorie . consumable protein per unit of consumed protein (in the base year).

For the majority of countries, the norms calculated in this manner proved to be roughly 25 kg consumable protein per capita per annum ($\simeq$ 250 kg wheat). Some countries (e.g. Ghana) showed extremely high efficiency possible due to incorrect data, the computed norm amounting to 18 kg. On the other hand, countries such as the USA, Japan, etc. showed great inefficiency and had very high norms. We have therefore assumed an upper limit, starting from the principle that it is not the average level of processing that is decisive, but that a minimum food supply should be available even at a lower level of processing. We have taken as limits 20 and, somewhat arbitrarily, 30 kg/ per capita/per annum.

Some of the results of our calculations are shown in Table 8.12.

Table 8.12

Food consumption and consumption norm in terms of consumable protein, per region

	(1) Calories from protein %	(2) Calorie norm kcal/day/caput	(3) Consumed kcal/day/caput	(4) Cal.norm /cons.cal. 2/3	(5) Consumable protein kg/caput/year	(6) Consumed protein per consumable protein	(7)* Norm in kg consumable protein/cap./year
North America	12	2400	3180	.75	104	.34	30
Western Europe	12	2395	3070	.78	81	.41	30
Japan	14	2150	2501	.86	55	.58	30
Australia etc.	12	2330	2942	.79	55	.59	30
East. Europe (incl. USSR)	12	2350	3169	.74	74	.46	30
Latin America	11	2254	2485	.91	43	.57	24
Middle East	11	2266	2237	1.01	33	.70	27
Tropical Africa	11	2179	2161	1.01	25	.89	21
Southern Asia	10	2064	2002	1.03	26	.73	22
China c.s.	12	2250	2060	1.09	30	.75	30
WORLD AVERAGE	11	2227	2398	.93	45	.55	25
DC	12	2352	3047	.77	80	.42	30
KDC	11	2170	2100	1.03	29	.72	22
Income Classes							
< 100 $/caput	11	2119	1999	1.06	24	.82	
100 - 200	11	2078	2062	1.01	27	.73	
200 - 400	11	2246	2148	1.05	32	.69	
400 - 800	12	2271	2714	.84	49	.59	
800 - 1600	12	2307	2988	.77	70	.47	
> 1600	12	2412	3150	.77	98	.35	

*approximate

NOTE: regional presentation. The model itself operates on country level and uses country data.

Source: own calculations, based on W.H.O. data.

Chapter 9

A SUMMARY VIEW OF MOIRA

9.1 *A SHORT SURVEY OF THE MODEL*

In the preceding chapters, the structure of MOIRA has been discussed at some length. This chapter gives a short summary of the basic structure of the model, in an attempt to help the reader to see how the various parts of the model are interrelated. Policy simulations will be discussed in Part III of this volume.

(1) The study aims at investigating the causes of hunger and malnutrition in the world, and at identifying the policy measures - particularly those at the international level - that will contribute to solving the hunger problem.

(2) Limitation of natural resources needed for agricultural production is not the primary factor responsible for hunger in the world. These natural resources are presently being used with rather low intensity only. The physical possibilities to increase agricultural output are large indeed, though these possibilities obviously are not equally large in all countries and regions.

(3) present levels of world food production are high enough to provide everyone with an adequate diet if food were distributed equally over all people.

(4) Hunger and starvation occur because food is distributed by and large on the basis of income or purchasing power; hence, levels of food consumption differ widely between countries and between people.

(5) Limited mobility of factors of production, and of labour in particular, forces a large part of the poor to earn their income in agricultural production. This implies that poor countries can improve their food consumption only by expanding their own production (in terms of the population numbers involved, most poor countries are net importers of food). The agricultural sector will increase its output only if it is worthwhile to do so. In the model the most important incentive for increased production is a higher domestic food price. It should be noted that this price is not (only) the price actually paid in the market; in the model, the food price includes also other current transfers of resources to the food producing sector.

(6)   The agricultural population is interested in higher food prices, but the urban or non-agricultural population is in favour of lower domestic food prices - primarily as they are consumers of food. Also, in case of exporting countries the urban sector will benefit from low internal prices because of the greater receipt of export duties that will accrue to them. This creates a conflict of interests between agricultural and non-agricultural population. The socio-political power of these two groups determines government policy concerning the desired domestic price level, via the ratio between agricultural and non-agricultural incomes per head that the government is compelled (or sees fit) to aim at. Thus in any country the income ratio between the two sectors is primarily determined by institutional forces, and is therefore the cause (rather than the consequence) of the desired domestic food price level.

(7)   Domestic price levels also depend, to a varying extent, upon the world market price level. Changes in the world market price level for food are due to changes in the net position in food (i.e. the difference between food supply and demand) of the various countries. Countries influence the world market, and therefore each other, through their net foreign trade position in food. (This implies, by the way, that from the point of view of development cooperation a rich country has to control and adapt its net foreign trade position only, so that its national food production and consumption levels may be oriented towards other goals like e.g. environmental protection).

(8)   In view of the ratio between agricultural and non-agri-cultural per capita incomes that is aimed at, governments try to avoid undesirable effects of the world market price level on the domestic price level by means of trade policy measures. These measures take the form of taxes or subsidies on exports or imports of food, or can be "translated" into such taxes or subsidies. The extent to which these trade policy measures can be pursued, is, however, subject to con-straints. Subsidies cannot take up more than a certain part of the government budget.

(9)   The constraints on trade policy measures aiming at a regulation of the domestic food price hold for all countries; generally speaking, however, they become active more rapidly in the poor countries than in the rich countries. By and large, the rich countries are able to realize their desired agricultural/non-agricultural income ratio almost irrespec-tive of the world market price level. Their level of eco-nomic development is such, that they can effectively pursue their own income policy as regards agricultural versus non-agricultural incomes; the trade policy measures they take for this purpose (affecting their exports or imports of food) may strongly influence world market food prices.

(10) Poor countries have basically the same objectives in their agriculture and food policy; however, as the latter countries have only limited resources for trade policy

measures that provide protection against possible undesirable effects of changing world market prices on the domestic
food price, they often cannot pursue this policy as effectively as the rich countries can. Therefore, to a large
extent the developing countries are forced to have their
domestic food price level follow the world market price
level. The food importing developing countries in particular
find themselves in a weak position in this respect. National
policies of the rich countries, via their effect on the
world market food price, may influence the domestic price
level of food (and hence the domestic production of food) in
the poor countries. Also, in the latter countries food
consumption is more sensitive to price changes as they
affect a larger part of the consumer's income.

(11) In centrally-planned economies, decisions on production
are assumed to be made by governments on the basis of material targets, not on the basis of prices. It is assumed that
centrally-planned countries strive for self-sufficiency in
food supply. Labour only is attracted from the agricultural
sector for as far as it is needed in non-agricultural sectors.
When self-sufficiency is not realized exactly, exports or
imports will take place.

(12) The effect of a change in the world market price on
domestic food prices is quite intricate and admittedly somewhat uncertain. For a food exporting country, an increase in
the world market price means an increase in wealth. At a
given domestic price level this implies an increase in food
demand. Under a constant income distribution between the
agricultural and non-agricultural sectors, an increase in
the food price will occur. Moreover, it is in the long-run
interest of a (small) exporting country to increase its
supply when prices are rising in the world market. Thus, for
both reasons one may expect an exporting country to have at
least some tendency to follow world market price changes in
its domestic food price policy. The situation is more complex
for a food importing country - especially when it is poor.
In this case, long-run and short-run interests of the non-
agricultural sector are conflicting. An increase in the
world market price decreases the wealth of this sector. At a
constant distribution of income, this would imply a decrease
in the domestic food price. This *perversity* will be counter-
acted by long-run substitution arguments, by smuggling food
out of the country, etc. The final outcome of all this is by
no means obvious.

(13) The balance between production and consumption in the
various countries, corrected for possible changes in world
stocks, gives initial net supply or demand of agricultural
products on the world market. In an iterative procedure a
world market price is calculated which would make through
its effect on domestic prices and on real income, total
consumption equal to supply. The domestic price level that
results plays a part in the decisions concerning next year's
production.

The analytical description of world food production and consumption, given in detail in the model and summarized above,
is used in Part III for a discussion of national and international policy measures in the field of food and agriculture. The next section tries to further clarify the model
structure by illustrating some important interrelations with
the help of arrow schemes.

9.2 *THE FUNCTIONING OF THE MODEL ILLUSTRATED WITH ARROW SCHEMES*

The arrow schemes presented below are sometimes slightly
simplified representations of the relationships actually incorporated in MOIRA, as will be clear from a comparison with
the text of the previous chapters. They are given for the
world market and for the market-economy countries only, as
the model for the centrally-planned economies is very simple
and easy to understand (see Chapter 4.6). Total net supply
of food by the centrally planned countries on the world
market will be indicated by NETEX.

We will discuss now the arrow schemes for the world market,
for the government's price policy, and for the reaction of
the agricultural producer, in this order. Finally, these
relations will be brought together in a (simplified) overall
arrow scheme. Country and sector variables are mentioned
without their sector or country subscripts. Resulting equilibrium values of variables are indicated by a horizontal
line above the label of the variables, as e.g. $\overline{CONS}$.

9.2.1 *The world market food price*

International trade is assumed to take place in
unprocessed food, in foodstuffs at the *raw material* stage.
Its price is defined, both at the national level and at
the world market, as the deviation from the base-year value:

DFPE = domestic price level of unprocessed food, measured
       as deviation from the base-year value;
DFP = world market price level of unprocessed food, measured
       as deviation from the base-year value.

The domestic price DFPE is a weighed average of the world
market price and the desired domestic price level DFPE*:

$$DFPE = \delta.DFP + (1-\delta)DFPE* \qquad\qquad (6A.4)$$

with $0 < \delta \leq 1$.

Given DFPE*, the domestic price level will move in the same
direction as the world market price. Also, given the world
market price the domestic price will vary in the same direction as the desired domestic price DFPE*. This is shown in
fig. 9.1.

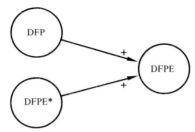

Fig. 9.1

Direct effects on the domestic food price

The domestic food price DFPE, as a component of the *total domestic food price* TFP, directly affects the level of food consumption in the non-agricultural sector[1]NCONS; its effect is negative - see Chapter 5.2. Disposable income in the non-agricultural sector NVLUE has a positive effect on consumption, through its effect on real income figuring in the consumption function. See figure 9.2.

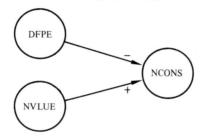

Fig. 9.2

Direct effects on non-agricultural food consumption

This picture is complicated by the fact that disposable income NVLUE is influenced by the domestic food price as well as by the food consumption level and still other factors. This effect on NVLUE runs through the tariff receipts (or the subsidy burden) modifying the - exogenously given - level of nominal non-agricultural income NVLU, as can be seen from Appendix 6A.2:

$$NVLUE = NVLU + (DFP-DFPE)(CTYC-NCONS) \qquad (6A.37)$$

In the case of a food-exporting country (i.e. CTYC-NCONS > 0), a lowering of the domestic food price DFPE will increase the tariff revenue, while at the same time an increase in NCONS

---

[1]Recall that food consumption in the agricultural sector is completely inelastic in the short run, as it follows from last year's production decision.

will reduce tariff revenue; also, an increase in the world
market price DFP will increase tariff receipts. As observed
already, NVLU and CTYC are given magnitudes. Thus, for a
food exporting country fig. 9.3 results.

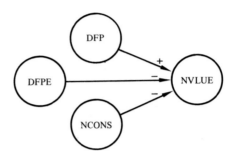

Fig. 9.3

*Direct effects on disposable income in non-
agriculture in a food-exporting country*

For a food-importing country, the arrows of fig. 9.3 will
have the opposite sign.

The world market price DFP is affected by the net foreign
trade position of the individual countries, i.e. by CTYC-
NCONS, of which the net food supply by the agricultural
sector CTYC is given. This variable and the given values of
DFPE* and NVLU determine in any specific year the equilibrium price on the world food market $\overline{DFP}$, together with the
corresponding equilibrium values of $\overline{DFPE}$, $\overline{NVLUE}$ and $\overline{NCONS}$
for the individual countries. This is shown in fig. 9.4, in
which figs. 9.1-9.3 are incorporated.

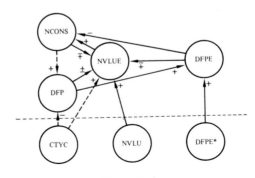

Fig. 9.4

*Interrelations between the main variables
influencing the world market price level*

The equilibrium value $\overline{DFP}$ is determined in an iterative procedure. The country variables CTYC, NVLU and DFPE* are exogenous variables in the equilibrium mechanism.

9.2.2 *The government's food price policy*

How do the equilibrium values $\overline{DFPE}$ and $\overline{NVLUE}$
affect the food price policy pursued by the government?
Together they determine the desired domestic price level of
the next year $DFPE^*_{t+1}$. Several links are involved in this
relationship

Disposable non-agricultural income, together with the politically desired income ratio PAR*, determines the desired
income level in agricultural VLUPOL:

$$VLUPOL = NVLUE/PAR* \qquad\qquad (6A.10)$$

Substitution of the desired income level VLUPOL in the
equation defining the producer's income - see Appendix 6A.1 -
gives the desired domestic food price for the next year
$DFPE^*_{t+1}$. These relations are illustrated in fig. 9.5.

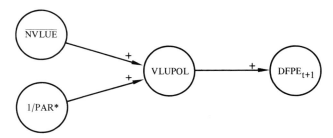

Fig. 9.5

*Direct effects on the desired domestic
food price for the next year*

The politically desired income ration PAR* depends, among
other factors, on real income in agricultural RVLU; see
Chapter 6.3.2. Real income in agriculture increases when
nominal agricultural income VLU increases as a consequence
of a higher food price DFPE, provided that the agricultural
sector consumes not only food products; a higher real income
in agriculture RVLU is assumed to influence the income
ratio PAR* between non-agriculture and agriculture in favour
of a larger share for agriculture (i.e. PAR* will take a
lower value). Introducing these effects in fig. 9.5 gives us
fig. 9.6.

Fig. 9.6 remains a simplified picture, as the ratio
NVLUE.NPOP/VLU.L = NV/V is another explanatory variable determining the level of PAR*. Note also that a change in
$\overline{DFPE}$ at the same time induces a change in $\overline{NVLUE}$, as is seen

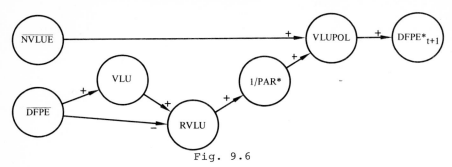

Fig. 9.6

*Interrelations between the main variables
influencing the desired domestic food price*

in fig. 9.4. The two effects on VLUPOL and $DFPE^*_{t+1}$ may work
in opposite direction.

9.2.3 *The agricultural producer's reaction*

The reaction of the agricultural producer on the
development of the food price and of incomes is twofold: his
production decision, and his possible decision to leave the
agriculture sector. We will first discuss labour outflow
from agriculture.

Agricultural population and labour force increase because of
(exogenously given) population growth g_{POP} and decrease as a
consequence of labour outflow LO. The latter variable is a
function of the ratio between the real incomes per capita in
non-agriculture NR and agriculture RVLU; see Chapter 4.5 and
(4.28). RVLU appeared already in fig. 9.6, while NR depends
on NVLUE and DFPE.

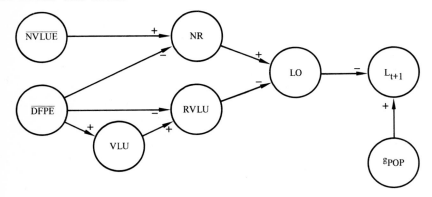

Fig. 9.

*Interrelations between the main variables influencing
labour outflow and the agricultural labour force*

In (4.27), labour outflow is influenced also by the distribution of population over the two sectors, i.e. by L/NPOP;
this long-term effect is not shown in fig. 9.7. Note that in
the long term the development of $\overline{\text{NVLUE}}$ is largely exogenous,
as the growth rate of total non-agricultural income NV is
exogenously given. As mentioned before, it is a shortcoming
of the present model that the growth of NV is not affected
by labour inflow from agriculture (as part of the non-
agricultural population).

Now we turn to the production decision. At a given quantity
of labour in agriculture L_{t+1} and at given prices of agricultural inputs, planned agricultural production will increase
when the expected price received by the producer P^*_{t+1} increases; see Chapter 4.4. (Note that this reaction is weaker
the smaller the amount of inputs bought by the agricultural
producer, i.e. the closer we are to subsistance agriculture).
As discussed in Chapter 4.4.5.5, the expected producer price
is the weighed average of the price actually received in the
previous year and expected price of the previous year; DFPE
is a component of this producer price. Hence, expected total
yield TY^*_{t+1} is positively related to DFPE.

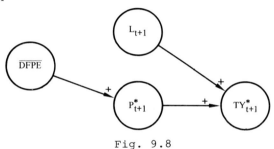

Fig. 9.8

Direct effects on expected total food production

Expected agricultural income VLU^*_{t+1} is also positively
linked to P^*_{t+1} and hence to DFPE. For the agricultural
sector in a rich country this means that net food supply to
the non-agricultural sector CTYC will increase; for a poor
agricultural sector this need not be the case. Introducing
these effects in fig. 9.8, we obtain fig. 9.9.

As mentioned in Chapter 5.2.3, the consumption plan of the
agricultural sector is linked to the production plan: the
actual ratio $CONS_{t+1}/TY_{t+1}$ will be equal to $CONS^*_{t+1}/TY^*_{t+1}$.
Due to uncontrollable weather conditions etc., in general
$$CTYC_{t+1} \neq TY^*_{t+1} - CONS^*_{t+1}$$

9.2.4 *A simplified arrow scheme of MOIRA*

Figs. 9.4, 9.6, 9.7 and 9.9 are brought together
in fig. 9.10. The variable NVLU in fig. 9.4 is represented
now by total non-agricultural income NV (exogenous) and non-

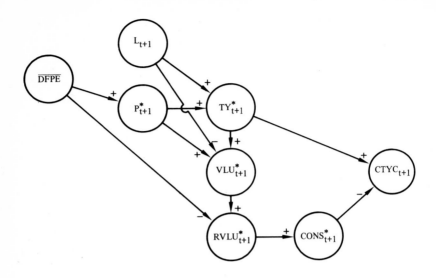

Fig. 9.9

*Interrelations between the variables influencing
net food supply to non-agriculture*

agricultural population NPOP, as NVLU = NV/NPOP. In fig.
9.10 the exogenous magnitudes are NV and g_{POP}; for the sake
of simplicity, also net food exports of centrally-planned
economies NETEX is shown as an exogenous variable. The
rectangle labelled *world market* denotes the iteration procedure by which the equilibrium values are computed, as
described in Chapter 7. As observed before, several simplifi-
cations have been introduced in order to keep the arrow
scheme relatively clear.

The equilibrium values resulting from world market equilibrium have their effects on many current-year variables as
well as on the agricultural sector's decisions regarding
next year's production and consumption of food, and on the
government's decision regarding the desired domestic food
price level for next year. The resulting values for $DFPE^*_{t+1}$
and $CTYC_{t+1}$ are (part of the) data for determining the world
market equilibrium in the following year.

9.3   *THE STRUCTURE OF THE COMPUTER PROGRAMME*

The arrow schemes of the above section and in particular
fig. 9.10 facilitate the understanding of the main structure
of the computer programme of MOIRA. The programme itself is
available upon request (see the addresses given in the Preface)
Keeping in mind the basic structure of the programme, as

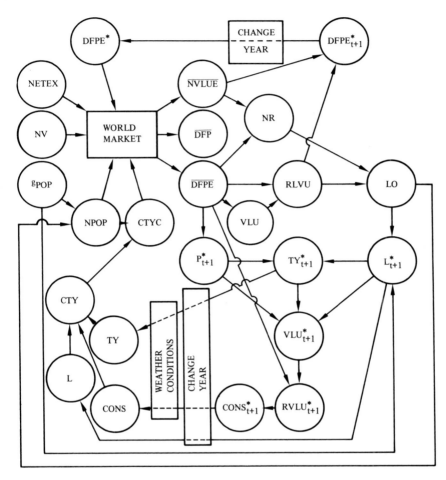

Fig. 9.10

Interrelations between some of the main variables in MOIRA

shown in fig. 9.11, may help the reader in digesting the full
programme.

The various *boxex* of fig. 9.11 show the sequence in which the
major variables and functions appear in the programme.
Reference is made to the chapter or chapters in which the
variables and functions concerned are discussed in detail.
The diagram gives, again, a stylized picture only. More
particularly, it excludes the additional equations needed
for simulation of alternative food policies to be discussed
in Part III.

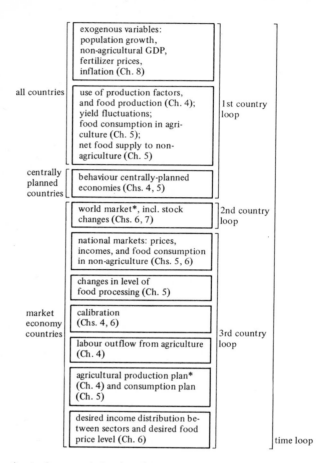

* = simultaneous solution through iterative procedure.

Fig. 9.11

*General structure of the computer programme
(without policy simulations)*

PART III

MOIRA AND THE WORLD FOOD PROBLEM

Chapter 10

THE WORKING OF MOIRA AND ITS SENSITIVITY TO
EXOGENOUS INFLUENCES

10.1 *INTRODUCTION*

Parts I and II have given a picture of the world food
situation and an analysis of the causes of hunger and malnutrition. The model MOIRA as presented in Part II is an
analytical description of the world food problem - and
especially of the international trade relations and their
implications. Part III focusses on results of MOIRA simulations. Simulation runs will be discussed in order to
assess MOIRA's sensitivity for alternative assumptions
regarding the future development of exogenous variables
(this chapter), and in order to investigate the consequences
of alternative international food policies aiming at lowering
and possibly abolishing hunger in the world (Chapter 11).
Before doing so, a few comments are called for regarding the
measurement of the crucial endogenous variables *world hunger*
and *world market price*.

World hunger

As stated already in section 5.3, the variable hunger is
defined as the positive difference between food norm and
food consumption of income class i of sector s of country j,
multiplied by the population size of the income class
concerned. Summation over i and s gives total hunger for
country j $HUNG_j$ for any specific year. Summation over all j
gives world hunger WHUNG:

$$\sum_j (HUNG_j)_t = WHUNG_t \qquad (10.1)$$

HUNG and WHUNG are measured in terms of consumable proteins;
the food norms involved in their actual computation are discussed in section 8.5. The variables $HUNG_j$ and WHUNG could
also be expressed in terms of the imaginary number of people
having no food at all, by dividing the variables by the
(average) food norms. Alternatively, if it is assumed that
people suffering from hunger and malnutrition consume on the
average 2/3 of the food norm, the variables in (10.1) should
be divided by 1/3 of the food norm to obtain an estimate of
the total number of hungry people. The latter assumption is

made in this and the next chapter whenever - for illustrative
purposes only - numbers of people affected by hunger and
malnutrition are mentioned.

In view of the divergence of interests between agricultural
and non-agricultural population as regards food prices, the
model distinguishes between hunger inside and outside the
agricultural sector. The variable AWHUNG represents that
part of WHUNG which is located, according to MOIRA, in the
agricultural sector.

Indicator world market price (DFP)

For every year the model calculates to what extent the
equilibrium price in the world food market differs from the
international price level in the base year 1965 (see Chapter 9).
This positive or negative price deviation is therefore an
indicator for the relative level of the world market price
of food in a specific year, while year-to-year mutations in
DFP show the direction and magnitude of price changes in the
world market over time.

DFP is expressed in 1965 U.S. dollars per 100 kg consumable
protein. A DFP of for instance 200 indicates that the world
market price is $200 per 100 kg above the 1965 level. DFP =
0 implies a price equal to the base year price.

From the historical world market prices in 1965 of the main
internationally traded primary food products, a weighed
average price of about $100 per 100 kg consumable protein
(of both vegetable and animal origin) can be derived. Consequently, a DFP_t of 200 indicates that the international
price level in year t is roughly threefold the 1965 level.
Sometimes the model generates negative DFP's of an absolute
magnitude near or even greater than 100. This indicates the
world market price to be near zero or even negative. Evidently, the equilibrium mechanism in MOIRA is not able to simulate
in a realistic way actual market performance under extreme
conditions of oversupply in the international market. In
those conditions exporters and possibly importers too make
special adjustments; this behaviour could not adequately be
incorporated in MOIRA. Consequently, a strongly negative
DFP - although in any case implying a very low price level -
is a less reliable indicator of the level of the world
market price than a positive DFP is.

10.2 *FUTURE DEVELOPMENT OF THE WORLD FOOD SITUATION ACCORDING
TO THE STANDARD RUN*

In the first instance MOIRA has been used to examine
how the world food situation will develop in the period
until 2010 under the assumptions mentioned in Chapter 8
regarding the exogenous variables.

According to the model, the comparatively fast economic
growth in the non-agricultural sector (more than 7 percent
in poor, and more than 4 percent in rich countries) and the
related increase in food demand will cause a relative scarcity on the world market (see Appendix 10A, run 111). The
international prices will fluctuate around a level which is
substantially higher than the price level in the base year
1965 (see figure 10.4). In the year 2010, world food production will be more than 2.5 times as high as in 1975 (a
growth rate of 2.7 percent a year); thus, it increases
faster than population growth (see figure 10.1). Nevertheless,

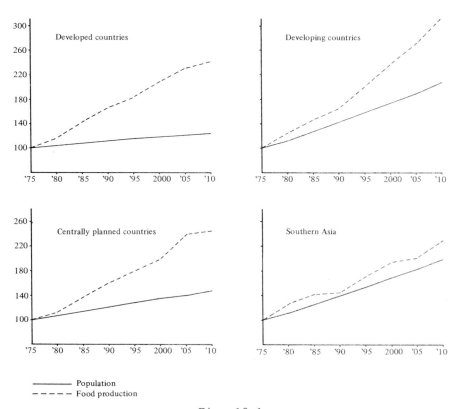

Fig. 10.1

*Development of population and volume of food production in
selected regions (1975-2010; indices, 1975 = 100) under the
assumptions of unchanged policy and relatively high income
growth in the non-agricultural sector
(standard run, cf. Appendix 10A, run 111)*

during this period, the number of people who have less than the minimum necessary amount of food will more than triple to a total of about 1.1 billion (figure 10.3). Average consumption per head of population will hardly increase in the densely populated developing countries (in particular South and Southeast Asia) (figure 10.2); hunger will mostly expand in these countries, especially among the non-agricultural population whose numbers will increase strongly. In the rich countries, but also in Latin America, Tropical Africa and the Middle East, per capita food consumption will burgeon considerably. The differences in the world will thus grow even greater (figure 10.2). According to these model results, North America will strengthen its position as important exporter of basic foods.

As has been said already in Chapter 4, the country model for the three centrally-planned groups of countries in MOIRA is rather crude and limited; as a consequence, the results of the simulation runs are for these countries not particularly interesting. They are assumed to aim at a selfsufficiency ratio of 100, and apart from very minor deviations due to weather fluctuations they succeed in maintaining the ratio at this level. The *passive* impact of these countries (given their assumed behaviour) on the world market is not very considerable; hence, in Appendix 10A and in the discussion of the simulation runs the centrally-planned economies will not be referred to explicitly.

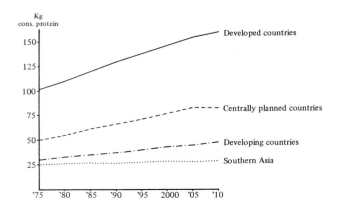

Fig. 10.2

Food consumption (in kg consumable protein per caput
in selected regions
(assumptions as in fig. 10.1)

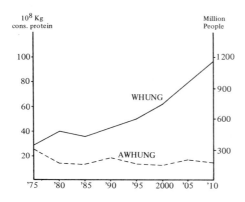

Fig. 10.3

*Development of hunger in the world (WHUNG)
and its component located in the agricultural sector (AWHUNG): number of people
with a consumption below the minimum food
standard and their total food deficit
(in 10⁸ kg consumable proteins);
assumptions as in fig. 10.1*

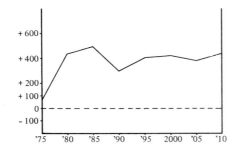

Fig. 10.4

*Development of the indicator for the world
market price of food (DFP = deviations
from the world price level in 1965);
assumptions as in fig. 10.1*

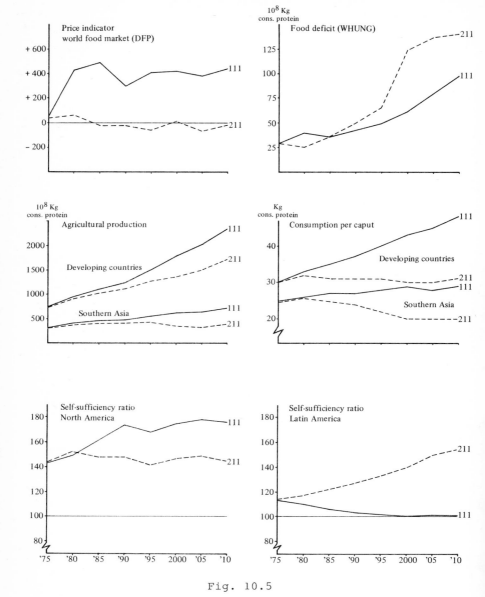

Fig. 10.5

*Impact of a lower growth rate of the non-agricultural sector
on selected indicators; comparisons between the standard
run 111 and the run in which growth rates of
income outside agriculture are half of
those in the standard run (run 211)*

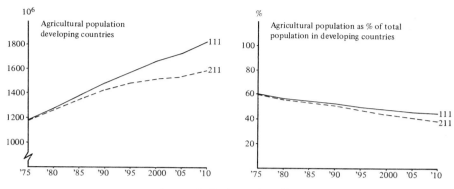

Fig. 10.5 *(continued)*

10.3 *THE IMPACT OF ECONOMIC GROWTH OUTSIDE AGRICULTURE*

Developments in the world food situation prove to be rather sensitive to the growth rate of non-agricultural GDP. An alternative simulation run in which growth rates for income outside agriculture were half as large as those in the standard run - see Appendix 10A, run 211 - generates far lower world market prices. World food production will only double in the period 1975-2010, nearly keeping pace with population growth. Hunger in that period is on average 35 percent larger than in the standard run, mainly because hunger in agriculture is much higher. In the densely populated Asian countries average per caput consumption decreases.

The differences in results between this simulation run and the standard run of section 10.2 (graphically shown for some of the variables in figure 10.5) are a good point of departure for illustrating again the functioning of MOIRA. This illustration and explanation is of use not only for understanding the implications of varying the assumed growth rate of non-agricultural incomes in MOIRA but also for the discussion of other simulation runs by keeping in mind the various points made in the present explanation.

A slower rate of growth of non-agricultural income (as compared to the one in the standard run) has domestically, i.e. within the countries, the following *primary* effects:
(a)   the demand for food by the non-agricultural population
        will grow less rapidly. According to the estimated consumption function (see Chapter 5) the sensitivity of food consumption - expressed in terms of consumable protein - to income changes is relatively high, not only at lower income levels but also for the higher income classes. Therefore, also in the rich countries a slower rate of growth of non-agrarian income clearly slows down the growth in demand for consumable protein.
(b)   a lower rate of income growth of the non-agricultural

sector leads (all other things being the same) to a
lower attraction or pulling force of this sector for the
agrarian population. Consequently, labour outflow from agriculture will be smaller.
(c)   given domestic policy as regards the distribution of
       income between agriculture and non-agriculture (the
income disparity equation of Chapter 6), a lower growth rate
of non-agricultural income leads to a lower domestic food
price level.

These primary effects - and in particular the one mentioned
under (c) - cause again several *secondary* effects:
(a)   the lower increase in the domestic price of food results
       in an income level of the agricultural population that
is lower than the agricultural income level corresponding
with a high rate of growth of non-agricultural income. This
effect in itself increases the tendency to leave the agricultural sector and will lead to increased labour outflow;
it works in a direction opposite to that of the primary
effect under (b).
(b)   inasmuch as these two opposite forces have the net
       effect of a slower increase (or a more rapid decrease)
of the volume of labour in agriculture - as compared to the
standard run with higher non-agricultural income growth -,
agricultural production growth will also be slowed down.
According to the estimated production function (see Chapter
4), the marginal productivity of labour has a substantial
magnitude, at least in the long run.
(c)   the lower level of domestic food prices resulting from
       a slower growth of non-agricultural income means a
reduced incentive for expanding the use of purchased inputs
in agriculture, and therefore also leads to a slower increase
in agricultural production. This price effect on agricultural production volume is larger when the economic relations
between agriculture and the rest of the economy are more intensive.

There is a possible *tertiary* effect that has to be mentioned.
A reduced rate of growth of non-agricultural income implies
that a larger number of countries will remain for a longer
period of time under the $400 level of non-agricultural in-
come per caput. As explained in Chapter 8, below this per
caput income level the assumed rate of growth of non-agricultural income may have to be adapted downwards in case the
rate of growth of the agricultural sector is lagging behind
considerably.

Thus far, possible influences of the world food market on
domestic developments have not come into the picture. In
fact, all effects mentioned above have their consequences
for the net export position (the difference between domestic
supply and demand) of a country. These consequences in turn
affect price formation on the world food market. According
to the results of the two simulation runs presently being
compared (see figure 10.5), a lower rate of growth of non-
agricultural income results - because of all its domestic

consequences - in an appreciably lower world market food
price level, even below the 1965 level. Note, however, that
this result is at the same time due to the influence a lowering of the world market food price exerts in turn on the
domestic food price level and hence on (agricultural and
non-agricultural) incomes of the countries, and consequently
on food production and consumption.

Food consumption is not particularly sensitive to price
changes on the world market, especially in the rich countries.
This is primarily a result of their high level of prosperity;
the price elasticity of the total demand for food is consequently small, while the national incomes of these countries
are also relatively insensitive to changes in the value of
food imports and exports. Secondly, the rich nations protect
their domestic food prices to a large extent against international price fluctuations. The result is that consumers in
these countries are very little affected by possible scarcity or surplus on the world market. Consequently, a lower
international price is not able to induce an increase of
consumption in the richer part of the world.

For the developing countries, the situation is somewhat
different. In the model, the domestic food price level of
developing countries is more readily affected by the world
market food price. Still, in the case of food-importing poor
countries the effects of a change in the international food
price partly offset each other and the consequences for the
domestic food price level can not immediately be predicted
(see Chapter 9).

Over the years, supply of agricultural products in the
richer countries shows the greatest sensitivity to price
changes. When the agricultural sector becomes more market-
oriented - both as regards the sale of products and the
purchase of means of production - an increase in food
prices, *ceteris paribus*, has a relatively greater effect on
income and therefore is a stronger incentive to invest, and
vice versa. It is true that producer prices in the rich
countries are protected by government against price movements on the world market, but the model suggests that even
the assumed restricted percolation of international price
influences has undeniable effects on total supply.

The fact that in MOIRA a reduction of the growth rate of
non-agricultural income by fifty per cent results in a much
lower world market food price, indicates that all simultaneously operating national and international forces and
relations have a negative effect on demand increases that
surpasses the negative effect on production increases. That
is at least the case in the greatest part of the world, viz.
the developing countries. In the rich countries, however,
the increase of food supply - because of its greater sensitivity to prices - does not surpass the growth of domestic
food consumption. As a consequence the self-sufficiency
ratio of North America - contrary to the standard-run case -
does not increase, whereas Latin America takes over part of

the role of exporter to the food importing developing countries, particularly the Southern Asian Region (see figure
10.5).

As observed already, the magnitude of hunger (WHUNG) is much
larger in the case of slower growth of non-agricultural
income than in the standard run. This is caused by a lack of
purchasing power of the agrarian sector in developing countries, which in turn is due to the effect of a low world
market food price on the producer price in these countries.
While in the standard run agricultural hunger AWHUNG does
not increase over the period 1975-2010, its magnitude is
trebled in the run of a fifty per cent lower growth rate of
non-agricultural income.

Finally, attention may be drawn to the difference between
the two runs as to the development of agricultural population.
In case of reduced income growth in the non-agricultural
sector agricultural population will increase less rapidly,
according to MOIRA, than in the standard-run case of a
rather high growth rate of non-agricultural income (fig.
10.5). Apparantly the migration-stimulating effect of the
lower income level in the agricultural sector is stronger
than the migration-reducing effect of lower incomes outside
agriculture.

10.4 *THE IMPACT OF POPULATION GROWTH*

In order to test the sensitivity of the model for
changes in the growth rate of population, a simulation run
was made in which the population growth rates were set at
half of their values in the standard run (average annual
population growth rates in the standard run: 0.7 in rich
countries, 2.2 in poor countries). The other exogeneous
variables were kept at their standard value. This implies a
strong increase in income per caput outside agriculture,
particularly in the developing countries, which in turn
positively influences domestic food prices, agricultural
incomes and agricultural production. On the other hand,
growth of agricultural supply is negatively influenced by a
smaller increase of the labour availability while total
demand is negatively influenced by the smaller population
size.

The outcome in MOIRA (see figure 10.6 and Appendix 10A run
112) is that world market prices are substantially lower
than in the standard run. Evidently, export supply is effected more strongly than import demand. In Latin America agricultural production remains almost at the same level as in
the standard run, as a consequence of a relatively high
marginal productivity of investments in agriculture. This
region therefore is able to strengthen its position as an
exporter, while at the same time its per caput consumption
is increasing. Production in the rich countries and their
self-sufficiency ratio are at a lower level than in the
standard run mainly because of the lower world market prices.

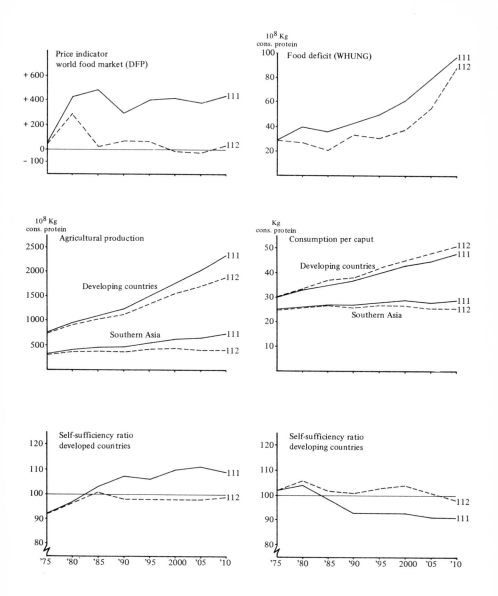

Fig. 10.6

*Comparison between the standard run 111 and run 112
in which growth rates of population are assumed
to be half of those in the standard run*

In Southern Asia food production hardly rises because the
agricultural population hardly increases; the assumed high
per caput income growth outside agriculture strengthens the
outflow of labour out of agriculture. On the other hand,
domestic food prices have to be raised substantially in
trying to realize the income parity goal. Consequently, the
buying power of food consumers is negatively affected to
such an extent that the average per caput consumption in
this region of the world is growing even slower than in the
standard run.

Over the period 1975-2010 world hunger is on average 30 per
cent lower than in the standard run mainly because hunger
outside agriculture decreases more than agricultural hunger
is increasing. However, expressed per head of total world
population hunger is only 15 per cent lower than in the
standard run.

As a general statement one could say that the much slower
rate of population growth which was assumed alleviates the
world food problem but does not solve it. One should especially keep in mind that it was assumed that a lowering of the
growth rate of population would not directly affect the
growth rate of non-agricultural GDP.

10.5 *SENSITIVITY TO INCOME DISTRIBUTION OUTSIDE AGRICULTURE*

In order to test MOIRA's sensitivity to the distribution
of income within the non-agricultural sector, the effect on
the food situation of gradually decreasing income inequalities was considered. In this run the share of income earned
by an income class of the non-agricultural sector ($distm_i$)
is progressively moved towards the share of the income class
in the non-agricultural population (d_i) by an amount of 2
per cent per year. For every country this implies:

$$distm_{i,t} = distm_{i,t-1}(1-NIVN) + d_i.NIVN \qquad (10.2)$$

with NIVN = 0.02.

Consequently, over the period 1975-2010 income inequality is
gradually reduced to about half of its initial magnitude.

As a result of the reduced relative income differences in
the non-agricultural sector, world hunger is substantially
decreased in comparison with the standard run (see figure 10.7).
In the lower income brackets income increases more rapidly
than at the assumed rate of growth of average non-agricultural GDP. Consequently, average food consumption per caput
in both the rich and the poor countries is growing faster
than in the standard run. On a global scale this greater
demand induces a relative shortage in the world market and
an international price level which is still substantially
above the already high DFP in the standard run.

Mainly due to this very high international food price level

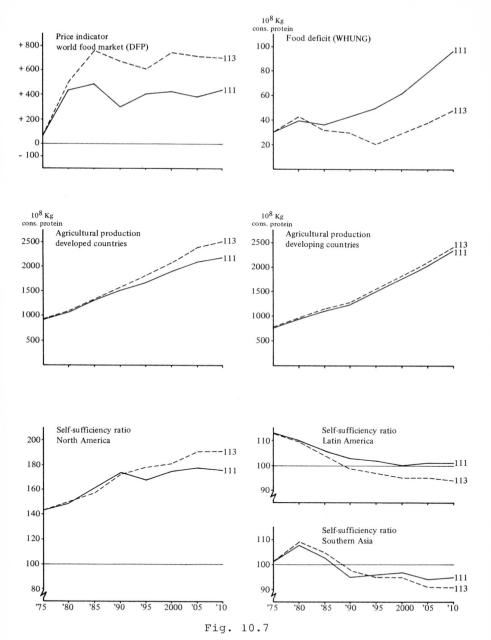

Fig. 10.7

*Comparison between the standard run 111 assuming fixed
income distribution and run 113 assuming gradually
decreasing income inequalities outside agriculture*

food supply in the rich countries is induced to expand
faster than the increase of domestic consumption: the self-
sufficiency ratio of these countries is rising to a higher
level than in the standard run.

In the developing countries agricultural production is, by
and large, only slightly higher than in the standard run, in
spite of the stimulus of a high international price level
for production increases in market-oriented agriculture.
Notably in Latin America the agricultural output level
remains unaffected by this incentive. The reason is that
under the assumptions of the standard run already the Latin-
American production growth rate comes close to the upper
limit of production growth of four per cent per annum built-
in in MOIRA. This constraint (explained in Chapter 4.4.4)
prevent additional effects from further incentives to production growth. Due to consumption increases caused by
reduced inequality in income distribution, Latin America
looses in the present run its position as food exporter.

In Southern Asia the rate of growth of agricultural production is still far below the upper limit mentioned above.
Nevertheless, production in this region of the world increases only slightly more than in the standard run. In
agriculture the use of purchased inputs is at a low level;
food supply, therefore, is much less sensitive to the large
increase of world market prices than in the rich countries.
As food consumption per caput is increasing according to the
equalizing of the income differences, the need for food
imports of Southern Asia is increasing.

This simulation run illustrates the thesis that the hunger
problem is to a large extent a problem of income distribution.
The gradual reduction of inequality in income distribution
within the non-agricultural sector is accompanied by considerably lower food deficits in the world. In the years after
1990 WHUNG is less than half of the extent of hunger in the
standard run. A relatively large part of the remaining
hunger is located in the agricultural sector. Note that in
this run the assumed improvement of income distribution is
limited to the non-agricultural sector only. It is not
possible to study the consequences of a less uneven income
distribution in agriculture in the same way; an assumption
on this point would have to take into account also the
implicit changes in the agricultural production structure
and their consequences for production growth. In its present
form, MOIRA is not able to cope with this problem.

10.6 *COMPARING THE VARIOUS SIMULATION RUNS*

      A survey of the numerical results (for selected variables)
of a limited number of simulation runs of MOIRA is given in
Appendix 10A. In the preceding sections of this chapter, the
reader has been referred already to some of the columns of
this table; the larger part of these runs will be discussed

in Chapter 11 only.

It should be emphasized here - and the authors feel that this point can hardly be overstressed - that the main figures given in Appendix 10A may suggest to the reader an accuracy and preciseness that are not warranted by the coarseness of MOIRA as a picture of reality. In view of the imperfections of MOIRA as a model of the real world, the numerical results should not be taken too *literally*. The seemingly *hard* numbers and their variations over time may be interpreted only as indicating tendencies that will manifest themselves in the world food situation under specific assumptions - and the reader will have noticed that many *ad-hoc* assumptions had to be made. This general proviso will have to be kept in mind when the numerical results of MOIRA simulation runs are studied and interpreted.

The discussion in the above sections regarding the effects of alternative assumptions concerning the exogenous variables has been used at the same time to illustrate the functioning of MOIRA on certain points. By way of comment on the findings presented in Appendix 10A it may be useful to list summarily some important factors underlying the differences between the world regions in future development over time as they operate in MOIRA.

(a)   Intensity of use of natural production conditions.
      As we have seen in Chapter 4, a country's natural con-
ditions for agricultural production are introduced in MOIRA
as a given factor of production taking the shape of the
maximum level of output per hectare YASY and the area potentially suitable for agricultura A. The actual level of
intensity of use of potential arable land is given by the
variable Z which is a function of the amounts of labour and
capital employed in production. The variables YASY and Z
together determine the yield level Y. For lower values of
the intensity of land use Z marginal productivity of labour
and capital will be higher; also, these marginal productivi-
ties of L and C will be higher, for a given value of Z, the
higher the value of YASY is.

As the (average) value of YASY and Z differ between the
regions, production response to a (domestic) price incentive
also differs considerably. In a region with a high YASY and
a low Z, on the average, production will respond relatively
strongly to price increases; also, agricultural population
growth will have a relatively large effect on the output
level. The fairly rapid expansion of agricultural production
in Latin America is a good case in point. It was mentioned
already that in this region the upper limit on annual production growth is often effective in the model. In densely
populated Southern Asia these conditions are less favourable:
a production increase requires relatively more labour and
capital inputs and consequently production growth shows a
slower development over time in that region. Within the
group of rich countries, a similar difference can be traced
between the North-American region, on the one hand, and the

European Community on the other.

(b)   Intensity of interrelations between agriculture and the
      non-agricultural sector.
The larger the extent to which the agricultural sector
interacts with the non-agricultural sector (for selling its
produce and for buying its inputs), the larger is also its
sensitivity to the relative prices of output and inputs; see
Chapter 4.4.3.2. The more intensive these interrelations
are, the greater are also the magnitude and the speed of
reactions of production to price changes. Obviously, agriculture in the industrialized countries and regions meets
this condition to a larger extent than that in the poor
countries where a considerable part of agriculture is still
functioning in relative isolation of the rest of the economy.

(c)   Position in international trade in food, or self-
      sufficiency ratio.
The effect of a change in the world market food price on the
economy of a country depends on the level of self-sufficiency.
For a food-importing country, a lowering of the world market
price DFP increases national income in real terms (as output
is given in the short run); depending on the measure of use
of compensatory import duties, this increase in real income
takes the form of a lower domestic food price or a higher
disposable (nominal) income of the non-agricultural sector.
Both effects lead to increased food consumption in non-agriculture. For a food-exporting country the direct effect of a
lower world market price is of course in the opposite direction. The more the self-sufficiency ratio for food of a
country or region deviates from 100 (either upwards or
downwards), the greater is the impact of a change in DFP. It
is also obvious that the effect on national income is greater
when the volume of imports or exports of food is larger
relative to the level of total economic activity.

(d)   Level of per caput income.
      The price elasticity of demand for food decreases with
increasing per caput income; see Chapter 5.2.2. Therefore,
in rich countries food consumption is less sensitive to
price changes. Moreover, the capacity of these countries to
protect their domestic food price level against undesired
influences from the world market price is greater than that
of the developing countries. In countries or regions with a
lower level of per caput income, the effect of changes in
the world market price DFP on the domestic food price level
is more pronounced, and the relatively price-elastic food
consumption is affected more easily. Also, the producer
price received by the farmer has to follow world market
price developments more closely in poor countries than in
the rich. At the same time it remains true, however, that
agricultural output in poor countries is less sensitive to
price changes because of the factor mentioned under (b).

The four factors (a) to (d) operate continuously and simultaneously, and generate various secondary effects. Their
combined interaction shows up in the numerical results of

the simulation runs as given in Table 10A. It is well to remember them in trying to interpret and understand the alternative regional patterns of development of food production and consumption shown in the table, even though the entire *mechanism* of MOIRA is more complex than the above four factors might suggest. (For a general comment on the time pattern of food policy effects, see Chapter 11.1.4).

10.7 *MOIRA AS A SECTOR MODEL*

At the end of this chapter, we come back to its main theme: MOIRA's sensitivity to exogenous influences. We have seen that the results of the simulation runs are strongly influenced by the assumptions one makes about the future development of such exogenous variables as population, non-agricultural income and income distribution. As MOIRA is basically a sector model, a model of the agricultural sector of the world economy, it is not surprising that it is sensitive to such *outside* influences.

In reality, varying degrees of uncertainty exist with regard to future developments of all these exogenous variables. In view of the sensitivity of the results to these developments, MOIRA has only very relative value for prognostic purposes. Its usefulness lies mainly in its ability to illustrate the cumulative short- and long-term effects of a certain external influence or of a purposeful political intervention on developments in world food production and consumption. It is therefore used to evaluate different forms of international coordinated food policies whose aim is to eliminate hunger in the world, or at least to minimize it. This objective is relevant under all circumstances. All simulation runs with alternative assumptions regarding exogenous variables have one thing in common: if policies remain unchanged the number of people who cannot obtain sufficient food will increase. The authors feel that MOIRA conveys this impression rather convincingly.

Appendix 10A

SELECTED RESULTS OF MOIRA SIMULATIONS:
Trends in agricultural production, food consumption, agricultural population, international food price level and
hunger under alternative assumptions regarding exogenous variables and policies; world and selected
regions (three-year averages)

Appendix 10A: SELECTED RESULTS OF MOIRA SIMULATIONS

RUN 111   : Unchanged policies, relatively *high* growth rate non-agricultural
              GDP; *standard run*

	1966	1975	1980	1990	2000	2009
TOTAL AGRICULTURAL PRODUCTION $(10^8$ kg cons. prot.)						
World	1943	2495	2970	4094	5340	6530
Developed countries	743	910	1067	1517	1896	2194
North America	403	497	580	855	1009	1151
European Community	147	182	218	297	377	434
Developing countries	599	749	941	1237	1774	2344
Latin America	181	241	297	434	631	905
Tropical Africa	66	82	96	145	208	297
Middle East	58	72	96	128	220	287
Southern Asia	265	321	409	467	624	736
FOOD CONSUMPTION PER CAPUT (kg cons. prot.)						
World	46	50	53	61	68	73
Developed countries	86	102	110	130	147	160
North America	107	121	129	148	163	173
European Community	90	103	108	126	141	153
Developing countries	30	30	33	37	43	48
Latin America	43	48	52	63	76	89
Tropical Africa	25	25	27	34	40	47
Middle East	38	40	46	56	71	78
Southern Asia	26	25	26	27	29	29
SELF-SUFFICIENCY-RATIO CONSUMABLE PROTEIN						
Developed countries	96	92	97	107	110	109
North America	142	143	149	174	175	176
European Community	59	60	67	74	81	82
Developing countries	106	102	104	93	93	91
Latin America	123	113	110	103	100	101
Tropical Africa	111	104	102	98	93	92
Middle East	87	85	88	58	65	65
Southern Asia	100	101	108	95	97	95
PERCENTAGE OF POPULATION IN AGRICULTURE						
World	52	46	42	36	32	29
Developing countries	66	60	57	53	48	45
Latin America	45	38	36	32	28	25
Southern Asia	70	64	61	57	52	48
PRICE INDICATOR WORLD FOOD MARKET (DFP; 1965 = 0)	-8	60	431	301	422	442
WORLD HUNGER						
Total food deficit (WHUNG) $(10^8$ kg cons. prot.)	15	29	40	43	62	97
Million people below minimum food standard	180	350	480	520	740	1160
% of WHUNG located in agricultural sector	76	85	35	42	19	15

Appendix 10A (continued)

RUN 112   : Unchanged policies; relatively *high* growth rate of non-
                 agricultural GDP; low growth rate of population

	1966	1975	1980	1990	2000	2009
TOTAL AGRICULTURAL PRODUCTION (10^8 kg cons. prot.)						
World	1943	2486	2908	3728	4639	5387
Developed countries	743	909	1063	1350	1606	1826
North America	403	497	580	722	811	930
European Community	147	182	216	277	325	372
Developing countries	599	745	910	1144	1559	1871
Latin America	181	241	296	434	625	890
Tropical Africa	66	81	96	142	196	210
Middle East	58	71	96	126	206	258
Southern Asia	265	317	380	381	455	419
FOOD CONSUMPTION PER CAPUT (kg cons. prot.)						
World	46	50	55	64	74	80
Developed countries	86	102	112	133	153	167
North America	107	121	132	151	166	178
European Community	90	103	110	130	147	160
Developing countries	30	30	33	38	45	51
Latin America	43	48	54	69	88	109
Tropical Africa	25	25	27	34	40	48
Middle East	38	40	48	59	80	95
Southern Asia	26	25	26	26	27	26
SELF-SUFFICIENCY-RATIO CONSUMABLE PROTEIN						
Developed countries	96	92	97	98	98	99
North America	142	143	150	156	153	158
European Community	59	60	66	70	71	73
Developing countries	106	102	106	101	104	98
Latin America	123	114	116	116	117	121
Tropical Africa	111	106	108	113	117	93
Middle East	87	80	84	78	83	80
Southern Asia	100	101	107	96	100	87
PERCENTAGE OF POPULATION IN AGRICULTURE						
World	52	46	41	34	29	25
Developing countries	66	60	57	51	46	40
Latin America	45	38	35	31	27	23
Southern Asia	70	64	61	55	49	42
PRICE INDICATOR WORLD FOOD MARKET (DFP; 1965 = 0)	-8	43	293	72	-15	27
WORLD HUNGER						
Total food deficit (WHUNG) (10^8 kg cons. prot.)	15	29	27	33	38	88
Million people below minimum food standard	180	350	320	400	460	1060
% of WHUNG located in agricultural sector	76	86	54	61	36	26

Appendix 10A (continued)

RUN 113 : Unchanged policies; relatively *high* growth rate of
non-agricultural GDP; gradually decreasing income
inequalities outside agriculture

	1966	1975	1980	1990	2000	2009
TOTAL AGRICULTURAL PRODUCTION (10^8 kg cons. prot.)						
World	1943	2495	2971	4169	5570	6899
Developed countries	743	910	1068	1565	2071	2497
North America	403	497	580	888	1148	1380
European Community	147	182	218	304	400	473
Developing countries	599	749	942	1264	1829	2411
Latin America	181	241	297	434	630	908
Tropical Africa	66	82	96	145	209	298
Middle East	58	72	96	128	220	288
Southern Asia	265	321	409	495	678	795
FOOD CONSUMPTION PER CAPUT (kg cons. prot.)						
World	46	50	53	62	71	77
Developed countries	86	102	110	134	157	175
North America	107	121	128	156	180	192
European Community	90	103	109	129	150	167
Developing countries	30	30	33	38	46	52
Latin America	43	48	52	65	80	96
Tropical Africa	25	25	27	35	41	49
Middle East	38	40	46	58	74	86
Southern Asia	26	25	26	28	32	33
SELF-SUFFICIENCY-RATIO CONSUMABLE PROTEIN						
Developed countries	96	92	96	107	112	115
North America	142	143	150	172	181	191
European Community	59	60	67	74	81	82
Developing countries	106	102	105	92	90	86
Latin America	123	113	110	99	95	94
Tropical Africa	111	106	102	92	89	88
Middle East	87	80	80	64	68	63
Southern Asia	100	101	109	98	95	91
PERCENTAGE OF POPULATION IN AGRICULTURE						
World	52	46	42	37	33	30
Developing countries	66	60	57	53	49	46
Latin America	45	38	36	32	28	26
Southern Asia	70	64	61	57	53	50
PRICE INDICATOR WORLD FOOD MARKET (DFP; 1965 = 0)	-8	60	498	671	745	700
WORLD HUNGER						
Total food deficit (WHUNG) (10^8 kg cons. prot.)	15	29	43	30	30	48
Million people below minimum food standard	180	350	520	360	360	580
% of WHUNG located in agricultural sector	76	86	33	51	33	25

Appendix 10A (continued)

RUN 121   : Relatively *high* growth rate of non-agricultural GDP;
                   reduction of food consumption in the rich countries

	1966	1975	1980	1990	2000	2009
TOTAL AGRICULTURAL PRODUCTION (10^8 kg cons. prot.)						
World	1943	2495	2951	3833	4586	4237
Developed countries	743	910	1065	1319	1402	704
North America	403	497	580	703	683	109
European Community	147	182	217	268	291	217
Developing countries	599	749	925	1175	1513	1541
Latin America	181	241	296	434	619	730
Tropical Africa	66	82	96	131	154	171
Middle East	58	72	96	128	216	210
Southern Asia	265	321	393	421	445	334
FOOD CONSUMPTION PER CAPUT (kg cons. prot.)						
World	46	50	53	57	58	49
Developed countries	86	102	105	110	91	28
North America	107	120	124	126	103	22
European Community	90	103	103	108	88	35
Developing countries	30	30	33	36	40	38
Latin America	43	48	52	63	77	82
Tropical Africa	25	25	27	31	66	34
Middle East	38	40	46	55	72	77
Southern Asia	26	25	26	25	24	18
SELF-SUFFICIENCY-RATIO CONSUMABLE PROTEIN						
Developed countries	96	93	101	110	131	204
North America	142	143	155	168	187	136
European Community	59	60	70	79	100	184
Developing countries	106	102	101	91	84	74
Latin America	123	113	110	103	98	91
Tropical Africa	111	106	102	92	73	72
Middle East	87	79	80	67	68	51
Southern Asia	100	101	102	91	82	69
PERCENTAGE OF POPULATION IN AGRICULTURE						
World	52	46	42	35	30	26
Developing countries	66	60	57	51	45	39
Latin America	45	38	36	31	27	22
Southern Asia	70	64	61	55	48	41
PRICE INDICATOR WORLD FOOD MARKET (DFP; 1965 = 0)	-8	43	260	-28	-338	206
WORLD HUNGER						
Total food deficit (WHUNG) (10^8 kg cons. prot.)	15	29	24	43	79	333
Million people below minimum food standard	180	350	290	520	950	4000
% of WHUNG located in agricultural sector	76	85	67	64	55	26

Appendix 10A (continued)

RUN 122   : Relatively *high* growth rate of non-agricultural GDP;
               large-scale food aid financed by the rich countries

	1966	1975	1980	1990	2000	2009
TOTAL AGRICULTURAL PRODUCTION $(10^8$ kg cons. prot.)						
World	1943	2495	2971	4175	5432	6721
Developed countries	743	910	1068	1567	1964	2338
North America	403	497	580	888	1061	1253
European Community	147	182	219	307	388	453
Developing countries	599	749	942	1268	1797	2391
Latin America	181	241	297	434	631	907
Tropical Africa	66	82	96	145	209	298
Middle East	58	72	96	128	220	287
Southern Asia	265	321	409	498	646	777
FOOD CONSUMPTION PER CAPUT* (kg cons. prot.)						
World	46	50	53	62	70	75
Developed countries	86	102	106	129	147	160
North America	197	121	124	150	163	174
European Community	90	103	105	124	141	152
Developing countries	30	30	34	39	46	51
Latin America	43	48	52	64	77	90
Tropical Africa	25	25	29	35	41	48
Middle East	38	40	46	56	71	82
Southern Asia	26	25	27	29	32	34
SELF-SUFFICIENCY-RATIO CONSUMABLE PROTEIN*						
Developed countries	96	92	99	111	114	117
North America	142	143	154	180	184	191
European Community	59	60	69	78	83	86
Developing countries	106	101	101	90	89	87
Latin America	123	113	111	101	99	100
Tropical Africa	111	105	95	89	89	88
Middle East	87	79	80	66	71	66
Southern Asia	100	100	104	92	90	87
PERCENTAGE OF POPULATION IN AGRICULTURE						
World	52	46	42	37	33	30
Developing countries	66	60	57	54	49	46
Latin America	45	38	36	32	29	26
Southern Asia	70	64	61	58	53	49
PRICE INDICATOR WORLD FOOD MARKET (DFP; 1965 = 0)	-8	60	623	573	451	586
WORLD HUNGER						
Total food deficit (WHUNG) $(10^8$ kg cons. prot.) :gross	15	29	59	47	54	88
net	15	29	27	0	0	0
Million people below minimum food standard: gross	180	350	710	560	650	1060
net	180	350	320	0	0	0
% of WHUNG (gross) located in agricultural sector	76	85	23	31	20	15

*food aid included

Appendix 10A (continued)

Run 123   : Relatively *high* growth rate of non-agricultural GDP; large-scale
               food aid financed by the rich countries; adjustment of food
               consumption in rich countries according to the extent of hunger

	1966	1975	1980	1990	2000	2009
TOTAL AGRICULTURAL PRODUCTION (10^8 kg cons. prot.)						
World	1943	2495	2887	3887	5093	6234
Developed countries	743	910	1020	1363	1718	1975
North America	403	497	548	743	900	1039
European Community	147	182	213	275	341	392
Developing countries	599	749	907	1184	1705	2267
Latin America	181	241	296	434	629	902
Tropical Africa	66	82	88	139	199	280
Middle East	58	72	96	125	216	283
Southern Asia	265	321	384	425	575	690
FOOD CONSUMPTION PER CAPUT* (kg cons. prot.)						
World	46	50	52	58	65	70
Developed countries	86	100	97	114	124	133
North America	107	119	114	131	140	148
European Community	90	101	98	111	118	126
Developing countries	30	30	34	37	43	49
Latin America	43	48	53	63	76	90
Tropical Africa	25	25	28	32	38	44
Middle East	38	40	48	56	71	81
Southern Asia	26	25	27	27	29	30
SELF-SUFFICIENCY-RATIO CONSUMABLE PROTEIN*						
Developed countries	96	94	104	110	118	19
North America	142	146	159	171	181	185
European Community	59	61	72	78	87	91
Developing countries	106	101	96	89	89	87
Latin America	123	113	109	103	100	99
Tropical Africa	111	105	88	94	92	91
Middle East	87	79	76	65	69	66
Southern Asia	100	100	96	85	88	85
PERCENTAGE OF POPULATION IN AGRICULTURE						
World	52	46	42	35	31	28
Developing countries	66	60	57	51	46	42
Latin America	45	38	35	31	27	24
Southern Asia	70	64	61	55	49	45
PRICE INDICATOR WORLD FOOD MARKET (DFP; 1965 = 0)	-8	43	1	169	247	327
WORLD HUNGER						
Total food deficit (WHUNG) (10^8 kg cons. prot.) :gross	15	29	25	48	68	124
net	15	29	0	0	0	0
Million people below minimum food standard: gross	180	350	300	580	820	1490
net	180	350	0	0	0	0
% of WHUNG (gross) located in agricultural sector	76	85	73	55	24	14

*food aid included

Appendix 10A (continued)

RUN 124   : Relatively *high* growth rate of non-agricultural GDP;
            world market price policy, DFP-target = 0

	1966	1975	1980	1990	2000	2009
TOTAL AGRICULTURAL PRODUCTION (10^8 kg cons. prot.)						
World	1943	2496	2923	3810	4887	5865
Developed countries	743	910	1044	1307	1589	1850
North America	403	497	565	699	817	971
European Community	147	182	215	266	313	357
Developing countries	599	749	918	1164	1628	2023
Latin America	181	241	296	434	628	893
Tropical Africa	66	82	96	126	161	234
Middle East	58	72	96	124	201	254
Southern Asia	265	321	387	418	553	537
FOOD CONSUMPTION PER CAPUT (kg cons. prot.)						
World	46	50	52	57	63	66
Developed countries	86	102	101	113	122	128
North America	107	120	119	130	137	142
European Community	90	103	102	111	117	122
Developing countries	30	30	33	35	40	43
Latin America	43	48	52	63	76	89
Tropical Africa	25	25	27	30	35	41
Middle East	38	40	47	53	65	72
Southern Asia	26	25	26	25	25	23
SELF-SUFFICIENCY-RATIO CONSUMABLE PROTEIN						
Developed countries	96	93	102	106	111	116
North America	142	144	158	162	168	181
European Community	59	60	70	76	81	86
Developing countries	106	102	100	92	92	86
Latin America	123	113	110	104	100	99
Tropical Africa	111	106	103	90	79	81
Middle East	87	79	79	68	70	65
Southern Asia	100	101	100	92	99	84
PERCENTAGE OF POPULATION IN AGRICULTURE						
World	52	46	42	35	30	27
Developing countries	66	60	57	51	45	41
Latin America	45	38	35	31	27	24
Southern Asia	70	64	61	55	48	42
PRICE INDICATOR WORLD FOOD MARKET (DFP; 1965 = 0)	-8	43	-7	25	15	14
WORLD HUNGER						
Total food deficit (WHUNG) (10^8 kg cons. prot.)	15	29	24	47	64	139
Million people below minimum food standard	180	350	290	560	770	1670
% of WHUNG located in agricultural sector	76	85	73	63	37	41

Appendix 10A (continued)

RUN 125   : Relatively *high* growth rate of non-agricultural GDP;
                world market price policy, DFP-target = 200

	1966	1975	1980	1990	2000	2009
TOTAL AGRICULTURAL PRODUCTION (10^8 kg cons. prot.)						
World	1943	2495	2965	4030	5235	6354
Developed countries	743	910	1066	1473	1831	2066
North America	403	497	580	804	939	1066
European Community	147	182	218	284	351	402
Developing countries	599	749	938	1217	1734	2296
Latin America	181	241	297	433	628	902
Tropical Africa	66	82	96	145	207	292
Middle East	58	72	96	128	220	286
Southern Asia	265	321	406	450	590	700
FOOD CONSUMPTION PER CAPUT (kg cons. prot.)						
World	46	50	53	59	67	71
Developed countries	86	102	104	123	141	152
North America	107	121	123	142	157	165
European Community	90	103	103	120	135	146
Developing countries	30	30	33	36	42	46
Latin America	43	48	53	62	76	89
Tropical Africa	25	25	27	32	38	45
Middle East	38	40	46	55	69	78
Southern Asia	26	25	26	26	27	27
SELF-SUFFICIENCY-RATIO CONSUMABLE PROTEIN						
Developed countries	96	92	101	108	109	108
North America	142	143	156	171	168	170
European Community	59	60	70	75	78	80
Developing countries	106	102	102	93	94	92
Latin America	123	113	109	104	101	100
Tropical Africa	111	106	101	98	95	94
Middle East	87	80	80	67	73	68
Southern Asia	100	101	105	95	97	97
PERCENTAGE OF POPULATION IN AGRICULTURE						
World	52	46	42	36	31	28
Developing countries	66	60	57	52	47	43
Latin America	45	38	36	31	27	24
Southern Asia	70	64	61	56	50	46
PRICE INDICATOR WORLD FOOD MARKET (DFP; 1965 = 0)	-8	60	278	300	277	228
WORLD HUNGER						
Total food deficit (WHUNG) (10^8 kg cons. prot.)	15	29	29	46	70	106
Million people below minimum food standard	180	350	350	550	840	1270
% of WHUNG located in agricultural sector	76	85	51	47	21	16

Appendix 10A (continued)

RUN 127   : Relatively *high* growth rate of non-agricultural GDP;
                large-scale food aid; world market price policy,
                DFP-target = 0

	1966	1975	1980	1990	2000	2009
TOTAL AGRICULTURAL PRODUCTION $(10^8$ kg cons. prot.)						
World	1943	2495	2939	3820	4904	5894
Developed countries	743	910	1056	1310	1582	1769
North America	403	497	574	699	814	924
European Community	147	182	216	265	310	337
Developing countries	599	749	921	1170	1652	2133
Latin America	181	241	296	434	628	902
Tropical Africa	66	82	96	129	172	239
Middle East	58	72	96	128	218	283
Southern Asia	265	321	389	418	551	605
FOOD CONSUMPTION PER CAPUT* (kg cons. prot.)						
World	46	50	72	57	63	65
Developed countries	86	101	96	108	113	106
North America	107	120	112	125	128	119
European Community	90	103	96	105	108	101
Developing countries	30	30	34	37	42	47
Latin America	43	48	53	63	77	90
Tropical Africa	25	25	28	32	37	43
Middle East	38	40	49	57	74	80
Southern Asia	26	25	28	27	27	28
SELF-SUFFICIENCY-RATIO CONSUMABLE PROTEIN*						
Developed countries	96	93	109	111	119	134
North America	142	144	169	169	179	203
European Community	59	60	75	80	87	98
Developing countries	106	101	97	88	88	84
Latin America	123	113	108	103	99	100
Tropical Africa	111	105	97	88	80	79
Middle East	87	79	76	65	67	67
Southern Asia	100	100	96	85	91	80
PERCENTAGE OF POPULATION IN AGRICULTURE						
World	52	46	42	35	30	27
Developing countries	66	60	57	51	45	41
Latin America	45	38	36	31	27	24
Southern Asia	70	64	61	55	48	43
PRICE INDICATOR WORLD FOOD MARKET (DFP; 1965 = 0)	-8	60	10	61	56	45
WORLD HUNGER						
Total food deficit (WHUNG) $(10^8$ kg cons. prot.) :gross	15	29	23	45	89	147
net	15	29	0	0	0	0
Million people below minimum food standard: gross	180	350	280	540	1070	1760
net	180	350	0	0	0	0
% of WHUNG (gross) located in agricultural sector	76	85	74	65	25	22

*food aid included

Appendix 10A (continued)

RUN 128   : Relatively *high* growth rate of non-agricultural GDP;
                   large-scale food aid; world market price policy;
                   DFP-target = 200

	1966	1975	1980	1990	2000	2009
TOTAL AGRICULTURAL PRODUCTION (10^8 kg cons. prot.)						
World	1943	2495	2971	3799	5033	6389
Developed countries	743	910	1068	1311	1844	2275
North America	403	497	580	717	1034	1253
European Community	147	182	219	262	339	402
Developing countries	599	749	942	1148	1518	2123
Latin America	181	241	297	417	600	863
Tropical Africa	66	82	96	140	196	276
Middle East	58	72	96	111	181	230
Southern Asia	265	321	409	420	452	635
FOOD CONSUMPTION PER CAPUT* (kg cons. prot.)						
World	46	50	53	57	66	70
Developed countries	86	102	101	108	136	137
North America	107	121	120	125	152	152
European Community	90	103	99	105	132	130
Developing countries	30	30	34	35	42	48
Latin America	43	48	53	61	75	89
Tropical Africa	25	25	29	32	36	44
Middle East	38	40	47	56	70	82
Southern Asia	26	25	28	25	27	30
SELF-SUFFICIENCY-RATIO CONSUMABLE PROTEIN*						
Developed countries	96	92	105	112	116	133
North America	142	143	160	173	191	219
European Community	59	60	73	79	78	90
Developing countries	106	101	99	91	81	82
Latin America	123	113	108	103	98	96
Tropical Africa	111	105	94	96	97	92
Middle East	87	79	78	58	59	153
Southern Asia	100	100	105	94	72	81
PERCENTAGE OF POPULATION IN AGRICULTURE						
World	52	46	42	36	31	27
Developing countries	66	60	57	52	46	42
Latin America	45	38	36	31	26	21
Southern Asia	70	64	61	56	50	45
PRICE INDICATOR WORLD FOOD MARKET (DFP; 1965 = 0)	-8	60	526	496	51	144
WORLD HUNGER						
Total food deficit (WHUNG) (10^8 kg cons. prot.) :gross	15	29	41	121	116	115
net	15	29	0	0	0	0
Million people below minimum food standard: gross	180	350	490	1450	1390	1380
net	180	350	0	0	0	0
% of WHUNG (gross) located in agricultural sector	76	85	34	20	53	20

*food aid included

Appendix 10A (continued)

RUN 129   : Relatively *high* growth rate of non-agricultural GDP; large-scale
                 food aid; world market price policy, DFP-target = 200; smaller
                 income gap between agriculture and the non-agricultural sector;
                 gruadually decreasing income inequalities outside agriculture

	1966	1975	1980	1990	2000	2009
TOTAL AGRICULTURAL PRODUCTION $(10^8$ kg cons. prot.)						
World	1943	2495	2971	4037	5344	6501
Developed countries	743	910	1068	1450	1863	2135
North America	403	497	580	784	966	1119
European Community	147	182	219	285	359	408
Developing countries	599	749	941	1247	1811	2374
Latin America	181	241	297	437	633	907
Tropical Africa	66	82	96	145	208	297
Middle East	58	72	96	128	220	288
Southern Asia	265	321	409	475	653	762
FOOD CONSUMPTION PER CAPUT* (kg cons. prot.)						
World	46	50	53	61	68	72
Developed countries	86	102	102	123	131	135
North America	107	121	121	144	152	154
European Community	90	103	101	120	126	128
Developing countries	30	30	34	39	47	53
Latin America	43	48	54	66	82	98
Tropical Africa	25	25	29	35	41	49
Middle East	38	40	47	59	75	86
Southern Asia	26	25	28	28	32	33
SELF-SUFFICIENCY-RATIO CONSUMABLE PROTEIN*						
Developed countries	96	92	104	107	119	126
North America	142	143	158	164	180	192
European Community	59	60	72	75	86	93
Developing countries	106	101	99	89	87	84
Latin America	123	113	108	99	94	91
Tropical Africa	111	105	93	91	88	87
Middle East	87	79	78	63	67	63
Southern Asia	100	100	101	91	91	87
PERCENTAGE OF POPULATION IN AGRICULTURE						
World	101	98	101	99	100	100
Developing countries	66	60	57	53	49	46
Latin America	45	38	36	32	29	26
Southern Asia	70	64	61	57	53	49
PRICE INDICATOR WORLD FOOD MARKET (DFP; 1965 = 0)	−8	60	505	255	274	307
WORLD HUNGER						
Total food deficit (WHUNG) $(10^8$ kg cons. prot.) :gross	15	29	40	32	29	43
net	15	29	5	0	0	0
Million people below minimum food standard: gross	180	350	480	380	180	520
net	180	350	480	0	0	0
% of WHUNG (gross) located in agricultural sector	76	86	33	57	37	33

*food aid included

Appendix 10A (continued)

RUN 131 : Relatively *high* growth rate of non-agricultural GDP;
liberalization of international trade in food (no
protection of domestic food markets in rich countries)

	1966	1975	1980	1990	2000	2009
TOTAL AGRICULTURAL PRODUCTION (10^8 kg cons. prot.)						
World	1943	2496	2966	4123	5111	6311
Developed countries	743	911	1073	1567	1860	2438
North America	403	498	582	891	1017	1382
European Community	147	182	219	303	343	428
Developing countries	599	749	932	1215	1581	1881
Latin America	181	241	296	434	603	865
Tropical Africa	66	82	96	145	173	215
Middle East	58	72	96	128	208	270
Southern Asia	265	320	400	447	509	421
FOOD CONSUMPTION PER CAPUT (kg cons. prot.)						
World	46	50	53	61	65	70
Developed countries	86	102	108	129	145	159
North America	107	120	126	145	159	170
European Community	90	103	107	127	141	154
Developing countries	30	30	32	37	38	43
Latin America	43	48	52	63	74	87
Tropical Africa	25	25	26	33	34	41
Middle East	38	40	46	55	67	80
Southern Asia	26	25	26	27	23	23
SELF-SUFFICIENCY-RATIO CONSUMABLE PROTEIN						
Developed countries	96	92	98	111	108	123
North America	142	144	153	186	182	217
European Community	59	60	68	75	74	81
Developing countries	106	102	103	91	92	79
Latin America	123	113	110	103	99	100
Tropical Africa	111	106	103	95	89	74
Middle East	87	79	81	67	71	63
Southern Asia	100	100	106	91	99	67
PERCENTAGE OF POPULATION IN AGRICULTURE						
World	52	46	42	36	31	27
Developing countries	66	60	57	52	46	41
Latin America	45	38	36	31	26	22
Southern Asia	70	64	61	56	49	43
PRICE INDICATOR WORLD FOOD MARKET (DFP; 1965 = 0)	-8	10	393	79	159	-6
WORLD HUNGER						
Total food deficit (WHUNG) (10^8 kg cons. prot.)	15	29	37	35	105	156
Million people below minimum food standard	180	350	440	420	1260	1870
% of WHUNG located in agricultural sector	76	86	41	60	27	48

Appendix 10A (continued)

RUN 211   : Unchanged policies; relatively *low* growth rate of
                   non-agricultural GDP

	1966	1975	1980	1990	2000	2009
TOTAL AGRICULTURAL PRODUCTION (10^8 kg cons. prot.)						
World	1943	2491	2860	3452	4055	4796
Developed countries	743	909	1047	1221	1409	1559
North America	403	497	566	639	709	771
European Community	147	182	216	252	292	333
Developing countries	599	749	918	1118	1352	1721
Latin America	181	241	296	430	604	848
Tropical Africa	66	82	96	109	142	169
Middle East	53	72	96	113	174	204
Southern Asia	265	321	386	407	351	395
FOOD CONSUMPTION PER CAPUT (kg cons. prot.)						
World	46	50	51	52	52	53
Developed countries	86	101	106	113	120	125
North America	107	120	123	130	136	140
European Community	90	103	107	114	120	126
Developing countries	30	30	32	31	30	31
Latin America	43	47	49	51	53	55
Tropical Africa	25	25	26	27	25	27
Middle East	38	39	43	42	46	48
Southern Asia	26	25	26	24	20	20
SELF-SUFFICIENCY-RATIO CONSUMABLE PROTEIN						
Developed countries	96	93	98	98	100	100
North America	142	144	152	148	147	145
European Community	59	60	67	70	74	77
Developing countries	106	103	105	100	99	100
Latin America	123	114	117	127	140	155
Tropical Africa	111	106	105	88	96	88
Middle East	87	81	86	77	85	79
Southern Asia	100	101	103	94	75	70
PERCENTAGE OF POPULATION IN AGRICULTURE						
World	52	46	44	40	35	30
Developing countries	66	60	57	51	44	39
Latin America	45	38	36	31	26	22
Southern Asia	70	64	61	54	47	41
PRICE INDICATOR WORLD FOOD MARKET (DFP; 1965 = 0)	-8	43	60	18	13	17
WORLD HUNGER						
Total food deficit (WHUNG) (10^8 kg cons. prot.)	15	29	25	50	124	141
Million people below minimum food standard	180	350	300	600	1490	1690
% of WHUNG located in agricultural sector	76	85	72	68	64	57

Appendix 10A (continued)

RUN 222   : Relatively *low* growth rate of non-agricultural GDP;
                 large-scale food aid financed by the rich countries

	1966	1975	1980	1990	2000	2009
TOTAL AGRICULTURAL PRODUCTION (10^8 kg cons. prot.)						
World	1943	2491	2885	3543	4204	5007
Developed countries	743	909	1065	1293	1489	1686
North America	403	497	580	686	750	857
European Community	147	182	217	263	308	352
Developing countries	599	749	926	1137	1420	1804
Latin America	181	241	296	429	611	863
Tropical Africa	66	82	96	129	158	191
Middle East	58	72	96	110	179	212
Southern Asia	265	321	394	410	388	433
FOOD CONSUMPTION PER CAPUT* (kg cons. prot.)						
World	46	50	52	53	54	55
Developed countries	86	101	105	113	120	125
North America	107	120	123	130	136	140
European Community	90	103	105	114	121	126
Developing countries	30	30	33	33	34	35
Latin America	43	47	50	51	54	57
Tropical Africa	25	25	27	29	29	31
Middle East	38	40	45	44	48	49
Southern Asia	26	25	27	26	25	25
SELF-SUFFICIENCY-RATIO CONSUMABLE PROTEIN*						
Developed countries	96	93	101	104	105	108
North America	142	144	156	159	155	160
European Community	59	60	69	73	77	81
Developing countries	106	102	102	96	93	93
Latin America	123	114	116	125	138	152
Tropical Africa	111	105	99	96	94	88
Middle East	87	80	83	72	84	80
Southern Asia	100	100	100	87	67	62
PERCENTAGE OF POPULATION IN AGRICULTURE						
World	52	46	44	40	35	31
Developing countries	66	60	57	51	45	39
Latin America	45	38	36	31	26	22
Southern Asia	70	64	61	55	48	42
PRICE INDICATOR WORLD FOOD MARKET (DFP; 1965 = 0)	-8	43	231	-4	19	23
WORLD HUNGER						
Total food deficit (WHUNG) (10^8 kg cons. prot.) :gross	15	29	31	58	118	163
net	15	29	4	0	0	0
Million people below minimum food standard: gross	180	350	370	700	1420	1960
net	180	350	50	0	0	0
% of WHUNG (gross) located in agricultural sector	76	85	53	56	55	44

*food aid included

Appendix 10A (continued)

RUN 224   : Relatively *low* growth rate of non-agricultural GDP;
                 world market price policy, DFP-target = 0

	1966	1975	1980	1990	2000	2009
TOTAL AGRICULTURAL PRODUCTION $(10^8$ kg cons. prot.)						
World	1943	2491	2780	3422	4094	4777
Developed countries	743	909	991	1200	1425	1569
North America	403	497	527	627	704	753
European Community	147	182	211	249	292	327
Developing countries	599	749	894	1109	1374	1692
Latin America	181	241	295	424	596	834
Tropical Africa	66	82	83	115	148	182
Middle East	58	72	95	112	176	176
Southern Asia	265	321	379	399	373	394
FOOD CONSUMPTION PER CAPUT (kg cons. prot.)						
World	46	50	51	51	52	53
Developed countries	86	101	102	111	118	124
North America	107	119	119	128	136	139
European Community	90	102	104	113	120	125
Developing countries	30	30	31	31	30	31
Latin America	43	47	48	51	53	55
Tropical Africa	25	25	25	27	27	28
Middle East	38	39	43	43	47	46
Southern Asia	26	25	26	23	21	20
SELF-SUFFICIENCY-RATIO CONSUMABLE PROTEIN						
Developed countries	96	93	96	99	102	102
North America	142	145	146	148	146	142
European Community	59	61	67	70	74	76
Developing countries	106	103	103	101	99	98
Latin America	123	114	118	126	139	153
Tropical Africa	111	106	92	94	95	93
Middle East	87	81	85	76	85	70
Southern Asia	100	101	101	94	78	69
PERCENTAGE OF POPULATION IN AGRICULTURE						
World	52	46	44	45	35	30
Developing countries	66	60	57	51	44	39
Latin America	45	38	35	31	26	22
Southern Asia	70	64	61	54	47	41
PRICE INDICATOR WORLD FOOD MARKET (DFP; 1965 = 0)	-8	42	-41	-59	-4	-13
WORLD HUNGER						
Total food deficit (WHUNG) $(10^8$ kg cons. prot.)	15	29	26	53	105	140
Million people below minimum food standard	180	350	310	640	1260	1680
% of WHUNG located in agricultural sector	76	84	74	68	65	57

Appendix 10A (continued)

RUN 225   : Relatively *low* growth rate of non-agricultural GDP;
                 world market price policy, DFP-target = 200

	1966	1975	1980	1990	2000	2009
TOTAL AGRICULTURAL PRODUCTION $(10^8$ kg cons. prot.)						
World	1943	2491	2859	3453	4168	4853
Developed countries	743	909	1046	1163	1200	1153
North America	403	497	564	573	487	391
European Community	147	182	216	252	293	312
Developing countries	599	749	918	1177	1675	2183
Latin America	181	241	296	432	618	876
Tropical Africa	66	82	96	143	200	274
Middle East	58	72	96	125	213	263
Southern Asia	265	321	386	418	561	661
FOOD CONSUMPTION PER CAPUT (kg cons. prot.)						
World	46	50	51	51	53	54
Developed countries	86	101	105	111	117	122
North America	107	120	123	130	135	138
European Community	90	103	106	111	117	122
Developing countries	30	30	32	31	33	34
Latin America	43	47	49	51	54	57
Tropical Africa	25	25	26	28	30	32
Middle East	38	39	43	44	49	50
Southern Asia	26	25	26	23	24	23
SELF-SUFFICIENCY-RATIO CONSUMABLE PROTEIN						
Developed countries	96	93	99	96	87	76
North America	142	144	152	133	103	76
European Community	59	60	67	72	76	74
Developing countries	106	103	105	105	114	120
Latin America	123	114	117	126	138	152
Tropical Africa	111	106	105	110	117	125
Middle East	87	81	86	83	99	99
Southern Asia	100	101	103	98	104	108
PERCENTAGE OF POPULATION IN AGRICULTURE						
World	52	46	44	40	36	32
Developing countries	66	60	57	51	46	42
Latin America	45	38	36	31	27	24
Southern Asia	70	64	61	55	49	45
PRICE INDICATOR WORLD FOOD MARKET (DFP; 1965 = 0)	-8	43	60	155	199	202
WORLD HUNGER						
Total food deficit (WHUNG) $(10^8$ kg cons. prot.)	15	29	25	56	72	116
Million people below minimum food standard	180	350	300	670	860	1390
% of WHUNG located in agricultural sector	76	85	72	56	25	20

Appendix 10A (continued)

RUN 226   : Relatively *low* growth rate of non-agricultural GDP;
             world market price policy, DFP-target = 400

	1966	1975	1980	1990	2000	2009
TOTAL AGRICULTURAL PRODUCTION (10^8 kg cons. prot.)						
World	1943	2491	2792	3449	4105	4589
Developed countries	743	909	978	1116	1082	802
North America	403	497	508	534	406	169
European Community	147	182	213	260	290	263
Developing countries	599	749	919	1220	1730	2271
Latin America	181	241	296	431	619	886
Tropical Africa	66	82	96	144	203	282
Middle East	58	72	96	128	219	270
Southern Asia	265	321	388	454	605	723
FOOD CONSUMPTION PER CAPUT (kg cons. prot.)						
World	46	50	51	51	53	51
Developed countries	86	101	103	108	114	95
North America	107	120	123	129	132	109
European Community	90	103	104	108	113	96
Developing countries	30	30	31	32	34	35
Latin America	43	47	49	52	54	58
Tropical Africa	25	25	26	30	31	35
Middle East	38	39	42	43	49	49
Southern Asia	26	25	26	24	25	24
SELF-SUFFICIENCY-RATIO CONSUMABLE PROTEIN						
Developed countries	96	93	94	95	81	69
North America	141	144	137	126	87	41
European Community	59	60	68	76	77	80
Developing countries	106	103	105	106	115	121
Latin America	123	114	117	124	139	152
Tropical Africa	111	106	105	108	115	115
Middle East	87	81	87	87	102	103
Southern Asia	100	101	104	102	107	112
PERCENTAGE OF POPULATION IN AGRICULTURE						
World	52	46	44	41	37	34
Developing countries	66	60	57	52	48	44
Latin America	45	38	36	31	28	25
Southern Asia	70	64	61	56	51	48
PRICE INDICATOR WORLD FOOD MARKET (DFP; 1965 = 0)	-8	43	185	387	407	841
WORLD HUNGER						
Total food deficit (WHUNG) (10^8 kg cons. prot.)	15	29	27	59	84	163
Million people below minimum food standard	180	350	320	710	1010	1960
% of WHUNG located in agricultural sector	76	85	66	38	18	9

Appendix 10A (continued)

RUN 227   : Relatively *low* growth rate of non-agriculturalGDP;
              large-scale food aid; world market price policy,
              DFP-target = 0

	1966	1975	1980	1990	2000	2009
TOTAL AGRICULTURAL PRODUCTION $(10^8$ kg cons. prot.)						
World	1943	2491	2820	3451	4205	4894
Developed countries	743	909	1019	1218	1443	1630
North America	403	497	547	641	725	828
European Community	147	182	213	251	298	335
Developing countries	599	749	906	1120	1468	1748
Latin America	181	241	296	429	607	854
Tropical Africa	66	82	90	115	155	188
Middle East	58	72	95	111	182	198
Southern Asia	265	321	382	406	442	404
FOOD CONSUMPTION PER CAPUT* (kg cons. prot.)						
World	46	50	50	52	53	54
Developed countries	86	101	98	108	116	118
North America	107	119	115	124	132	134
European Community	90	102	100	109	116	119
Developing countries	30	30	33	33	33	35
Latin America	43	47	49	51	54	56
Tropical Africa	25	25	27	29	29	30
Middle East	38	40	44	45	48	49
Southern Asia	26	25	27	25	25	25
SELF-SUFFICIENCY-RATIO CONSUMABLE PROTEIN*						
Developed countries	96	94	103	103	106	111
North America	142	145	158	156	154	162
European Community	59	61	71	73	78	82
Developing countries	106	102	100	95	97	91
Latin America	123	114	116	125	137	152
Tropical Africa	111	105	93	87	93	88
Middle East	87	80	82	71	85	74
Southern Asia	100	100	97	87	78	58
PERCENTAGE OF POPULATION IN AGRICULTURE						
World	52	46	44	40	35	30
Developing countries	66	60	57	51	44	39
Latin America	45	38	36	31	26	22
Southern Asia	70	64	61	54	47	41
PRICE INDICATOR WORLD FOOD MARKET (DFP; 1965 = 0)	-8	43	-24	-27	14	7
WORLD HUNGER						
Total food deficit (WHUNG) $(10^8$ kg cons. prot.) :gross	15	29	26	51	87	154
net	15	29	0	0	0	0
Million people below minimum food standard:gross	180	350	310	610	1040	1850
net	180	350	0	0	0	0
% of WHUNG (gross) located in agricultural sector	76	84	73	68	51	51

*food aid included

Appendix 10A (continued)

RUN 228   : Relatively *low* growth rate of non-agricultural GDP; large-scale food aid; world market price policy, DFP-target=200

	1966	1975	1980	1990	2000	2009
TOTAL AGRICULTURAL PRODUCTION (10^8 kg cons. prot.)						
World	1943	2491	2884	3475	4282	5006
Developed countries	743	909	1064	1214	1353	1358
North America	403	497	580	617	613	542
European Community	147	182	217	256	301	329
Developing countries	599	749	925	1148	1636	2131
Latin America	181	241	296	430	617	876
Tropical Africa	66	82	96	131	184	250
Middle East	58	72	96	116	199	245
Southern Asia	265	321	394	412	551	653
FOOD CONSUMPTION PER CAPUT* (kg cons. prot.)						
World	46	50	51	52	54	55
Developed countries	86	101	104	110	117	122
North America	107	120	122	129	135	138
European Community	90	103	104	111	117	122
Developing countries	30	30	33	33	35	36
Latin America	43	47	50	52	55	58
Tropical Africa	25	25	28	29	31	33
Middle East	38	40	45	44	49	50
Southern Asia	26	25	27	26	26	27
SELF-SUFFICIENCY-RATIO CONSUMABLE PROTEIN*						
Developed countries	96	93	102	100	98	89
North America	142	144	157	144	128	105
European Community	59	60	69	73	78	79
Developing countries	106	102	102	97	105	109
Latin America	123	114	114	125	136	150
Tropical Africa	111	106	99	97	103	110
Middle East	87	80	82	76	93	92
Southern Asia	100	100	100	88	92	92
PERCENTAGE OF POPULATION IN AGRICULTURE						
World	52	46	44	40	36	32
Developing countries	66	60	57	51	46	42
Latin America	45	38	36	31	27	23
Southern Asia	70	64	61	55	49	45
PRICE INDICATOR WORLD FOOD MARKET (DFP; 1965 = 0)	-8	43	207	168	198	182
WORLD HUNGER						
Total food deficit (WHUNG) (10^8 kg cons. prot.) :gross	15	29	31	62	77	114
net	15	29	1	0	0	0
Million people below minimum food standard: gross	180	350	370	740	920	1370
net	180	350	10	0	0	0
% of WHUNG (gross) located in agricultural sector	76	85	55	54	26	21

*food aid included

Chapter 11

ANALYSIS OF INTERNATIONAL FOOD POLICIES

11.1 *AIMS AND INSTRUMENTS OF WORLD FOOD POLICIES*

11.1.1 *The aim of minimizing world hunger*

The principal aim of an international food policy should be to provide an adequate food basket to every human being. Other aims may be important also, such as e.g. self-sufficiency in food, but none of them ultimately carries greater weight from a humanitarian point of view than the eradication of hunger. As the previous chapter has shown, according to MOIRA hunger and malnutrition in the world must be expected to increase considerably in the decades to come if present-day policies remain unchanged. The present chapter analyzes to what extent alternative international food policies could change and improve this gloomy prospect.

The various policy runs to be discussed in this chapter will have to be compared and assessed in terms of their efficacy in contributing to the aim of eradicating hunger. For instance, for certain specific years (including the terminal year) the level of world hunger WHUNG resulting from the various policy simulations may be compared. It is also useful to have a criterion for comparing the seriousness of the food situation over the entire period of the simulation run. For a model run, over T years, a reasonable criterion would seem to be:

$$J_1 = \sum_{t=0}^{T} WHUNG_t \qquad (11.1)$$

This criterion could, of course, be brought on an annual base again by dividing by the number of years T.

It should be noted here that hunger as defined thus far is the extent or amount of hunger that results from the economic process as described by MOIRA, i.e. before any food aid takes place. Earlier already reference has been made to the possibility and actual existence of food aid; in this study the concept of food aid refers to the physical supply of food not affecting effective demand for food in the receiving country and income groups. As food aid will be one of the policy instruments , a distinction will have to be made between hunger before food aid is given and hunger after

receiving aid. For lack of a better expression, the level of
hunger before food aid takes place is called gross hunger,
while the amount of hunger that remains after food aid is
given is labelled net hunger.
The criterion for assessing food policies as given in (11.1)
is based on the concept of gross hunger. Alternatively, a
criterion J_2 defined in terms of net hunger WHUNGP might be
used:

$$J_2 = \sum_{t=0}^{T} WHUNGP_t \qquad\qquad (11.2)$$

The difference in meaning between the two criteria is obvious;
while (11.1) primarily indicates the seriousness of the world
food situation from a socio-economic point of view, in (11.2)
the health aspect predominates.

It would have been attractive to use (11.1) and (11.2) in a
formal procedure for minimizing J_1 and J_2, respectively,
given a set of alternative food policies. This procedure
would have indicated what combination of policies and what
intensity of use of the various instruments would have led
to the lowest level of world hunger. Nevertheless, this line
of approach has not been followed, for several reasons:
(a)   optimization of a rather complicated model (such as
      MOIRA) over a given period of time is computationally
very hard to realize;
(b)   one of the most important tasks in trying to contribute
      to a solution of the world food problem is to devise
alternative policies and effective decision structures.
Optimization is possible only once the entire structure of
the model is given, including the decision structure. In
other words, optimization requires that the specification of
the model is already given in such a way that the alternative
policies are represented exclusively by variations in the
level of instrument variables. Therefore, even though optimization may facilitate the choice between given alternatives,
it cannot devise and develop the alternatives themselves.
(c)   a third problem of optimization is the well-known issue
      of the stability of the optimal solution. The values of
the instrument variables pertaining to the optimal solution
are relevant only if they do not imply a *walking on the
ridge*. Put otherwise, small variations around the optimal
values should not lead to large deviations in the value of
the criterion function.

For these reasons, it is not attempted to develop a formal
procedure for minimizing J_1 and J_2. Instead, attention will
focus on devising acceptable strategies for fighting hunger.
These strategies are discussed in the next section. From the
various strategies, aspiration levels serving as intermediate
objectives can be derived. Deviations of reality (as simulated
by the model) from these aspiration levels will lead to corrective policy action.

11.1.2 *Derived criteria and strategies*

What are the strategies the international community can adopt to fight the problems of hunger and malnutrition? Three international strategies present themselves:
international investment in food production in the developing
countries, food aid and international food trade policy. The
first strategy cannot be explicitly simulated with MOIRA, as
it is assumed in the modelling of the production decision
that investment resources will always be available (at a
cost) whenever it pays to invest. In other words, it is
assumed that no investments will take place unless it will
be profitable to do so. In fact, it is hardly likely that
international capital would be made available to the agricultural sector in developing countries unless the conditions
are created for its productive and remunerative use. This
requires among others an appropriate domestic food price
policy in developing countries, which in turn depends in
part on the world market food price policy (cf. Chapters 6
and 7). International investment in food production thus
depends on an adequate incentive to invest, and the latter
condition is obviously analyzed in MOIRA. It remains true,
however, that the model does not distinguish between local
and international sources of investment; as there are no
capital transfers incorporated in MOIRA in its present form,
all investment in agriculture is implicitly assumed to be of
national origin. The following analysis will therefore
concentrate on food aid and trade policy as international
strategies.

A food aid strategy is composed of several elements:
(a)   acquisition of financial means, which is in MOIRA as-
      sumed to take place in the rich countries only;
(b)   buying of food on the world market;
(c)   establishment of a food stock for aid and a distribution
      net work;
(d)   physical distribution of food, in MOIRA to people with
      consumption below the minimum food norm only.

International food aid is typically a measure aiming at redistribution of available food. As such, its effects may be
compared to those of a similar approach sometimes advocated
in the rich countries, namely a voluntary reduction of food
consumption by populations living in affluence.

As distinct from policies at redistribution of available
food, international food trade policy should basically aim
at stimulating agricultural production in the developing
countries. Increased production in the poor countries is in
the long term the only viable and lasting solution of the
hunger problem, as it generates additional income, reduces
balance of payments problems, and precludes unwarranted
political dependence. The analysis of Chapters 6 and 7 has
shown, that agricultural production growth in developing
countries depends among others on the domestic food price
that in turn is subject to the internal political objective
with respect to the income distribution between agriculture

and non-agriculture, and moreover to the influence exerted
by outside factors, notably the variations in the world
market food price. International trade policy should be
oriented towards the elimination of the latter disturbances,
and if possible towards the use of the world market food
price level for positively supporting and encouraging domestic
incentives for food production growth in poor countries.

An appropriate measure for international price policy would
seem to be, therefore, the regulation of the world food
market in order to (a) stabilize world prices, and (b)
maintain a world price level offering the largest (indirect)
incentive for production growth in the developing world.
Stabilization of the world market may be pursued by means of
a food buffer stock. Regulation of the *level* of stabilization
requires in addition that the net exports or imports of food
of (some of the) world market parties be brought under
control. Again, it is only reasonable to put this burden on
the shoulders of the strongest parties, i.e. the rich countries. These countries can perform this task by adapting,
whenever necessary, their domestic food production or their
food consumption, or both. In the policy simulation runs of
MOIRA it is assumed that they can and will do so. The instrument for a downward adaptation of food production used in
MOIRA is a food tax per unit of output, reimbursed to the
producer as a lump-sum deficiency payment in order to protect
the farmer's income position. Downward adaptation of food
consumption in the rich countries is assumed to be a voluntary decision of the population, with stronger consumption
cuts at higher income levels. For a more detailed discussion
of these instruments, the reader is referred to Appendix
11A.

It is likely that not everyone will agree to the need to
regulate the world food market. Particularly those that have
a strong position on the market are often inclined to believe
that the free play of market forces will necessarily lead to
the best result. As an alternative to deliberate international
price policy, a simulation run showing the effects of international trade liberalization in food can be performed with
MOIRA. In this run it is assumed that the rich countries do
away with all impediments to exports or imports of food;
consequently, in these countries also the income disparity
equation becomes inoperative.

Although strictly speaking not constituting an international
food policy in itself, a relaxing of the internal political
constraint of the sectoral income distribution policy (based
on internal power relations) in developing countries is
worth studying as well, as it might effectively support the
international measures. Thus, it will be analyzed - as part
of a larger package of policy measures - what the consequences
would be of an improved sectoral income distribution in
favour of the agricultural sector in poor countries allowing
a higher domestic food price level as incentive for agricultural producers.

In summary, the following policy measures were examined to
see in how far they could eliminate or reduce the extent of
hunger in the period 1975-2010.
(a)   Measures intended to achieve a redistribution of avail-
      able food in the world:
      - reduction of food consumption by the rich countries
        (Appendix 10A, run 121);
      - food purchases by an international food aid organi-
        zation (financed by the rich countries) which will
        distribute this food to the underfed population
        groups (Appendix 10A, run 122, 123 and 222).
(b)   Measures intended to stimulate food production in the
      developing countries:
      - regulation of the world food market in order to
        stabilize international prices; the price target
        pursued on the world market is a policy variable
        whose influence is tested (Appendix 10A, run 124,
        125, 224, 225 and 226).
      - on the other hand, the effect which liberalization of
        international trade would have on developments in the
        world food situation is also examined (Appendix 10A,
        run 131).
In the first instance, these policy measures were tested as
to their individual influence on the development of world
hunger. Based on these findings, combinations were designed
in order to establish which package of measures within the
framework of international policy would be of the greatest
benefit to world food supply during the coming 35 years
(Appendix 10A, run 127, 128, 227, 228 and 129).

11.1.3 *A criterion function for steering international price policy*

            Before discussing the various policy simulation
runs, the adaptation mechanism that controls the intensity of
use of some of the policy instruments has to be introduced.
As mentioned above, a world market price level policy uses in
MOIRA two *instruments:* the food production level in the rich
countries, and the food consumption level in these countries.
Both instruments affect, in opposite direction, the world
market food price level as they influence the volume of exports or imports of the country concerned. Assume now that international food price policy would aim at a world market price
level DFPTARG, and that the actual price level DFP is below
this desired level. Restricting food production in the rich
countries would bring DFP closer to DFPTARG. If next year's
world market price level would still be below DFPTARG, the
instrument of production restriction will have to be used
with greater intensity.

The extent to which the actual level of a target variable (in
this case the world market price level) deviates from the
desired level determines the intensity of use of the instrument variable (here the adaptation in the rich countries of
food production or consumption). However, the desired price

level DFPTARG is not the only target variable, and the adaptation of production or consumption may and will also affect
these other target variables. Therefore, a criterion function
is used to judge the overall success, or lack of success, of
international policies. The criterion function combines the
three elements of price stability, food aid to eliminate
(gross) hunger, and the desired world market price level of
food. To each element, a weight is assigned, and their weighed
sum is used as indicator of the overall success or failure of
the policies pursued.

The technical aspects of the criterion function are discussed
in the appendix to this chapter. The first element of it,
the lack of price stability, is measured by the initial discrepancy between food supply and demand on the world market;
the price stabilization function of food stocks has been described already in Chapter 7. The weight of this element in the
criterion function is larger than zero in all MOIRA runs. The
second element is the amount of hunger that remains after food
aid has been given; its weight is zero in policy runs without
food aid. The third element is the discrepancy between desired and actual world market food price, DFPTARG - DFP, as
discussed above; when no price level policy is pursued, its
weight is zero. The numerical value of the criterion function
steers the use of the price level instruments, after magnify-
ing the effect of this numerical indicator by a reinforcing
factor ensuring speedy but not excessive adaptation.

11.1.4 *Time pattern of policy effects*

          The following sections will review the effects
of alternative international food policies, as shown in the
various simulation runs. A general comment regarding the
time pattern of these effects is in place. Firstly, it has
to be borne in mind that the yearly growth rate of agricultural production (disregarding weather disturbances) is
subject to an upper limit, for the reasons discussed in
Chapter 4; this upper limit is set at 4 per cent in the
simulation runs. Another constraint that may restrict production growth is the maximum permissable change in the labour/
capital ratio; see again Chapter 4. Therefore, a policy
stimulating production growth (in the developing countries)
will necessarily have a sizeable impact only after a number
of years: the higher the absolute level of production in any
given year, the larger next year's increase can be (other
production conditions permitting). At the same time this
implies that larger production increases during the second
half of a simulation run should not be attributed solely to
the policies during that period itself.

Secondly, several less-developed countries find themselves
in a position of a lowering self-sufficiency ratio towards
the end of the simulation period. This is due to the specific
assumptions made with regard to population growth and growth
of non-agricultural GDP; another set of exogenous growth
assumptions would change their position. In the case of

food-exporting countries, such lowering of the self-sufficiency ratio leads to a decreasing sensitivity to the world
market price and therefore, indirectly, to a decreasing
supply sensitivity. For food-importing countries, these
sensitivity-effects of a lower self-sufficiency ratio are
less clear (see Chapter 6).

The upshot of these considerations is that a comparison of
the levels of variables between different policy runs, or
between a policy run and the standard run, should pay due
attention to the fact that the particular constellation at a
given moment is the outcome of developments over the entire
preceding period. In other words, one should be careful in
attributing a difference between simulation runs in, say,
1995 to a specific policy action one or a few years earlier;
the interrelations are too complex to warrant such a simpli-
fication.

11.2 *REDUCTION OF FOOD CONSUMPTION IN THE RICH COUNTRIES*

According to MOIRA, moderation of food consumption in
the rich countries will in itself (i.e. if it occurs as a
change in taste) not lead to an improvement in the food
supply in the countries where hunger prevails (see figure
11.1 and Appendix 10A, run 121). In this simulation run the
consumers in developed countries are assumed to cut their
food consumption according to the extent of WHUNG. Per caput
consumption in these countries will, according to this
assumption, go down very considerably in the years after
1990 when WHUNG - instead of diminishing - is rising steeply.
The reduction of effective demand, which is what such a
consumption restriction amounts to, will lower world market
prices (the model calculates irrealistic low price levels)
and thus curb the growth of agricultural production; this
will occur in both the rich and the poor countries. On
balance, therefore, such a policy would increase hunger more
than if policies remained unchanged. Although in the short
run a poor importing country might take advantage of the
situation, in MOIRA a very low world market price has in the
long term an adverse effect on food production and food
consumption in the developing countries.

11.3 *FOOD AID ON A LARGE SCALE*

Secondly, we examined whether food aid, financed by the
rich countries would be able to banish hunger from the world
(see figure 11.2 and run 122 in Appendix 10A). It was assumed that food aid could be supplied with 100 per cent
efficiency, i.e. that the total food shortage of all hungry
people (WHUNG) could be cancelled-out by the provision of
food without disturbing the functioning of the local markets.
It is further assumed that the necessary food will be purchased with the aid of funds contributed by the rich countries.
MOIRA shows that it will thus be possible to reduce hunger
to almost zero - if sufficient financial means become available. On the average, over the period 1975-2010, this re-

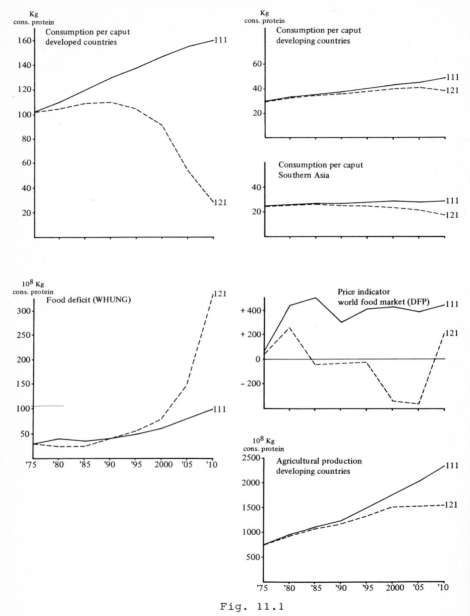

Fig. 11.1

*The impact of a reduction of food consumption in the rich
countries on the food situation in developing
countries; comparison between run 121
and the standard run (111)*

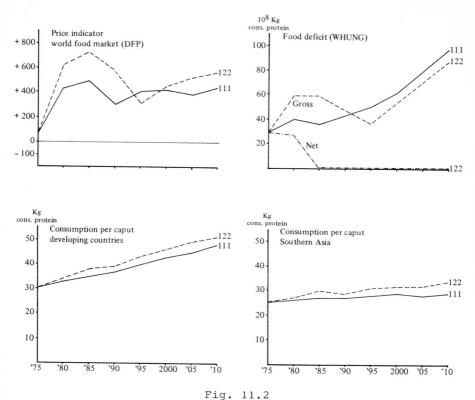

Fig. 11.2

Fighting hunger by food aid financed by the rich countries;
run 122 in comparison with the standard run (111)

distribution of food would demand each year about 0.5 per
cent of the national incomes of the rich countries. Such
food purchases would be accompanied by the phenomenon of a
higher world market price level for food, notably in the
first two decades of the period under consideration. On the
one hand this higher international price would stimulate
production, particularly in the rich countries, but on the
other hand it would have a negative effect on the purchasing
power of the non-agricultural population of the importing
developing countries. In the first half of the period 1975–
2010 gross hunger (i.e., before food aid is given) is therefore remarkably higher than in the standard run. After the
high DFP has induced food production to increase, gross
hunger is at a slightly lower level than in the standard
run.

Under the assumption of a lower growth of the non-agricultural
sector, the extent to which food aid affects DFP and gross

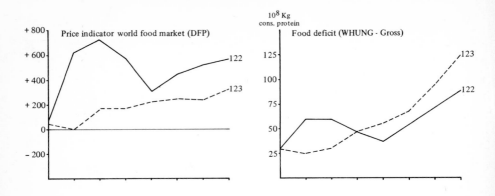

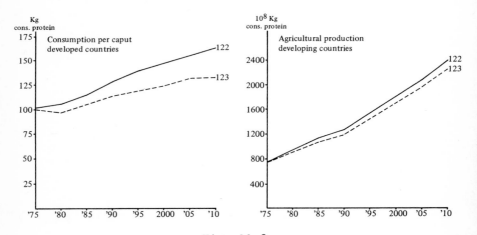

Fig. 11.3

Combination of food aid and voluntary reduction of food consumption in the rich countries; comparison of run 122 (food aid only) with run 123 (food aid + adjustment of consumption according to the extent of hunger)

hunger is less distinct (see run 222 in Appendix 10A). This is due to the fact that under these conditions the world market prices are low. At this low level a price increase induced by purchases for food aid is a stronger incentive for agricultural production to grow. The effects of food aid on DFP and WHUNG (gross) will therefore earlier and to a greater extent be offset by a greater supply of food.

The very high world market price level for food (in case of run 122) and the accompanying negative effect on the purchasing power of the non-agricultural sector, will both be mitigated if food aid policy is combined with a voluntary reduction of food consumption in the rich countries. In a simulation run (with relatively high income growth outside the agricultural sector) combining these two policies (see figure 11.3 and run 123 in Appendix 10A), the world market price is at a lower level and agricultural production increases less rapidly than in the case of food aid only. As a consequence, gross hunger is found to be somewhat higher, partly because the food deficit in the agricultural sector increases. Reduction of consumption of food in the rich countries may change the distribution of hunger over the sectors, but it does not bring the hunger problem closer to its solution. As a result of the lower food price level in the world market, the magnitude of the food aid fund required for fighting gross hunger is smaller than in the case of food aid only.

11.4 *RELEVANCE OF THE INTERNATIONAL FOOD PRICE LEVEL*

Food aid, however necessary it may be to alleviate acute need, is a measure that must in principle be temporary. The developing countries will have to achieve a structural improvement of their food supply primarily by increasing their agricultural production, because the relatively large agricultural sector uses a great deal of labour and land which has little if any alternative use. With this in view, measures which would stimulate this development were considered; in particular, the importance was examined of the world market food price level, which the rich countries are able to influence by means of their policies.

A deliberate world market price policy, aimed at maintaining a relatively high and stable price level, proved in MOIRA to stimulate in the long term production growth in the poor countries. This favourable impact is particularly effective under the assumption of a relatively low economic growth of the non-agricultural sector (see figure 11.4 and Appendix 10A run 211, 224, 225 and 226). If policies remain unchanged the world market will have to contend with surplusses and low prices (see Chapter 10); average per caput consumption in the developing countries will not increase in the period 1975-2010; in the densely populated countries of South Asia food consumption per caput will even decline. The introduction of an international policy of stable and relatively

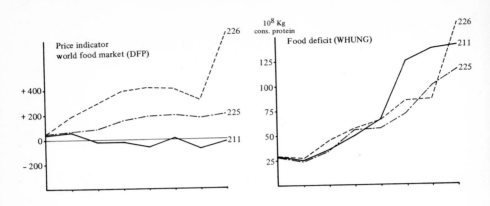

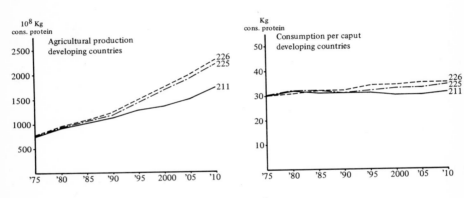

Fig. 11.4

*Impact on the food situation in developing countries of a
stabilization of the world market price at different levels
under conditions of a slower income growth outside agriculture: comparison of run 211 (unchanged policy)
with run 225 (DFP-target = 200) and with
run 226 (DFP-target = 400)*

high prices on the world market, realized by the rich nations
(see para 11.5), would cause the food situation in developing
countries to improve as a result of faster production growth.
The deliberate raise of the world market price level will
induce the domestic food prices in developing countries to
increase which in turn will mitigate the outflow of agricultural labour and will stimulate the agricultural sector
to use purchased inputs.

The corresponding simulation runs assuming a relatively high
growth rate of non-agricultural income (see figure 11.5 and

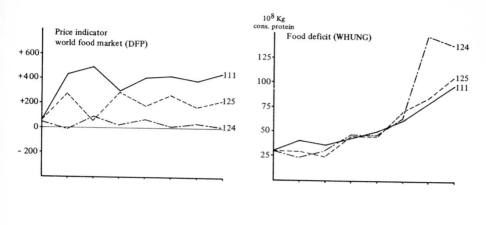

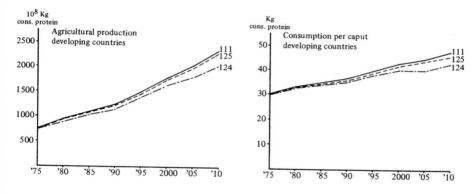

Fig. 11.5

Impact on the food situation in developing countries of a stabilization of the world market price at different levels under conditions of a relatively fast income growth of non-agricultural income: comparison of the standard run 111 with run 124 (DFP-target = 0) and with run 125 (DFP-target = 200)

run 124 and 125 in Appendix 10A) show a similar impact of the world market price level on the food situation in developing countries. As, however, by unchanged policy (the standard run, 111) the world market price is already at a relatively high level, the introduction of a policy of stable and high international prices will not affect the future development positively. On the other hand, a policy that under these conditions aimed at lowering the international price level would undoubtly worsen the perspective of the food situation in the poor countries.

11.5 *BUFFERING IMBALANCES BY THE RICH COUNTRIES*

Regulation of the world market, as intended under 11.4 above, assumes a fundamental change in the position which the rich countries take in the international trade in food. It is assumed, namely, that these countries will jointly fulfil a buffer function on the world market by operating stockpiles which will be sufficient to bridge the yearly fluctuations in supply and demand. In addition, it is assumed that the rich nations will absorb the structural imbalances in world food supply by a coordinated import and export policy that is oriented towards maintaining a particular world market price level. To fulfil this latter function, the wealthy countries will need to be able to influence their own production or consumption (dependent on the circumstances) in such a way that their net position on the world market will support the internationally agreed price policy.

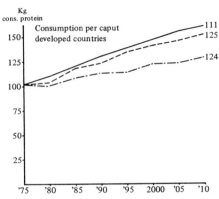

Fig. 11.6

Necessary restriction of domestic food consumption in the rich countries in order to stabilize DFP at various levels under the assumption of a relatively high growth rate of non-agricultural income; comparison of the standard run (111) with run 124 (DFP-target = 0) and with run 125 (DFP-target = 200)

According to the model simulations, such regulation of the import or export balance is essential if the long-term target is to be achieved. Under the assumption of rapid economic growth, the maintenance of a relatively high price level on the world market will not demand much effort on the part of the rich countries (see figure 11.6 and run 125 in Appendix 10A). It might be necessary to restrict their own consumption somewhat, in order to prevent the world market price from rising above the intended price level. The higher this target price, the less the necessary consumption res-

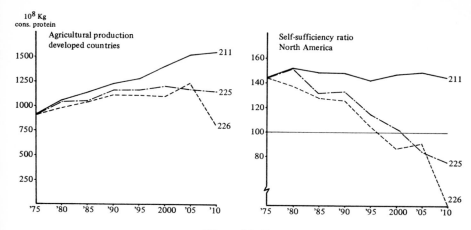

Fig. 11.7

*Necessary restriction of domestic food production in the rich
countries in order to stabilize DFP at various levels under
the assumption of a relatively low growth rate of non-
agricultural income; comparison of run 211 (unchanged
policy) with run 225 (DFP-target = 200) and with
run 226 (DFP-target = 400)*

triction. However, if the world's economic growth were to
slow down, the envisaged regulation of the world market
would require fairly drastic measures (see figure 11.7 and
run 225 and 226 in Appendix 10A). In fact, the rich countries
will have to significantly curb their supply to the world
market if the desired price level is to be maintained. In
the relevant simulation run, North America would even have
to give up its position as food exporter.

11.6 *WORLD MARKET STABILIZATION AND THE EXTENT OF HUNGER*

Stabilization of the world market price at a relatively
high level thus enables gradual improvement of the food
supply of poor countries (measured in average food consumption per capita). The extent of hunger, however, is not very
sensitive to such a policy. It is true that hunger decreases
somewhat as a higher international price level is pursued,
but there is no chance of its being eliminated (compare in
Appendix 10A, run 124 and 125, respectively run 224, 225,
and 226). This is due to the contrasting influences which
the food price level has on the purchasing power in the poor
countries of the urban population on the one hand, and of
the rural population on the other hand. High prices favour
the farmers (and therefore their consumption), but operate
to the disadvantage of non-agricultural consumers, and vice
versa.

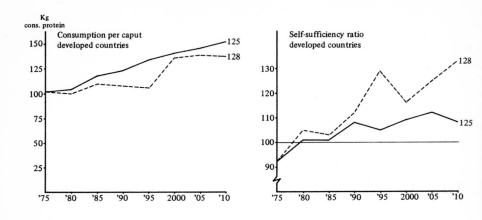

Fig. 11.8

The impact of food aid on the necessity to restrict consumption in the rich countries in order to stabilize DFP around 200 under the assumption of a relatively high growth rate of non-agricultural income: comparison of run 125 (DFP-target = 200) with run 128 (food aid, DFP-target = 200)

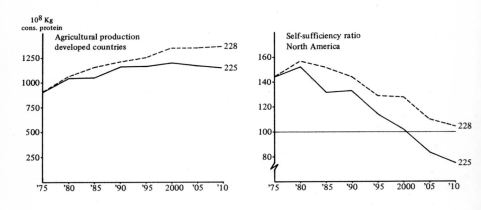

Fig. 11.9

The impact of food aid on the necessity to restrict food production in the rich countries in order to stabilize DFP around 200 under the assumption of a relatively low growth rate of non-agricultural income: comparison of run 225 (DFP-target = 200) with run 228 (food aid, DFP-target = 200)

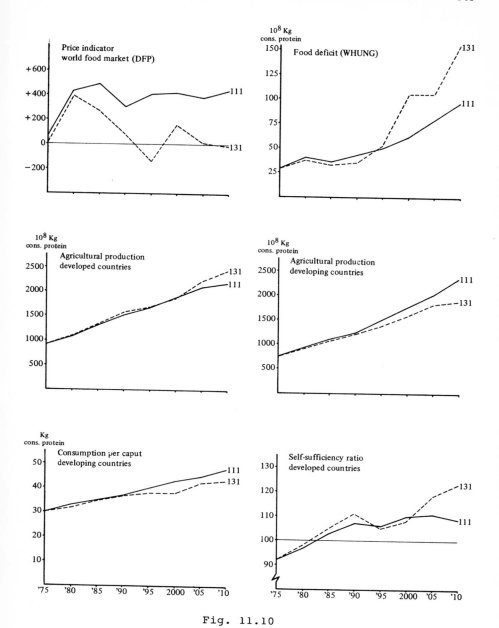

Fig. 11.10

*Impact of liberalization of international trade in basic foods
on the food situation in developing countries: comparison of
the standard run (111) with run 131 in which rich countries
are assumed not to protect their domestic food markets*

Regulation of the world market, therefore, notwithstanding
its positive effects, is not likely to render food aid
unnecessary. As we have ascertained earlier, hunger is
caused, above all, by the unequal distribution of income
within the developing countries. And this cause can hardly
be eliminated with the aid of the international policy
measures introduced above.

All the same, the hunger that prevails in the world cannot
be ignored. A world market policy combined with large-scale
food aid could alleviate hunger and also stimulate the
development of food production in the poor countries (Appendix 10A, runs 127, 128, resp. 227, and 228). MOIRA has shown
that purchases on behalf of food transfers can both support
and obstruct the world market price policy, dependent on the
demand and supply position. Under conditions of rapid economic growth the extra demand for food is more likely to oblige
the rich nations to reduce their consumption (figure 11.8).
Under conditions of moderate growth, food aid will reduce
the necessity for rich countries to limit their production
growth (see figure 11.9).

11.7 THE IMPACT OF TRADE LIBERALIZATION

As an alternative to the deliberate influencing of
world market prices, MOIRA was used also to evaluate the
effect of a liberalization of international trade in basic
foods. It is assumed that the rich countries in particular
would no longer protect their domestic food markets (see
figure 11.10 and run 131 in Appendix 10A). Under this assumption, hunger in the period 1975-2010 will average 25 per
cent more than if policies remain unchanged; in the second
half of the period WHUNG will increase considerably faster
than in the standard run. After 1990 the growth rate of
production in the developing countries, particularly in
Southern Asia, will be affected negatively by the low world
market price level that in turn is induced by the extension
of agricultural output in the rich countries. Supply in
these countries, notably in North America, had already
rather high elasticities with respect to domestic prices but
in this simulation run also shows high sensitivity to world
market prices. Supply is lagged; this causes some cycles in
production and destabilization of world market prices. In
the long run the rich countries, where food consumption has
a very limited price sensitivity, will increase their self-
sufficiency ratio; in 2010 North America reaches, according
to MOIRA, a self-sufficiency ratio of more than 200. On the
other hand, the import dependence of Southern Asia will be
increased.

The overall conclusion that MOIRA suggests is that a policy
of trade liberalization in basic foods is primarily in
favour of the rich exporting countries at the expense of
agricultural development and food supply in the economically
less-developed countries.

11.8 *THE ROLE OF THE RICH COUNTRIES WITH REGARD TO WORLD FOOD SUPPLY*

11.8.1 *Interdependencies*

The influence which the rich countries are able to bring to bear to safeguard the world food supply is based on the (direct and indirect) relations between the development of the production and consumption of food in the industrialized nations on the one hand, and that in the developing countries on the other hand. However, the capacity of rich countries to favourably influence the structure of world food supply in this way proves to be fairly restricted. This is chiefly due to the preponderant role that is to be played by the national policies of the developing countries with regard to agricultural development and income distribution. According to MOIRA, a deliberate change of income distribution in these countries could remarkably strengthen the positive effect of food aid and world market regulation (see figure 11.11 and run 129 in Appendix 10A). For the distribution of income primary responsibility lies - as has been stated - with the developing countries themselves.

Nevertheless, the rich nations should be expected to do everything within their power to create international conditions which will be conducive to the improvement of the food situation in the poor countries. Technical and financial development aid in the agricultural sphere can only achieve its full effect if the desired production growth does not peter out because of lack of purchasing power. This applies not only on the regional level but certainly also on the international level. For this reason, a purposeful world market price policy - effectuated by the rich countries - will form an essential complement to the increasing international effort that is being made to improve the food supply of the poor countries.

It has to be emphasized, in this connection, that a world market price policy along these lines cannot and should not be considered in isolation of other measures. Food importing developing countries, for example, cannot be expected to subscribe to an international policy of relatively high food prices when considered in isolation, because their balance of payments position will deteriorate as a consequence (at least in the short run). A regulation of the world food market aiming at a relatively high price level will therefore have to be accompanied by measures giving financial compensation to those developing countries that suffer a price rise of their food imports. Such measures can be seen as a complement to the programme of stabilization of export receipts as incorporated in the Lomé agreement between the European Community and the ACP countries, and as envisaged also in the UNCTAD proposals concerning the regulation of international commodity markets.

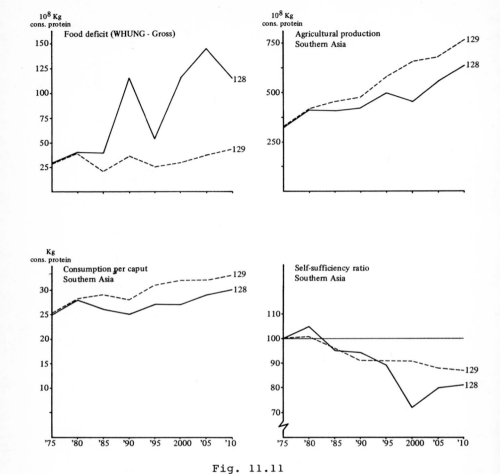

Fig. 11.11

*Impact of a reduction of income differences within poor countries on
the effects of world market regulation and food aid: comparison of
simulation run 127 (food aid, DFP-target = 200) with run 129
(food aid, DFP-target = 200, gradually decreasing income
differences outside agriculture, smaller income gap
between agriculture and the non-agricultural sector*

11.8.2 *The need for adaptation of national agricultural policies*

The international policy for agriculture and food supply advocated above, requires that the rich countries significantly reorientate their agricultural policies. The rivalry between the economic blocs within the western world (i.e. between North America and the Common Market) with regard to agricultural policies will have to be replaced by a concerted effort towards a global food supply policy. In pursuing their national agricultural policies, the rich countries will have to make allowances for the targets of this international policy. The desire to stabilize world market prices at a fairly high level entails that the rich nations should make more of an effort to adapt the volume of their own food production (and if necessary also their own consumption) to the international demand and supply situation. A more flexible agricultural policy is then necessary, as the OECD has ascertained.[1]
With this purpose in mind, the rich countries will have to extend and complement the instruments of their agricultural policies so that both national and international targets can be realized. As far as the European Common Market is concerned, this would signify that efficient measures, by which to influence the size of production, must be given greater significance in the instrument arsenal. In view of the international interests which this would serve, it should be possible to overcome any technical difficulties.

The conditions under which regulation of the world market would be possible are not likely to be fulfilled from one day to the next. All too frequently, in fact, international cooperation founders on the priority of national interests. It is to be hoped that the MOIRA study will be able to support the efforts to put international economic relations at the service of a target transcending narrow national interests, in this case: sufficient food for all.

---

[1] Study of trends in world supply and demand of major agricultural commodities; OECD, Paris 1975.

Appendix 11A

INTERNATIONAL FOOD POLICIES IN MOIRA

11A.1 *INTERNATIONAL FOOD AID*

The financial means for international food aid are acquired by taxing income of the non-agricultural sector in the rich countries. (As this tax reduces disposable income of the sector, its incidence will be partly passed on to the agricultural sector through the domestic food price policy). The food-aid tax is constrained by an upper limit, expressed as a percentage of total value added of the non-agricultural sector. The food-aid tax receipts of all developed countries together constitute the annual donations to the food-aid fund.

Every year food for aid is bought in the world market. The volume of the food purchases is equal to the moving average of annual gross hunger WHUNG, multiplied by a factor FOODAIDFR. The moving average of WHUNG indicates the magnitude of *structural hunger* and is labelled WHUNGT. The multiplication factor FOODAIDFR is defined as the minimum of the relative capacity of the fund (its financial magnitude, divided by the world market food price of last year, and divided by WHUNGT) and the desired fraction of gross hunger to be covered by food aid (FOODAIM) multiplied by a safety margin (1 + AIDSAFE). Thus, the value of the parameter FOODAIDFR is determined by the food-aid fund's financial resources, or by the political decision to eliminate only part of gross hunger by aid - whichever is limiting most.

A short technical comment may be added here as regards the use of last year's food price in determining the relative capacity of the food-aid fund. It would have been better to use the current year's food price, but this would create considerable computational complications as the capacity of the fund would come to depend on the outcome of the world market forces while at the same time influencing them.

The quantity of food aid available in any given year is allocated and distributed to countries (and income groups) in proportion to gross hunger $(HUNG_j)_t$. The level of *structural hunger* $WHUNGT_t$ and the world market food price in year t determine the required magnitude of next year's food-aid fund and hence the tax rate for food aid. The upper limit to this tax rate, TAXMAX, has been set at 3 per cent of non-agricultural income.

11A.2 *INTERNATIONAL FOOD PRICE POLICY*

As observed before, international food price policy in MOIRA has two immediate purposes: stabilization of the world market food price, and to stabilize it at the proper level. The instruments are the operation of food buffer stocks and the adaptation of food production or food consumption, or both, in the rich countries. Instrument use will be discussed in more detail shortly. First, a criterion function will be introduced that will serve to evaluate the relative success or failure of a policy package and to determine the required adaptation of instrument use.

The criterion function (or target function) used in the policy simulation runs of MOIRA contains the three derived or intermediate objectives of stabilization policy, food aid policy, and price level policy, weighed by the coefficients W_1, W_2, and $(1 - W_1 - W_2)$, respectively. The weighed sum of the three terms is divided by total world market food supply FSUP which transforms the expression into a dimensionless number; this number is used as (rough) indicator of the degree in which the present policy package has been unsuccessful. The indicator is labelled ERFACT and has a distributed time lag.

Food stock policy for price stabilization has been discussed already in 7.3.3. Initially planned net exports to the world market (assuming no change in the world market price level) are indicated by FSUP, while initially planned net imports (again assuming that last year's price would prevail) are given by FCONS. Initial world market food surplus is DIF; hence DIF = FSUP - FCONS. As mentioned before (7.3.3), a fraction STABFR of DIF is added to the world food stock; when DIF is negative this is obviously a withdrawal. Note that FSUP refers to net world market supply after stock adjustment for weather fluctuations and after food-aid purchases have been made. The way in which food-aid policy is modelled has been outlined already in paragraph A above. Price level policy determines a desired level of the world market price DFPTARG; this price level is compared with the actual level of DFP. The price level difference (DFPTARG-DFP) has to be translated into a quantity difference; this is done by multiplying it with WQ which is the reciproke of the slope of the world market demand curve in the equilibrium point.

Consequently, the criterion function has the following form:

$$ERFACT_t = [-W_1.DIF+W_2\{FOODAIM.(1+AIDSAFE) - FOODAIDFR\}.$$
$$.WHUNGT + (1-W_1-W_2).(DFPTARG-DFP).WQ].WER/FSUP+$$
$$+(1-WER).ERFACT_{t-1} \qquad (11A.1)$$

with the constraint of ERFACT $\geq$ -1. All variables and parameters have been defined in the text. The delay parameter
WER could contribute to the stability of the policy adaptation process; in the simulation runs to be discussed below
its value is put equal to one, however.

The objective of an international food policy can now be
described as the stabilization of the criterion function
around the value zero. It will be clear that this is a
derived objective. The policy simulation runs of MOIRA show
how alternative food policies - characterized by different
weights W_1, W_2 and $(1-W_1-W_2)$ in the criterion function -
will influence the value of the criterion ERFACT.

11A.3 *THE INSTRUMENTS OF AN INTERNATIONAL PRICE LEVEL POLICY*

The level of world market price stabilization plays an
important part in the policy simulation runs, as it affects
the domestic food price levels and through these the incentive
for food production growth in the developing countries. The
rich countries may influence the world market price level by
their net position in food exports and imports. The instruments at the disposal of the rich countries for an international food price level policy are therefore the adaptation of domestic food production and domestic food consumption. They will be discussed now, in this order.

Adaptation of food production in the rich countries is
possible only in a downward direction. Governments of rich
countries may try to reduce production in various ways, e.g.
by administrative measures limiting agricultural land use,
or by introducing production-related taxes combined with
deficiency payments to maintain incomes in the agricultural
sector. In MOIRA, the latter approach is chosen. Obviously,
this type of constraint on agricultural production can also
be removed again, but it cannot become negative.

Consider the equation (6.13) defining value added of the
agricultural sector:

$$V = P.TY - PCOST$$

Income per capita VLU follows from dividing both sides by
agricultural population L"

$$VLU = (P - \frac{PCOST}{TY})\frac{TY}{L} \tag{11A.2}$$

Suppose that a tax is levied per unit of output which is
entirely paid back to the producer:

$$VLU = [(P-DFPG) - \frac{PCOST}{TY}]\frac{TY}{L} + DFPT.\frac{TY}{L} \tag{11A.3}$$

with DFPG > 0.

Obviously, the farmer's income remains unaffected at given
TY, etc. Assume, however, that the tax reimbursement DFPG.TY/L

is a fixed amount guaranteed by the government. This affects
the marginal returns to the producer which are lowered by an
amount DFPG.

A lowering of the marginal returns in this manner will influence the farmer's decision concerning production growth;
the changed relation between costs and returns will have a
downward effect on production. The sectoral income distribution policy will see to it that agricultural incomes
are maintained at their proper level through domestic food
price changes, if necessary.

Thus, the introduction of a tax on agricultural output will
not in this constellation do harm to the income position of
the agricultural sector; in terms of MOIRA, the income disparity equation (6.1) remains operative. The non-agricultural
consumer pays the food price that results from the income
disparity equation. However, the agricultural producer
receives the corresponding amount only partly in the form of
the price paid for his product; the remaining part - i.e.
the food tax revenue DFPG.TY - is transferred to the producers as a lump sum independent for the farmer of the
actual volume of production.

In this way, a gradual increase of the parameter DFPG will
cause a lowering of agricultural production; a decrease in
the parameter value is also possible. However, it is assumed
that a negative value of DFPG is impossible (i.e. a lump-sum
taxation of agricultural incomes to be paid out as a subsidy
per unit of output). The reason is that policy measures with
DFPG > 0 imply in fact the creation of underutilization of
resources, and that the opposite case of creating *overutili-
zation* is hardly possible.

Turning now to the instrument of restricting food consumption
in the rich countries, we consider again the consumption
function (5.3):

$$CONS_{is} = min\left[\frac{R_{is}}{FP^s}, \; ACONS+BCONS(\sqrt{R_{is}+CCONS} - \sqrt{CCONS})\right]$$

If it is assumed that restricting food consumption in the
rich countries will not apply to the poorest income groups
spending all income on food (if they exist at all in these
countries), we have to deal only with the non-linear part of
the function:

$$CONS_{is} = ACONS+BCONS(\sqrt{R_{is}+CCONS} - \sqrt{CCONS}) \qquad (11A.4)$$

In rich countries an increase in the food price will have a
limited effect only on food consumption as the part of income spent on food is relatively small and hence the effect
on real income will be little. As has been said before, the
substitution effect is not taken into account in this study.

It is well-known, however, that total demand for food in terms of its raw materials (in this study consumable protein) is certainly price-inelastic in rich countries. This implies that a reduction of food consumption in rich countries cannot be achieved easily by instruments operating through the market, and that the major role will have to be played by a deliberate decision of the consumers - particularly the rich ones - to consume less food. (The possibility of food rationing is not considered here).

Therefore, in MOIRA the adaptation of food consumption in rich countries takes place by means of adaptation of the parameter CCONS in (11.6). The effect of varying CCONS on CONS can be seen from differentiation of (11.6):

$$\frac{dCONS_{is}}{dCCONS} = BCONS \left(\frac{1}{2\sqrt{R_{is}+CCONS}} - \frac{1}{2\sqrt{CCONS}} \right) \qquad (11A.5)$$

As BCONS, R_{is}, and CCONS are positive, we find that

$$\frac{dCONS_{is}}{dCCONS} < 0$$

In order to decrease $CONS_{is}$, CCONS should be increased.

Let us call the original parameter value of CCONS now OCCONS, with CCONS > OCCONS; furthermore, let the reduction in food consumption level be indicated by DIFCONS:

$$DIFCONS \equiv CONS_{is}(OCONS) - CONS_{is}(CCONS) \qquad (11A.6)$$

From (11A.5) and (11A.6) we have

$$\frac{dDIFCONS}{dR_{is}} = BCONS \left(\frac{1}{2\sqrt{R_{is}+OCCONS}} - \frac{1}{2\sqrt{R_{is}+CCONS}} \right) \qquad (11A.7)$$

As CCONS > OCCONS, we find

$$\frac{dDIFCONS}{dR_{is}} > 0$$

Thus, the reduction of food consumpiton is larger in absolute terms at higher income levels.

Having explained the functioning of the instruments DFPG and CCONS, their use should now be related to the criterion function (11A.1). The criterion function gives a certain value for ERFACT that can be positive or negative. A negative figure means that, in order to come closer to zero, food production in the rich countries has to be decreased or the restriction on food consumption (if existing) has to be relaxed. The opposite holds in case of a positive value of ERFACT.

For the policy simulation runs, the adaptation mechanism has been designed in such manner that the value of ERFACT determines, with a reinforcing factor ADFACT, the required adaptation of DFPG and CCONS. For instance, for CCONS we have

$$CCONS_{t+1} = CCONS_t \cdot (1+ERFACT)^{ADFACT2} \qquad (11A.8)$$

The parameters ADFACT1 and ADFACT2 determine the degree of reinforcement of the original impulse. Their numerical value has been set at 25 and 30, respectively, after a series of experiments with alternative values. The actual values have been chosen as they guarantee an adequate but not too fast rate of adaptation; very fast adaptation of DFPG and CCONS might lead to (possibly even explosive) oscillations.

11A.4 *THE COMPATIBILITY OF INTERNATIONAL FOOD POLICY MEASURES*

The three elements of an integrated international food policy - price stabilization, food aid, and price level policy, as figuring in the criterion function - require the use of various instruments. Are these instruments mutually compatible, or might they be in conflict and counteract each other? For example, both world market price stabilization policy and food aid make use of food stocks (and so does, for that matter, stabilization policy offsetting supply variations due to weather fluctuations). However, these food stocks serve different purposes and are technically two different things. In point of fact, the food stock performing a price stabilization function by withholding from the market the larger part of DIF - see (11A.3) - is included in MOIRA already as a *regular* institution that forms part of the existing world market mechanism. As described in 7.3.3, it is an existing instrument, the importance of which needs only to be underlined here. In the policy simulation runs, the food-aid fund and the food-aid stock enter as a new instrument, for an entirely different purpose; the two stocks can very well function side by side.

Nevertheless, we cannot completely rule out beforehand the possibility of a certain conflict between short-term measures (fighting hunger by redistributing food) and long-term objectives (fighting hunger by encouraging food production in developing countries). Might not food aid lower the incentive for expanding domestic production in the receiving countries? How does food aid influence the world market price level? And how does the latter affect the possibility of giving food aid? These matters need some clarification, and are therefore discussed below. The discussion will lead to the conclusion that, as long as the rich countries are able and willing to provide the funds needed for buying food for aid purposes and provided these transactions do not constitute a large part of total world market transactions, there is little possibility of conflict between the objective of a stable and relatively high (see 11.4) world market

food price on the one hand and international food aid
(actually given to people under the food norm only) on the
other.

Firstly, food aid need not lower the domestic food price
level in the receiving developing country. The way to implement food aid adhered to in MOIRA is to increase the
level of food consumption of the population by physical
distribution of food to those people whose income and hence
consumption is not high enough to reach the food norm. This
can be achieved by realizing an *autonomous* shift of the
supply and demand functions; see fig. 11A.1).

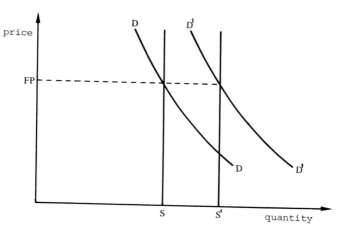

Fig. 11A.1

*An autonomous shift of supply and demand
functions leaving the price level
unchanged*

In fig. 11A.1, the quantity of food aid received is SS', and
the supply curve shifts to the right. The problem is, of
course, to shift the demand curve over the same distance as
there is no direct control over it. However, the elasticity
of food demand will be very close to one as long as the food
norm has not been reached; in this case, a policy of physical
distribution of food to the hungry in the form of free meals
will hardly affect their expenditure on food and consequently
shift the demand curve to the right-hand side as shown in
fig. 11A.1. In the model the condition of a demand elasticity
of one is usually met as most income groups with consumption
below the food norm generally still find themselves on the
linear part of the consumption function (see Chapter 5).
Nevertheless it is true that the assumption of a shift of
the demand function equal to the quantity of food aid received
is a rather bold one.

Secondly, buying food in the world market for the sake of

food aid will increase the world market price level. The
financial means for giving food aid will have to be acquired
by some form of taxation of higher income groups with an
income elasticity of demand for food lower than one. Trans-
ferring these resources in the physical form of food bought
on the world market to income groups with a demand elasticity of one (or very close to one) implies an autonomous
increase in market demand for food. Given perfectly inelastic
supply of food this increase in demand will result in a
price increase of food in the world market. To the extent
that the latter is desired, there is no conflict between a
food aid policy and an international food price policy.

Thirdly, if the resources available for food aid are inadequate
in view of the immediate requirements for fighting hunger, a
conflict may arise between the two strategies. In the event
that the financial means available for giving food aid are
clearly insufficient, the food aid strategy will be in
favour of reducing (exogenously) food consumption in the
rich countries, as this will result in a larger net supply
to the world market. As a consequence of the increase in net
food supply to the world market, (a) food will be bought by
traders and governments, increasing their stocks and contributing to price stabilization, (b) the food price in the
world market will decrease in as much as stabilization is
not fully achieved, and (c) this lowering of the food price
increases the purchasing power of the food-aid fund. Effect
(c) obviously is desirable from the point of view of the
food-aid strategy, and even effect (b) will somewhat reduce
hunger in the short run (although the increase in food
consumption that it allows will be dispersed widely over all
non-agricultural income groups in all countries, and therefore benefit the hungry only very marginally). At the same
time, however, effect (b) conflicts with the international
stabilization strategy. The latter strategy would advocate a
reduction of food consumption in the rich countries only in
case of major production shortfalls and exclusively with the
objective of contributing to price stability. (Actually this
potential conflict between the two strategies is not likely
to be of great importance; as is shown in 11.2 in discussing
the relevant simulation run, an autonomous cut in food
consumption in the rich countries is not particularly help-
ful as a contribution to eradicating hunger in the world).

Fourthly, it should be quite clear that a stabilization
policy aiming at a relatively high world market price is by
no means a policy aiming at maximum food prices. It has to
be borne in mind that a policy aiming at a stable and
relatively high international food price has basically two
objectives to be realized through its effect on domestic
food prices in the developing countries : (a) increasing food
production in these countries, and (b) increasing agrarian
incomes in these countries. With respect to (a) it has to be
noted that a relatively high domestic food price is needed
as an incentive for production growth in agriculture only
insofar as production is not growing already at the highest

rate that is technically and institutionally possible. In
other words, when the capacity to step up the rate of growth
of output reaches its upper limit, no further domestic food
price increases will be warranted. Similarly, as regards
objective (b) there is no need to overshoot the mark by
raising agrarian incomes above those in the urban sector.

Finally, it has to be kept in mind that high world market
prices negatively affect food consumption levels in the non-
agricultural sector of food-importing countries. Even though
food consumption levels in the non-agricultural sector may,
generally speaking, compare favourably with those of the
agricultural population, very high food prices in the world
market would lead to large increases in hunger in the non-
agricultural sector of food-importing countries. For this
reason, a policy of relatively high world market prices is
by no means a policy of *maximum* food prices.

In summary, reflection on the above four points shows that
there need be no conflict between the food-aid strategy and
the international price policy. In particular, potential
conflict can be avoided if a food-aid policy uses the instrument of taxation in the rich countries as its sole means
for obtaining the required quantity of food, and if the
instrument of adapting food production and consumption
levels in the rich countries is reserved for exclusive use
in the context of an international food price policy.

Chapter 12

SOME FINAL COMMENTS

The reader who has worked his way through the chapters of
this book may perhaps feel tired and dissatisfied. Tired,
because parts of the text may not be easy to read; the
authors have had considerable trouble in putting the results
of their modelling work on paper in a manner that would be
both lucid as to the main ideas and accurate as to details
- and no doubt they have failed in several instances. Dissatisfied, because of the numerous assumptions and simpli-
fications that had to be made in the course of developing
the model, with their consequent restrictions on policy
conclusions to be drawn from the analysis. In short, has it
been worth while to construct MOIRA? What knowledge and insights have been gained that did not exist already?

Misgivings of this sort did steal upon the authors as well.
And yet, looking back upon the entire exercise, they feel
they have gained considerably (at least for themselves) in
terms of their understanding of the world food problem.
Perhaps the model should be looked upon primarily as a
learning tool for the modellers themselves. Nonetheless,
others too may learn from MOIRA, provided its limitations are
clearly kept in mind. Let us briefly summarize the main
limitations and weaknesses of MOIRA, as seen by the authors.
To be sure, objections can be raised in general against any
mathematical (economic) model; these objections are not our
concern at the moment, but rather the specific weak spots of
the model presented here. These specific weaknesses of MOIRA
might be cured in future improvements of the model and are
therefore worth mentioning.

First, the basic framework that was chosen for the analysis
- i.e. the equilibrium approach - has not been fully adhered
to. It has been followed at the output side of the model,
but the input markets have not been modelled explicitly. The
non-agricultural sector is treated in a rudimentary fashion
only. Also, balance-of-trade consequences would have to be
dealt with more explicitly.

Second, the model generalizes too strongly over countries and
is too aggregated. Government policy as well as production
and consumption deserve a more detailed treatment, differentiating between types of products. The distinction between
agriculture and animal husbandry is only one (though impor-

tant) case in point. Also, the instruments of government
policy would have to be differentiated further if the actual
institutional setting in which the agricultural sector operates is to be depicted more realistically.

Third, monetary phenomena and their possible impact on real
processes and magnitudes have been neglected altogether.

Fourth, the empirical basis of MOIRA is (necessarily) weak,
due to the scantiness of relevant time series for longer
periods. As a consequence, the dynamics of the model is
rather artificial.

Fifth, ecological aspects of agricultural production are in-
adequately dealt with; they play a part only in establishing
the upper limit to agricultural production under otherwise
ideal production conditions.

Sixth, the interrelations between economic development and
income distribution within the countries have not been incorporated. In particular, income distribution within the
agricultural sector, as it may be influenced by alternative
agricultural development strategies, has not come into focus.

Seventh, the interrelation between the food situation and
demographic development has not been analyzed and introduced,
mainly because of lack of expert knowledge on the subject
matter.

This list is not exhaustive, but already it is impressive.
It underlines that the predictive value of the MOIRA simulation runs should not be overestimated as these are fraught
with uncertainties. There are obvious uncertainties with
respect to the assumed development over time of the exogenous
variables (population growth, growth rates of non-agricultural income, income distribution, prices of agricultural
inputs). But also within these conditional assumptions about
crucial external influences the endogenously generated variables are still subject to a large margin of uncertainty due
to the high level of generalization as regards the behaviour
of the actors in the world food system (farmers, consumers,
governments) and as regards the description of the technical,
economic and institutional environment in which these actors
are assumed to operate.

For these reasons, MOIRA has only limited value for purely prognostic purposes. Its usefulness lies chiefly in
analyzing and illustrating the structure of the complex of
technical, economic and political factors that affects and
interrelates agricultural production and food consumption
in the various regions of the world. MOIRA simulations intend
primarily to show the cumulative short-term and long-term
effects of external influences or political interventions on
the direction in which food production and food consumption
in different parts of the world will develop.

Thus, MOIRA is not meant to be, in its present form, a readily

available instrument for prediction and policy making. The
single most important function of a model such as MOIRA is
that it provides an internally consistent framework for a description of the world food problem - a framework that because of its structure as an algorithmic model lends itself
conveniently to an analysis of alternative scenarios. A number of scenarios has been discussed in Chapters 10 and 11; in
future work, a greater variation in international policies
may be introduced (the *New International Economic Order*),
and the mode of description of such policies be made more
formal.

In order to gain improved understanding of the international
economic interrelations, also in the field of agricultural
production and food consumption, the development (and linkage)
of country models that are conceptually similar still appears
to be a sensible and fruitful approach. The requirement that
the national models be conceptually similar implies that it
would be of little use to develop highly sophisticated and
refined models for one part of the world while the other
part would be described in very simple and crude national
models only. Unfortunately this means that the tune is set
by the (relatively large and important) country or countries
for which information is scantiest.

In MOIRA, the problem had to be faced that very little is
known about the agricultural sector of the centrally-planned
economies. This has led to the factual exclusion from the
world food system of the economies of the centrally-planned
countries - which may or may not be realistic in the long run.
Apart from these countries, all other countries are treated
in MOIRA on an equal footing. On this point again, further
differentiation may be desirable (if not in fact required)
in a future improvement of the model.

This catalogue of caveats regarding the use of MOIRA should
not be read as to imply that the authors do not believe themselves in the usefulness of building global models. They are
convinced that such models can be useful indeed in deepening
our understanding of both global and national problems. The
services that global modelling may be able to render are not
to be found in *absolute* prediction, however, but rather in
showing alternative paths and their implications. Continuous
adaptation of the conditional forecasts on the basis of additional data and improved formulation of interrelations will
be needed. In this way, world models may gradually contribute
to sound and timely policy making.

In ancient Greece, fate was supposed to be in the hands of
the three Moirae: Clotho spun the thread, Lachesis measured
it, and Atropos cut it with her shears. In the description of
the model MOIRA, the thread is cut off here, but the spinning
is fortunately going on. After the completion in 1976 of the
modelling work as described in the present volume, research
efforts along these lines did continue. The activities of the
MOIRA research team have been incorporated in the newly-

established Centre for World Food Studies at Amsterdam and
Wageningen, as mentioned already in the Preface (where also
the address is given). The enlarged team closely cooperates
with the Food and Agriculture Programme of the International
Institute for Applied Systems Analysis (IIASA) at Laxenburg,
Austria. This cooperation will hopefully lead to an improved
and adapted version of MOIRA. One of the present authors,
M.A. Keyzer, has undertaken a study on An interlinked system
of open exchange models, which is forthcoming as an IIASA
research report. If all or some of these ventures come to a
successful end, MOIRA might become MOIRAE. Of course, this
is still in the hands of the Moirae. Suffice it to say now
that in the field of international food and agriculture policies, MOIRA is intended to make its own, modest contribution
- even if it is to be seen in its present form as a first
step only.

Annex

THE DATA ON AGRICULTURAL PRODUCTION AND FOOD
CONSUMPTION IN MOIRA

A.1 *GENERAL CONCEPTS*

A.1.1 *Food and non-food products*
        The set of data necessary for MOIRA includes data
on total agricultural production and consumption, per country,
as an average for the period 1964-1966.[1] Although food
production and food consumption is emphasized, agricultural
production of non-foods cannot be neglected for several
reasons. The production of non-foods is part of agriculture.
The farmer earns an income from it and compares production
of food products to that of non-foods; both products therefore compete with regard to land use. The same crop supplies
in several cases both food and non-food products (cotton
seed, used as feed, versus cotton; mutton versus wool). For
reasons mentioned in Chapter 3.4.3, however, it is impossible
to generate in the model changes in the farmer's mix; the
production of non-foods is therefore considered as production
of vegetal proteins, and in this sense it is possible to add
it to the production of food products.

A.1.2 *Consumable protein as a yardstick for the volume
      of food production and consumption*

A.1.2.1 *The concept 'consumable'*
        Very often food is not consumed in the
location where it was produced, neither is it often produced
immediately in its final form. After harvesting it is processed
into all kinds of products; usually these are processed once
more by the consumer before eating. Moreover, the consumer
does not eat all parts of his food, and the nutritional
value of his meals also depends on his particular metabolism.
In short, it is not possible to establish with any accuracy
the final nutritional value of food to a consumer. Therefore,
supply and consumption have to be measured at a specific
point in the processing chain; waste before this measuring

---

[1] FAO *Food Balance Sheets* provide the best data available on food production and consumption for this period. The lack of such data on the
consumption of non-foods prevents its calculation.

point is considered to be a production inefficiency, and
waste after this point is considered as a consumption inefficiency.

Food is defined as everything that can be consumed by man;
all products edible for man (after waste due to storage) are
called *consumable*. When an animal is fed, slaughtered and
finally eaten, the meat is considered to be consumption of
vegetal food, i.e. consumption of the original consumable
food that fed the animal in as far as these vegetal feedstuffs
are also edible for man. The resulting inefficiencies in
this transformation process are regarded on a par with those
arising when brewing beer or throwing away potato peelings.
Consumable therefore does not necessarily mean *consumed*.

In a number of cases the consumable product has not been
converted into the original vegetal material from which it
was derived. Fish feed on algae; algae, however, are not
edible for man. Therefore the protein content of fish has
been measured directly. In the case of chicken, however,
which may have been fed on grain, the original protein
content of the grain has been established and the lower
protein content of the chicken thus means an inefficiency in
consumption. The case of cattle grazing on pastures (the
grass of which is inedible for man) will be dealt with below
in Annex 1.2.3.

A.1.2.2 *The concept of 'protein'*
                    From the definition of the concept *con-*
sumable just given, it follows that especially vegetal
proteins are considered. Although it is well known that
vegetal proteins may vary greatly in nutritional value,
these differences have been disregarded in this study. The
use of the protein concept as a yardstick has already been
discussed in Chapter 3.4.3, the advantage of protein being
that it can be linked both to the process of photosynthesis
and to the quantity of nutrients required by the plant.
Proteins are therefore an indicator of the volume of production,
but not of its nutritional value, as a considerable part may
have to be thrown away.

The processing of the original data, i.e. the conversion of
the quantities of product into quantities of proteins,
necessarily gives rise to several inaccuracies, falling in
two broad classes:

- Inaccuracies connected with the unit used.
    (a) quantities of products have to be converted into quanti-
        ties of proteins. In doing so a set of conversion factors
        is used which are uniformly applied to the data for
        all countries; regional differences in the protein
        content of the harvested part of production of a
        certain good are assumed to be nil.
    (b) when a particular product does not contain proteins,
        it does not appear in the results. This is the case

with sugar, a product which is very important for
certain countries but would be totally ignored by
this method. A solution for this problem has been
reached by assigning to sugar a hypothetical protein
content based on the protein content of a grain crop
grown on the same area.
(c)   the conversion factors of non-food products are of a
different nature; the concern here is not with consumable proteins but with the quantities of proteins
required for the production of the non-food product.
In the case of rubber e.g. - which in itself contains
no proteins at all - an estimate has been made of the
quantity of proteins required by the tree to sustain
production. The production figures of food are thus
not fully comparable to those of non-foods, as the
respective conversion figures differ conceptually.

- Inaccuracies connected with the statistical material used.
The *Food Balance Sheets* (subsequently called FBS) represent
the most important source of statistical information; however, FBS have been drawn up primarily to indicate food
consumption per country and (agricultural) non-foods are
not included. Hence, many data gaps are encountered when
trying to compute from this source total net production
for the model, making it necessary to use additional
statistical material. This material does not fully correspond with the FBS data, neither does it fill all gaps.

A.1.2.3 *Proteins from roughage*
            In the calculation of production figures
the so-called *production on the basis of roughage* plays a
special and very important role. Roughage (or herbage, and
especially grass) is not edible for man, but it is *harvested*
by cattle and transformed into food in the form of meat,
milk, etc. Hence, the final products of roughage can be
considered in two alternative ways:
(a)   Gross calculation of proteins.
Production of meat (and other products of animal origin)
is multiplied by a commodity-specific factor expressing
the quantity of vegetal proteins necessary to obtain
this production.[2] From the total *animal* and *derived
animal* production obtained in this way, the total
vegetal protein content of feedstuffs edible for man is
subtracted. The residual is defined as the gross production on the basis of roughage (GPBR).
(b)   Net calculation of proteins.
Roughage is converted into food in the form of meat and
milk. In the case of food, we are primarily interested

---

[2] This data corresponds to a 'standard' cow (or other animal) and is
applied to the herd as a total, under the assumption of a constant age
tructure of the livestock. 'Standard' refers to an animal of average
ge, normally bred and functioning, living under normal circumstances.

in really consumable proteins. The above approach does not really indicate the consumable proteins if we assume that the soil on which roughage grows has no immediate alternative application. Roughage therefore cannot provide man with more than the protein yield of cattle in the form of meat, milk, etc. Hence the production on the basis of roughage has to be reduced by an inefficiency factor that expresses the ratio between the quantity of vegetal proteins required and the production of animal proteins.[3]

In order to calculate the net protein production on the basis of roughage (PBR) it has to be established which animals have most likely been feeding on roughage. When this is known, the average ratio between the quantity of vegetal proteins required and the resulting production of animal proteins can be calculated. For this purpose the types of animals have been ranked in decreasing order of feeding on roughage. For each class of animals - indicated by the subscript j - the ratio t_j between vegetal proteins required and animal proteins produced is known. In decreasing order of feeding on roughage, the classes of animals and animal products are shown below, together with the corresponding value of the ratio t_j:

(1)	game, rabbit, other meat	7.58
(2)	sheep, mutton, lamb	8.68
(3)	goat, camel	8.81
(4)	buffalo	8.81
(5)	cattle, beef, veal	8.81
(6)	cow milk	4.77
(7)	horsemeat	8.80
(8)	poultry	8.33
(9)	pig	
	- developed countries	2.89
	- less-developed countries	7.33
(10)	eggs	3.88

The quantity of animal proteins produced on the basis of roughage is calculated after determining how many classes of animals feed entirely or almost entirely on roughage. If RB_j is the quantity of vegetal protein required for animal class j, and GPBR the gross production on the basis of roughage according to the FBS, we have

$$GPBR = \sum_{j=1}^{n} \lambda_j \, RB_j$$

in which, for j = 1, . . ., i,

(a) as long as $\sum_{j=1}^{i} RB_j < GPBR: \lambda_i = 1$

---

[3] Animal and vegetal proteins are assumed to be perfectly substitutable in this case; in the same way we multiply the consumption of animal and derived animal proteins (see Annex 2.2) by this inefficiency factor.

(b) as soon as $\sum\limits_{j=1}^{i} RB_j > GPBR$: $\lambda_i = 1 - \dfrac{\sum\limits_{j=1}^{i} RB_j - GPBR}{RB_i}$

(c) for all higher values of i, up to n : $\lambda_i = 0$.

In other words, GPBR is allocated to those classes of animals most likely to feed on it, until all of it is *used up*; one class may be feeding partly on roughage.

If we have n' classes feeding wholly or partly on roughage, net production of consumable protein from roughage PBR is calculated as

$$PBR = \sum_{j=1}^{n'} \lambda_j \frac{RB_j}{t_j}$$

with λ_j defined as above. The reduction factor RF for the conversion of gross production on the basis of roughage is

$$RF = \frac{PBR}{GPBR}$$

This factor is used as a reduction factor, applied to both production and consumption; see also below (Annex 3.8).

A.2 *CONSUMPTION*

A.2.1 *Remarks on statistical data*

The FBS are grouped into three parts:

Part   I, including most developing countries,
Part II, including East European countries and some developing
          countries,
Part III, including OECD-countries.

Although the presentation of data in each of these Parts is different, requiring a corresponding distinction when stating how these data are processed, for the sake of clarity we have chosen a uniform formulation (viz. that valid for Part I). The changes in approach when processing data from Parts II and III have been specifically indicated.

A.2.2 *Notation*

The following can be stated about the notation of the symbols:
- symbols which are written in small characters are conversion factors and have no dimension;
- barred symbols such as $\bar{H}_2$ correspond to main products in the Food Balance Sheets (FBS Part I); symbols with

an asterisk such as H* correspond to derived products.[4]
The group *derived* animal food refers to non-meat animal
products such as milk and eggs;
-   symbols used in this Annex do not appear in the main
    text of the present study, or have a different meaning
    in the main text.

A.2.3 *Calculation procedures*

(a) $CNA = 1000\Sigma_i \{\overline{FO}_i + \overline{MF}_i - \Sigma_j a^*_{ij}(NE^*_j + \Delta S^*_j - MI^*_j + F^*_j)\}\ p^{NA}_i$

(b) $CDA = 1000\Sigma_i\Sigma_j \{\overline{FO}_i p^{DA}_i \cdot t^{DA}_i + (FO^*_j + W^*_j)p^{DA}_j \cdot t^{DA}_j\}$

(c) $CA = 1000\Sigma_i \{\overline{FO}_i + \overline{MF}_i - \Sigma_j a^*_{ij}(NE^*_j + \Delta S^*_j + MI^*_j)\}\ p^A_i \cdot t^A_i \cdot q_{L/C,i}$

(d) $CW = 1000\Sigma_i \{\overline{FO}_i + \overline{MF}_i - \Sigma_j a^*_{ij}(NE^*_j + \Delta S^*_j + MF^*_j + F^*_j)\}\ p^F_i$

(e) $CL = CNA + CDA + CA$

(f) $C = CL + CW$

i is an index pertaining to main products
j is an index pertaining to derived products.

A.2.4 *Explanation of the symbols*

ad a   CNA   = consumption of non-animal food in 10^3 kg
                      proteins
           $\overline{FO}_i$ = availability of commodity i for food use
                      in 10^6 kg (Gross Food in Parts II and III)
           $\overline{MF}_i$ = availability of commodity i for processing
                      for food in 10^6 kg
           a^*_{ij} = quantity of commodity i, required for the
                      production of the processed commodity j
           NE^*_j = net exports of the processed commodity j in
                      10^6 kg
           MI^*_j = processing for non-food use of commodity j
                      in 10^6 kg
           ΔS^*_j = increase in stock of the processed com-
                      modity j in 10^6 kg
           F^*_j = processed commodity j, used as feed in
                      10^6 kg
           p^{NA}_i = quantity of proteins in kg per kg harvest-
                      able product i, non-animal food.

ad b   CDA   = consumption of *derived* animal food in 10^3
                      kg proteins

---

[4] Main products are the original products (e.g. wheat, potatoes, etc.);
    derived products are processed main products (e.g. wheat flour, beer,
    wine, etc.).

$$p_i^{DA} = \text{quantity of proteins in kg per kg/product,}$$
derived animal food, commodity i

t_i^{DA} = quantity of vegetal proteins, standard required for the production of animal proteins, contained in commodity i, *derived* animal food

FO_j^* = processed commodity j, used as food in 10^6 kg

W_j^* = waste of processed commodity j in 10^6 kg

$p_j^{DA} \cdot t_j^{DA}$ = analogous to $p_i^{DA} \cdot t_i^{DA}$

ad c   CA = consumption of animal food in 10^3 kg proteins

p_i^A = quantity of proteins in kg per kg liveweight product, animal food, commodity i

t_i^A = quantity of vegetal proteins, standard required for the production of animal proteins, contained in liveweight meat, commodity i

$q_{L/C,i}$ = liveweight/carcass weight, commodity i.

Capital symbols are in 10^6 kg carcass weight and refer to meat.

ad d   Capital symbols are in 10^6 kg liveweight, except CW, in which CW = consumption of water-produced food in 10^3 kg proteins. Other symbols are self-evident.

ad e   CL = consumption of land-produced food in 10^3 kg proteins

ad f   C = consumption of food in 10^3 kg proteins.

A.2.5 *Notes on consumption*

(a) The consumption in proteins of food i has to be reduced by the protein value of the by-product, whenever the processing of commodity i into commodity j yields a by-product that serves as feed (e.g. bran).
(b) CDA is calculated in another way than the remaining consumption fractions, as a consequence of the greater obscurity of the input-output relations (Part I); several derived products in the same process result from one main product.
(c) CNA is not corrected for W_j^*, because this waste is considered to be an inefficiency in consumption; therefore it is consumable. For CDA we have to add W_j^* to FO_j^*.
(d) Define $s_i^{DA} = p_i^{DA} \cdot t_i^{DA}$; the s^{DA} for cowmilk is fixed at 0.167. All other s_i^{DA} and all s_j^{DA} are derived by multiplying s^{DA}(cowmilk) with p_i^{DA}/p^{DA} (cowmilk) resp.

p_j^{DA}/p^{DA} (cowmilk); in other words, t^{DA} is assumed to be uniform for all main and derived products from the group *derived* animal food. This is not valid for eggs, which factor is derived from data on *poultry*.

(e)   Standard refers to normal circumstances: animal of average age, normally functioning (no draft animals), normally bred.

(f)   The $s_i^A = t_i^A p_i^A$ is derived from s^A (cattle) as in note (e), for game, buffalo, goat, sheep and horse meat. s^A (cattle) is put at 1.295.

(g)   Non-consumption of part of the proteins embodied in the living animal is considered as consumption (offals such as bones, etc.).

(h)   The symbol F_j^* is not incorporated in the formula for CA; that is to say, processed meat is not fed. Also meatmeal, which really is a feed product, falls outside the scope. In other publications it is impossible to find the quantity of meatmeal fed in the countries of Part I and II, estimates existing only for OECD countries. This has the consequence that consumption may turn out to be a little too high, particularly for those countries where stock-breeding is one of the most important means of existence. For production, the consequence is that the feed deduction is not very accurate (see Annex 3.5). The small importance of meatmeal in the OECD publication concerned makes it reasonable to assume that the omission of meatmeal in the countries of Part I and II is of little consequence.

(i) $\overline{MF}_i$ is not included as far as oil is produced from it (out of oil seeds or out of fish); it is assumed that the protein content of $\overline{MF}_i$ is fed.

(j)   In parts II and III the distinction between main product and derived product is hardly made. For some goods this distinction is expressed through a so-called extraction rate, indicating the weight of the processed commodity as a percentage of the weight of the original product (e.g. for cereals: wheat as *food gross* yields a percentage of wheat flour as *food net*). For other goods Parts II and III only indicate that they enter into the manufacturing stage. Whenever the derived products are given as food products, their *main product equivalent* has been calculated, using input-output ratios from Part I. Any residual value in the manufacturing column not shown to be turned into processed food has been considered as *for industrial use*. This method proved unworkable with milk, as for example in the case of cheese a great many input-output ratios are feasible. As it seems likely that all derived milk products are consumed as food, no attempt has been made to calculate a residual value for the manufacturing column. The derived products stated in the *food gross* column have merely been converted into proteins in order to arrive at consumption.

(k)   CNA comes out too high (and has to be corrected accordingly) if procedure (a) is simply applied to the FBS data; this is because a number of by-products, rich in proteins, get lost when converting cereals into flour. The protein content of these by-products (which are fed to livestock) can be determined by means of the FBS, namely, with the help of the assumptions given for each country in Part I. This knowledge is used for Parts II and III by applying an average factor to $\overline{FO}_i$.

(1)   As stated above (Annex 1.2.3), CA and CDA are divided by a reduction factor RF in order to obtain the really consumable proteins.

A.3 *PRODUCTION*

A.3.1 *Introduction*

As mentioned in the first paragraph of the Annex, the FBS are primarily drawn up to give consumption of food per country. Hence we can expect some gaps in the information concerning production. What is finally needed is the production of food for human consumption, which will be called net production. This is arrived at in the following way: taking the output figures from the FBS, waste, seed and processing for industrial use are subtracted. The figure thus arrived at is still to some extent a gross production figure, as output includes both animals and feed. To obtain net production, feed has to be deducted. This procedure can be indicated in simplified symbols as

$$\{(Y-W-S-MI) - F\} + NETIMP = D$$

in which

Y	= output
.W	= waste
S	= seed
MI	= processing for non-food use
F	= feed
NETIMP	= net imports
D	= demand

The part of the equation between curly brackets represents net production. Waste, seed, processing for industrial use, and feed are considered as claims on domestic output only. This assumption may occasionally lead to a negative net production, especially in the case of mini-states. The assumption may also lead to underestimating food production and over-estimating non-food production, as the input of processing for industrial use may have been imported. In order to avoid this error, however, one would need a data matrix of all international trade flows in agricultural products for the period 1964-66. As this is not available, the above assumption had to be used.

A.3.2 *Notation*

The comments regarding consumption are also valid here.

A.3.3 *Calculation procedures*

(a) $\text{PNA} = 1000\Sigma_i(\overline{O}_i - \overline{MI}_i - \Sigma_j a^*_{ij}MI^*_j - \overline{S}_i - \overline{W}_i)p_i^{NA}$

(b) $\text{PDA} = 1000\Sigma_i(\overline{O}_i - \overline{MI}_i - \Sigma_j a^*_{ij}MI^*_j - \overline{S}_i - \overline{W}_i)p_i^{DA}t_i^{DA}$

(c) $\text{PA} = 1000\Sigma_i(\overline{O}_i - \overline{MI}_i - \Sigma_j a^*_{ij}MI^*_j - \overline{W}_i)p_i^{A}t_i^{A}q_{L/C,i}$

(d) $\text{PW} = 1000\Sigma_i(\overline{O}_i - \overline{MI}_i - \Sigma_i a^*_{ij}MI^*_j - \overline{W}_i)p_i^{F}$

A.3.4 *Explanation of symbols*

(a) PNA = production non-animal food in 10^3 kg proteins

$\overline{O}_i$ = output in 10^6 kg harvestable product

$\overline{MI}_i$ = processing for non-food use in 10^6 kg

$\overline{S}_i$ = seed in 10^6 kg

$\overline{W}_i$ = waste in 10^6 kg

(b) PDA = production *derived* animal food in 10^3 kg proteins

(c) PA = production animal food in 10^3 kg proteins

(d) PW = production water-produced food in 10^3 kg proteins

The production figures as calculated here are still semi-gross production figures, as feed has not yet been deducted.

A.3.5 *Notes on food production*

(a) In the first instance those commodities that are wholly or partly used as fodder (such as oil seeds) are also included in production. The feed part of these commodities is subsequently subtracted from production by means of the feed deduction. For Parts II and III this method gives rise to some problems, because in these Parts only the processed product of vegetable oils is stated and not the original production of oilseeds. As there are no proteins in vegetable oils, these could not be considered. Therefore the production figures of oilseeds in the FAO Production Yearbooks have been used.

(b) With regard to *derived* animal production it is not necessary to introduce a different procedure as in the case of consumption, procedure (b) being useful for many countries. Nevertheless, there are some problems in production because of obscure input-output ratios. For Parts II and III a different computation procedure has to be adopted, because the input-output ratios are totally unknown and no distinction is made between processing for nonfood (industrial) use and for food. This procedure is:

$$\text{PDA} = 1000\Sigma_i\Sigma_j\{(\overline{O}_i - \overline{MI}_i - \overline{S}_i - \overline{W}_i)p_i^{DA}t_i^{DA} + (O^*_j - MI^*_j)p_j^{DA}t_j^{DA}\}$$

$\overline{MI}_i$ and MI_j^* meaning input in the processing sector of commodity i and its processed commodity j; O_j^* is output of the processed commodity j. This input in the manufacturing sector must not be added to the production of non-food because we can assume that the total input in the manufacturing sector, as stated in FBS, returns as a food product.

(c)   From Part I the input-output ratios between main product and derived product, for instance cereals-beer, grapes-wine, are known. This knowledge is used in Parts II and III by assuming an average input-output ratio for the products concerned; this ratio is applied to the input figures of the manufacturing sector. For instance, the input of barley in the manufacturing sector is split into a component destined for the production of beer and therefore to be added to food production, and a second component which must be added to production of feed.

(d)   As has been noted in Annex 3.1, mini-states may cause computational problems (there are no fundamental differences with larger nations) because relatively large net imports are wasted and used for manufacture for industrial use, and as a consequence production may sometimes appear negative. In such a case production is assumed to be nil; if only part of production is negative, it is treated as such in the construction of the figure for total production.

(e)   For the computation of animal production we have started from the output of meat, as given in the FBS. In Part I, however, a distinction is made between meat in kgs and the number of animals. Trade in live animals would be neglected if only meat were taken into account. For this reason the figure is corrected by adding the net export of livestock, assuming that the age structure of imported livestock is the same as the age structure of the domestic livestock. This problem does not figure in Parts II and III, where output is given in kgs only and trade figures include trade in meat as well as trade in live animals.

A.3.6 *The feed deduction*

Before it is possible to calculate production on the basis of roughage it is necessary to determine what is fed to the total livestock apart from grass. A distinction can be made between feedstuffs of animal origin except fish (e.g. skimmed milk) and products of other origin. The protein content of feed of animal origin is subtracted from the production of animal- and derived animal proteins, use of these products by livestock being considered a sort of internal cycle.

$$PADA = PDA + PA - 1000 \{\Sigma_k (\overline{F}_k + \Sigma_l a_{kl}^* F_l^*) p_k^{DA} \cdot t_k^{DA} + F_v p_v^A \cdot t_v^A\}$$

PADA = production of animal and *derived* animal food in 10^3 kg vegetal protein

$\overline{F}_k$ = feed in 10^6 kg according to the FBS-column *derived* animal

F_l^* = feed of the processed commodity l in 10^6kg according to the column concerned in FBS

F_v = meatmeal fed in 10^6kg.[5]

All other feed is included in the feed deduction:

$$FDD = 1000 \{\Sigma_i (\overline{F}_i + \Sigma_j a_{ij}^* F_j^*) p_i^{NA} + \Sigma_s F_s p_s^{NA} + \Sigma_f F_f p_f^{F} + \Sigma_b F_b p_b^{NA}\}$$

FDD = feed deduction in 10^3kg proteins

$\overline{F}_i$ = feed in 10^6kg according to FBS column

F_j^* = feed of the processed commodity j in 10^6kg according to FBS column

F_s = feed in the form of cake, converted into 10^6kg oil-seeds

F_f = feed in the form of fishmeal, converted into 10^6kg liveweight fish

F_b = feed in the form of bran, pollard and other by-products of the processing of cereals, converted into 10^6kg main product.

(a) Computation of feed for Part I

(1) Oil-cakes as feed, F_s

$$F_s = \overline{MF}_s - a_{sc} NE_c$$

$\overline{MF}_s$ = input of oilseeds in the sector *processing for food* in 10^6kg

NE_c = net exports of oilcakes in 10^6kg

a_{sc} = quantity of oilseeds required for the production of one unit of oilcakes

$\overline{MF}_s$ and a_{sc} are provided by FBS, NE_c by FAO *Trade Yearbooks*.

(2) Fishmeal as feed, F_f

$$F_f = \overline{MF}_f - a_{fm} NE_m$$

$\overline{MF}_f$ = input of fish in the sector processing for food in 10^6kg, as far as this input results in the production of fishmeal and marine oils

NE_m = net exports of fishmeal in 10^6kg

---

[5] Data on meatmeal are lacking for Parts I and II, implying that for the countries concerned the computed value of PADA may be somewhat too high. Data on meatmeal for Part III are provided broadly by the statistics mentioned in the OECD *Study on the factors influencing the use of cereals in animal feeding* (Paris, 1971).

a_{fm} = quantity of fish required per unit of fishmeal

$\overline{MF}_f$ and a_{fm} are provided by the FBS, NE_m by FAO *Yearbooks of Fishery Statistics*.

    (3) Bran etc. as feed, F_b

$$F_b = O_b - NE_b$$

O_b = production of bran, etc. in 10^6kg

NE_b = net exports of bran, etc. in 10^6kg

O_b is computed with the help of the assumptions from the FBS given for each country; NE_b is provided by FAO *Trade Yearbooks*.

(b) Computation of feed for Part II

    (1) Computation of F_s; see under (a)

    (2) Computation of F_f

Fishmeal is not included in the FBS statistics for Part II. Therefore F_f is calculated with the aid of data provided by the FAO *Yearbook of Fishery Statistics*:

$$F_f = O_m - NE_m$$

O_m = output of fishmeal in 10^6kg

NE_m = net exports of fishmeal in 10^6kg

In this case fishmeal is not converted into the original product (liveweight fish). When calculating FDD fishmeal is multiplied by its *own* conversion factor (p_f^m).

    (3) Computation of F_b, see under (a)

Information from the assumptions of Part I has also been applied here.

(c) Computation of feed for Part III

    The feed-column of the FBS again forms the basis for the OECD countries. However, the additional data required for the computation of FDD such as data on fishmeal, oilcakes and bran, are more accurately available in the OECD *Study on the factors influencing the use of cereals in aminal feeding*, which provides data on quantities actually fed.

In this study fishmeal is grouped together with meatmeal under the heading of animal meals. For this reason meatmeal is included in FDD here and not directly subtracted from animal production. This is justified because fishmeal is more important than meatmeal as feed product in terms of proteins.

A.3.7 *Production on the basis of roughage*

Defining the animal and derived animal production in vegetal proteins and subtracting the feed deduction gives the gross production of proteins on the basis of roughage (GPBR):

GPBR = PADA - FDD

A.3.8 *Net production of food*

Net production of food is constructed by adding net water-production (fish) to net land-production:

Net land-production: NPL = GPBR . RF + PNA

in which

RF = reduction factor, representing an average $t_i^{A,DA}$ (see Annex 1.2.3(b)).

Therefore

NP = NPL + NPW

A.4   *PRODUCTION OF NON-FOODS*

As mentioned already, data are needed on the production of non-foods as well as on the production of food products. The procedure for non-foods is as follows:

$$PNF = PR.Q_r + 1000 \{\Sigma_i (\overline{MI}_i + \Sigma_j a_{ij}^* . MI_j^*) P_i + PW.p_w^A . t_w^A + \Sigma_n PN_n . P_n\}$$

PNF = production of non-food products in 10^3kg proteins

$\overline{MI}_i$ = input in the processing sector for industrial (non-food) use in 10^6kg according to the FBS

MI_j^* = input in the processing sector for industrial (non-food) use of processed product j in 10^6kg according to the FBS

PR = production of roundwood in 1000 m³.[6]

Q_r = kg proteins per m³ roundwood

PW = production of wool in 10^6kg

p_w^A = kg proteins per kg of wool

t_w^A = vegetal proteins necessary for producing animal proteins in the form of wool

PN_n = production of other non-foods (e.g. tobacco, cotton lint, rubber) in 10^6kg

P_n = kg proteins per kg of these products

---

[6] For roundwood and also for other perennial crops we have to assume a constant age structure.

A.5   *STATISTICAL PUBLICATIONS USED*

FAO *Food Balance Sheets, 1964/66,* Rome 1971
FAO *Trade Yearbooks*
FAO *Production Yearbooks*
FAO *Yearbooks of Fishery Statistics*
FAO *Yearbooks of Forest Products*
FAO *Food Composition Tables – Minerals and Vitamins,* Rome
    March 1954
OECD *Study on the factors influencing the use of cereals
    in animal feeding,* Paris 1971.

INDEX